Pre-Code Hollywood

Sex, Immorality, and Insurrection in American Cinema, 1930–1934

Thomas Doherty

COLUMBIA UNIVERSITY PRESS / NEW YORK

Columbia University Press
Publishers Since 1893
New York   Chichester, West Sussex
Copyright © 1999 by Columbia University Press
All rights reserved
Library of Congress Cataloging-in-Publication Data
Doherty, Thomas Patrick.
    Pre-code Hollywood : sex, immorality, and insurrection in American
cinema, 1930–1934 / Thomas Doherty.
      p.   cm. — (Film and culture)
    Filmography: p.
    Includes bibliographical references and index.
    ISBN 0-231-11094-4 (cl. : alk. paper). — ISBN 0-231-11095-2 (pa. :
alk. paper)
    1. Motion pictures—Censorship—United States—History.   2. Sex in
motion pictures.   I. Title. II. Series.
PN1995.62.D65   1999   99–11956
302.23'43'097309043—dc21

For Sandra, again

Contents

Preface   xi

1. ON THE CUSP OF CLASSICAL HOLLYWOOD CINEMA   1
   Patrolling the Diegesis   3
   Pre-Code Contexts   15

2. BREADLINES AND BOX OFFICE LINES: HOLLYWOOD IN
   THE NADIR OF THE GREAT DEPRESSION   21
   The Lost Millions   27
   A Synchronized Industry   31
   "Mike Fright"   34

3. PREACHMENT YARNS: THE POLITICS OF MERE ENTERTAINMENT   39
   Telegraphing Ideology   45
   Class Distinctions   53
   Professional Malfeasance   58

4. DICTATORS AND DEMOCRATS: THE RAGE FOR ORDER   69
   Hankering for Supermen   70
   "The Barrymore of the Capital": The Newsreel
      Presidency of Franklin Delano Roosevelt   77
   A New Deal in the Last Reel   85
   The Mad Dog of Europe   93

5. VICE REWARDED: THE WAGES OF CINEMATIC SIN   103
   Packaging Vice   107
   Models of Immorality   113
   Figurative Literalness   118

Queer Flashes   120
"Women Love Dirt"   125
Working Girls   131

6. CRIMINAL CODES: GANGSTERS UNBOUND, FELONS
    IN CUSTODY   137
    Rushing Toward Death: The Gangster Film   140
    Men Behind Bars: The Prison Film   157

7. COMIC TIMING: CRACKING WISE AND WISING UP   171
    Commentators on the Action   174
    Story, Screenplay, and All Dialogue by Mae West   182
    Newspaper Patter   187
    The Blue Eagle and *Duck Soup* (1933)   192

8. NEWS ON SCREEN: THE VIVIDNESS OF
    MECHANICAL IMMORTALITY   197
    Library Stock   204
    The Newsreel Ethos   208
    Covering Up the Great Depression   213

9. REMOTE KINSHIPS: THE GEOGRAPHY OF THE
    EXPEDITIONARY FILM   221
    Points on the Compass   225
    Faking It: Phoney Expeditions and Real Deaths   235
    The Dark Continent   245

10. PRIMITIVE MATING RITUALS: THE COLOR WHEEL OF THE
    RACIAL ADVENTURE FILM   253
    "He's White": *Tarzan, the Ape Man* (1932) and *Tarzan
      and His Mate* (1934)   256
    Red Skin, Red Lips: *Massacre* (1934)   262
    East Mates West   267
    "The Ethiopian Trade"   274
    Nerve and Brains: Paul Robeson and *The Emperor
      Jones* (1933)   284
    Beauty and the Beast: *King Kong* (1933)   289

11. NIGHTMARE PICTURES: THE QUALITY OF GRUESOMENESS 295
    Rugged Individualism: *Dracula* (1931), *Frankenstein*
      (1931), and Their Progeny 299
    The Lower Orders Rise Up: *Island of Lost Souls* (1933)
      and *Freaks* (1932) 308

12. CLASSICAL HOLLYWOOD CINEMA: THE WORLD ACCORDING
TO JOSEPH I. BREEN 319
    "The Storm of '34" 320
    Hollywood Under the Code 336
    Post-Code Hollywood Cinema 342

Appendix 1: The Text of the Production Code 347
Appendix 2: Particular Applications of the Code and the
    Reasons Therefore [Addenda to 1930 Code] 361
Appendix 3: Amendments 365
Appendix 4: The Critical and Commercial Hits of 1930–1934 369

Notes 373
Index 411
Film Index 425

 **Preface**

A few years ago, MGM released a fully restored version of *Tarzan and His Mate* (1934), an uncensored print that included heretofore unseen footage: an eye-opening underwater swim scene featuring Johnny Weismuller, barely clad in a loin cloth, and a body double for Maureen O'Sullivan, an Olympic swimmer named Josephine McKim, clad not at all. I saw the film at the Brattle Theater in Cambridge, Massachusetts, a vintage repertory house and a mecca still for film buffs who prefer their celluloid straight up, no videotape. The aquatic nudity generated a curious and memorable reaction from the packed house. Good-natured laughter at the rear-screen projection and embarrassed wincing at the offhand racism turned suddenly to shocked silence. Some people actually gasped. Obviously, the nudity per se wasn't shocking to the sophisticated crowd of pallid cineastes. What shocked was the motion picture context: none of us had seen anything like it in classical Hollywood cinema and the glimpse of an alternate film universe was fascinating and a bit disorienting. Before diving into that universe, the world of pre-Code Hollywood cinema, I'd like to offer some explanation, thanks, and caution.

Cultural-historical in cast, this study takes its critical methodology not from a French structuralist or British semiotician but from an American poet with an eye for cinema. In 1930, felicitously enough, Hart Crane published his visionary epic *The Bridge*, a journey in language through the contours of American myth that, like the Brooklyn Bridge that was its overarching symbol, sought to link art and technology. An orbic bard in tune with his democratic vistas, Crane began by evoking the mystery of film and history with a motion picture vision:

> *I think of cinemas, panoramic sleights*
> *With multitudes bent toward some flashing scene,*
> *Never disclosed but hastened to again,*
> *Foretold to other eyes on the same screen.*

Crane's outlook suggests a poetics for film history that grasps the visceral power of the medium (those multitudes bending toward the "flashing scene"), that speaks to its cultural persistence ("foretold to other eyes"), and that wrestles with its resistance to interpretation ("never disclosed"). The "panoramic sleights" is a nice insight too, granting permission to gaze admiringly at the spectacle without being hoodwinked by the magic of the dreamwork.

Of course, the films themselves are the primary documents to hasten to, but I've also relied heavily on the motion picture trade press to eavesdrop on the dialogue between Hollywood and American culture. No less than the *Congressional Quarterly* or the *New York Times*, the pages of *Variety*, *Motion Picture Herald*, the *Film Daily*, and the *Hollywood Reporter* registered the tremors of Great Depression America in the early 1930s, and with wittier headlines. Another point of orientation concerns the nettlesome matter of definition. Although the "pre-Code" tag is something of a misnomer (strictly speaking, any film produced before 1930 would be nominally pre-Code), I have retained the common practice of cinema scholars and film programmers and bracketed the pre-Code era between 1930, when the Production Code was officially adopted, and 1934, when the Production Code was rigorously enforced—a convention that I hope is justified in the following pages.

A convention requiring no justification is the pleasant task of thanking many kind and generous people. Like all film scholars, I depend on the kindness of archivists: Madeline Matz, Rosemary Hanes, and Joe Belian at the Motion Picture Division of the Library of Congress; Mary Corliss and

Terry Geeskin at the Museum of Modern Art Film Stills Archive; Scott Curtis and Janet Lorenz at the Margaret Herrick Library; Dace Taube at Special Collections at the University of Southern California; Jill Costill at the Indiana State Historical Society; as well as the staffs of the Lincoln Center for the Performing Arts, the National Archives at College Park, Maryland, the Film and Television Library at UCLA, and the FDR Library at Hyde Park. At Columbia University Press, Jennifer Crewe, Roy Thomas, and Mary Ellen Burd shepherded the project to completion with sensitivity, professionalism, and an understanding attitude toward deadlines. With good spirit and keen insight, many friends commented and kibbitzed: Diane Bernard, Dana Benelli, Steve Biehl, Laura Browder, Jim Deutsch, Bob Eberwein, Doug Gomery, David Lugowski, Dan Leab, Chuck Maland, Dane Morrison, Bob Moses, Bill Paul, Jeff Ruoff, Luke Salisbury, Jim Schwoch, Laura Shea, and Kathy Whittemore. I owe special thanks to John Belton, Henry Jenkins, and John Raeburn for reading the work in manuscript; to Felicia Herman for help with the Yiddish; and to Susan Carruthers for help with the Briddish. My colleagues in the American Studies Department at Brandeis University were generous in lending their ears and encouragement and the university's Sachar Fund provided welcome financial assistance. Above all, as ever, I owe my wife Sandra more than thanks.

Finally, in the spirit of the weaselly precredit warnings posted before the classic gangster films to deny evil intent and sidestep full responsibility for the mayhem that followed, a disclaimer must preface this production. Besides eye strain, one of the occupational hazards of film criticism is target fixation, a cognitive misfiring wherein the topic the critic finds most congenial—a turning point in Hollywood history, a brilliant director, a landmark film—just happens to be absolutely vital to the evolution of the medium and the course of American history. Fortunately, the nexus between a four-year chapter of Hollywood history and America in the nadir of the Great Depression lives up to the billing.

Pre-Code Hollywood

On the Cusp of Classical Hollywood Cinema

On or about July 1934 American cinema changed. During that month, the Production Code Administration, popularly known as the Hays Office, began to regulate, systematically and scrupulously, the content of Hollywood motion pictures. For the next thirty years, cinematic space was a patrolled landscape with secure perimeters and well-defined borders. Adopted under duress at the urging of priests and politicians, Hollywood's in-house policy of self-censorship set the boundaries for what could be seen, heard, even implied on screen. Not until the mid-1950s did cracks appear in the structure and not until 1968, when the motion picture industry adopted its alphabet ratings system, did the Code edifice finally come crumbling down.

Hollywood's vaunted "golden age" began with the Code and ended with its demise. An artistic flowering of incalculable cultural impact, Hollywood under the Code bequeathed the great generative legacy for screens large and small, the visual storehouse that still propels waves of images washing across a channel-surfing planet. The synergistic spread of American entertainment, the whole global kaleidoscope of films, television, video games, computer graphics, and CD-ROMs, draws on the censored heritage for archival material, deep backstory, narrative blueprints, and moral ballast. Whether conventional retread or postmodern pastiche, Hollywood under the Code is the prime host to a long line of moving image parasites.

But what of Hollywood "before the Code," the motion picture record that predates the censorship that polished up the golden age heritage? For four years—from March 31, 1930, when the Motion Picture Producers and Distributors of America formally pledged to abide by the Production Code, until July 2, 1934, when the MPPDA empowered the Production Code Administration to enforce it—compliance with the Code was a verbal agreement that, as producer Samuel Goldwyn might have said, wasn't worth the paper it was written on. Relatively and in context, Hollywood was free to roam far and wide, or at least to venture farther out on the frontiers of free expression than would be permitted after the Code, when the range was fenced in and the deputies were on duty.

That four-year interval marks a fascinating and anomalous passage in American motion picture history: the so-called pre-Code era, when censorship was lax and Hollywood made the most of it. Unlike all studio system feature films released after July 1934, pre-Code Hollywood did not adhere to the strict regulations on matters of sex, vice, violence, and moral meaning forced upon the balance of Hollywood cinema. In language and image, implicit meanings and explicit depictions, elliptical allusions and unmistakable references, pre-Code Hollywood cinema points to a road not taken. For four years, the Code commandments were violated with impunity and inventiveness in a series of wildly eccentric films. More unbridled, salacious, subversive, and just plain bizarre than what came afterwards, they look like Hollywood cinema but the moral terrain is so off-kilter they seem imported from a parallel universe.

In a sense pre-Code Hollywood *is* from another universe. It lays bare what Hollywood under the Code did its best to cover up and push off screen. Sexual liaisons unsanctified by the laws of God or man in *Unashamed* (1932), *Blonde Venus* (1932), and *She Done Him Wrong* (1933); marriage ridiculed and redefined in *Madame Satan* (1930), *The Common Law* (1931), and *Old Morals for New* (1932); ethnic lines crossed and racial barriers ignored in *The Bitter Tea of General Yen* (1933), *The Emperor Jones* (1933), and *Massacre* (1934); economic injustice exposed and political corruption assumed in *Wild Boys of the Road* (1933), *This Day and Age* (1933), and *Gabriel Over the White House* (1933); vice unpunished and virtue unrewarded in *Red Headed Woman*

(1932), *Call Her Savage* (1932), and *Baby Face* (1933)—in sum, pretty much the raw stuff of American culture, unvarnished and unveiled.

Of course Hollywood after 1934 is a rich index of all the above too. The fractures of American life, still less the open embrace of sex, did not close up when the Code clamped down. No matter how rigid the body cast, Hollywood cinema is too supple and expressive an art to constrain what Walt Whitman celebrated as "nature without check with original energy." The Code seal stamped on Alfred Hitchcock's *Notorious* (1946) did not keep Ingrid Bergman and Cary Grant from simmering with erotic passion and flaunting the sacrament of marriage, nor did it temper the plight of the dispossessed or strangle the voice of protest in John Ford's version of John Steinbeck's *The Grapes of Wrath* (1940). Always too, in the hidden recesses of the cinematic subtext, under the surface of avowed morality and happy endings, Hollywood under the Code is fraught with defiance of Code authority.

But in pre-Code Hollywood the fissures crack open with rougher edges and sharper points. What is concealed, subterranean, and repressed in Hollywood under the Code leaps out exposed, on the surface, and unbound in Hollywood before the Code. Often what is seen and heard in pre-Code Hollywood is not so much as glimpsed or whispered in Codified Hollywood. Images, language, ideas, and implications are projected on screen with blunt force and unmistakable meaning. Aptly dubbed "the motion picture industry's Magna Charta of official decency," the Production Code set down strict laws of moral gravity. The universe of pre-Code Hollywood operated under rules of its own.

Patrolling the Diegesis

To movie buffs, film professors, and inside dopesters, the phrase "classical Hollywood cinema" is a loaded term liable to go off whenever the dialogue turns philosophical at a postscreening postmortem. The classic work on classical Hollywood cinema is David Bordwell, Janet Staiger, and Kristen Thompson's *The Classical Hollywood Cinema: Film Style and Mode of Production to 1960*, published in 1985. A magisterial and synoptic study, it refined a set of notions percolating in academic film studies since the early 1970s, around the time the field became a secure university discipline with its own departmental stationery and tenure-track teaching slots. As Bordwell, Staiger, and Thompson told it, the vital components of classical Hollywood cinema were a conventional visual style and a sturdy economic structure: how the films looked and how they were produced, distributed, and exhibited. That bifocal vision on film culture and studio commerce—looking at the means of art and the means of production, the "show" and the "business" of moviemaking—remains the best way of understanding the hybrid medium.

As an art, Hollywood's creative unit is the narrative feature film, which became its flagship product around 1912–1915, the traditional touchstone being D. W. Griffith's *The Birth of a Nation* (1915). Griffith's "twelve-reel photoplay" deployed full blown the still-emergent grammar of the moving image, a morphology evolved from snippets of documentary "actualities," picaresque slapstick, and one-reel vignettes. After two decades of moving-image spectatorship, roughly from Thomas Edison's perfection of the kinetoscope in 1894 to the nickelodeon era of 1907–1912, the building blocks of visual literacy had been mastered by filmmaker and spectator alike: the close-up, parallel editing, point-of-view shots, eyeline matches, montage sequences, and so on. The same period marked another crucial transition, the shift from film-as-spectacle to film-as-fabula, from looking at things move to being moved by things on screen. Though anything might be filmed, the movies were now primarily a story machine.

As a business, the medium underwent a concurrent standardization. The pioneer days of rough-and-tumble hustle settled into a civilized arrangement wherein the fittest of moviemakers survived by crushing competition, gobbling up the leavings, and consolidating assets. A technologically complex, capital-intensive business dependent on circuits of national distribution, the motion picture industry made no room for small entrepreneurs or corner shops. Hollywood, a place name that became synonymous with the American motion picture industry around 1920, came to describe not just a location but an economic practice. The vertical integration of motion picture production, distribution, and exhibition—in which a single corporate entity produced, sent out, and screened the film product—crystallized into the mature oligopoly of the Hollywood studio system. Like the items on a grocery shelf or automobile lot, the familiar brand names—Columbia, Fox, MGM, Paramount, RKO, Universal, and Warner Brothers—were defined by their trademark stars, consistent styles, and signature genres.

Bordwell, Thompson, and Staiger set the rough boundaries of classical Hollywood cinema from 1917 to 1960. However, since the gambit of historians dealing with matters of priority is to backdate a genesis farther and farther into the past, and since research into the archaeology of early cinema continues to unearth prior claimants, some film scholars have pushed back the original birth date of classical Hollywood cinema to about Edwin S. Porter's *The Great Train Robbery* (1903). Eventually, an enterprising graduate student will discover that the first true exemplar of classical Hollywood cinema was originally shot in the back of Thomas Edison's Black Maria in 1894.

Yet whether the date is 1903 or 1917, the problem with placing silent cinema under the rubric of classical Hollywood cinema is that no one watches it. For all its influence on descendants, the forebearer is forgotten and the debts unacknowledged. If "classical" means primal and formative, then the Bordwell-Staiger-Thompson time clock seems punctual enough, but if it means alive in the mind's eye, it runs slow. Except to antiquarians and preservationists, silent cinema has little presence on the cultural radar screen, its landmark films unrented on video, its iconic images spotted only as fodder for video collage on MTV. Synchronized sound is so intimately embedded in the structure of motion picture grammar that it takes an effort of imagination to realize that American cinema lived quite well without it for over thirty years.

The introduction of sound to the cinema in 1927 beckons as a likely starting point for a true classical era, but not until 1930, when the major studios announced the cessation of silent film production, did the death knell for the silent screen toll for certain. If film style and mode of production yoked to sound are the prime ingredients of classical Hollywood cinema, then 1930 seems the logical birth date, especially since it coincides so fortuitously with the formal adoption of the Production Code.

Yet to think of classical Hollywood cinema is to think not solely of means of production and film style, silent or sound, but to conjure a moral universe with known visual and ethical outlines. This is not to say that Hollywood cinema in the silent and pre-Code era refused to bow to official virtue and popular expectations. Still less is it to imply that the grammar deployed by the embryonic sound cinema was not first cast by the previous three decades of silent cinema. It *is* to say that the Code gave Hollywood the framework to thrive economically and ripen artistically and that Hollywood in turn gave the Code provenance over a cultural commodity of great price—the visible images and manifest values of American motion pictures. What makes Hollywood's classic age "classical" is not just the film style or the studio system but the moral stakes.

Naturally, motion picture morality, or the lack of it, had been monitored by guardians of civic virtue since the chaste peck between the middle-aged lovebirds in *The Kiss* (1896). For progressive reformers and cultural conservatives who beheld in the embryonic medium the potential for social damage and moral blight, the products of the motion picture industry (no less than the methods of meat packing or the distribution of demon rum) warranted regulation and prohibition as a public health measure. Especially after World War I, when Hollywood began spinning out whole film cycles devoted to the sins of wild youth, dancing daughters, straying wives, and dark seducers, the moral guardians tried their damndest to break up the parade of wastrels marching in the vanguard of the Jazz Age assault on Victorian values. In 1922, after a cascade of sordid scandals offscreen and shocking antics onscreen, their agitations compelled studio executives to recruit Presbyterian elder and model of probity Will H. Hays, postmaster general from the administration of Warren G. Harding, to clean up, or at least put a more respectable face on, the motion picture industry. For the next quarter century, as president of the Motion Picture Producers and Distributors of America, Hays was Hollywood's man in the crosshairs of controversy, the official who defended the industry from attacks, recited soothing nostrums, and negotiated treaties to cease hostilities. The most significant pact between the censors and the censorable was the Production Code itself, adopted in 1930 to roll back the profligacy of the 1920s and set a reformed America again on the path of righteousness in the new, harsher decade.

The Production Code, the enabling legislation for classical Hollywood cinema, was written by Father Daniel Lord, a Jesuit priest, and Martin Quigley, a prominent Roman Catholic layman and editor of the influential exhibitors' journal *Motion Picture Herald*. Their amalgam of Irish-Catholic Victorianism colors much of the cloistered design of classical Hollywood cinema, not just the warm-hearted padres played by Spencer Tracy, Pat O'Brien, and Bing Crosby, but the deeper lessons of the Baltimore catechism—deference to civil and religious authorities, insistence on personal responsibility, belief in the salvific worth of suffering, and resistance to the pleasures of the flesh in thought, word, and deed.

As theological prolegomenon and cultural guidebook, the Code was a sophisticated piece of work. Contrary to popular belief, the document was not a grunted jeremiad from bluenose fussbudgets, but a polished treatise reflecting long and deep thought in aesthetics, education, communications theory, and moral philosophy. In the context of its day, the Code expressed a progressive and reformist impulse akin to that other emblem of elite cultural management, the "noble experiment" of Prohibition. It evinced concern for the proper nurturing of the young and the protection of women, demanded due respect for indigenous ethnics and foreign peoples, and sought to uplift the lower orders and convert the criminal mentality. If the intention was social control, the allegiance was on the side of the angels.

In good Jesuit fashion, the Code was divided into two parts, a set of "general principles" (the moral vision) and "particular applications" (a precise listing of forbidden material). Deeply Catholic in tone and outlook, the animating rationale for the Code held that "art can be morally evil in its effects," that both "as a product [of a mind] and the cause of definite effects, it has a deep moral significance and an unmistakable moral quality." As such, motion pictures demanded responsible handling from those who traffic in them and careful monitoring from those who shepherd the flock.

Though the tones echoed the intellectual lineage of Ignatious Loyola, the Code rightly presumed a broader constituency, a well-founded confidence that sound-thinking Americans, Catholic and non-Catholic alike, need not debate the right or wrong of some issues or even utter aloud certain unpleasant matters. Pronouncing the document "consonant with public opinion ... censorship or no censorship," the poet and biographer John Drinkwater detected "nothing in the moral aspects of the Code to which reasonable objection can be taken." In an age of moral consensus, at least among the moral guardians, the zone of agreement was large, the areas of legitimate controversy small, and the realm "beyond the pale" self-evident. "Even within the limits of pure love," asserted the Code delicately, "certain facts have been universally regarded by lawmakers as outside the limits of safe presentation." Father Lord and Mr. Quigley saw no need to defile the document by typesetting long lists of "pointed profanity" or "vulgar expressions." Likewise, the prohibition against homosexuality dared not speak the name, but it didn't need to. "*Impure love*, the love which society has always regarded as wrong and which has been banned by divine law ... must not be presented as attractive and beautiful." However, another kind of forbidden love did warrant prohibition by name: "Miscegenation," precisely defined as "sex relationships between the white and black races," was never permitted.

Lending the Code moral authority and widespread acceptance was the composition of Hollywood's audience, conceived to be a great undifferentiated Public comprised of all ages, classes, and moral sensibilities. On the universality of Hollywood cinema, both the censors and the studios agreed: everyone goes to the movies. "Most arts appeal to the mature," declared the Code. "This art appeals at once to every class—mature, immature, developed, undeveloped, law-abiding, criminal." Given the nature of the mass medium, an "'adults only'" policy would never be "completely satisfactory" and "only partially effective" even were Hollywood willing to shut out its most loyal customers, the young and gregarious. "Films, unlike books and music, can with difficulty be confined to certain selected groups," asserted the Code. So reasoned Dr. Harlan T. Horner, assistant commissioner of education for New York, in upholding a statewide ban on *The Mystery of Life* (1931), a nature documentary featuring trial lawyer Clarence Darrow discoursing upon the theory of evolution. "What constitutes decency in a plan of general public amusement open to both sexes and all ages may be vastly different from what constitutes decency before a restricted audience brought together for scientific or educational purposes," explained Dr. Horner. "In this case, the presentation of such views taken in connection with the explanation of them in a public moving picture house, wholly unrestricted, constitutes indecency." Graduate students in medicine might watch the love life of one-cell animals, snails, and spiders, but not the young and the old, the male and the female mixed together indiscriminately.

In 1930, to circumvent government regulation and squelch the protests of religious and civic groups, the Motion Picture Producers and Distributors of America pledged to abide by the Lord-Quigley commandments. Yet the men charged with bringing studio productions into line with the Code—the weak-willed factotums Col. Jason S. Joy and Dr. James Wingate of the Studio Relations Committee—lacked the fortitude and vision to enforce it. More importantly, the regulatory and oversight process was a rigged game: members of the MPPDA could appeal unfavorable decisions by Code administrators to the next level of executive authority, namely themselves. By gentleman's agreement, material that violated both the letter and spirit of the Code was granted a transit visa for theatrical release. The lax oversight was an open secret in Hollywood. "Does any producer pay attention to the Hays Code?" the *Hollywood Reporter* inquired archly in 1931, knowing none did. "Producers have reduced the Hays Production Code to sieve-like proportions and are deliberately out-smarting their own document," declared *Variety* in 1933. The same year a prominent screenwriter asserted that "the Hays moral code is not even a joke any more; it's just a memory."

Looking at the gunplay of James Cagney and listening to the wordplay of Mae West, American Catholics agreed. Beginning in late 1933 and with escalating vehemence throughout the first half of 1934, they launched a crusade against Hollywood immorality. When the New Deal in Washington insinuated the probability of federal censorship, and a reformist educational group called the Motion Picture Research Council published a series of reports linking bad behavior to bad movies, the studios found themselves fighting a three-front war against church, state, and social science. Desperate to negotiate a peace treaty, they agreed to reorganize the internal enforcement

The public face of motion picture morality: Will H. Hays, president of the MPPDA, strikes a familiar pose at a dedication ceremony at the Koster and Bial Theater, New York, 1938. (Courtesy of the Museum of Modern Art)

mechanism to ensure that the Code, so long a paper tiger, acquired teeth. The old Studio Relations Committee and the Producers Appeal Board were abolished and replaced with the Production Code Administration. The PCA derived its authority from, and ultimately answered to, the board of directors of the MPPDA, the New York bankers and moneymen behind the industry, not the on-site studio executives in Hollywood.

To head the new agency, MPPDA president Will H. Hays appointed Joseph I. Breen, a former newspaperman and influential Roman Catholic layman. As chief of the Production Code Administration from 1934 until 1954, he became one of the most influential figures in American culture. Upon his death in 1965, *Variety* summed up Breen's preeminent role: "More than any single individual, he shaped the moral stature of the American motion picture." With the exception of a brief and unhappy term as an executive at RKO from 1941 until 1942, Breen enforced the Code commandments with a potent mix of missionary zeal and administrative tenacity. Interpreter of the law and court of last resort, he presided over and upheld the moral universe of classical Hollywood cinema.

Thus, just as the term "pre-Code" has erroneously come to designate the 1930–1934 interregnum between adoption of the Code and enforcement of it, "the Hays Office," the shorthand designation for the perceived nexus of Hollywood censorship, is also a misnomer: "pre-Breen" or "Breen Office" would be more accurate.

Even for moral guardians of Breen's dedication, however, film censorship can be a tricky business. Images must be cut, dialogue overdubbed or deleted, and explicit messages and subtle implications excised from what the argot of academic film criticism calls the "diegesis." Put simply, the diegesis is the world of the film, the universe inhabited by the characters existing in the landscape of cinema. "Diegetic" elements are experienced by the characters in the film and (vicariously) by the spectator; "nondiegetic" elements are apprehended by the spectator alone. For example, in *Casablanca* (1942), when Sam performs "As Time Goes By" on the piano for Ilsa at Rick's Cafe, the music is diegetic, heard by Sam, Ilsa, and Rick ("I told you never to play that song!") as well as by the spectator. When the orchestral score reprises "As Time Goes By" on the soundtrack as Rick bids Ilsa goodbye at the airport, the music is nondiegetic, heard by and affecting the heartstrings of the spectator but not Rick, Ilsa, Victor Lazlo, and Captain Renault.

The job of the motion picture censor is to patrol the diegesis, keeping an eye and ear out for images, language, and meanings that should be banished from the world of the film. The easiest part of the assignment is to connect the dots and detect what is visually and verbally forbidden by name, snipping out a flash of flesh or cutting out a vulgar epithet. Anyone can see that Claudette Colbert's milk bath in *The Sign of the Cross* (1932) is exposing more of her breasts than section VI, part 3, of the Production Code permits, or hear that the fifth word in the closing line from *The Front Page* (1931) ("That son of a bitch stole my watch!") must be drowned out by ambient noise on the soundtrack. More challenging is the work of textual analysis and narrative rehabilitation that discerns and redirects hidden lessons and moral meanings. The astute and dedicated censor knows that correct images and proper words do not alone a moral universe make.

Breen saw his errand in the Hollywood wilderness in grander terms than the concealment of skin and the deletion of curses. He wanted to remake American cinema into a positive force for good, to imbue it with a transcendent sense of virtue and order. To earn Breen's imprimatur, the moral meaning of the picture needed to be clear, edifying, and preferably Catholic.

Not for nothing was he called the "supreme pontiff of motion picture morals." Hollywood might show the evil that men do but only if it were vanquished by the last reel, with the guilty punished and the sinner redeemed. "Compensating moral value" Breen called it, the dictum that "any theme must contain at least sufficient good in the story to compensate for, and to counteract, any evil which it relates." Moral compensation was the only justification for a glimpse of the snake in paradise.

Adhering to the catechism's injunction that sin resided in three places ("thought, word, and deed"), the genius of Hollywood's system of censorship lay in the sophisticated critical scrutiny accorded not only what was seen, said, and meant onscreen but what was apprehended from offscreen as well. True dream police, the Code censors extended their surveillance beyond the visible world and into the space of the spectator's mind. For example, in *The Office Wife* (1930), the camera follows Joan Blondell's legs into a bathroom, where her lingerie drops to the floor as she disrobes. The camera remains focused on her legs as she slips out of her chemise, her arms entering the frame from above, thereby conjuring an image of the naked actress bending over, her dorsal exposure beckoning in offscreen space should the camera tilt upward just a few inches higher. In pre-Code Hollywood, even what the spectator *doesn't* see is more nakedly suggested. Under the Code, so explicit a mental image—that is, an image not even depicted on screen but merely planted in the spectator's mind—would be too arousing to summon up.

Just as the Code monitored explicit images in offscreen space, so too did it regulate images that existed only contingently if at all. Where the unseen body of Joan Blondell from *The Office Wife* is sharply outlined, the offscreen images in Hollywood under the Code are blurred and indistinct. The very obscurity of the image, its openness to varied interpretations, was precisely what allowed the Code to grant it a conditional existence. Under this formulation, sophisticated and morally fit adults picked up on the shady implications their guileless but susceptible children missed. The Code itself recognized the two levels of comprehension: "Maturer minds may easily understand and accept without harm subject matter in plots which does younger people positive harm." Provided the children were quarantined and the meaning was elliptical, the Code permitted the possibility of a cinematically inspired thought crime. Two examples—one from the fully operating years of Code regulation, one from the lax enforcement of the pre-Code interregnum—illustrate the universe of difference.

Leo McCarey's *Make Way for Tomorrow* (1937) is a heartbreaking melodrama about an impoverished elderly couple, played by Victor Moore and

After the diegetic ellipsis: Beulah Bondi (*right*) has communicated the unspeakable to Anita Cooper in Leo McCarey's *Make Way for Tomorrow* (1937). (Courtesy of the British Film Institute)

Beulah Bondi, who are forced to depend on the kindness of familiars, the ungrateful brats who are their grown children. Farmed out to two sets of homes, separated for the first time in fifty years of marriage, they endure the humiliation of being the recipients of filial charity unwillingly given. The grandmother finds shelter but not welcome in the apartment of her eldest son, whose upscale wife and teenage daughter resent the old lady putting a crimp in their styles. In a subplot apprehensible only to the alert and sophisticated, granddaughter Rhoda (Barbara Read) is seeing a married man on the sly. The spectator who left for refreshments midway into the plot might have missed the hints: the girl, roped into taking her grandmother to the movies, sneaks out of the theater to meet secretly with a man; later, she returns from the assignation to pick up granny after the show. In the mannered world of 1930s cinema, the mere fact she consorts with a man who does not come to the door to meet her parents is a portent of trouble. The man in question is not so much as glimpsed; all is rendered elliptically.

One night Rhoda doesn't come home. Next morning, grandmother and mother wait nervously by the telephone. The phone rings and only the grandmother's side of the conversation is heard. A description of the scene and a verbatim transcription of the dialogue leaves much unsaid:

"Hello? Yes? This is Mrs. Cooper," says the grandmother, forgetting she shares the name with her daughter-in-law. "What? Don't talk so fast . . ." Her eyes widen, her jaw drops. "You don't want *me*—uh, hello?"

"Why didn't you let me talk?" demands the mother.

"She hung up. Talked about Rhoda."

"What did she say?"

The grandmother glances nervously over at an eavesdropping maid. "I'll tell you," she says, leading the mother into a back bedroom, tut-tutting all the way, "Oh, dear . . . oh, my, my . . ."

The door closes behind the pair and the camera remains outside the room, fixed on the door. The maid (Louise Beavers) sneaks over, pretending to dust, and leans down by the keyhole to listen, a surrogate for the spectator.

After a slow fade, the scene shifts to the two women behind the closed door. "You don't know how awful I feel about this," says the grandmother, signaling that the unspeakable contents of the phone conversation have been exchanged during the ellipsis.

In 1937 few spectators under the age of fourteen would have been able to figure out the message of the unscreened conversation, namely that a betrayed wife has called to tell the mother about her wayward daughter and threaten scandal. An early draft of the screenplay confirms the suspicion: Rhoda holes up with her lover in a hotel room in New Jersey and must be brought back to her family by the authorities. During the preproduction review process, Breen precisely pinpointed the moral flashpoint ("the indication on page F-22 that the granddaughter, Rhoda, spends the night in a hotel room with a married man") and decreed the solution ("this sequence should be rewritten to remove any flavor of adultery or loose sex").

McCarey complied, making the flavor of adultery a challenge for adults to detect. Since to speak the transgression is to call down judgment upon the sinner, the revelation is neither depicted nor uttered aloud. "Out of regard for the sanctity of marriage and the home, the *triangle*, that is, the love of a third party for one already married, needs careful handling," intones the Code. "The treatment should not throw sympathy against marriage as an institution." Perhaps the girl has slept with someone, perhaps she has not. Regardless, the (possibly) adulterous subplot is tangential, a device to trigger a crisis involving the continued housing of the grandmother in the family's apartment. Director McCarey's real concern is the shabby treatment of the elderly in American culture, not the indiscretion of the frisky granddaughter. *Make Way for Tomorrow* employs an elaborate conceit, above the heads of children and the dim, in which adultery receives such "careful handling" as to be almost opaque. But though murky even in the mind's eye of the alert spectator, what might be called the "diegetic ellipsis"—an ambiguous interlude occurring offscreen—is still subject to Code authority.

Victor Fleming's *Red Dust* (1932) is a hot-blooded romance, produced smack in the middle of the freewheeling pre-Code interregnum. Bare-armed and frequently bare-chested, Clark Gable plays the hard-drinking owner of an Indochinese rubber plantation who has the good fortune to find Jean Harlow squirming in his lap. Warmed by hard liquor and soft flesh, he embraces her with a frank lust she returns in kind. Dissolve to a morning six weeks later, when a smitten and satiated Harlow is to leave the plantation and travel downriver to Saigon, where she works as a "bar hostess." Misunderstanding her needy affection for the bill come due, Gable forks over some cash. As Harlow temporarily walks out of his life, Mary Astor walks in, with a husband in tow. Dispatching the husband to the jungle interior and ignoring Harlow's competitive come-ons, including a titillating, open-air bath scene, Gable seduces the mildly resistant wife. During a symbolic monsoon, a soaked Astor is swept away and the couple kiss passionately. A fade-out settles upon Astor, reclining languidly in bed, glowing with satisfaction.

Ultimately, Gable resolves to relinquish Astor, a decision he confides to a delighted Harlow. As the two tussle drunkenly, Astor walks in, Gable insults her, and she shoots him. Distraught and repentant, the wife retreats into her husband's arms, whereupon Harlow lies brazenly to conceal Astor's complicity in the illicit affair. "This bozo's been after her every minute," she declaims in mock outrage. "And tonight he comes in drunk and tries to break into her room and she shoots him"—here, Harlow puts a sardonic spin on the words—"the way any *virtuous* woman would with a *beast* like that!" None the worse for a flesh wound, Gable is nursed back to virility by the platinum blonde and the randy pair, abed, fall back into each other's arms. The End.

In 1932 no one would have had trouble figuring out that Harlow is a hooker, Astor an adulterer, and Gable a double-dealing rake. As Gable leaps between trashy blonde and classy brunette, he violates propriety and the bonds of matrimony with impunity—as do, respectively, Harlow and Astor.

Un-Codely conduct: Jean Harlow distracts Clark Gable in Victor Fleming's *Red Dust* (1932). (Courtesy of the Museum of Modern Art)

No one suffers for the sins of the flesh, and Gable and Harlow clinch happily in unsanctified lust in the final shot. Although the camera moves away from the consummations of desire, what happens when the camera retires is utterly lucid. Not only does the diegesis proper violate the Code (the triangle does not receive "careful handling"), not only is the offscreen imagery explicitly conjured (spectators are invited to unspool their own carnal images), but nothing in *Red Dust* is in any way subtle or ambiguous in meaning. There is nothing truly "elliptical" in the diegesis at all.

PRE-CODE CONTEXTS

The arc of pre-Code Hollywood cinema spanned a historical epoch of singular upheaval and rare misfortune. Between 1930 and 1934, the great smothering fact of American life was, of course, the Great Depression during its first, and worst, years. Other maladies, specific to Hollywood, also descended with a dreadful sense of timing. Two media revolutions in sound technology—commercial radio broadcasting and synchronized sound cinema—reached a quickening just as the full impact of the fiscal catastrophe was being realized. With the nation crippled economically, with expenses for sound technology skyrocketing and revenues nosediving, and with radio looming to erode the market further, the motion picture industry confronted an unprecedented cultural and financial crisis.

The historian of American cinema confronts a more familiar crisis: how to link the films to their times. Like any excursion into motion picture history, this study of pre-Code Hollywood presumes a relationship between the contents of the screen and the contexts of the culture. Vivid and vital before the eye, motion pictures freeze history despite themselves, permanently locking in time the lingo, manners, and values of their moment. Though the suitability of the medium to historical inquiry is commonsensical (film titles being marked by the date of issue), establishing a sensible fix between film and history is uncommonly difficult. To render the conflicted relationship, historians reach for line-of-sight metaphors: film reflects the moment, mirrors the zeitgeist, screens the past, opens a window on its age, spies reality through a glass darkly, and so on. A variation on the motif tries to filter out the distortion via the critical eye of the beholder, who modifies the focal length and angle of vision with each new setup, figuring that while some films invite a political interpretation others require a technical assembly-disassembly.

In the interest of getting on with it, the links between the unguarded moments of pre-Code Hollywood and the convulsions of American culture in the early 1930s are reckoned accordingly:

INSURRECTIONS ON SCREEN   The economic catastrophe of the 1930s, not the threat to national security in the 1940s, was the central American trauma of the twentieth century, the last time that the foundational beliefs of the nation were seriously up for grabs—not only its political system and economic structure but (more to the Hollywood point) its animating myths and cultural values. Whereas the challenges of the Second World War affirmed and reinvigorated American values, the ordeal of the Great Depression cruelly denied them. The myths of rugged individualism, upward mobility, material progress, frontier opportunities, and American exceptionalism, canons of the national faith since John Winthrop envisioned his gleaming City on a Hill in Puritan New England, wilted before a wasted landscape of breadlines and Hoovervilles, forgotten men and fallen women.

As the most visible purveyor of the national mythos, pre-Code Hollywood negotiated the cultural dislocations by venting insurrectionist impulses and re-formulating American myths during a time uncongenial to their straight-faced assertion. Newly audible and becoming articulate, relatively free and open to risk, it uttered challenges to traditional verities and flirted with polit-ical controversy, anything to lure back a lapsed audience with depleting re-serves of discretionary income. The pre-Code era begins in the nadir of the Great Depression, the most desperate passage in the American century, and closes with the rise of Franklin D. Roosevelt and the New Deal, the within-the-system salvation of the American experiment. After three years of wrenching disillusionment and social upheaval, the launching of the New Deal in March 1933 and its validation in the November 1934 midterm elec-tions restored not just the Democrats but America's democratic vistas. Though the Great Depression endured until the eve of World War II, the threat of a radical overthrow of capitalism and constitutionalism was averted—in part, by the cultural work performed by and enforced upon Hollywood cinema.

REVOLUTIONS IN SOUND   In the wake of *The Jazz Singer* (1927), Holly-wood's first articulate feature film, an expensive retooling of motion picture machinery and a sweeping realignment of film grammar jarred Hollywood just as the Great Depression settled over the country. A media revolution at once technological and aesthetic, the conversion from silent cinema to syn-chronized sound cinema required enormous outlays in costly new equip-ment (cameras, sound stages, recording booths, film prints, and theatrical sound systems) and the refinement of a new cinematic syntax (dialogue, sound effects, and music). Already strapped for ready cash because of the conversion to sound, holding huge speculative investments in theater chains purchased in the boom days of silent cinema, the motion picture industry was caught by the stock market crash of October 1929 at the very moment it was most vulnerable financially and unsteady aesthetically.

The gift of speech abetted the turn to morally daring and politically charged material. Where the unspoken interludes and ethereal auras of silent cinema were interrupted only by polite intertitles, the early talkies traded in rough vernacular and sophisticated wordplay. Hollywood's "all talking" movies meant fast talking, wisecracking, and double entendres. Some of the cracks were not just wise but seditious, the talk not just naughty but down-right dangerous.

Moreover, cinema was not the only popular art with something to say. Invented in 1920, commercial radio was second only to the automobile as the engine for the economic boom of the Roaring Twenties. Yet not until the early 1930s did radio become a true mass medium, a nationally shared network of signals sending out music, news, and entertainment, all free, all in the home. The living room medium of the day, radio was the first serious threat to the cultural centrality of the movies, emerging at a time when the movies could least afford the competition. Hollywood responded by co-opting radio when it could and cooperating when it had to.

The uneasy symbiosis between Hollywood and radio was intimate enough to appear a united front to Washington. The rise and regulation of radio parallels the ascendancy of the sound motion picture and its containment under the Code. No less than the contest for Hollywood's cultural capital, the regulation of radio expressed official misgivings about the politically disruptive potential of popular culture, a powerful and possibly threatening force during troubled times. In 1934, the same year that self-censorship came to Hollywood, Congress passed the Federal Communications Act, the law annexing the airwaves for "the public interest, convenience, and necessity" as determined by the federal government. Even as Hollywood was renegotiating the morality and tonality of the sound moving image, Washington was setting the ground rules for a selfsame regulation of the broadcast industry. Still distant on the mass communications horizon, sound motion pictures of Production Code quality, broadcast over airspace regulated by the government, would converge into a medium more influential and pervasive than either movies or radio.

RUMBLINGS IN THE THEATERS   Throughout the early years of the Great Depression, even as the evaporation of discretionary income cut weekly attendance in half, Americans remained passionately invested in Hollywood. Against the logic of many family budgets, the lure of the medium was still strong enough for sixty million Americans per week to steal away for a matinee or splurge on a night out. What drew them to Hollywood and what they left with were perennial questions given new urgency by the temper of the times. The standard answer, then and now, was simple escapism, the notion that Hollywood provided a psychic release from the cares and woes of life outside the theater. The more lighthearted and fantastical the film, the better the relief. Why seek depression in an imaginary world when the real world poured on more than enough, at no charge and around the clock?

Yet the proliferation of whole genres devoted to dark, dangerous, distressing, and macabre doings—gangster films, expeditionary films, tragic melodramas, and horror films—gives the lie to the popular notion of high-kicking musicals and slap-happy comedies as the exclusive low-nutrition sugar diet of Depression moviegoers. To chart the place of American cinema in the imaginative life of a people whose imaginative vistas were being foreclosed fast is inevitably a more open-ended and speculative inquiry, but the motion picture screen is always more than a blank slate. Inducements to immorality and incitements to insurrection, said one set of critics; the opiate of the masses, dulling revolutionary fervor with two-hour doses of false consciousness, said another set. The best proof of how many agreed on how high were the stakes in the allegedly escapist fare was the ferocious debate that culminated in the Production Code of 1934.

No less than the films, the motion picture theater itself was a site for clamorous and politically charged tumult. Congregated together under cover of darkness, attending to representations of American life that ranged from the inflammatory to the imbecilic, moviegoers reacted with audible expressions of approval and discontent. They hissed at images of Herbert Hoover, cheered the communist speeches of George Bernard Shaw, and sneered at the experts from government and industry who, week in and week out, insisted that the economy was on the upswing, prosperity just around the corner. At the Paramount Theater in New York, on the eve of the 1932 elections, newsreel images of President Hoover elicited so many "boos, catcalls, and whistles from the audience" that the disturbance "menaced the progress of the opening show." Nor, observed *Variety*, were such manifestations of an angry vox populi an isolated incident. "[The] situation has also been noticeable in other programs—wherein political subjects meeting with the dissension of audiences, have engendered a mocking attitude that endangers the entire performance." And, with American capitalism and constitutional democracy receiving the worse notices ever, the motion picture program was not the only performance endangered by the dissension of audiences.

LEGACIES FROM THE PAST   Although some pre-Code films have attained a secure place in the American imagination, particularly the classic gangster epics, the Universal horror twins *Dracula* (1931) and *Frankenstein* (1931), and the indelible *King Kong* (1933), the better portion of the motion picture legacy of 1930–1934 is lost to memory. When Joseph Breen took the reins of the Production Code Administration, unsavory pre-Code films were pulled from circulation and not rereleased unless rendered moral. Perhaps few pre-Code films would have warranted rerelease under any circumstances, having met their historical moment and passed with it. The early years of the Great Depression were so painful and aberrant a passage in American history that the films most intimately in touch with their times tend to perplex or put off later generations. Economically distraught, politically befuddled, and aesthetically off-balance, they have an otherworldly quality to them—due, not least, to their un-Codely conduct. After completing their original run, most pre-Code films gathered dust in studio vaults, some vanished entirely.

Television, the most powerful medium for keeping history before the eyes of the present, also blacked out the pre-Code heritage. In the early 1950s, when the major studios began selling their film libraries to the small screen, the networks found that the images and values of the 1930–1934 catalogue were as unacceptable to Cold War broadcasting standards and practices as to Joseph Breen. Television censors either rejected pre-Code films outright or sliced them so drastically that they have not lived in the popular memory with anything like the intensity of the post-Code cinema of Hollywood's golden age. Only with the advent of cable narrowcasting, where specialty channels such as American Movie Classics and Turner Classic Movies cater to obsessive cineastes, have pre-Code films found a venue for revival.

To point to a pre-Code lacuna in motion picture history, however, is not to argue for the existence of a bursting treasure trove of neglected classics and unjustly maligned masterpieces. Unfortunately, the sad lesson of film archaeology is that quite a few forgotten movies have earned their consignment to oblivion. Fortunately, the happy compensation is that many gems lie amid the quarry of pre-Code ephemera, films well worth romancing for aesthetic value and inspecting for reflections of their historical moment.

This being Hollywood cinema, the reflections seldom disclose a photographic resemblance to historical reality. Sprung from the bleakest years of the Great Depression, grappling uncertainly with a new technology, undisciplined by regular supervision but still beset with meddlesome intrusions, pre-Code Hollywood is as mediated and compromised as any popular art cursed by trade and controlled by the timid. Yet the motion pictures produced on the cusp of classical Hollywood cinema had more reason to traffic in the risqué and the risky than its mature and secure descendent. The dislocations in American culture opened up new spaces on screen and, before the territory was placed off limits, filmmakers rushed in to test the air. After 1934 the machinery of classical Hollywood cinema would operate at full throttle, under strict surveillance. For four short years, though, pre-Code Hollywood entertained, even embraced, visions of immorality and insurrection.

2

Breadlines and Box Office Lines
Hollywood in the Nadir of the Great Depression

The cultural transition from the 1920s to the 1930s turns neatly in time with the pages of the calendar, one epoch flipping over into the other almost precisely on cue. With the stock market crash of October 29, 1929, the knockout bell for a flattened decade tolled the cold-water awakening for the next round. In print and on screen, popular renderings soon cast the passage as a kind of temporal morality play wherein the frenetic excesses of the Jazz Age lead inevitably into the long penance of the Great Depression. After a wild night spent burning the candle at both ends, gyrating to the Charleston, and sloshing around in bathtub gin, the dull pain of the next ten years is the deserved hangover, just punishment for straying so far from the traditional American virtues of temperance, hard work, and deferred gratification.

Glancing back from no great distance in 1931, the novelist F. Scott Fitzgerald and the historian Frederick Lewis Allen each contemplated the 1920s as if gazing upon a strange horizon from across a huge gulf of time. They speak with detachment and dissonance, not nostalgia for the lost glory, but incredulity that such an age once existed, and so recently. "It is too soon to write about the Jazz Age with perspective," wrote Fitzgerald, who did just that in his poignant memoir, "Echoes of the Jazz Age." "After two years the Jazz Age seems as far away as the days before the war," he marveled. "It is as dead as were the Yellow Nineties in 1902." Fitzgerald could still muster a wistful regard for his age of miracles, art, excess, and satire ("It all seems rosy and romantic to us who were young then, because we will never feel quite so intensely about our surroundings any more"), but he was too sensitive a tuning fork to the pitch of his times not to admit that most Americans looking back at the 1920s readily "summoned the proper expression of horror" and succumbed "to violent retching when they happened upon any of its characteristic words."

The very title of Frederick Lewis Allen's *Only Yesterday* expresses a disbelief that such giddy follies had lately been abroad in the land. Though somewhat apologetic for "the writing of a history so soon after the event," Allen correctly surmised that the eleven-year period from Armistice Day to the 1929 crash "in the future may be considered a distinct era in American history." In chronicling the ebb and flow of what he dubbed "the ballyhoo years," Allen predicted that the mists of time would doubtless come to soften the memory of those "charming, crazy days," but in summing up the late past he pronounced a harsher verdict. Of the 1920s, he remembered all too well "the frustrated hopes that followed the war, the aching disillusionment of the hard-boiled era, its oily scandals, its spiritual paralysis, the harshness of its gaiety." The end of Coolidge-Hoover prosperity was "a bitter draught to swallow" but was needed medicine for the sickness in the American soul.

Both Fitzgerald and Allen were evoking not some remote era, a lost empire of distant memory, but a period that should still have been green in memory. Yet both are astonished by the recent past and not yet able to come to terms with the grim present. Even before the full pain and persistence of the Great Depression was comprehended, the vibrant zeitgeist of the 1920s seems to have given up the ghost overnight. What would have been the thoughts of Fitzgerald, Allen, and their fellow Americans in 1931 had they known how prolonged and dreadful the economic trough before them would be, how bleak the outlook for so long?

From sin to retribution, debauchery to convalescence, gaiety to gloom, the "morning after" imagery and moral shadings of the historical shift settled over the atmospherics of Hollywood cinema. Wild party scenes fade to

Après le déluge: Joan Crawford (*center*) and the jazz babies of the 1920s in *Dance, Fools, Dance* (1931). (Courtesy of the Museum of Modern Art)

wasted flappers passed out on sofas; tires screech as drunken frat boys in speeding flivvers miss the curve; frenzied trading on Wall Street dissolves to piles of ticker tape swept up in trash bins. In *Dance, Fools, Dance* (1931), reckless young Fitzgeraldians at a yacht party strip down to their underwear and leap into the ocean, bootleg drinks in hand. When the Crash comes, the ruined yacht owner staggers to the floor of the New York Stock Exchange and keels over from a heart attack, leaving his helpless jazz babies (Joan Crawford and William Bakewell) to fend for themselves. She gets a job as a cub reporter and acquires a backbone; he drifts into bootlegging and a murder rap. A 1930s film with a 1920s title, *Dance, Fools, Dance* flashbacks to the Jazz Age with the mixture of wide-eyed wonder and moral censure that was now the cultural consensus. Like the retrospective cinema of World War II, where December 7, 1941, looms like a ticking bomb awaiting detonation at a pivotal plot point, pre-Code Hollywood looks back at the 1920s with rueful anticipation of the calamity of October 29, 1929. The wild party, the Great Depression spectator knows, will come crashing down on these blissfully ignorant revelers, shimmying as their inheritance burns.

As for the present, the early 1930s begin with denial, turn to despair, settle into numb endurance, and, slowly, work toward recovery with FDR. Initially, in the immediate aftermath of the Crash, the extent of the catastrophe was simply denied. To read the pronouncements of businessmen and politicians in the first years of what was by 1932 already being called the Great Depression is to be struck by the pathos in their desperate boosterism, almost grateful that they don't yet comprehend the duration and depth of what awaits them.

Cold statistics render the magnitude of the wreckage. In any graph of economic indicators between 1929 and 1933, the lines plunge downward almost at right angles, bottoming out at a "cyclical trough in March 1933" before inching upward with an agonizing slowness that slumps again in 1937 and will not truly reverse itself and quicken until the eve of World War II. In the wake of the Crash, production of goods contracted by 33 percent. One-fifth of all commercial banks failed. Nationally, 25 percent of the labor force was idle, but in some stricken regions the figure was twice that or more. When looking at the bottom lines of the Great Depression, conservative economists drop their normal reserve, indulge in superlatives, and admit that the sky really was falling. "The great contraction" of 1929–1933, concluded Milton Friedman and Anna Jacobson Schwartz, was "the most severe business cycle contraction" in the whole of U.S. history. "Real income fell by 11 percent, 9 percent, 18 percent, and 3 percent in the four successive years. These are extraordinary declines for individual years, let alone for four successive years."

Anecdotal evidence backs up the statistics, with both ends of the economic spectrum recalling the early 1930s as the worst of bad times. "I've been in a Depression ever since I've been in the world," a former West Virginian coal miner told historian Studs Terkel. "Still, it's better and worse. '31, '32, that's about the worst we ever been through." From his infinitely more secure vantage, Gen. Robert E. Wood, a vice president at Sears, Roebuck and founder of All-State Insurance, held the same opinion. "We had to lay off thousands of people. It was terrible. '32 was bad, '33 was bad, '31 was the worst of all."

Yet government and business leaders seemed oblivious to conditions on the streets. "The only real and lasting remedy for unemployment is employment," Herbert Hoover declared blankly in the midst of the calamity. In 1932 the president suggested to crooner Rudy Vallee that he write a tune to drive the Great Depression away, a magic incantation to erase the bad times. Though Hoover was jesting, the remark reflected his impotence before the present emergency. Elected in 1928 on a platform of continuity and confidence, unable to cope with or speak plainly about the nationwide destitution, Hoover paid the bill for the paper margins of Coolidge prosperity. "You was handed a balloon that was blowed up to its utmost," Will Rogers reproached him, the "unofficial president of the United States" addressing the real one as an equal. "You held it as carefully as anyone could, but the thing busted right in your face." Hoover's paralysis was soon taken for complicity and the once-respected name of the president became an all-purpose, derisive prefix. In the 1920s "to hoover" meant to take care of things efficiently. In the 1930s his surname christened the detritus of the Great Depression. Newspapers were "Hoover blankets," outturned pockets "Hoover flags," and hobo encampments "Hoovervilles."

The invincible ignorance of officialdom inspired Edward Angly, a reporter for the *New York Herald Tribune*, to compile into a bitter little volume the unruffled utterances of politicians, bankers, economists, columnists, and other esteemed experts. Published in 1931, the book simply reprinted newspaper headlines, editorial cartoons, and quotations from the rich and powerful that denied the reality of the past two years or predicted its imminent reversal. Hoover and his cabinet were well represented in a catalogue of blithe reassurances now ringing so hollow as to be funny. Two examples:

"The worst is over without a doubt."
> *–James J. Davis, Secretary of Labor, June 19, 1930*

"We have hit bottom and are on the upswing."
> *–James J. Davis, Secretary of Labor, September 18, 1930*

The only editorial response to the litany of false prophecies is the defiant title Angly gave to the book: *Oh Yeah?* "The discrepancy between fact and fiction had a profound effect on the minds and hearts of the American people," remarked the critic Gilbert Seldes in 1933, by which time the veil had lifted. "A hundred more obscure and subtle shades of feeling all were determined by this one thing,"—and here Seldes italicizes the crucial fact—"*that we were not permitted for many months to confront the reality of our situation.*"

Beset with adversity severe and undeniable, ordinary Americans responded to the upbeat slogans, glib reassurances, and serene self-delusions with despair and ridicule. A Kansas farmer claimed that Hoover was the greatest engineer in the world because "he had drained, ditched, and damned the United States in three years." In "The Hobo's Psalm," a widely recited satire of the twenty-third Psalm, the president's name is invoked for a double blasphemy on religion and politics:

> *Hoover is my shepherd, I shall not want*
> *He maketh me to lie down on park benches*
> *He leadeth me beside the still factories*
> *He arouseth my doubt in the Republican Party*
> *He leadeth me in the path of Destruction*
> *For his party's sake*
> *I fear evil, for thou art with me.*

With conditions under Hoover seemingly a visitation immune to human action, the biblical backdrop was a persistent frame of reference, the fire and brimstone rained down on Sodom and Gomorrah by an angry God a fit precedent for the punishing onslaught of the Great Depression. In Cecil B. DeMille's *Madame Satan* (1930), a Jazz Age bacchanalia aboard a zeppelin echoes the gaudy debauches in the director's biblical spectacles and egyptomaniac epics. Scantily clad damsels parade before salivating men in a mock slave auction, waitresses serve up bootleg booze, revelers exchange salacious bon mots, and flappers croon hot songs. Celestial wrath is visited upon the sinners when a bolt of lightning crashes the party and rips the zeppelin apart. Strapping on parachutes, the revelers leap from the plummeting airship and float to earth, the skirts of the women billowing high in the updraft—but though the wild party has ended in a crash, DeMille's chastened wastrels, unlike the investors on Wall Street, can come in for a soft landing. In literature and criticism too, allusions to Old Testament plagues and divine vengeance swirled around descriptions of the early 1930s. "The years of the locust," Gilbert Seldes called them, before B-movie screenwriter Nathanael West made the allegory his own in 1939 with his phantasmagorical vision of a Hollywood-filtered apocalypse, *The Day of the Locust*.

The two nostrums of reassurance and optimism, now uttered with ironic bitterness, were the catch phrase "prosperity is just around the corner" and the Tin Pan Alley tune "Happy Days Are Here Again." The premature song, written for *Rain or Shine* (1930) by Milton Ager and Jack Yellin, was a jaunty melody that came to sound like a dirge, its lyrics a rebuke ("our cares and troubles are gone/they'll be no more from now on"). Throughout American cinema in the early 1930s, it is sung, hummed, and played sardonically. In *Under 18* (1932), the tune is whistled by an impoverished Marian Marsh after her sister, with a new baby and ne'er-do-well husband in tow, move into the cramped tenement apartment she shares with her mother. In *20,000 Years in Sing Sing* (1933), when doomed inmate Spencer Tracy walks onto death row, the condemned men greet him with the song's chorus. "Happy days," he mutters. "Mighty few of 'em. These guys got a sense of humor."

In the long night that was the Great Depression, the period between 1930 and 1933 measured out the blackest hours. Historians of the era dig deep for metaphors that emphasize the extremities of distress in an already extreme time, stretching the language to render the bottommost depths, the trough in an abysmal decade, the nadir of the Great Depression. Prior to March 1933, when the vigorous Franklin Roosevelt took the reins from the hapless Herbert Hoover, the condition of the country seemed critical and the attending physician inept. Recalling the period years later, the literary critic Edmund Wilson ventured the appraisal that "the whole structure of American society seemed actually to be going to pieces." Writing in 1932, as America neared "the third anniversary of that fatal October day which wrote finis to the turbulent 'twenties," the literary critic Ernest Gruening asked a series of feverish questions. "What lies ahead for all of us? Is the old America gone forever? Is the promise of American life irretrievably broken? Is the Depression a mere passing phase from which we shall awake as we always have? Will there be revolution in the United States?" In the last moments of *Heroes for Sale* (1933), a hobo gestures hopelessly into a rain-swept night and speaks one of the bleakest lines in Hollywood cinema: "It's the end of America."

The Lost Millions

No less in a steady state of denial about the true magnitude of the crisis than their brothers in banking and government, executives of the motion picture industry repeated the rosy predictions and recited the return-to-good-times mantras. In 1930 Samuel Katz, president of Paramount Publix Corporation, delivered a typically buoyant prognosis. "We are passing through a temporary period of changing values and confusion," he said reassuringly. "The firm foundation upon which the United States rests with its free, educated people, its natural resources and national resources, is a permanent, unchanging factor for optimism." Speaking in the bleak summer of that same year, Harold B. Franklin, president of Fox West Coast Theaters, cheerfully contemplated the next season: "Business is better. Much better. We look for

Breadlines not box office lines: an army of the unemployed lines up at Al Capone's Soup Kitchen, Chicago, 1931 (Courtesy of the National Archives)

continued improvement and a return to normalcy." But it was not the old expression ("normalcy," a characteristic word of the 1920s) but the new coinage, still lower case ("depression") that stuck. Every year, prosperity was just around the corner and outlooks for the future were bright. "Hooray!" bellowed a trade ad in 1931. "Breadlines are becoming box office lines!" Every year, around the corner was another corner.

By 1931 box office returns had dropped 10 percent to 35 percent in most localities. Tens of millions of once loyal moviegoers, up against it and forced to cut back, forswore the luxury of motion picture entertainment. By the middle of 1932, 6,500 moviehouses had gone "dark," an all-time high that left the remaining 13,000 at an all-time low. According to *The Film Daily Year Book of 1934*, between the happy days of the 1920s and the first years of the Great Depression, attendance plummeted from "a boom high of more than 100,000,000 weekly to a Depression low of less than 40,000,000," before leveling off at around sixty million. On Wall Street, motion picture stocks sank to record lows. In 1932 industry pioneer Adolph Zukor tearfully confronted a meeting of Paramount stockholders. "My pride is broken, my heart is torn—I want to help restore the company to its former position. I do not want money. I want to rebuild this company for which I have given my life," pleaded Zukor, weeping unashamedly. "Some mornings I have left home feeling that I could tear the world apart, and before I went home I marveled that the world had not torn me apart." Teetering on the brink of ruin, the major studios scrambled to cut costs and squeeze out profits. By January 1933 both Paramount Publix Corporation and Radio-Keith-Orpheum had gone into financial receivership to avoid the onus of bankruptcy.

In public, official voices remained upbeat. Allowing that "the depression, unemployment, and fear for the future undoubtedly have interfered with the regular attendance at entertainment," Will Hays declared in 1932 that "the inherent stability of motion picture entertainment has been proven as never before" and predicted the "fullest possible prosperity for the industry." "There is no depression to a showman!" boomed the unsinkable Harold B. Franklin, still putting the best face forward, still unwilling to admit that aggressive salesmanship couldn't turn business around. "I believe that the depression is at an end and that conditions are improving," avowed Universal's Carl Laemmle at the beginning of 1933.

In private, however, Hollywood insiders were becoming downright panicky. In 1932 Paramount's once optimistic Samuel Katz bore the bad news to the managers of Fox Theaters. "Nothing would give me greater pleasure at this time than to be able to forecast an immediate return to prosperity. In all honesty, I cannot do it. There is no use kidding ourselves. We are not half-grown boys, but mature, seasoned men and we should look things squarely in the face. As I see it, we have not as yet come to the turn in the road. There is still a hard pull ahead of us." To the boosterism of Hays, Franklin, and their ilk, the *Hollywood Reporter* printed a one word rejoinder: "Bunk."

In fact the motion picture industry was better off than many American businesses, but the winds of the Great Depression hit Hollywood harder because the town had never before known so precipitous an economic downturn. From kinetoscope to nickelodeon to motion picture palace, box office had been all boom and no bust. Born and reared in flush times with a monopoly on the most alluring medium in popular culture, having not only weathered but prospered during recessions and world war, the motion picture industry was supposed to be immune to the normal business cycles of ups and downs, bull and bear markets, humming merrily along to an ever-expanding profit margin. The early period of sound from 1927 to 1929, when audiences flocked to discover the new wonder of the cinema, encouraged the fat complacency. Confronting mortality in the early 1930s, Hollywood was traumatized by the sudden withdrawal of its privileged status. The industry retained its monopoly over a precious commodity, but it was no longer assured of guaranteed profits on just any "all talking" picture. Like everyone else, filmmakers had to work harder for less money, with no guarantee of deliverance from the creditors in the last reel.

By the close of 1931, industry executives were looking back glumly at what they called "the only serious business recession in the history of the industry" or "the first serious storm that has beset us in our history." The judgment from *Variety* verged on the apocalyptic: "The decline was such that it leaves an open question whether the moving picture will ever again know the popularity of those peaks it reached in the silent era and then again with sound." Two years later, the prognosis was still grim. "The studios are in trouble," moaned the *Hollywood Reporter*. "The picture business is in trouble. The whole of America is in trouble."

From their perch on Wall Street, the bankers who backed the moguls looked at the hemorrhaging on the West Coast and took emergency action: rolling heads, slicing payrolls, and rewriting corporate flowcharts. Cost-cutting measures and strict accounting practices came to a business notorious for extravagant spending, padded payrolls, and creative bookkeeping. Sometimes the moneymen made matters worse by intruding into production meetings and bungling about sound stages. "These Wall Street guys are going to ruin pictures," griped a studio executive. "They send out a wire to cut the payroll $10,000 and everybody on the lot who knows anything about making pictures is fired."

Taking note of "the tightening of loose spots and the elimination of waste in the most rigorous manner," Paramount founder and president Jesse L. Lasky called the belt-tightening "the most thorough and far-reaching reorganization that I have ever seen sweep through the studios." Universal's Carl Laemmle agreed, but insisted that "the industry is merely eliminating waste [and] dead overhead" in order to make "every dollar invested in screen entertainment visible on the screen."

At the exhibition end of the business, theater owners slashed prices, fired ushers, eliminated stage shows, and scrambled to attract the "lost millions" with raffles and giveaways. Purchase a movie ticket and win a chance at grocery baskets, hams, china, Japanese tea sets, crockery, waffle irons, vacuum cleaners, refrigerators, home furnishings, cash, automobiles, trips to Yellowstone and Hollywood, and in one case (soothing the Depression-racked mind and body at one session) free psychoanalysis and ice cream served up in the lobby.

But behind the economic travails was the sense too that Hollywood was simply off its game, that business was bad, sure, but so were the movies. Film for film, the studios were not turning out quality product, as if the combination of the bad economy and the new sound technology had fostered an industry-wide creative block. "It's all bunk that the best writing is done under the stress of worry and necessity," said Fox president Sidney R. Kent. "Writers worrying about their losses in the stock market and often when they will eat has resulted in a mediocre type of product getting into print." In 1932 MGM president Nicholas Schenck uttered a remark that was to be repeated every time the industry suffered a slump in attendance. "There is nothing the matter with the picture business that good pictures will not cure."

That a few big hits of manifest merit and originality—*Little Caesar* (1930), *Frankenstein* (1931), and *King Kong* (1933)—racked up record business only heightened the perception that something beyond economics and technology was at the core of Hollywood's troubled times. When the public really wanted to see a film, even the Great Depression couldn't keep them away. In 1931 Groucho Marx diagnosed what was wrong with the movies. "So far as the movies go, everything is simply swell," wisecracked Groucho, who had lost a fortune in the Crash but had profited from the shift from physical comedy to verbal dexterity as much as anyone. "The only thing that happens to be wrong, unfortunately, is the public. The good people (damn them) seem suddenly to have decided not to go to the picture shows. God knows where they do go. They certainly don't go to legitimate theaters. They don't go to bed and, judging from business conditions, they don't go to work."

In the long run, the Great Depression was good for the motion picture industry, requiring it to streamline operations, facilitating its realignment along modern lines of business management, and helping it to crush independent producers. But in the early 1930s few in Hollywood were taking the long view. Eyes fixed on the present, they saw only black days and red ink.

A SYNCHRONIZED INDUSTRY

Woven into the economic troubles and exacerbating the artistic self-doubts were the disruptions wrought by the conversion to sound technology. When *The Jazz Singer* (1927) rendered the silent cinema obsolete, Hollywood was forced to retool the means of motion picture production and revamp the art of cinema, to create a whole new industry from the skeleton of the old one. In mastering the technology and perfecting the art, the Hollywood studio system forged the dominant medium of the twentieth century, the audible moving image.

The transition to sound spawned two related synchronizations. First, as a new, complex component in motion picture production, sound refined the machinery of filmmaking. Synchronized sound recording demanded more precision, care, and expense at all levels of production, distribution, and exhibition. The second synchronization was quite literal: the fluid integration of the wonder of talk, music, and noise into motion picture art.

Purely as an industrial revolution, the speed and ruthlessness of the sound revolution was dizzying. By 1930 fully 70 percent of motion picture theaters were wired for sound, the balance being comprised mainly of small neighborhood houses ("nabes" in the jargon) seating under five hundred. That same year the major studios announced total cessation of silent film production, and the trade press published the obituary. The all-sound studio releasing schedule for 1930–31 meant that "the final nail has been driven into the silent picture's wooden kimono." A few paused to eulogize the sad plight of a great art form made superfluous in one technical stroke. Most took pride in the march of progress and gaily consigned "the unobtrusive quiet movie of the old days" to the "cinematic happy hunting grounds." Hollywood "has been completely revolutionized from a muted but successful business to a loquacious, dynamic and powerful new art in a period of approximately two years," boasted the *Film Daily* in 1930. "Silents have reached the antique stage and are now approaching the curio era."

Live sound recording required a scrupulous attention to moviemaking detail, a greater reliance on rehearsals, scheduling, written directives, and work charts. In case anyone missed the point, two shouted phrases summed up the new regime: "Quiet on the set!" and "Stick to the script." To help close the margin for error, director Lewis Milestone improvised a permanent contribution to the Hollywood battle plan, the storyboard (then called a "scene chart"), a series of cartoon panels roughly illustrating mise-en-scène and camera angle. By 1931 the major studios took only sixteen working days to complete a standard talkie, twenty-five to fifty days for a special production. "In silent pictures, I was accustomed to take at least five shots of each scene and ofttimes upwards of a dozen of the same scene," reported Cecil B. DeMille. "In my current talkie, *The Squawman* [1931], two takes were enough."

The most significant managerial revolution was the shift to unit production. The old model for motion picture production, in which a single chief executive oversaw a studio's entire slate of films, was administratively inefficient and physically killing. "No one man—and I know this from my experience as head of production for Paramount—can hope to be responsible for 50 or 60 productions a year and not have to pay the price, through loss of perspective from a succession of 18-hour days," confessed B. P. Schulberg in 1932. Unable by temperament to heed the advice of his colleague at Paramount, MGM's Irving Thalberg worked himself to death by 1936, burnt out at age thirty-seven. The new model for production likened the studio mogul to a general at the head of several regiments, delegating command authority to executives in charge of production, who in turn appointed "junior associate producers" as field lieutenants. The moguls still had final say (and final cut) and still took a passionate interest in projects close to their hearts. But the sheer complexity and size of the task made on-site supervision too big for any one man.

Other modifications visibly refined and refashioned the American screen. In 1931, in a qualitative upgrade in the look of the celluloid image, Eastman Kodak introduced a high-speed panchromatic negative film stock. Officially designated as Eastman Supersensitive Panchromatic Negative Type 2, it was twice as "fast" as previous stocks and noticeably enhanced the clarity of the studio-quality 35mm motion picture image. The same year also witnessed the standardization of the dimensions of the motion picture frame. After a brief flirtation with a widescreen 70mm process, the aspect ratio (the relationship of height to width in the motion picture screen) was designated as 1 to 1.33, a standard settled on with an eye already to the future contours of the television frame. Until CinemaScope extended the horizontal space of the screen in the early 1950s, the so-called Academy ratio was the platonic ideal for the American screen image.

Finally, sound standardized reel sizes and running times. In the silent era, the running time of a film varied depending on how fast it flowed through the projector. Sound meant twenty-four frames per second: the speed of an image was readily variable, the soundtrack wasn't. Though the "one reel" and "two reel" coinage survived in the vernacular of the trade, running times were now officially measured to the second.

Though the changes from film frame to film production convulsed Hollywood's physical plant, the technical transformations and economic adjustments remained offscreen happenings, not registering consciously in the experience of moviegoing. What spectators could not help but see—and hear—were the new styles and sounds of American cinema.

The dual maladies of static staging and frenzied talking remain the two abiding clichés of the early sound cinema. Like a lot of stereotypes, truth is at the back of each. For every fleet-footed innovation like Rouben Mamoulian's *Applause* (1929) or Lewis Milestone's *All Quiet on the Western Front* (1930), with their mobile cameras and double-tracked recordings, dozens of proscenium stage productions were filmed with cameras bolted to the floor, little more than preserved vaudeville shows interrupted with cutaways to applauding audiences.

At the other extreme was the nonstop talkfest where a cacophony of speech cluttered the diegesis from title card to end credits. Having advertised an "all talking" movie, it was as if filmmakers feared that audiences would demand their money back were not every second of screen time filled with a human voice. As early as 1930, Carl Laemmle criticized the "continuous barrage of speaking or music" in the "chattering dialogue pictures." Heedless of the pleas for peace, though, the actors on screen would not just shut up. "What do we have a camera for?" director Ernst Lubitsch exclaimed in frustration. "Why talk about things that happen or have happened? Show them!"

"MIKE FRIGHT"

Sound was the essential element in another ongoing media revolution, this one vexing Hollywood not from within but without. Just when motion picture theaters were being rewired for the talkies, American homes were undergoing a selfsame transition. From the early 1930s to the late 1940s, the free broadcasting medium of radio linked the nation in a web of news events, musical performance, comedic byplay, and the original soap operas. A transcontinental causeway paved in a few short years, radio, not cinema, permeated the atmosphere of daily life with an ambient soundtrack for work and leisure.

The relation of radio to the motion picture industry was competitive and symbiotic. As an alternative entertainment option, radio shows siphoned off potential box office customers. Yet radio also provided a network of national advertising for Hollywood and a farm team for motion picture performers. The well-spoken and verbally adroit radio personality might sashay easily into films and back again to radio for bimedia exploitation, double-dipping into the two most popular media of the day.

Fearing encroachments on its turf, the motion picture industry warily monitored the progress of the broadcast industry. Beginning in the mid-1920s, radio static was a steady hum in the background of Hollywood production decisions, goading the industry into experiments with sound film and the production of spectacles such as *Ben-Hur* (1926) and *The King of Kings* (1927). Not until the early 1930s, however, when radio penetration passed 50 percent of the population and the Great Depression dried up discretionary income, did it become corrosive competition to Hollywood. "Radio broadcasting of headline performers is making severe inroads in box office receipts," warned *Motion Picture Herald* in a series of alarmist articles in 1933. "Radio audiences are growing daily; theater attendance reacts accordingly, and, while authorities in both fields are unable to estimate definitely to what extent radio is making inroads on box office receipts, exhibitors almost everywhere are complaining that the competition is serious if not menacing." As a simple matter of dollars and cents, the trade-off in media could be calculated in food on the table. "The average family of five can sit home Sunday nights and listen to the biggest stars, offering the best music and entertainment in the world," a radio station manager pointed out. "If they went downtown to the picture house, they would pay a minimum of $1.75 plus cost of transportation. In these times, $1.75 plus transportation would provide the average family with bread, butter, and milk for the week."

Exhibitors tried to co-opt the enemy by playing radio shows in theater lobbies and sometimes even interrupting the motion picture program for a broadcast interlude, with the radio set placed on the stage before the screen. Anticipating the media theories of Marshall McLuhan, however, exhibitors concluded that communal listening to Amos 'n' Andy "was lost on a large audience in unaccustomed surroundings for this so-called 'intimate' or home entertainment."

However much Hollywood feared and disdained the home entertainment, radio advertising was too potent a force not to compel collaboration. By 1931 the major studios not only spent huge sums on "spot" advertising to plug current releases, but all were involved in elaborate programming tie-ins with radio. Paramount sponsored a weekly "Paramount Hour" over the NBC network, Warner Brothers operated KFWB in Los Angeles as an adjunct publicity unit, and RKO's "Theater of the Air" functioned as a thirty-minute commercial for studio releases ("pre-sold direct to the whole family every night"). Entertainers cross-pollinated between the media, with film actors appearing on radio to perform bits and plug features and radio personalities making the transition the other way. On the debit side, radio extravaganzas promoting motion pictures kept audiences at home listening to the stars publicizing their movies on radio. Exhibitors objected to motion picture talent appearing on radio and proposed a "code of ethics" whereby studio contract players would be prohibited from broadcast appearances between the prime moviegoing hours of 6:00 P.M. and 10:00 P.M.

Not wanting to validate the competition, Hollywood only grudgingly depicted the emerging prominence of radio as essential furniture in the American household. Two comparable film moments register both the speed of radio penetration and the reluctance to acknowledge it onscreen. In *Speedy* (1928), Harold Lloyd's last silent comedy, the comedian plays a sports-crazed soda jerk in downtown New York. To obtain the updates on a baseball game from Yankee Stadium, he depends on a telephone relay system. Harold calls up a friend who in turn receives his own up-to-the-inning reports by telephone from a source at the stadium. Though the first simultaneous coast-to-coast radio broadcast of the World Series occurred two years earlier in 1926, *Speedy* labors to avoid the existence of the rival medium. Two years after *Speedy*, four years after the fact, cultural reality could no longer be ignored. In *They Learned About Women* (1930), a World Series game in Yankee Stadium is broadcast live over the air by real life sportscaster Graham McNamee, the very man who announced the 1926 games. Cutaway shots show a young boy and his father listening at home before a gargantuan radio set. No one uses the telephone any longer to hear the latest baseball scores.

Not unlike the way Hollywood later sought to denigrate the allure of television in the early 1950s, the films of the early 1930s insulted the rival medium at every opportunity. In *State's Attorney* (1932), John Barrymore shuts off the radio when the announcer begins an annoying commercial spiel. "I wonder what radio announcers do for a living?" he muses. In an earnest review of *Arrowsmith* (1931), a prestige project and a serious film, *Motion Picture Herald* praised the ambition of Hollywood ("It took nerve to invest a large sum of money in the making of this psychoanalytic study of a scientist and his problems") and sniffed at the lowbrow competition ("To the minds who prefer to turn on the radio and listen to a broadcast phonograph of 'The Peanut Vendor' the reaction is not likely to be enthusiastic").

Despite the snide remarks, the human traffic between the two media was unstoppable. Underemployed screen entertainers happily auditioned for the quick cash radio paid out for live performances requiring no rehearsals. In turn, vocally confident radio performers eyed the new sound cinema as a lucrative career move. But if giving a voice to a silent screen face was hit or miss, giving a screen face to a radio voice was mostly miss. Although virtually all the big radio stars of the 1930s ventured into the movies, few radio-born personalities achieved first-rank success as motion picture performers. Often even the most high-priced radio talent was relegated to short features, supporting-player status, or single numbers in cavalcade productions. In the pre-Code era, the Marx Brothers, Al Jolson, Lawrence Tibbet, and Eddie Cantor were considered the only radio "headliners whose screen efforts enjoyed any appreciable success," and all but Tibbet had already achieved fame in vaudeville. Promiscuous crossbreeding between radio and motion pictures would be regulation practice by the mid-1930s (with W. C. Fields jousting memorably with wooden dummy Charlie McCarthy, and Bing Crosby and Bob Hope, singly and together, crossing over back and forth), but purely radio-fueled successes (Amos 'n' Andy, Burns and Allen, Jack Benny, Ed Wynn, and Kate Smith) fared poorly in the movies only to thrive a media generation later in the descendent broadcast medium, television.

For their part, motion picture performers tended to freeze up when placed before a radio microphone. Just as silent screen actors with untested voices grappled with the transition to sound cinema, faces from the screen seemed unable to render personality as mere voices in the ether. Many were said to be afflicted with "mike fright," a malady defined as "an unreasonable fear of an unseen audience."

The "mike fright" of the screen thespian paled beside Hollywood's quite reasonable fears of its unseen audience. The convergence of economic, technological, and artistic forces pummeling the motion picture industry in the early 1930s would not have been so cumulatively debilitating had not the core source of sustenance been withdrawn so abruptly. Reorganizing the business for maximum efficiency, mastering the technology of sound, and facing down the radio competition meant nothing unless the lost millions were once again found.

3

Preachment Yarns
The Politics of Mere Entertainment

A parade of disgruntled and bedraggled men marches forward ominously, locked shoulder to shoulder. Once hopeful and vigorous, they are now worn out and beaten down, threadbare in dress and slightly deranged, sometimes quite literally bearing torches. As the mass of humanity moves from back frame to center screen, shouted slogans rise above the single animal roar filling the soundtrack. Long shots scan the angry assembly and close-ups pick out a montage of faces—emaciated laborers, rugged farmers, ethnic types of all varieties, even the random black man. A wide-eyed desperation fires their revolutionary fervor and something unnatural pervades the sight of Americans taking to the streets like so many French peasants or Russian serfs.

Always on the edge of chaos and violence, part demos and part mob, the group portrait of the unemployed, the radicalized, and the panic-stricken unspools with grim regularity in pre-Code Hollywood. From every side, rebels and recalcitrants converge menacingly, whether as the workers on strike in *Heroes for Sale* (1933), the army of the unemployed in *Gabriel Over the White House* (1933), or the delinquent riff-raff in *The Mayor of Hell* (1933). Panoramic long shots survey dozens, sometimes hundreds, of teeming extras, and fluid editing builds in intensity as individual men merge into a single mass organism, barely constrained, it seems, by the hand of the director off screen. "One of the most excitingly realistic mob scenes ever pictured on the screen," raved the *New York World Telegram* about the surging multitudes in the bank run sequence in *American Madness* (1932), Frank Capra's chilling portrait of the thin line between investor confidence and panic in Hoover's America. "Ah, they've gone crazy," says the noble bank president, watching helplessly as the hysteria creates the very insolvency the depositors fear. "You can't reason with a mob."

Insurgents of all persuasions seethe with anger and, when the collective will comes to realize its power in numbers, erupts into spontaneous, cathartic violence. "There are hundreds of us and ten of them!" shouts a voice from the herd of juvenile hoboes in *Wild Boys of the Road* (1933), inciting a counterattack on a squad of railroad dicks. Dispersed by firehoses and clubs, beaten up by goons, fired on by deputies, they are pushed back only by the application of police force. (For a counterspectacle of disciplined, coordinated action, the geometric precision and military order of the chorus lines in Busby Berkeley's musicals celebrated a communal harmony on the stage unknown on the streets. Not until the eve of the World War II would Americans outside the musical genre parade with calm and deliberate purpose, lining up on behalf of state power, not breaking ranks to run riot and assault the citadel.)

Whether shuffling in breadlines, milling in parks, swarming in hobo camps, or rallying in hunger marches and "red strikes," restless men at the end of their rope haunt the early years of the Great Depression. For many Americans, the frightening images of the mad mob inspired the not unreasonable suspicion that, like France under the Bourbons and Russia under the Czar, America was coming unglued. Walter Lippmann, dean of newspaper commentators and font of conventional wisdom, expressed the fear that the established order felt before the mob and the fear that individuals in the mob felt when they realized what they were capable of en masse. "Individual fears," warned Lippmann, "spread like an hysteria in a crowd which is trapped in an inclosure and cannot find the exits, and the hysteria itself accelerates the very evils which men fear." The soothing reassurance from FDR's first inaugural

The Great Depression mob: Walter Huston and Constance Cummings face crazed depositors during the bank run sequence in Frank Capra's *American Madness* (1932). (Courtesy of the Museum of Modern Art)

address ("we have nothing to fear but fear itself") admitted that men like Lippmann had good reason to fear the pervasive fear.

The story of the Bonus Army may stand for many instances of the Great Depression mob and fear itself. In May 1932, some 15,000 hungry and ragged veterans of the Great War descended on Washington, D.C., to demand from Congress an early payment on a promised cash bonus for their wartime service. Some were encamped within sight of the White House on Pennsylvania Avenue, others in a ramshackle village on the flatlands across the Anacostia River. Dressed in the remnants of old uniforms, carrying American flags, and executing a rusty imitation of parade drill, the so-called Bonus Expeditionary Forces marched up to the very doors of the Capitol to make their appeal. Hoover remained deaf, but most of the nation expressed sympathy for the plight of proud men driven to beg for recompense. Will Rogers, the oracle of the common man, broadcast the opinion that the Bonus Marchers were "the best behaved of any 15,000 hungry men ever assembled anywhere

Flames under the Capitol: the Bonus Army encampment goes up in smoke, July 28, 1932. (Courtesy of the National Archives)

in the world." Besides, no survivor of trench warfare could be accused of shirking good honest work to be on the dole.

As the summer dragged on, with no action from Congress and no hearing from Hoover, the political problem became a social crisis in Washington. On July 28, 1932, after a district policeman killed two veterans during a scuffle, Hoover gave the order to disperse the petitioners. With sabers and bayonets drawn, in line and on horseback, a contingent of regular Army troops under the command of Maj. Gen. Douglas MacArthur waded into the Bonus Marchers, scattering them in a mad melee of cavalrymen and tear gas. That night the troops set fire to the Anacostia encampment, the glow of the flames visible from the White House. Suiting up before the battle, General MacArthur smelled "incipient revolution in the air." He turned to Maj. Dwight D. Eisenhower and said, "That mob down there was a bad looking mob. It was animated by the essence of revolution." The next day he told the press the marchers had been comprised of "insurrectionists and revolutionaries." Hoover's comment: "Thank God, we have a government in Washington that knows how to deal with a mob."

Imprinted on the national psyche by wirephotos and the newsreels, the rout of the Bonus Army with tanks and tear gas became an ugly symbol of how far things had gone: one force of government soldiers battling another. Universal Newspaper Newsreel called it "the most critical situation in the Federal District since the Civil War" and "the most cataclysmic domestic event of the decade." "It's war!" yelled commentator Graham McNamee. "The greatest concentration of fighting troops in Washington, D.C., since 1865." Over images of MacArthur's troops ("grim and relentless") and Great War vintage tanks, McNamee recites the official version: "Mr. Hoover doesn't blame the veterans entirely. He claims that the disorder and defiance were caused by foreign reds and a large criminal element in the ranks of the veterans." Still, "it's a spectacle unparalleled in the history of the country—a day of bloodshed and riot reminiscent of actual conditions in France in '17. Sullen, disgruntled, the veterans give way unwillingly before the steady advance of the soldiers. Tension is terrific. Real drama of the highest rank."

The tone of the newsreel commentary modulates between severity ("the orders of the President and the Secretary of War must be obeyed") and frivolity (resisting veterans get "a free ride to jail"). The footage, however, is jolting: scenes of street violence amidst clouds of tear gas and the shacks at Anacostia engulfed in flames. Not a few newsreel audiences hissed the U.S. Army when it waded into the Bonus Army. The newsreel report closed with an image that became a metonymy for the regal callousness of the Hoover administration, the impression of the president as an emperor fiddling about while America burned. "And the roaring flames sound the death knell to the fantastic Bonus Army," winds up McNamee, "the adventure that failed and ends so disastrously in the shadow of the beautiful dome of the Capitol of the United States of America."

Though the roaring flames under the Capitol did not exactly light a path for American cinema, the popular resistance and official reprisal it symbolized was too heated to ignore. Long oblivious to or agnostic about politics, temperamentally wary of involvement and above the fray, Hollywood went against its own grain to reflect and express the dissent of the day.

Traditionally, political ideology lies dormant in American cinema, hidden in the recesses of the text, under the surface of manifest meaning. It is a measure of the trauma of the Great Depression, and especially the early 1930s, that politics crystallized into a species of screen entertainment. Sometimes dubbed "Warner Brothers social consciousness" after the studio that most assiduously mined socioeconomic realities for screen fiction, the films do not fit between the brackets of a well-defined genre, still less do they advocate a coherent course of political action. Instead, they expose what so much else of the Hollywood product line suppressed: economic dislocation, grinding poverty, government corruption, official incompetence, injustice under the law, and rotten treatment all around. The focal point where all the misfortunes converged was the Great Depression itself. To speak its name or screen its images was to raise to consciousness the brutal realities outside the walls of the motion picture theater.

Almost as if against its better judgment, Hollywood tackled the Great Depression—if not head-on and without compromise, then with more vigor and directness than is usually credited. Taking stock of the anomaly, film historian Robert Sklar called the sudden lurch into polemics "one of the most remarkable challenges to traditional values in the history of mass commercial entertainment." Not only did the studios produce feature-length tracts on the human costs of the Great Depression, but social commentary and political asides slipped into the effervescent escapism of backstage musicals, anarchic comedies, and syrupy melodrama. In *Mystery of the Wax Museum* (1933), a montage of raucous New Year's Eve revels welcoming in 1933 fades to a conversation between two morgue attendants wheeling a gurney into place, the occupant covered by a white sheet. "New Year's Eve isn't what it used to be," muses one of the men, considering the cadaver. "You know, this is only the second one tonight. Times sure are tough." In the Marx Brothers comedy *Horse Feathers* (1932), a bum hits up Harpo for a dime for a cup of coffee; Harpo pulls a freshly brewed cup from his trouser cuff. Sometimes even the most refined atmospheres were sullied with intimations of the extreme conditions of offscreen life. "Tough season, isn't it?" asks an out-of-work actor at an audition in the sprightly backstage comedy *Morning Glory* (1933). "Pretty tough, yes," replies his friend, almost whispering, "but I'm afraid nowadays they're *all* tough seasons."

To be sure, the bulk of Hollywood output between 1930 and 1934, and throughout the decade, tried to pretend that the Great Depression did not exist, and scores of films and even whole genres succeeded moderately well. "Playing soft music on the screens while political fireworks fill the newspapers," was how *Variety* described the diversionary tactics "to elevate the public mind from everyday surroundings." "We are now in what might be called a headache recovery period," declared MPPDA secretary Carl Milliken in 1931, prematurely diagnosing the end of the national migraine. Articulating the reigning aesthetic, he claimed Americans "don't want problem plots on the screen. They want light romances. No stark realism."

But sometimes the blithe pretense was insupportable, the suspension of disbelief too much to ask if a film—set in the present, seeking to connect with adults—were to maintain a semblance of credence and legitimacy. At such moments, the narrative collapses under the weight of its own conceit. All the politically charged films of the pre-Code era were undermined by the Hays Office and state censorship boards, the conventions of popular entertainment, and interference from politicians and exhibitors alike. Yet the weight of the worst years of the Great Depression was too heavy not to register in a high-definition photographic medium. Sometimes if only in shunning its presence, in the "structured absence" that is nascent but unmentionable, the Great Depression lurks at the edge of the frame.

TELEGRAPHING IDEOLOGY

Throughout the pre-Code era and beyond, the official stance of the motion picture industry was emphatically apolitical, a firm and repeated denial that the movies were in any way ideological or contained anything like political impact or partisan purpose. "The function of motion pictures is to ENTERTAIN," insisted Will Hays in 1932. "This we must keep before us at all times and we must realize constantly the fatality of ever permitting our concern with social values to lead us into the realm of propaganda." Of course, Hays acknowledged, motion pictures "deliberately and consciously" contributed to international good will and properly upheld the forces of law and order against the depredations of criminals. "But on every other topic the American motion picture preserves its impartiality, owes no civic obligation greater than the honest presentment of clean entertainment and maintains that in supplying effective entertainment, free of propaganda, we serve a high and self-sufficing purpose."

In fact, during such dark times, Hollywood's steady avoidance of overt politics in favor of buoyant escapism was a positive public service the government should cultivate. In 1932, testifying before the House Ways and Means Committee, MPPDA counsel C. C. Pettijohn argued against a proposed tax on theater tickets by reminding congressmen of how the industry helped maintain the domestic tranquility:

An admissions tax strikes at a critical time at the very existence of an institution which the nation requires today more than ever before—a focal center in every city and town where people go in orderly fashion and find relief through recreation in entertainment from the strains imposed by depression and unemployment.

In case his listeners missed the point, Pettijohn conjured the kind of mischief idle minds might make were not the movies keeping them busy:

> Every darkened motion picture theater is a victory for the forces of discontent and disorder in the United States. Every time you destroy a place of decent cheap amusement for the masses, you cut off the supply of a vital necessity—entertainment—and you leave taut nerves, strained loyalties, and no escape except the contemplation of destructive processes that bitterness breeds. A federal admissions tax would be far more than a nuisance tax. It would be a threat against the maintenance of morale in the United States at a time when depression and unemployment are fertile sources of discontent and disorder.

In providing a zone for a catharsis that alleviated pent-up radical tensions, Pettijohn was proud to say that, yes, the movies were the opiate of the people—and in this they served a salutary social purpose. "In the dark days of depression, the motion picture has been a great refuge for humanity," proclaimed Hays in a national radio broadcast in 1934, "the courage and sanity of nations" being assured by regular sessions of screen therapy.

Hollywood's aversion to political controversy was exemplified by producer Sam Goldwyn, credited with the famous advice to those who would make motion pictures to telegraph ideology: "If you want to send a message, call Western Union." Goldwyn's own timorousness about politically charged material, no matter how safely mainstream, showed he followed his own aphorisms. In 1932 the producer decided to forgo a contemplated film version of a story of the Russian Revolution that sympathized with the White Russians, because he did not want to risk offending the partisans of the Red Russians, namely American communists. "We can't take sides in our film stories," insisted Goldwyn. Scanning the New York stage or the newspapers for potential story ideas, studio executives employed a mechanism of preemptive self-censorship, knowing certain material was simply "too hot for use on the screen." In 1934, when the Theater Guild staged John Wexley's *They Shall Not Die*, a dramatization of the plight of the Scottsboro Boys, nine African-Americans then under sentence of death in Alabama for the alleged rape of two white women, motion picture producers didn't need the Hays Office to tell them that a Hollywood version was beyond the realm of realization.

Looking for direct calls to action and programmatic policies, many politically minded critics took Hollywood at its apolitical word. For them, the introduction of sound offered little hope that American cinema would find a revolutionary voice. "A movie with dialogue," sniffed *The Nation*, "will be merely a movie made more ghastly because it has learned to say in words the nonsense which it formerly could only imply in pantomime." Walter Lippmann ventured to pun that "the body politic is one kind of body that Hollywood has not learned about." In 1937, looking back at a film landscape that was "sterile of any political interest," Gilbert Seldes asserted that "a straightforward, direct tackling of the problems brought about by the depression under Hoover or the zigzag course of recovery under Roosevelt was not attempted in Hollywood."

But if old-line, print-based critics looked upon motion picture images as beneath serious consideration, observers with keener insight, on the right and the left, acknowledged the political import of American cinema and reacted in characteristic ways to its distorted vision. From both ends of the ideological spectrum, they cast a cold eye on Hollywood for, respectively, sins against God and affronts to the People.

On the right, religious and cultural conservatives thought the movies were corrupting and corrosive: they favored metaphors of illness and degeneration, configuring the medium as a parasite eating away at a healthy organism, an active agent in the all-too-evident decline of American civilization. The decadence that had led to the Great Depression was still an insidious force sapping the nation's vitality in the present emergency.

The adoption of the Production Code in 1930 was an early attempt to restore good habits, but slippery artifice by the unsanctified had subverted the wholesome regimen. In 1937, shuddering to recall the libertinism of the pre-Code era, Olga J. Martin, Joseph Breen's secretary at the Production Code Administration, put the triumphant 1934 campaign in cultural historical terms. "To an impoverished country which had become religious and serious-minded, the sex attitudes of the post-war period became grotesquely unreal and antedated. The public at large wanted to forget its own derelictions of the 'gay twenties,' " she asserted. "The stage was set for the moral crusade." In 1970, Jack Vizzard, another longtime official in the Production Code Administration, conjured the zeitgeist in the same moralistic terms. "One thing which, I think, is generally forgotten in accounting for the inception of the Code is that the mood of the times was one of severe backlash. Psychologically, I think it is very important to recognize this," Vizzard argued. After the flappers, speakeasies, and money-grubbing of the Jazz Age, "an enormous sense of guilt set in" with the Crash. "A creeping fear that Big Daddy was striking back set in. In a mood of sobriety, a chastened citizenry reacted against those symbols of the great debauch and began to punish them."

The greatest symbols were the movies themselves, whose great debauches had managed to escape the putative new mood of sobriety. With Prohibition having long since lost moral stature and cultural consensus, a likeminded prohibitionist impulse sought to protect Americans from imbibing other kinds of toxic spirits.

On the left, critics were animated by the aesthetic of social realism, the notion of art-for-Stalin's-sake, where popular culture (or "mass culture" as they scornfully called it) should further the Revolution, a dim prospect they realized in a capitalist system rigged against party line values. The radicals favored metaphors of narcosis, sleep, and drug addiction, the movies being the new opiate of the people, the benighted masses too stuporous to awake to the revolutionary dawn, lulled to sleep by visions of clinches with Gable or Garbo. Audiences watched screens like zombies, hypnotized by "the flashing panoramas that unfold as if in promised hope for them," as Wolf W. Moss, a critic-activist for the Theater Guild, expressed it. "For a few brief moments, submerged in darkened picture palaces they sink beneath the sedatives of blissful forgetfulness." Or worse: subliminally seduced by the likes of Shanghai Express (1932), wherein "virulent counter revolutionary sentiment" lay hidden in the lush chiaroscuro of a Josef von Sternberg–Marlene Dietrich melodrama. Blind to the austere beauty of Robert Flaherty's Man of Aran (1934), communist critics saw only "a film patently in accord with the ideology of the capitalist class and, unlike the indubitable screen masterpieces of the Soviet Union, not in the least dangerous socially."

As a force for progressive change, Hollywood cinema was a lost cause, its tripe merchants beneath contempt. "Is it possible to create a proletariate cinema in America?" queried Harry Alan Potamkin, the film critic for the communist monthly, the New Masses. Not likely, given the resistance by "the monopoly invested in Hollywood, Hays, and Wall Street." Subversion of the capitalist model was the only viable alternative. Formed in 1931, the communist-backed Workers Film and Photo League envisioned "a great counter-offensive to vicious and nauseating Hollywood productions" by "bringing revolutionary films to workers organizations throughout the country." The group produced its own newsreels, taught seminars on working-class film criticism, organized protests against "reactionary pictures," and screened the glories of the Soviet Union to cadres of radical cineastes. Though the league reported that entertainment fare such as *Storm Over Asia*, *Cannons or Tractors*, and *Volga to Gastonia* was "welcomed by workers everywhere," in truth all levels of the class structure preferred the "bourgeois sentimentality" of Hollywood to any imported alternatives. The seductions of mass culture distressed and bewildered Marxist critics who spent most of the 1930s reprimanding their fellow Americans for flocking to the movies instead of manning the barricades.

With neither the gospel of the fundamentalists nor the manifestos of the communists outlining a bankable scenario, Hollywood created its own brand of issue-oriented film fare. Beginning in mid-1932, with a momentous presidential election around the corner, the major studios ventured tentatively into partisanship, or at least an admission that such things as partisanship existed. "The political trend," noted *Variety*, "is absolutely new, producers having [historically] avoided the subject as worthless for picture purposes." Though the political film remained the exception to the Goldwyn rule, the pre-Code era produced more exceptions because, in the absence of systematic censorship and the presence of political upheaval, it was an exceptional time.

Never a model of rhetorical consistency, the MPPDA talked out of both sides of its official mouth about politics and the movies. Testifying before Congress, it claimed to be a purveyor of mere entertainment. Defending controversial material, it claimed to be a beacon for an enlightened citizenry. "The public demand for realism in its entertainment has resulted in treating current local and world politics, penal institutions, marriage and divorce, and even religion with a frankness not hitherto approached," declared an official overview of the product line from the MPPDA in 1932.

Yet so against the Hollywood grain was the foray into issue-oriented cinema that the definition, even the very name, of the ragged genre was mercurial. Any film addressing any argument about any social policy was liable to be labeled a "propaganda picture" or, more glibly, a "preachment yarn." For example, *American Madness*, which dramatized a frenzied bank run, *I Am a Fugitive from a Chain Gang* (1932), which depicted the brutality of the southern chain gang system, and *The Wet Parade* (1932), MGM's adaption of the Upton Sinclair novel against Prohibition, all fit the elastic phrase. Warner Brothers, the studio that carved out a niche with the genre, preferred the less contentious designation "Americanism stories."

Whatever the label, two recurrent markers signpost the preachment yarns. Each device appears in other films at other times, but their proliferation in the early 1930s is a leading indicator of pre-Code Hollywood preachments. The first is the exculpatory preface; the second is the Jazz Age prelude.

The exculpatory preface gainsays in print what the images proceed to affirm. Designed to give plausible deniability to polemical purpose and partisan intentions, the precredit expression of pure motives acts as a preemptive apologia. Both misdirection and inoculation, the exculpatory preface appears before any film likely to offend any political persuasion.

Where the exculpatory preface denied political partiality, the Jazz Age prelude insisted on historical context. Whether as first act, flashback, or expository montage, the shameful sins committed in the previous decade are remembered with embarrassment and hard-won wisdom from the vantage of the present. Few pre-Code films that presume to speak plainly about current events do so without dredging up the 1920s as deep backstory, as if to say, "The mess we're in now came about because of the mess we made then."

A vintage example of an "Americanism story" according to Warner Brothers is *Cabin in the Cotton* (1932). Once controversial, obscure today, the dusty melodrama preaches a compromised yet compelling critique of capitalism. Directed by Hungarian émigré Michael Curtiz from the social realist novel by Harry Harrison Kroll, the film is a self-conscious exposé of stark class divisions, simmering resentment, and rank economic exploitation. Two years after its American release, the KINO commissars in Moscow deemed *Cabin in the Cotton* politically palatable enough to be the first Hollywood talkie to play in the Soviet Union.

In an unnamed southern state, a plantation system pits landowners and tenants, "big fish and little fish," against each other. In this food chain, the cotton pickers are in the thrall of serfdom. The exculpatory preface explains:

> In many parts of the South today, there exists an endless dispute between the rich land-owners, known as planters, and the poor cotton pickers, known as tenants or "peckerwoods." The planters supply the tenants with the simple requirements of every day life and in return, the tenants work the land year in and year out.
>
> A hundred volumes could be written on the rights and wrongs of both parties, but it is not the object of the producers of *Cabin in the Cotton* to take sides. We are only concerned with the effort to picture these conditions.

The picture immediately gives the lie to the prose. Dressed in an immaculate white suit, overbearing landowner Lane Norwood (Berton Churchill) surveys a family of cotton pickers from his sporty roadster. Dressed in tatters, father, mother, and daughter huddle dirt-poor on the ground. That night father dies of exhaustion. His son Marvin (Richard Barthelmess) is destined for bigger things. Spotting talent among the white trash, Norwood sends him to school and employs him in the price-gouging company store. Marvin is trapped between two worlds: on the one side, his blood ties with the tenants and his warm feelings for his down-home girlfriend Betty (Dorothy Jordan); on the other, his ambitions with Norwood and the planters, especially in the form of Norwood's randy daughter Madge (Bette Davis), who flirts mercilessly with Marvin: "I'd like to kiss you but I just washed my hair—bye!"

Director Curtiz crosscuts between the planters, who are stealing from the tenants by charging ruinous interest rates and high prices, and the tenants, who are stealing cotton from the planters and selling it on the side. However, moral equivalence this is not. At a lavish party in the big house, Madge goads Marvin into leading the uppercrust assembly in the "peckerwood wiggle," the dance of his people. From outside, the peckerwoods watch, furious at the theft of folk custom by the slumming aristocrats. "They're making fun of us!"

The class hatred explodes in violence when a tenant kills a planter. As Marvin protests helplessly, Norwood and his henchmen track the suspect down with bloodhounds, hurl a rope over a branch, and, offscreen, lynch him. When Norwood returns to his mansion, the company store is ablaze, set afire by the tenants to destroy the records of their indebtedness. Marvin retains another copy of the ledgers, but will he save Norwood or stand with his own people?

To end the "stealing and burning and murder and lynching," Marvin calls a meeting of tenants and planters. He demands the planters "play fair" and proclaims the grievances of the tenants with firebrand eloquence. Faced with the will of the people united, the planters can only accede to the terms of a new and better contract with the tenants. Outside, Marvin sees his childhood sweetheart Betty, winsome in a cotton dress, and Madge, luminous from behind the wheel of the roadster. He will join Betty next Sunday, in church, washing away the sins of his other Sundays with Madge.

Cabin in the Cotton confirms the old maxim that Hollywood is least articulate when most earnest, most subversive when least didactic. Intimately tied to their historical moment, caught between reformist impulse and restricted expression, the overtly political films of the 1930s look moldy

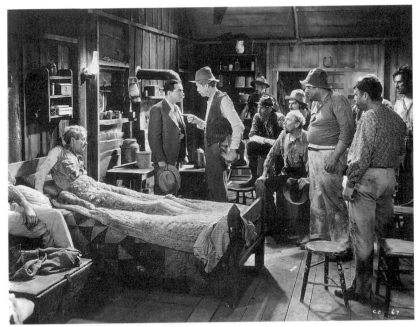

Peckerwoods and planters: Trading his overalls for a business suit, Richard Barthelmess crosses class lines in *Cabin in the Cotton* (1932). (Courtesy of the Museum of Modern Art)

and muddled in retrospect. Perhaps, in a sense, Sam Goldwyn was right—not because Hollywood was incapable of telegraphing a clear message but because, no less than government officials and economic experts, it was at a total loss about what message to send. Both in their pre-Code and Code-approved versions, the preachment yarns of the Great Depression are constrained not only by political censorship but by the enormity and complexity of the crisis. The Great Depression was the great incubator of discontent and insurrection, but who had a solution to the Great Depression? Not Hoover's cabinet, not FDR's brain trust, and not the contract screenwriters at Warner Brothers.

The second wave of politically charged films in classical Hollywood cinema, the "social problem" genre that emerged in the post–World War II era, provides a useful contrast with the preachment yarns of the 1930s. The postwar social problem films seek to do more than dramatize a crisis; they want to cure it and they know exactly what medication to prescribe. Tinkering around the edges of a basically sound social organism, they examine a slice of the human condition with an unbridled faith in their own ability to nurse the afflicted back to health. Whatever the problem besetting the American body politic— alcoholism (*The Lost Weekend*, 1945) returning war veterans (*The Best Years of Our Lives*, 1946), antisemitism (*Gentleman's Agreement*, 1947), racism (*No Way Out*, 1950), or physical disability (*The Men*, 1950)—they offer a sure solution: therapy, understanding, religious tolerance, racial tolerance, and rehabilitation, respectively. They exude the serenity of the missionary bringing the gift of modern medicine to a primitive tribe, confident that all can be put right with an injection of enlightened thinking.

The preachment yarns of the Great Depression express the anguish of the dispossessed and fearful, but they have no idea how to alleviate the symptoms of what seems a terminal case. Like their protagonists, men on the verge of a crack-up, at the end of their rope, the films have a fevered, pursued, despairing quality. After 1933, the magic bullet of the New Deal would provide a panacea for narrative closure, its slogans spoken like incantations before the end credits rolled. Yet even under FDR the treatments play out as quack remedies, disbelieved at the moment of utterance. Despite their billing, the preachment yarns do not so much administer a cure as watch helplessly while the patient howls in pain.

Class Distinctions

As much as any specific film in the unwieldy preachment yarn genre, a collage of discrete moments and a montage of images render the political dynamics of the early 1930s. In set design, lighting schemes, and social milieu, the polar oppositions of Great Depression experience found vivid expression. Pre-Code Hollywood's universe is either fantastically plush or starkly threadbare, Central Park West penthouses or Lower East Side tenements, ragged men or tuxedoed swells, hatcheck girls or high society dames, with no middle ground, no middle class, no modestly prosperous workers moving incrementally but surely up the ladder of respectability. Wish-fulfillment titles like *If I Had a Million* (1932), *Lady for a Day* (1933), and *We're Rich Again* (1934) promised the stuff of pipe dreams and presupposed that the only way to be propelled out of poverty was to be struck by a lightning bolt of amazing good luck—finding a lottery ticket, inheriting a fortune from a lost relative, being befriended by an eccentric millionaire or dotty dowager. The plight of Chaplin's tramp in *City Lights*

(1931) is emblematic. Bounced back and forth between two diametrically opposed economic strata, at the caprice of a millionaire who, when drunk, welcomes Charlie into his home and heart, and, when sober, consigns him back to trampdom.

In the best of all possible scenarios, a solvent prince or a madcap heiress fulfilled two daydreams at once. Secretaries and shopgirls catch the eye of the handsome boss, bored with the shallowness of society dames, longing for her spirited wholesomeness and refreshing frankness ("I've never met a woman like you!"). Construction workers peek into the window of the penthouse apartment and attract bored debutantes longing for *his* spirited wholesomeness and refreshing frankness ("You're not like other men").

Two studios came to symbolize the opposite ends of Depression era experience: MGM and Warner Brothers, run respectively by rock-ribbed Republican Louis B. Mayer and New Deal Democrat Jack L. Warner. On the one side perched the high-gloss top cat of the Hollywood studios with the growling Leo the Lion mascot and the fancy Latin motto ("ars gratia artis": not the foreign tongue Mayer was most conversant in). On the other, the scrappy upstart with the bare-bones decor and a chip on its shoulder.

To transcend the ground of the 1930s, MGM bragged about having "more stars than there were in heaven." Their trademark screen faces (Norma Shearer, Clark Gable, and Garbo) were enthroned beyond the reach of the arms of mortals. *Grand Hotel* (1932), one of the studio's most successful pre-Code films, is representative: a cavalcade of grand stars (Barrymore, Garbo, Crawford) wrapped in glitzy, self-contained architecture. Like Hoover's White House, Louis B. Mayer's studio often seemed insulated from the workaday world of its constituency. Audiences laughed out loud at a moment in MGM's *Faithless* (1932) when Robert Montgomery announces in all seriousness his intention to resume work "even though the job only pays $70 a week." No one in a Warner Bros. picture would have uttered such a line without winking at the gallery.

On the other side of the tracks, Warner Brothers stacked its working stiffs against MGM's leisured clientele. A stable of city-bred, ethnic performers, Irish and Jews mainly, incarnated the working-class ethos, struggling less for the big break than a weekly paycheck. Even the contract players at Warner Brothers seemed more class-conscious as wage earners, ready to strike and walk off the set for higher salaries and better treatment. (In 1932 James Cagney may have been the only worker in America who felt mistreated at $1,400 a week.) In *Taxi!* (1931), Warner Brothers took a swipe at the competition's product line when Cagney and Loretta Young go to the movies to

Art Deco, modern art, and more stars than heaven: Lionel Barrymore, Joan Crawford, director Victor Fleming, Lewis Stone, John Barrymore, and Wallace Beery in a publicity shot from the archetypal MGM production, *Grand Hotel* (1932). (Courtesy of the British Film Institute)

see a plush melodrama entitled *Her Hour of Love*, a film whose stilted romance amidst drawing rooms sends off none of the electric sparks of the streetwise couple in the film that is *Taxi!* (Actually, the satirized film is a Warner Bros., not an MGM, production. Jack Warner was willing to tweak the competition but not to pay royalties for the privilege.)

For the cultural historian of film, Warner Brothers manufactured the more dependably durable and interesting material. Its coarse edges have aged better than MGM's glimmering sheen, the films directed by workhorses like William Wellman, Michael Curtiz, Archie Mayo, Mervyn LeRoy, and Roy Del Ruth retaining their original vitality while the bulk of MGM's stiff reels is impossible to resuscitate. The very speed of the production machine at Warner Brothers allowed the historical moment to leave a fresh imprint, unmediated and unpremeditated, like snapshots taken before the models could assume an artificial pose. In an eighteen-month period from 1931 to 1933, director Roy del Ruth ("fastest of the fast set") sped through a nonstop string of ten films, each shot in roughly three weeks, one after the other, all worth looking at for the exposure of the raw nerves of Great Depression America: *Blonde Crazy, Taxi!, Beauty and the Boss, Winner Take All, Blessed Event, Employee's Entrance, The Mind Reader, The Little Giant, Captured!*, and *Bureau of Missing Persons*. If the studio's vaunted social consciousness was compromised and selective, the straightforward confrontation with everyday problems (hunger, work, money) and the topical subject matter ("ripped straight from today's headlines!") link it kinetically with the real world. MGM people just exist; Warner Brothers people must work.

Work or starve. Fulsome evidence of one common experience in the Great Depression, the palpable pangs of hunger afflict screen characters across the genres, men and women alike living hand to mouth, propelled by the basic biological urge to eat, to earn not even a decent day's wages but just a square meal. Food and eating are more than leitmotifs in pre-Code Hollywood; people literally faint from hunger. In the Warner Bros. blockbuster *42nd Street* (1933), undernourished hoofer Ruby Keeler collapses from exhaustion. In the follow-up musical *Gold Diggers of 1933* (1933), chorines steal a bottle of milk for a spartan breakfast. In *King Kong* (1933), down-and-out Fay Wray reaches weakly for sustenance from a fruit stand. In *It Happened One Night* (1934), spoiled brat heiress Claudette Colbert flings a hearty meal into the ocean, an act merely impulsive in flush times but wastefully sinful now. Later, she suffers for the transgression. On the road and penniless, she feels true hunger for the first time. Forced to forage in the woods like an animal for carrots, she learns the value of a single chocolate bar and the pleasures of dunking doughnuts.

Women can be bought for the price of a meal, tempted no longer by jewelry and fancy clothes but by nourishment. Decent girls are forced to put themselves in compromising positions, going against their better judgment to satisfy a basic need. Picked up by a flush fellow with loose pockets, the female ingenue eats ravenously as the man looks on, the two trading urge for urge. "Chorus girls used to get pearls and diamonds," cracks Joan Blondell in *Big City Blues* (1932). "Now all they expect is a corned beef sandwich and they yell if they don't get it." In *Blonde Venus* (1932), Marlene Dietrich begins her descent into prostitution by trading her virtue to feed her child and herself. The price of the meal is 85 cents.

No wonder the camera seems to linger lovingly over full course meals and bountiful spreads, to caress the sumptuous image of food with the certainty of having hit a sure audience pleasure point. In *I Am a Fugitive from a*

The hunger motif: Marlene Dietrich prepares to barter herself for a meal in *Blonde Venus* (1932).

Chain Gang the famished James Allen (Paul Muni) is unknowingly lured into a robbery by the prospect of a hamburger. Entering a diner, he takes in
the scene hungrily. The cook places a pair of burgers on the grill. They sizzle tantalizingly. The cook tops them off with diced onions, the aroma filling the diner and, one suspects, the nostrils of moviegoers across America.
Later, on the chain gang, a fellow convict asks Allen what he is in prison for.
"For looking at a hamburger," he replies bitterly.

In *Union Depot* (1932), when a jobless man (Douglas Fairbanks, Jr.)
stumbles upon a wad of cash, his first impulse is to rush to a restaurant and
stuff himself. "Woman, here's what I crave," he tells the pretty waitress,
with his desire focused on the meal not the girl. "I want a nice tomato sal-
ad, a thick sirloin steak smothered in onions, some brown potatoes in
creamy gravy, a flock of hot biscuits, and some honey"—he comes out of
his reverie and notices the girl—"from a honey." She laughs, "Coffee?" He
nods. "And a cut of raisin pie a la mode." The meal finished, the camera
salivates over the check as the waitress tallies the cost, savoring the spread
one more time:

Salad, L. T.	.15
T. Bone and Onions	.85
Brown Potatoes	.15
Biscuits	.15
Honey	.15
Coffee	.10
Raisin Pie a la mode	.20
	$ 1.75

Women, the privileged object for the pleasure of the gaze in Hollywood cinema, might be overlooked for another elemental satisfaction.

PROFESSIONAL MALFEASANCE

Less overt than the preachment yarns but no less direct in expressing cultural resentment was a series of films targeting the cupidity of the professional classes who had profited most publicly from the 1920s and who folded most pathetically in the 1930s. Typically cast as workplace melodramas or fictional biopics, they vented a breezy contempt for the American system by exposing the villainy of government officials, elite experts, and professionals of all job descriptions. Once guaranteed to garner prestige and profits, hagiographic biopics of great men from the American pantheon, such as *Abraham Lincoln* (1930) and *Alexander Hamilton* (1931), lagged at the box office. In film after film, the administration of justice and the practice of business appeared as scams and rackets, to be looked upon cynically and bypassed when possible. Corrupt politicians, crooked bankers, shyster lawyers, and quack doctors practiced professional malfeasance as part of the job.

No profession suffered more in public prestige than the businessman, a once unassailable figure. In the 1920s, the businessman was a secular saint, his financial wealth outward manifestation of moral worth. In the 1930s, he was dethroned, condemned as impotent at best and parasitic at worst. The portrait of the self-made man, the rags-to-riches individualist who had been an American exemplar since Ben Franklin paved his way to wealth, took on dark and sinister shadings. By the early 1930s, the cultural stock of the business class was as low as that other stock.

The titan of industry is a public enemy in *The Match King* (1932), a kind of biopic-à-clef of the notorious Swedish industrialist and swindler Ivar Krueger. A jaundiced look back at the economic practices of the Roaring

Twenties from the rueful perspective of the Great Depression, it tracks the criminal enterprise of ruthless international tycoon Paul Kroll (Warren William, pre-Code Hollywood's scoundrel of choice) who stops at nothing to corner the global market on matches, "the one indispensable commodity." Unscrupulous, contemptible, Kroll rockets up the financial ladder by betraying coworkers, girlfriends, and relatives and committing fraud, robbery, and murder. Whenever an obstacle disturbs the swathe he cuts through the commandments, Kroll repeats his favorite saying: "Stop worrying until something happens—then I'll take care of it."

Kroll incarnates the fast-talking 1920s businessman, a slick hustler constructing a financial house of cards on margin buying and worthless bonds. Not neglected is the 1920s obsession with advertising, as when Kroll concocts the "three on a match" superstition to encourage the use of more matches. Like the rest of his generation of rapacious and reckless businessman, however, market forces more malevolent than even Kroll set him up for a fall. When the stock market crashes, the debts come due. Encircled by creditors and threatened with prison, "something" has finally happened and he can't take care of it. "Gentleman," Kroll tells his board of directors, "it is my experience that bankers and pawnbrokers are reluctant to lend you money when you actually need it and frantic to accommodate you when you don't." With his past crimes swirling in double exposure around his head, Kroll shoots himself and falls into the gutter from whence he came.

In *Skyscraper Souls* (1932), a vertical version of *Grand Hotel*, an edifice taller than the Empire State Building houses a village of interconnected souls, from ruthless business mogul David Dwight (Warren William again) to winsome secretary Lynn Harding (Maureen O'Sullivan). To gain ownership of the skyscraper, Dwight and his partner manipulate the company's stock. Replaying the investment hysteria of the 1920s, every occupant of the skyscraper gets the "hot tip" to put their fortunes into "can't fail" stock, which they buy on margin. As ticker tape rolls, the stock goes through the roof only to plummet to the basement, ruining all save the evil mastermind David Dwight.

A cad in his personal life as well, Dwight betrays not only his wife but his longtime mistress and business associate, the unmarried career woman Sarah Dennis (Verree Teasdale). He sets his sights on Lynn, the innocent secretary entrusted into Miss Dennis's care. Repulsed by this final proof of Dwight's utter depravity, the scorned mistress shoots him. In a dreamy finale, she goes to the top of the skyscraper, her black dress billowing, and walks off into the air. In silence, without a scream, the camera watches her recede in space to the street below.

A close second to businessmen on any scale of loathsomeness were lawyers, known in the vernacular as mouthpieces, a guild of state-sanctioned jackals. Masters of courtroom chicanery and legal sophistry, they were willing to do anything to get their clients off in a judicial system rigged to pamper the pedigreed and impound the underdog. Helped along by Gene Fowler's *The Great Mouthpiece*, a popular biography of rakish New York trial attorney William Joseph Fallon published in 1931, Hollywood embarked upon a cycle of scurvy lawyer films featuring world-weary shysters molding an infinitely malleable legal system to devious ends. Among the indictments issued were *State's Attorney* (1932), with John Barrymore as a whiskey-soaked rogue; *The Mouthpiece* (1932), with Warren William as an unprincipled defense attorney for gangsters; and *Lawyer Man* (1932), with William Powell riding an ethical roller coaster from an honest practice on the Lower East Side to a shady partnership uptown and back again.

In *The Mouthpiece* the brilliant courtroom oratory of district attorney Vincent Day (William) convicts a simpering defendant of murder. On the eve of his execution, the condemned man is discovered to be innocent. Frantic, the chief DA tries to get word to the warden. The lights dim, the juice hums. Too late: the innocent man has gone to the chair. "There's only one chance in 10,000 for a miscarriage of justice like this," his superior assures the distraught prosecutor, misrepresenting the statistical likelihood for bad luck in Warner Bros. melodramas.

His faith in the law shattered, Day moves from "underpaid D.A. to high-priced mouthpiece," a blackleg lawyer who will defend embezzlers and murderers with courtroom theatrics and legal tricks. "Sensationalism! Ballyhoo! Barnum and Bailey!" is what the law is all about. With his smart-mouthed gal Friday (Aline MacMahon), he operates a lucrative if disreputable law practice. Ultimately, he resolves to make a judicious change in his own life, but his personal reformation does nothing to change the image of the courtroom as an arena for miscreants and the law as a high-priced racket.

Harsher still is the portrait of lawyering and American justice in MGM's Warner Brothers–like *Paid* (1931), wherein Joan Crawford plays a department store clerk wrongly accused of pilfering by her hard-hearted boss. Sent to prison for three years, she spends her term learning legal technicalities so she may steal within the law. Once outside, she runs an extortion racket against rich men and negotiates the "legal" settlements. A convoluted last act reveals the forces of law and order willing to intimidate and lie to make a conviction stick. Her true love goes to the electric chair rather than see the DA implicate Crawford in a crime she had nothing to do with. Again, the justice system is a farce, its representatives venal. Only the deviant classes—the prostitutes, con men, and petty criminals—are stand-up folks.

Not being complicit with the collapse of the banking system or the impotence of the political class, physicians were usually treated more kindly, as in the portraits of dedicated "heroes of science" in *Arrowsmith* (1931) and *Men in White* (1934). But even the noble doctor may wear a sullied white coat. In *Mary Stevens, M.D.* (1933) a surgeon shows up drunk for an operation; in *Heroes for Sale* (1933) a family doctor betrays the trust of his patient; and in *Massacre* (1934) a government physician lets Indian children die from tuberculous.

The uninhibited *Night Nurse* (1931) is the most cynical of the pre-Code excursions down hospital corridors. Directed by William Wellman from the novel by Dora Macy, the medicinal melodrama follows the rounds of spunky nurse Lora Hart (Barbara Stanwyck), who uncovers a plot by a wealthy society doctor to starve two children to death in order to seize their trust fund. Along with the evil chauffeur Nick (Clark Gable, clad in black), the doctor keeps the mother hopped-up on drugs and alcohol ("I'm a dipsomaniac and I like it!"). Medical ethics are elastic: Lora first meets her bootlegger beau Mortie (Ben Lyon) in the emergency room and agrees not to report his bullet wound to the police. At no point does a cop or judge appear; at no point does it occur to anyone to turn to the authorities for justice. The single force for moral order is the likeable Mortie, the bootlegger, who in the last reel nonchalantly informs Lora that Nick "has been taken for a ride." The startling coda replays the montage that began the film, the screeching sirens of an ambulance rushing a dead-on-arrival victim to the emergency room. The supine passenger is Nick, the chauffeur, his capital punishment administered not by the law but by the criminal.

Not even men of the cloth were sacrosanct, at least if they were women. In 1927, mining the deep background of the two most celebrated religious hucksters from the 1920s, the evangelists Billy Sunday and Aimee Semple McPherson, Sinclair Lewis's novel *Elmer Gantry* had created a scandal by revealing the sins of the flesh behind the faith of the fathers. The sure-fire material beckoned to Hollywood, but a screen version of the novel was specifically banned by Will Hays. "It's agin' God," Lewis explained. "Offensive to too many."

To circumvent the flash point in the name "Elmer Gantry," Columbia Pictures appropriated the outlines of Lewis's story for a distaff version. Directed by Frank Capra, *The Miracle Woman* (1931) was inspired by the antics

Warner Bros. class warfare: Barbara Stanwyck (*left*) grapples with the corrupt aristocracy (Charlotte Merriam) in William Wellman's *Night Nurse* (1931).

of Aimee Semple McPherson and the cynical ballyhoo of that old-time religion. The exculpatory preface comes in the form of two epigraphs designed to shield the exposé from charges of blasphemy. The first is a quote from Matthew (7:15) that cloaks the anti-Bible-thumping film in biblical authority: "Beware of false prophets which come to you in sheep's clothing." The second is from Frank Capra: "*The Miracle Woman* is offered as a rebuke to anyone who, under the cloak of religion, seeks to sell for gold, God's choicest gift of humanity—FAITH."

Before girl-boy stuff derails the critique of commercial Christianity, the film indicts the exploitation of the gullible by the greedy, exposing the backstage devices of mass-marketed religion as a Barnum sideshow, complete with cathedral set design, candle lighting, paid shills, and the shtick of born-again conversions and faith healing. The *Hollywood Reporter* welcomed Columbia's exposé of McPherson, a "religious mountebank in petticoats," noting that "the sin racket" had been woefully neglected "for the beer, alki, smuggling, political and other rackets."

The "political racket" (that is, the sovereign will of the American people) was the subject of two election-year manifestos that treated the democratic process as an exercise in subterfuge. Government officeholders warranted a special measure of contempt, and the cynicism about politicians did not exempt the gullible electorate from culpability.

In *The Dark Horse* (1932) a complete moron (Guy Kibbee) is accidentally tapped to run for governor. Making the best of the gaffe ("It isn't the first time a fool was nominated to a political office"), the party bosses hire political fixer Hal S. Blake (Warren William) to sell the boob to the booboisie as a modern-day Lincoln. "He's a human dynamo!" enthuse Blake's admirers, "the greatest manipulator of public opinion this country has ever produced!" Thus the man pulling the strings possesses all the leadership qualities the puppet on the ticket so conspicuously lacks. "He'll give the people a square deal," proclaims Blake, concocting a platform and catchy slogan on the spot. "That's what the public wants in these days of corruption and depression." Despite the best efforts of the bumbling candidate to sabotage his own campaign, Blake guides him to victory at the ballot. The last shot shows the happy idiot in formal wear, riding in the back of a convertible, acknowledging the cheers of an electorate as dense and manipulatable as himself.

Released to coincide with the 1932 election ("rips the lids off in the midst of the most important campaign since the Civil War!"), the very title of *Washington Merry-Go-Round* (1932) presumed the constant malfunctioning of a federal government spinning its wheels. A wry overture of American anthems accompanies the opening credits and an exculpatory preface explains that the film is "Dedicated to those public servants in Washington who despite the hidden malignant force which operates to defeat the principles of representative government, are serving their country sincerely and well."

The outline of *Washington Merry-Go-Round* anticipates Frank Capra's *Mr. Smith Goes to Washington* (1939). A freshman congressman (Lee Tracy) rides into the Capital to begin his first term. "If you knew what you were walking in to, you'd quit now," reads a letter from a mentor. As businessmen and politicos play poker in tuxedos, they chat provocatively. "It's high time that these Marines stopped acting as a private police force for those American dollar grabbers in South America," says a congressmen.

Timely enough to feature the Bonus Expeditionary Forces, the taglines for the film promised incendiary political content:

Don't vote until you've seen *Washington Merry-Go-Round!*
Where has government by, of, and for the people gone?

Give us back our United States!
Why is the U.S. in the red?

Yet so toothless was the film version of *Washington Merry-Go-Round* that Robert Sharon Allen and Drew Pearson, the authors of the original book, took out newspaper ads denying that they had anything to do with it. Columbia admitted that the title was the only element retained from the book and that screenwriter Maxwell Anderson had concocted the narrative from whole cloth. The first preview prints of the film climaxed with a scene in which the body of a lynched politician is dumped on the steps of the Capitol. Though Columbia Pictures chief Harry Cohn insisted the controversial scene would remain intact, it was ultimately cut. In the end, Columbia kept to its preproduction pledge that *Washington Merry-Go-Round* would "reach the screen with the approval of all political parties."

Sheltered from controversy by the cover of comedy and the medium of animation, another part of the motion picture program offered a dimmer view of the American political process. Betty Boop, Max Fleischer's cartoon sex object, tossed her hat, and garter, into the ring in *Betty Boop for President* (1932), an election-season release that asked voters to choose between paralysis and pandering. Betty runs for chief executive against a stick figure called "Mr. Nobody." Wiggling her hips, she tunefully promises voters the moon:

> *Some of you are rich,*
> *Some of you are poor, you know.*
> *If you send me to Washington,*
> *I'll just divide the dough.*

Her opponent, Mr. Nobody, takes the stage and pledges a program of Hoover-esque insensitivity:

> *When you're hungry, who feeds you?*
> *Mr. No-body.*
> *Who cares what becomes of you?*
> *Mr. No-body.*

After Betty wins the democratic mandate, she appears before Congress (donkeys on the left, elephants on the right) and pushes through a program of "boop-oop-e-doop and chocolate ice cream." The final frame dissolves into a tantalizing and prophetic prospect: a cold mug of beer.

The most excessive of the motion picture assaults on the political and professional classes was Cecil B. DeMille's *This Day and Age* (1933), an uncharacteristic lurch into social consciousness from the preeminent auteur of the biblical disaster film. In 1947 DeMille would represent the extreme right wing during the House Committee on Un-American Activities investigations into alleged communist subversion in Hollywood. In the early 1930s, however, when economic conditions unhinged even the most conservative sensibilities, the once and future right-winger found himself making common cause with his legions of extras. "I am not a radical, but now things are a question of right and wrong," declared DeMille in 1931. "The public has been milked and are growing tired of it. It is not [financial] speculation alone. There is something rotten at the core of our system." Like not a few American artists of the 1930s, DeMille looked to the Soviet Union as a lodestar, expressing his sympathy with the Bolshevik experiment and his opinion that capitalism was doomed. Almost as if planning the storyboards of a future epic, he envisioned the Soviet Union as "a great prehistoric beast shaking off its shackles and stepping into civilization." In 1931, DeMille toured the USSR and returned five months later still brimming with enthusiasm. "Russia offers many and marvelous opportunities," he gushed. "It packs more drama per square inch than can be found in a square mile elsewhere." He refused to confirm or deny reports that his next project for Paramount would be a dramatization of the Soviet Union's Five Year Plan.

Perhaps DeMille looked to the remote, faraway, and really big USSR because it offered a sprawling canvas for his own epochal aspirations, an impulse he later satisfied not with a Stalinesque paean to hydroelectric power but with two epics of classic antiquity, *The Sign of the Cross* (1932) and *Cleopatra* (1934). Each wallowed in an orgy of paganism before the Judeo-Christian deity broke up the Greco-Roman shenanigans in that way that is only His. In between the ancient spectacles, however, *This Day and Age* demonstrated DeMille's expertise with mob scenes of more contemporary shadings. As usual, the director is less surefooted on the streets of twentieth-century America than the antechambers of first-century Rome.

An establishing shot shows a bustling and conspicuously integrated swarm of high school students in a placid, sunlit all-American community. It is Career Day, when the most likely to succeed in the senior class exchange places for twenty-four hours with the civic leadership—mayor, judge, district attorney, police chief, and so on. A postcredit close-up of the honor roll of alumni killed in the Great War shows that these kids possess a patriotic backbone the nation can call on in the present crisis.

Across the street, Herman's Tailor Shop serves as an unlikely juvenile hangout. A lovable old-world Jew, Herman (Harry Green), caters without discrimination to the appetites of his multiethnic clientele. To the Jewish kid, he serves *tsimmis*, to the Italian kid, chicken cacciatore, to the Chinese kid, chop suey, and to the Irish kid, eggs and—ham. "For me," he chuckles, "that's something." Despite his soft exterior, Herman is a courageous independent businessman who refuses to knuckle under to the protection racket of gangster Louis Garrett (Charles Bickford) even after his tailor shop is bombed. Determined to make an example of the old man, Bickford barges into the shop and kills Herman.

Though young Steve Smith (Richard Cromwell) is an eyewitness to the murder, Garrett beats the rap, giving the kids a harsh civics lesson in a dysfunctional justice system. A montage of legal mumbo jumbo shows the gangster's "million dollar mouthpiece" tangling up the court in technicalities and derailing the wheels of justice. Found innocent, Bickford walks, grinning to his henchmen and fawned over by the press.

Stymied by the corruption infesting all levels of adult authority, the boys resolve to take justice into their own hands. In a sequence bizarre even by pre-Code standards, the fledgling vigilantes take Garrett to a deserted brickyard for a kangaroo courtroom session of ritualistic humiliation and rough justice. As mobs of boys from the area high schools roar their school cheers, Garrett is hoisted on ropes and slowly lowered into a pit full of rats. Two sets of squeals (Garrett's and the rodents') echo on the soundtrack. When the police arrive, rather than breaking up the juvenile saturnalia, they endorse it. "These kids are all deputies," the police chief decides. Whistling "Yankee Doodle Dandy" and singing "The Battle Hymn of the Republic," the youth movement rides Garrett on a rail through the town in a jubilant torchlit parade, hundreds of kids taking over the streets from their paralyzed, ineffectual elders. The mob rouses the local judge from his sleep ("Is it a revolution?" asks his wife nervously) to preside over another trial, in a civil courtroom not a brickyard, but with the certainty of the guilty verdict the community demands.

DeMille's paean to vigilante action was bound to run afoul of adult authorities. Incredibly, though, the Studio Relations Committee managed to miss the scent of revolution in the air. "We do not believe [*This Day and Age*] will be interpreted in any way as an attack upon constituted authority, or a portrayal of lynch law, inasmuch as we noticed that you took great care to portray the boys as under control and working in harmony with the police department, having been appointed special deputies by the sheriff, and at the end, the judge, mayor, and district attorney were portrayed as being in sympathy with the boys' actions," the helpful James Wingate informed Paramount after a preview screening.

Other censors were not so easily gulled. Wingate himself had cautioned Paramount that "censor boards lately (particularly the New York State Board) have been insisting on maintaining respect for established law and order and have stated specifically that they will not tolerate any attempt to undermine this sentiment." True to its threat, the New York board deleted the italicized portions of the lines "And we're going to try him *without any bunk or hokum*—just pure and simple justice" and "For once Garrett, you're going to be really tried for murder—and there isn't going to be any bail or habeas corpus *or any of the rest of that hocus pocus.*" In Maryland, sex not sedition caused the censor board to demand that a reference to the virginal charms of a high school girl ("I like my olives green") be deleted. In Wingate's obliviousness to the meaning of the Code and the variable standards of the state boards, the censorship experience of *This Day and Age* is a microcosm of the pre-Code regulatory problems that made the revisions in procedure and personnel so attractive to Hollywood in 1934: the head of the Studio Relations Committee possessed few cinematic smarts and less authority, and the attentions of the state censorship boards lurched unpredictably from political subversion in one state to sexual innuendo in another.

Partly impressed, partly troubled, the *Hollywood Reporter* described the fervid bloodlust *This Day and Age* inspired in a preview audience. "Cheers, and the final long burst of applause" marked a reaction "tempered by a touch of mob hysteria." "DeMille, always a genius in using crowds to arouse that hysteria, almost overreaches himself in this film," worried the uneasy reviewer, who nonetheless concluded that "anyone who would be moved by a parade or by any kind of mob demonstration, will be sufficiently overcome by *This Day and Age* to send all their friends scurrying to see it."

4

Dictators and Democrats
The Rage for Order

One of the most politically charged films of the pre-Code era came from an unlikely source, the drawing boards of the Walt Disney studio. First screened at Radio City Music Hall on May 25, 1933, *The Three Little Pigs* built steadily in popularity to become a national sensation. Playing multiple dates and return engagements throughout summer and fall of 1933, the cartoon was probably the most widely seen film of the 1930s. A record 350 prints circulated constantly and exhibitors ballyhooed the Disney "Silly Symphony" with more fervor than the feature films it preceded on the motion picture program. Standing-room-only crowds comprised mainly of adults with children "brought just to see the cute short subject" flocked to theaters.

The whimsical tale follows the adventures of a trio of pigs who experiment with three progressively sturdier options in home building material (straw, wood, and bricks) and their respective resistance to the lung power of a lupine predator. The jaunty theme song "Who's Afraid of the Big, Bad

Wolf?" permeated the air via radio, phonographs, and streetcorner singa-longs. Sometimes the tune was called "catchy," other times, more interest-ingly, "haunting." Either way, the cultural resonance of motion picture art is seldom so transparent. Even at the time, the animated fable took hold as a double-edged metaphor: the fear of life being blown away by the cold winds of the Great Depression and the hope that, with sound reconstruction poli-cies and honest statecraft, the wolf could be kept at bay, huffing and puffing outside the door.

HANKERING FOR SUPERMEN

In 1932 the American Legion passed a resolution declaring that "the princi-pal causes of the present situation are in general such that they cannot be promptly and efficiently met by existing political methods." Bereft of faith in the present occupant of the White House, holding out little hope that a shuf-fling in personnel would prompt a change in conditions, one of the most patriotic and conservative organizations in America was calling for the over-throw of the national government. "From what source come these unmanly fears that prevail among us? These dark forbodings? This despairing impo-tence? What is it that has shaken the nerves of so many?" asked Walter Lipp-mann, himself not a little shaken by the proposal. Perhaps, he wondered, "it is not only against the material consequences of the decade of drift and hallu-cination, but against the essence of the spirit that the best and bravest among us are today in revolt."

One troubling response to the hallucinatory sensation of drift was what Lippmann termed the "hankering for supermen," the rage for order that called out for a take-charge leader who would seize the wheel and right the ship of state. With democratic capitalism on its knees, with a hapless Hoover in the White House, the punctual virtues of authoritarian order and the forthright actions of charismatic dictators seemed attractive by comparison. Just as American communists looked dewy-eyed toward Joseph Stalin and the future that worked in the Soviet Union, homegrown authoritarians yearned for potent stewardship and doted on images of ordered men march-ing together in sharp uniforms.

Hollywood filled the leadership vacuum with what the trade press dubbed a "dictator craze": a series of films with strong tyrannical personalities who, whatever their flaws as human beings and citizens, at least knew how to take strong action. Four decisive models of benevolent dictatorship, two from the world of business and two from the world of politics (one domestic, one international), arrived with suggestive punctuality during the cultural transition from Hoover to FDR.

The Power and the Glory (1933) embodied the hankering for a superman in title, sentiment, and central character. Directed by William K. Howard from a screenplay by Preston Sturges, the film is often considered a precursor to *Citizen Kane* (1941) because of its pioneering use of voice-over narration, or "narratage" as Fox's publicity department grandly called "the first major experiment in sound dramatics!" Slowed down by remedial lessons in flashback film grammar (as a narrator conjures the past, the camera moves in on his face, tracks right, and dissolves into his recollection; an alternative visual cue deploys a tinted curtain wiping diagonally down from upper screen right to lower screen left), *The Power and the Glory* resurrects the deceased and unmourned railroad tycoon Tom Garner (Spencer Tracy) for a meditation of the price of greatness. Personally flawed but professionally flawless, Garner rises Horatio Alger-fashion from pauper to plutocrat. When his railroad workers strike and threaten violence, he marches alone into their ranks and brings them to heel through sheer dint of his haughty bearing. Once out of his presence, the workers strike and Garner makes good on his promise to suppress them by force, killing over four hundred men in a wild labor riot. Despite the massacre, and the fact that Garner's love life is a mess that drives him to suicide, the end reel judgment on the tycoon answers one question—is this any way to run a railroad?—affirmatively. The suicide and the massacre are acceptable trade-offs for the power and the glory.

The definitive incarnation of this autocratic personality type was the actor Warren William, who appeared in film after film as an electrifying if caddish professional (lawyer, businessman, producer, political fixer) whose mean exterior concealed a meaner interior. A joy to watch in action, William played men callous in character but commanding in presence, harsh dynamos with not a whit of self-doubt or common decency.

Released mere weeks before FDR's inauguration, Roy Del Ruth's *Employee's Entrance* (1933) showcases William at his magnetic worst. The film tracks the machinations of ruthless business executive Kurt Anderson (William) of the Franklin Monroe Department Store, the names of the founding fathers now an ironic rebuke. A Jazz Age montage shows the rising arc of prosperity the store traces from its establishment in 1878 on through the Roaring Twenties and up to the screeching halt of 1929. In business "there's no room for sympathy or softness—my code is smash or be smashed!" Anderson tells his calcifying board of directors. He proves as much by ruin-

Authority figures: Warren William in firm control in Roy Del Ruth's *Employee's Entrance* (1933). (Courtesy of the Museum of Modern Art)

ing a kindly old factory owner because the man failed to fulfill a contract due to labor unrest.

A workaholic with no home life, Anderson roams the store after hours and comes upon the unemployed Madeline (Loretta Young), trying to sneak a night in a "model home" exhibit in order to be first in line for a job the next morning. "With your looks you shouldn't have any trouble finding a job," Anderson flirts. "Thank, you," she replies virtuously, "but I'd rather be employed for my brain."

But it is her brain that tells her she is in no position to refuse the attentions of Mr. Anderson when he tempts her with "How about a little dinner?" The next scene finds the pair alone in his apartment. She thanks him for the wonderful dinner and the loan of ten dollars. She says she must go. Really, she must go. Anderson shuts the door and leans into her. "You don't have to go, you know," he purrs.

Next morning Madeline has a job in the women's department as a model. Anderson moves on to other business. Store revenues have dropped $45 million. "That's Depression!" he declares redundantly. When he asks for ideas on how to meet the crisis, a milquetoast executive named Higgins meekly states the official line. "I don't know if there's very much to be said. There's a depression and everybody's affected. Everything. I should say that the thing to do is retrench, economize." Anderson erupts. "Get out Higgins—you're dead weight!" Humiliated, Higgins commits suicide. "When a man outlives his usefulness, he ought to jump out a window," sneers the executive who drove him to his death. "But he's worked here thirty years," protests a co-worker. "Send him a wreath!" barks Anderson.

Anderson is a fierce businessman and avowed misogynist, but one thing he is not is timorous and vacillating. Moreover, his despotism is benevolent: he points out that if the department store fails, hundreds of employees will be out of work. His decisive actions and firm hand at the helm are infinitely preferable to the impotent board of directors and cowardly bankers who "couldn't go out and earn a nickel." Unlike the financiers, Anderson acts. Next to the simpering characters who surround him, his aggressive command style is captivating and admirable. The businessman he ruined in the first reel, now a worker in the department store, sees the cold necessity in Anderson's methods. "I thought there was such a thing as honesty and cooperation and sincerity in the business world. I found out differently. It's men like you who crush who succeed." Impressed, Anderson promptly writes the man a $5,000 check to stake him in a business venture. The man insults him and tears up the check. Anderson gives him a promotion and raises his salary.

The logical place to seek strong leadership was elected office, a platform from which to fantasize a figure without feet of clay or head of rock to take command in Washington. That impulse generated pre-Code Hollywood's most surreal excursion into the political realm, Walter Wanger's production of *Gabriel Over the White House* (1933), directed by Gregory La Cava and written by Carey Wilson with uncredited contributions by media mogul William Randolph Hearst. At once silly and chilling, it shows how acute the national malady was in Hoover's last year: better an energetic tyrant than a passive president.

Authentic newsreel images of the inauguration of Herbert Hoover are crosscut with the inauguration of President Jud Hammond (Walter Huston), a handsome party hack in the Warren G. Harding mold. A series of expository vignettes reveals that Hammond is not so much sinister as weak. Immature, inattentive, and prone to sins of the flesh (his mistress shows up at the White House and strolls across the presidential seal on the floor), he is the wrong man for troubled times. At a press conference, a swarthy member of the fourth estate launches into a fiery Bolshevik speech about the unemployed, but Hammond rejects pleas for presidential action. While a voice on the radio exhorts listeners to rally in Washington, D.C., to protest government inaction, Hammond crawls about on the Oval Office floor, playing with his nephew.

When Hammond's symbolic recklessness behind the wheel of a car knocks him into a coma, he looks to be a terminal case. But tingly music fills the soundtrack, a curtain in a window flutters, the light changes, and the president opens his eyes—not the eyes of the limp puppet who was Jud Hammond but the eyes of a man of deep wisdom and steely timber. Animated with a divine spirit, he calls Congress into session, declares martial law, and seizes dictatorial power. Brooking no opposition from his cabinet, he sets about bringing order to the chaos of Depression America.

As both his aide and his mistress look on, perplexed but delighted by the personality transplant, Hammond resolves two parallel threats to the social order: the Army of the Unemployed, who plan to march on Washington for relief (a stand-in for the Bonus Marchers of the summer of 1932), and the gangster Nick Diamond, who thumbs his nose at the law (a stand-in for Al Capone et al.). Hammond co-opts the one and wipes out the other. After a speedy military trial, the gangsters are executed by firing squad under the torch of the Statue of Liberty. Prophetically, the organs of mass communications, especially radio, over which Hammond communicates his plans to the American people via live nationwide hook-ups, figure prominently in the political revolution.

Title billing notwithstanding, the figure hovering over the White House is not the archangel Gabriel but the spiritual father Abraham Lincoln. Recognized as "the greatest crisis facing the nation since the Civil War," the Great Depression called upon the wartime rhetoric and symbology as a wellspring of sustenance. When the transformed Jud Hammond is first glimpsed, he sits upright in a chair, posed like the Daniel Chester French statue at the Lincoln Memorial. Gangster Nick Diamond manipulates the law ("My lawyer will habeas my corpus out of there"), and so, like Lincoln, Hammond suspends habeas corpus. The Army of the Unemployed sings a rousing chorus of "The Battle Hymn of the Republic." Like Lincoln too, when Hammond's work of reunification is done, he gives up the ghost and belongs to the ages.

Leading up to and upon its release, courtesy of shilling by the Hearst newspaper and radio syndicate, *Gabriel Over the White House* was a controversial, hugely publicized prestige project. Notwithstanding the powerhouse

The "dictator craze": Walter Huston (*left*) as the divinely inspired president in *Gabriel Over the White House* (1933). (Courtesy of the Museum of Modern Art)

backing of the media baron, however, the Hays Office "flatly refused to pass the picture in its original form declaring that its reality is a dangerous item at this time."

Yet Hays needn't have worried about the danger lurking in Hearst's message to the masses. In spirit a 1932 film, *Gabriel Over the White House* was released on March 31, 1933, which placed it not in the midst of Hoover paralysis but on the wave of FDR dynamism. "If you had voted for Hammond—there would have been no Depression!" screamed ads that flashed back to 1928 and failed to notice that Americans had already cast their vote for a new deal. Set in relief against FDR's first hundred days, a radical call to action was redundant on arrival. This, and the traditional antipathy to hectoring screen rhetoric, had the film "dying the death of a flop" throughout the country.

On the domestic front, *Gabriel Over the White House* expressed the last gasp of the "dictator craze" of 1932–33. Overseas, however, Jud Hammond's brand of tyranny was not the stuff of Hollywood fantasy. The consolidation of Fascism in Italy and the rise of Nazism in Germany presented two charismatic models for decisive leadership. If most Americans viewed the European examples with trepidation or detached curiosity, in some quarters the admiration was undisguised.

Columbia Pictures proposed Italian fascism as a punctual alternative to the clumsy inefficiency of American democracy in a 76-minute compilation of newsreel clips of Il Duce, *Mussolini Speaks* (1933), "described and interpreted" by NBC radio commentator Lowell Thomas and edited and compiled by Jack Cohn. The precredit inscription reads: "This picture is dedicated to a man of the people whose deeds for his people will ever be an inspiration to all mankind."

Natty in a sharp suit and sporting a carnation in his lapel, narrator Thomas speaks the exculpatory preface into a prop microphone. "Whether we agree with a man's policy or not doesn't matter," Thomas explains. "We're interested in a man if he marks himself a leader, if he molds history, if he's a man of achievement, and if he has that rare gift—personal magnetism." Casting Mussolini as an Italian Horatio Alger story, Thomas asks "how came this blacksmith's son to rise" to become "a modern caesar?"

Archival newsreel footage and adulatory commentary trace Mussolini's rise to power in the 1920s. Blackshirts march on Rome, a sea of humanity fills the screen, and (the cliché for the ages) "the trains run on time to the dot." "Fascism has scored its decisive triumph!" cheers Thomas. "He stands like a modern caesar," does Mussolini, "a man of tireless energy—he works incessantly." A litany of great European leaders places Il Duce in heady company: "Charlemagne, Richelieu, Napoleon, Bismarck, and now Benito Mussolini." New irrigation and construction projects fuel a roaring economy, and the seizure of North African colonies restores a national pride dormant since the Roman Empire. On land, sea, and air, Italy is a country on the move, on the upswing. "This is a time when a dictator comes in handy!" enthuses Thomas.

As Mussolini declaims, at length, to the multitudes, Thomas provides simultaneous translation and play-by-play commentary. "I like the way he makes faces. There's something ingratiating and exceedingly human in the way he puckers his mouth and wrinkles his brow. Sometimes it's funny and then again in a sudden flash you see the head of a Roman Emperor." The American curiosity in all this is not idle. "Well, for those of us in other countries who have been saying, 'What we need is a Mussolini,' here's our chance to size him up."

Released the week of FDR's inauguration, *Mussolini Speaks* was advertised as "the timeliest box office scoop of the year" both "because it appeals to all red-blooded Americans" and "because it might be the answer to America's needs." At the Palace Theater in New York, where over 175,000 saw the film in two weeks, press accounts reported "rounds of applause and handclaps" and audiences who "cheered time and time again." *Mussolini Speaks* "should be shown in both Houses of Congress, in every high school, club, and university," demanded syndicated columnist Arthur Brisbane in the *New York American*. "It illustrates as no picture has done, the role that talking pictures are destined to play as education." Making a foray into ethnic niche marketing, Columbia urged exhibitors to contact local Italian stores and fruit stands for publicity tie-ins and provided translated ad copy for insertion into Italian language newspapers.

But with FDR in the White House, neither Jud Hammond nor Benito Mussolini became motion picture stars. Invited to "size up" the Italian alternative against the new American president, the overblown stature of Mussolini shrank. The "dictator craze" was quashed by the impact of FDR on American popular culture. Onscreen and off, his good-humored manner and steady hand broke the fever and satisfied the rage for order.

"THE BARRYMORE OF THE CAPITAL": THE NEWSREEL PRESIDENCY OF FRANKLIN DELANO ROOSEVELT

After listening to one of FDR's first radio addresses in 1933, actress Miriam Howell remarked that the presidential timbre sounded "almost as good as Walter Huston." Due to a series of storied fireside chats on radio, mellifluously delivered and carefully parcelled out over the course of four terms, Franklin Delano Roosevelt is heralded as the first president to exploit with savvy the modern mass media. Yet FDR's cultivation of the motion picture screen as a transmission belt for political communication was just as farsighted and cunning as his pioneer radio broadcasts. Via the five commercial newsreels, FDR became not just a familiar radio voice, or the benevolent visage on the New Deal portraits that wallpapered the homes, stores, and offices of Great Depression America, but a vibrant cinematic personality. Beheld week in and week out on screen, his commanding presence and serene manner helped calm insurrectionist impulses that before his inauguration on March 4, 1933, had threatened to overturn both capitalism and the Constitution.

FDR had an easy presidential act to follow. His screen charisma contrasted sharply with the decidedly unphotogenic character and taciturn

A hopeless subject for the newsreels: Herbert Hoover at the podium, 1932. (Courtesy of the National Archives)

style of his predecessor, the dour Herbert Hoover. To the newsreel boys, Hoover was a hopeless screen subject. Refusing to play to the cameras, he was apt to be caught in unflattering profile or with eyes cast downward, to flub lines, or to freeze up. "Hoover can't speak six words without looking at his notes," wrote Fox Movietone cameraman Charles Peder. "You can't kid him in front of the mike. It is all a set performance or nothing." Looking back from 1935, a historian of the 1932 campaign remembered that "the pictures of [Hoover] on the screen and in the newspapers were almost never good; invariably he appeared solemn and sad, an unhappy man, a man without hope."

By contrast, FDR's quite calculated "eternal smile" exuded confidence and optimism. Even before his nomination and election in 1932, Governor Roosevelt was deemed "a natural subject for the film and mike . . . always a popular subject with the public" who "always gives the glad hand to the men who shoot him." Democratic partisans almost to a man, the newsreel boys glad-handed FDR in turn, favoring him with flattering camera angles and friendly sound bites.

Yet no media conspiracy was needed to make FDR a dynamic screen presence. Shortly after his inauguration, the newsreels recorded his induction into the National Press Club, a delightful appearance in which the patrician reformer "strongly registered the regular fellow spirit." Before long, newsreel editors realized they were in the presence of a political star of the first magnitude. "No chief executive in the recollection of newsreel men has possessed all the screen qualifications of Mr. Roosevelt," *Variety* reported, dubbing him "the Barrymore of the Capital." Consider a small but characteristic moment of public grace, good humor, and media smarts. While tossing out the first ball of the 1934 baseball season, FDR turns to the crowd and cracks, "Last year, I almost killed a photographer."

Besides FDR's native mediageniety and intuitive grasp of the importance of screen imagery in modern politics, a surfeit of motion picture-wise Democrats gave him a wide advantage over his rival. With the exceptions of MPPDA president Will H. Hays and MGM chief Louis B. Mayer, almost everyone in Hollywood was avowedly Democratic and ardently pro-Roosevelt. During the 1932 election campaign, Jack Warner headed up the motion picture division of the California Democrats, tithed his employees for donations to the campaign, and closed down production at Warner Brothers for two hours so crews could listen to Boston mayor James Michael Curley deride Herbert Hoover.

For his part, FDR courted the medium from the very start of his public career. As assistant secretary of the Navy in the Wilson administration, he recognized the causal relationship between bigger budgets from Congress and motion pictures of impressive military exercises, in one instance loaning the newsreels a destroyer to obtain pictures for Navy publicity. As governor of New York, he heightened his national profile by performing frequently in the newsreels and solidified his power base in special state issues screened only in New York. When the National Democratic Committee rejected a newsreel request to pay for the lighting and wiring needed to film and record the Democratic Convention of 1932, the candidate intervened on behalf of the newsreels and directed his delegates to reverse the decision. FDR knew that it paid in the long run to keep the newsreel boys happy.

Soon after his inauguration, FDR brought into the White House two former newsreel editors, Col. Marvin Hunter McIntyre of Pathé News and Stephen T. Early of Paramount News, both of whom had served as Wash-

A natural in the newsreels: a jovial FDR shares a laugh with son James Roosevelt, William McAdoo, campaign manager James Farley, and Will Rogers during a rally in Los Angeles, 1932.

ington bureau chiefs. They worked assiduously to accommodate the newsreels and massage editorial egos. Not content to delegate the nurturing of so important a symbiotic relationship, the president himself lavished personal attention on the newsreel boys. Pathé News featured a jovial FDR complimenting them on a hard day's work after the long trek of his inaugural parade. Turning to face the cameras, he quips, "You can say that the cameramen are all in very good physical condition—they've run five miles!"

Considered "probably the keenest motion picture and newsreel enthusiast that ever sat in the state chair at the White House," FDR watched movies and newsreels almost nightly at the White House or his residence in Hyde Park. "As an exhibitor, the President is showing such pictures as *The Power and the Glory* [1933] and *Cavalcade* [1933] on one night bookings," joshed *Variety*. "He has them exclusively in his zone—Hyde Park. The only policy that regular exhibs wouldn't like is that the President has no box office. Admissions are Annie Oakleys [free tickets], limited to family and friends."

Upon his entry into public life, FDR had begun keeping a personal copy of motion picture footage of himself. During his presidency, the newsreels stroked the chief executive by contributing to his collection. Truman Talley of Fox Movietone secured footage from all five newsreels, whereupon Fox's Washington editor "presented the film, mounted on a reel all ready for screening, at the front door of the White House." Pathé News made up special, personalized issues for James A. Farley, FDR's campaign manager, postmaster general, and dispenser of patronage. "This permanent record of the Great Democratic Presidential campaign is presented to the Hon. James A. Farley in recognition of his splendid and successful management that brought Franklin Delano Roosevelt to the White House," read one personalized title card.

After FDR's election, the newsreels played a pivotal role in the campaign to sell the New Deal and glorify its point man. Within four months, FDR had clocked more screen time in the newsreels than Hoover had during his first two years in office. The alliance between the newsreels and new president began with the release of special issues on the transition of presidential power, FDR's inauguration being the first to be recorded by sound-on-film motion pictures. In many theaters, the FDR films were given more marquee space than the accompanying feature film.

Fox Movietone's special issue *The Inauguration of Franklin D. Roosevelt* (1933) depicted the transfer of power from Hoover to FDR as far more momentous than the usual quadrennial passage. "The hour of destiny has struck," the narrator intones, as the "President and Mrs. Hoover, leaving the White House after four trying years, greet Mrs. Roosevelt on the portico." Observing that "the President-elect waits in the car in which he and Mr. Hoover will ride to the Capitol together," the commentary leaves unmentioned the reason for the departure from etiquette, why the wife of the president-elect walks to greet the defeated president.

Of course, walking was the structured absence in newsreel coverage of FDR, the great unspoken and unscreened fact about the president. Like still photographers and print reporters, newsreel cameramen and editors colluded with FDR and his inner circle to conceal the full seriousness of his paralysis from the polio which had stricken him in 1921. At a time when the American economy was itself crippled, an image of helplessness and dependence was considered symbolically discouraging to a nation craving the vigorous leadership of an activist president. Throughout the Great Depression, and on through the Second World War, the disabled and by 1944 visibly infirm president was never shown to disadvantage on the newsreel screen. On the contrary, the newsreels consistently played up the president's vitality and mobility, showing him riding by in cars, waving from trains, and frolicking at water polo ("Roosevelt at Play! Intimate Glimpses Show Democratic Candidate at Play!").

Not that FDR's infirmity was unknown or unremarked upon. In 1928 Al Smith responded to a whispering campaign questioning FDR's fitness for the New York governorship with a widely quoted wisecrack that, in shutting up the rumor-mongers, also revealed how commonplace was public awareness of his malady: "We do not elect him for his ability to do a double back flip or handspring." Abiding by the decorum of the time, however, the discussions of FDR's polio occurred more in private conversation than public commentary. In 1932 even the acerbic H. L. Mencken broached the topic with uncharacteristic delicacy when he wrote of the "grave uneasiness" on the part of Democratic electors about the "physical capacity" of FDR "for the job they were entrusting to him." Mencken noted that FDR "struggles against it in a most gallant manner, and will certainly never let it get him down, but all the same it would be idle to say that he is as fit as a normal man."

The newsreels adhered to the tacit agreement not to mention the unpleasant truth and certainly never to expose it on screen. As late as 1944, Terry Ramsaye of *Motion Picture Herald* approvingly cited such deference to the commander in chief on the grounds that "a reasonable and patriotic citizenry would be wanting him always to look his best." Still, week in, week out, FDR sits when the president should stand or walk; when he stands, he grips railings and podiums. Twenty-twenty hindsight or not, the newsreel image of FDR reveals what it tries to hide, a man who is not ambulatory.

Though FDR lacked candor about the full extent of his disability, his blunt talk and confident manner on radio and in the newsreels tolerated no mealy-mouthed euphemisms about the state of the nation. In his first inaugural address, he speaks of "a stricken nation in a stricken world" and promises to wage "the moral equivalent of war" against the Great Depression. Under Hoover, public statements from government and business leaders were exercises in double-talk and wishful thinking. FDR's articulate diagnosis, as much as his prescription for remedy, served to reassure Americans that sentient political leadership had returned to government. The contrast on screen emphasized the contrast in policy: Hoover's detachment and discomfort against FDR's warmth and grace.

Driving the difference home, two newsreel biopics of FDR followed close on the heels of the inauguration newsreels, Hearst Metrotone's *Roosevelt—The Man of the Hour* (1933) and Universal's *The Fighting President* (1933). "America cries out to its Fighting President: Show Us the Way and

We Will Follow!" pleaded the pathetic taglines. Chronicling the blizzard of legislative activity that marked FDR's first one hundred days in office, the film complements the presidential energy with its own nimble tempo. A fast-paced montage sequence checks off the day-by-day accomplishments on the pages of a calendar (March 1933, April 1933, May 1933), packing each second of screen time with action and accomplishment. Drenched in patriotic music and beatific lighting, the film closes with an image of FDR's serene, almost divine visage floating in double exposure over the White House. Anna Roosevelt Dall, the president's daughter, introduced *The Fighting President* at its premiere engagement in New York, where it played on the program with *Destination Unknown* (1933), a religious allegory set on board a stranded ship (and not a Republican scheme to undercut the president).

As if nurturing the career of a favored contract player, Hollywood doted on FDR in other ways. Within days of his inauguration, slides, trailers, and lobby cards filled moviehouses exhorting the public to:

STAND BY YOUR PRESIDENT

President Roosevelt is doing a great job. He is restoring order out of banking chaos. He is preparing for the resumption of business. He is paving the way for prosperity. All this can not be done in a day. In the meantime, all he needs is a continuance of the same cheerfulness and patience that the American people have displayed thus far. Our lot may be tough, but his is tougher, so let us all help him as best we can.

The motion picture industry followed its own advice. A national committee of ranking film executives, chaired by Harry M. Warner, was organized to "prepare propaganda pictures and recruit theater screens for showing them." For Hollywood, getting behind the New Deal meshed patriotic impulses and financial self-interest: patriotism because a revitalized America meant a revitalized box office; self-interest because the New Deal's National Recovery Act (NRA) governed the operation of motion picture production and distribution, a looming bludgeon that kept the industry nervously compliant throughout 1933–34.

Beginning on August 20, 1933, distributed without cost to over six thousand theaters by National Screen Service, a 15-second addition to the motion picture program arrived in the form of the New Deal symbol, a blue eagle against a red background, with white letters reading "This theater is a NRA member. We do our part." The "Blue Eagle" (in black and white) was

also added to the credits of Hollywood films, either in a title panel preceding the film proper or a small logo in the corner of the frame.

By the fall of 1933 all five of the major studios (Warner Brothers, Paramount, MGM, Fox, and RKO) had produced FDR-friendly short subjects,
a practice that continued throughout the New Deal era. Typically, the New
Deal shorts featured second-tier contract players in mini-playlets exhorting
administration policies such as the forty-hour work week or farm price
supports. In the spirit of the rest of the balanced program, the New Deal
propaganda was leavened with comedy and music. Even MGM, repenting
for backing Hoover, came on board with *Inflation* (1933), a short film
explaining the economics of inflation and closing with a triumphant pane-
gyric to FDR.

Characteristically, Warner Brothers took the mission from Washington
most to heart. In its premiere NRA entry, *The Road Is Open Again* (1933),
musical star Dick Powell plays a young composer trying to write an anthem
for the NRA. Visions of George Washington, Abraham Lincoln, and Woodrow Wilson materialize over Powell's head as inspiration. Each tells of his
contribution to America in the past and assures Powell that FDR is on the
right track for the future. Thus inspired by the presidential muses, Powell
sings a verse of "The Road Is Open Again" (written by Sammy Fein and
Irving Kahal) and turns to the camera to invite audiences to sing the chorus along with him.

Another prominent endorsement of FDR came by way of the motion
pictures from a rival radio voice. Before the priest and the president went
their separate ways, Father Charles E. Coughlin borrowed FDR's sobriquet
for his own vanity biopic, *The Fighting Priest* (1934). An independent release
from Shamrock Pictures Corporation, it was billed as a "pictorial review of
the man of the hour—the Reverend Charles E. Coughlin, famous Detroit
radio commentator." Besides being an advertisement for himself, *The Fighting Priest* baptizes FDR as the chosen agent of salvation on earth. "FDR, our
beloved president, is one of the closest friends of the Reverend Charles E.
Coughlin, who is himself a staunch supporter of the president in his fight
for the real betterment of the country," intones a prefatory benediction.

The paean to the radio priest closes with a Coughlin tirade praising the
monetary policies of FDR and the character of "this one single outstanding
gentleman" who is all that stands between America and damnation. In the
bracing tones that riveted thirty million listeners every afternoon at 4:00
P.M., Coughlin looks into the camera and implores "that you stand steadfast
in your loyalty to him who shall bring us out of the Depression and awak-

en in the hearts of every American a spirit of prosperity the like of which has never been dreamed in this world of ours. Today it is either Roosevelt or ruin!" Listening to Coughlin, and without the benefit of lowercase typeface, Great Depression audiences might be forgiven for momentarily confusing "loyalty to him" (FDR) with "loyalty to Him" (God).

In truth, the deification of FDR on the newsreel screen was one of the most successful and longest-running programs of the New Deal. Soon, as the full force of his vibrant personality registered in the newsreels and worshipful biopics, FDR became not just a friendly radio voice, or the benevolent face on the ubiquitous portraits, but a fully animated, moving and talking character. Ironically, the paralysis of the president proved a cinematic advantage: FDR sits commandingly behind desks, or casually in chairs, and speaks directly to the newsreel audience in the theater, not declaiming to an auditorium from a lectern. Often, too, he is behind the wheel of a car, disguising his personal immobility with the forward motion of the vehicle. Up close, looking squarely into the lens, he exuded confidence, vigor, and energy. Unlike Hoover, FDR knew his real audience was in the moviehouse, not immediately in front of him. So many of the men and women speaking before the early sound camera look stiff and formal, unfamiliar with the strange new toy, uncomfortable with the prospect of their image and voice on film. Not FDR: no less than on radio, he was a natural in the newsreels.

A NEW DEAL IN THE LAST REEL

Caught at the crossroads between 1932 and 1933, between Hoover's raw deal and FDR's New Deal, Hollywood cinema underwent a jarring sensibility transplant, sometimes within the very same film—an abrupt turnabout from despair to hope, contempt to respect, wisecracking cynicism to wide-eyed belief. Two somber preachment yarns register the realignment of the national temperature. Both were produced by Warner Brothers on the cusp of the Hoover-Roosevelt transition, both looked back on the 1920s from the present trauma of the 1930s, and both were directed by studio ace William "Wild Bill" Wellman, the master craftsman who helmed twenty-one films in the pre-Code era.

Bleaker than a women's weepie and more sadistic than a prison film, *Heroes for Sale* (1933) piles a Sophoclean weight of misfortunes upon its guiltless protagonist, a hero of the Great War discarded in its aftermath. Directed by Wellman from a screenplay by Robert Lord and Wilson Mizner, the film reaches back to the horrors of combat and the pressures of the upwardly mobile 1920s before casting out its hero into the dead ends of the early 1930s. The meteorology of the Great Depression is a steady torrent of misfortune until the New Deal forecasts a break in the clouds.

In the No Man's Land of the Great War, under a withering downpour of rain and machine-gun fire, a mud-caked squad of doughboys undertakes a suicide mission to capture a German officer. Wellman's overhead crane shot swoops above the soldiers as they go over the top, a panoramic long shot from the wartime perspective of the director, himself a veteran of the Lafayette Escadrille. Tom Holmes (Richard Barthelmess, the personification of American grit in the silent era chestnut *Tol'able David* [1921]) doesn't mind confessing his fear to hometown pal Roger (Gordon Westcott), but in the heat of battle it is Roger who cracks, leaving Tom to complete the mission alone. Returning with the captured German officer, Tom finds Roger quaking in a shellhole. Just then, an artillery shell blasts him from behind. Thinking Tom dead, Roger takes the German back to headquarters and earns a Distinguished Service Cross for his bogus heroism.

Tom is not dead. Found moaning on the battlefield, he is brought back to life by the German medical corps. When the war ends, a kindly doctor gives him morphine to ease the pain from the shrapnel that still remains in his spine. On the troopship back to the States, Tom encounters an abashed Roger, fearful of being exposed as a sham hero. Generous Tom bears no grudge, having learned his Great War lesson. "I've been in the shadow of death for so long that nothing in life seems very important any more," he tells Roger. Like so many retrospective memories of the Great War, the whole affair is rendered as a horrific farce, with medals meaningless tokens and the moral equivalence between the combatants assumed.

Back in the States, Roger, the son of the local bank president, and Tom, a teller, resume their positions in civilian life, but as Roger bathes in the accolades of a moronic home front, Tom pops morphine tablets and suffers. Behind the bars of his teller's cage, Tom is trapped by his addiction and tempted to embezzle money for the narcotics he craves. Frantic, he seeks help from a doctor, who refuses treatment and informs the bank president of the dope fiend on the payroll. Addiction is a "loathsome cowardly act," he lectures Tom, especially given the "good clean Christian life" Tom's mother provided him. When Tom blurts out a true account of Roger's exploits on the field of battle, Roger convinces his father that Tom's exclamations are "the ravings of a dope fiend."

A montage of file cards reveals that Tom has been shipped off to a narcotics farm for treatment. His day of admission is November 9, 1921. Dis-
charged a year later, he visits his mother's grave. Chiseled on the tombstone
is the date of her death: November 10, 1921. The news of Tom's morphine
addiction has killed her.

A nighttime skyline and the word "Chicago" signposts Tom's next destination. Mary (Aline MacMahon), a tender-hearted settlement house
worker, chats with the new arrival and shows him to a room. Tom plans to
reside elsewhere until he spies a fellow apartment dweller, Ruth (Loretta
Young). Their eyeline match can only mean love at first sight.

Taking a hint from Ruth, Tom obtains work at a laundry company,
where his go-getting ambition pushes him up the ladder of success. This
being the 1920s, business is on everyone's mind, even the communist Max
(Robert Barrat), who spouts party-line rhetoric about "doctrines of communism" and "the Great Lenin." No one takes him seriously. "All you do
is talk everybody into a stomach ache," cracks Mary. As Tom thrives at the
laundry, Max condemns his "dirty capitalist" ambitions. "Steam, sweat,
consumption, shame!" he bellows. "He's getting awfully red," says Mary
indulgently. The German-accented Max is a colorful eccentric, not a political menace.

But Max is no fool. Trading his Karl Marx and Vladimir Lenin for
Thomas Edison and Henry Ford, he invents a machine that industrializes
the laundry business. Initially, Max's invention improves life for the laundry
workers, and Tom, Ruth, and a new baby prosper throughout the 1920s. But
when cutthroat capitalists automate the laundry plant and fire the workers,
the unemployed men blame Tom and take to the streets, arming themselves
with bricks, sticks, and pickaxes. "Smash the machines!" scream the Lud-
dites. As Tom tries to quell the labor riot, Ruth runs into the mob after him.
Suddenly, too quick to see, Ruth is hit by a brick and the side of her face
explodes in blood. She falls to the street, her lifeless eyes staring upward.

Unbelievably, Tom's bad luck is just beginning. Falsely accused of leading the labor riot, he is sentenced by a faceless judge to five years in prison
"for the serious crime of leading a mob and inciting to riot, a heinous attack
on the stability of organized society resulting in the death of four officers of
the law." Ruth's death is unmentioned.

"Hire the best lawyers," Max counsels Tom during a prison visit. "Bribe
everybody. Buy your way out of here." Tom refuses the "blood money" he
has earned from Max's invention, but Max pledges to invest it anyway. "You
used to hate the capitalists," mutters Tom. "Naturally," replies Max. "That was

before I had money." Tom's years of confinement float by in montage—1929, 1930, 1931, 1932—before releasing him to freedom in the nadir of the Great Depression.

At the settlement house, lines of unemployed queue up for food. "Gee, there's more and more people every night," says Tom's little boy. Two thuggish members of Chicago's "Red Squad" come by to warn Tom against engaging in any "radical stuff." "Cossacks," snarls Max, reclaiming his Bolshevik roots. When a "red riot" wrecks a machine shop, the Red Squad rounds up the usual suspects (Italians) and orders Tom to hit the road. He bequeaths his fortune to Mary so she may continue to feed the homeless.

A dissolve-montage of feet walking over a roadmap tracks Tom's perambulations across the nation in search of work: east to Harrisburg, Pennsylvania, west to St. Louis, Missouri, northeast to Nashville, Tennessee. "Jobless Men Keep Going," reads a billboard outside of a city. "We can't take care of our own." Rousted out of boxcars by goon squads, Tom and his fellow hoboes are welcomed nowhere and cursed as labor agitators and bums. "Who you calling reds and hoboes?" Tom shouts defiantly. "We're ex-serviceman!"

In the rain and mud again, in a noirish vista echoing the landscape of the other No Man's Land that began the hard traveling of Tom Holmes, the ex-servicemen congregate around a fire. The rain thunders relentlessly and the breath of the men condenses in the cold night air. A voice asks for food. It is Roger, Tom's old nemesis. "The stock market crashed and we crashed with it," he explains. "Funny," he muses. "We end up here in the rain together."

Comrades again, in another kind of trench warfare, Roger and Tom discuss the state of the nation. "The country can't go on this way," whines Roger. "It's the end of America." Tom disagrees. "Did you read President Roosevelt's inaugural address? He's right. You know, it takes more than one sock on the jaw to lick 120 million people." With an irony as heavy as the rain, Tom's peroration is interrupted by a goon squad that rousts the men out of town. In a traveling shot, the bedraggled ex-heroes walk toward the camera. "Well at least we got something to be thankful for," observes Tom laconically. "It's stopped raining." A coda shows Mary and Tom's son back at the soup kitchen, doing what they can for the poor, praising the saintly Tom.

Released in June 1933, *Heroes for Sale* pulls back from the hour-long "radical stuff" of its 73-minute running time at the last seconds. Every figure of authority, every political and economic institution, is depicted as corrupt, unjust, and unfeeling. The military leadership can't tell a hero from a coward, the town physician betrays the confidence of a patient who came to him in pain, the bank president fires a veteran wounded in mind and body, the businessmen cheat Tom and the workers, the judge convicts Tom of a crime he did not commit, the Red Squad drives Tom from his home and family, and the goon squads attack Tom for no other reason than that he seeks work. The New Deal finale in the rain cannot wash away the downpour that floods what is not a Warner Brothers "Americanism story" but an anti-Americanism story.

Just as sleek and no less bleak, *Wild Boys of the Road* (1933) is a fast-paced road movie accelerating through flush times, hard times, and the promise of better times. Wellman's location shots of authentic rail yards and Hoovervilles contrast starkly with the studio scenes, a style that anticipates the aesthetic of documentary realism embraced by the Farm Security Administration photographers commissioned by the New Deal at mid-decade. Like the still photographers Dorothea Lange and Walker Evans and the documentary filmmaker Pare Lorentz, Wellman layers his own roadwork with a thick coating of "found" social reality, images available just footsteps outside the studio gates and soundstage hangers at Burbank.

In another rueful Jazz Age prelude, a quartet of boisterous adolescents on a double date pulls up to a high school dance in a jalopy, driven by the carefree male ingenue Eddie (Frankie Darro). Like the nation, he will move from frivolity to destitution in a matter of minutes. Eddie's pal Tommy (Edwin Phillips) is already "up against it." Shamefacedly, he confides that his widowed mother survives on waitressing and charity. Eddie feels more fortunate but only temporarily. Upon arriving home, he raids the refrigerator (not the icebox) for a huge slice of apple pie, a symbol of his transient affluence. Mom has been crying; Dad has been fired.

Debts pile up in montage (overdue rent notices, grocery and laundry bills), and Eddie is forced to sell his beloved jalopy to a junk dealer for scrap. Perceiving themselves as a burden at home ("Why should I stick around and have a good time while [my father] has to stand in a breadline?"), the boys resolve to hit the road and find work. They jump a freight car and begin a forlorn and dusty journey across America, seesawing between mild respites and dashed hopes.

Like so many Great Depression migrants on the road, the wild boys confront the end of a frontier both geographic and symbolic. For them, Huck Finn's option—to light out for the territory and fulfill the American birthright of restoration in the West—is foreclosed. Aimless and unwelcomed, they wander around in the desert with no promised land in sight, a particularly anguishing turn of events for Californians who have nowhere to go but backward. The perambulations of the American journey in the 1930s, no longer in a straight line east to west, but up, down, around, and over, is rendered on screen in a flurry of illustrations with lines backtracking and wiggling over maps of the United States.

Jumping onto a boxcar, the boys encounter another young hobo who turns out to be a girl, Sally (Dorothy Coonan, soon to be Mrs. William Wellman). As the road trip proceeds, ragged tribes of boys, hundreds of them, riding the rails and converging in juvenile Hoovervilles, show the scale of the social wreckage: America can no longer feed and shelter its own children. Outside Chicago, a stern official lines up the wild boys like refugee supplicants at Ellis Island. He consigns them to juvenile detention or allows them into the city if they have a letter from a relative. Sally holds an invitation from her aunt, so the trio makes the cut.

Against expectations, Sally's aunt is vivacious and friendly. As a prostitute, this is her job. She welcomes the young drifters into her apartment, but no sooner are they sitting in her kitchen—she has a chocolate cake waiting—than the cops raid the joint. The kids bolt through the window and escape, but not before Eddie reaches back to grab a handful of cake and falls into it face first.

Back on the road again, rape and riot converge. Inside a boxcar, a lone girl removes her wet shirt and unwittingly stirs the lust of the train brakeman. Meanwhile, outside along the tracks, the wild boys earn their name. Rising up against a squad of railroad dicks, they boot them off the train and pelt them with foodstuff. Eggs, potatoes, and fruit splatter down from on high. Two black kids atop a rail car toss a watermelon down upon a white man and score a direct hit. "A gift from Dixie!" they scream giddily. The exhilaration is short-lived, however, for the bruised rape victim sobs out her story. Spotting the perpetrator, the juvenile mob chases him down and pushes him off the train to his death. The boys pay no penalty for the act of vigilante justice.

As the train pulls into the next bone-dry railroad yard, Tommy falls on the tracks and a train runs over his leg. A kindly doctor does what he can, but the leg must be amputated. The three kids now form a nuclear family. Dependent, crippled Tommy is the child; plucky, good-natured Sally is the mom; and dominant, harried Eddie is the father, the natural leader of the wild boys, burdened with his role as decision-maker, a premature patriarch.

Another town, another hobo encampment. Eddie spies a shop for prosthetic devices and breaks in to steal an artificial leg for Tommy. The device doesn't fit. Frightened by the burglary, the city fathers order the police to

Juvenile hoboes: Frankie Darro, Edwin Phillips, and Dorothy Coonan in William Wellman's *Wild Boys of the Road* (1933). (Courtesy of the Museum of Modern Art)

clear out the camp. "If you ask me, this is a pretty low trick," says one of the cops as he attaches a fire hose. "How do you think I feel? I've got a kid at home," his companion retorts. Their exchange flips the hierarchy of official culpability under the Code after 1934: the men on the line are regular guys but the authorities higher up are brutes. After the rout of the wild boys by firehoses, Wellman's camera lingers on the aftermath of the chaos, a shot of the artificial leg in the dirt, an awful white against the mud.

In New York, Eddie has a chance at a job if he can purchase the required uniform, so the trio goes into the city to panhandle. Two con artists promise Eddie five dollars if he will simply hand a letter to the teller at a motion picture box office. It is, of course, a robbery demand. The teller screams and Eddie flees into the theater. Onscreen a James Cagney movie is playing and its soundtrack overlaps with the soundtrack of *Wild Boys of the Road*. Unlike the diegetic audience, harkening to a Hollywood fantasy, no escape from the Great Depression beckons for Eddie.

Hauled before a judge, the fourth representative of callous state authority encountered so far, the kids expect nothing but cruelty. A self-righteous lecture from the bench meets expectations. "You're an enemy to society," the judge tells Eddie, "and I've got to keep you off the streets." In an extended monologue that builds in passionate intensity, Eddie wails out a defiant speech for the young and the dispossessed:

> I knew all that stuff about you helping us was baloney. I'll tell you why we can't go home—because our folks are poor. They can't get jobs and there isn't enough to eat. What good will it do you to send us home to starve? You say you've got to send us to jail to keep us off the streets. Well, that's a lie! You're sending us to jail because you don't want to see us. You want to forget us. But you can't do it because I'm not the only one. There's thousands just like me—and there's more hitting the road every day.

Tommy chimes in:

> You read in the papers about giving people help. The banks get it. The soldiers get it. The breweries get it. And they're always yelling about giving it to the farmers. What about us? We're *kids*!

Voice cracking, Eddie breaks down sobbing: "Go ahead! Put me in a cell! Lock me up! I'm sick of being hungry and cold. Sick of freight trains. Jail can't be any worse than the street. So give it to me!"

But this judge is different. The stern close-up on him, from the low-angle subservience of Eddie's point of view, pulls back to reveal behind him . . . the Blue Eagle, symbol of the New Deal, and the slogan "WE DO OUR PART." Federal authority, once the cold enemy, looks down sympathetically. "Things are going to be better now, not only here in New York, but all over the country," the suddenly avuncular magistrate assures Eddie. "I know your father will return to work shortly."

Outside the courthouse, the trio is joyous. The agile acrobat Frankie Darro performs a series of backflips and spins on his head, cheerfully hot-dogging for his pals. Not so fast, though. Watching the exuberant gymnastics of his friend, a close-up of the crippled Tommy exposes his thoughts: that for him there will be no backflips. Even if the New Deal makes you jump for joy, not everybody, quite yet, will land on his feet.

THE MAD DOG OF EUROPE

As FDR was consolidating his newsreel presidency and acting as a benevolent deus ex machina in the end reels of preachment yarns, the presence of another forceful political leader shadowed Hollywood's screens. In 1932 Adolf Hitler made his first noteworthy appearances in the newsreels and, after January 30, 1933, the Nazi leader and his uniformed masses appeared regularly in spectacles staged especially for the motion picture medium. Delivered ready-made by the Reichsfilmkammer, the motion picture branch of Joseph Goebbels' Ministry for Propaganda and Popular Enlightenment, the clips proved irresistible to American newsreel editors who needed to cover a newsmaking regime that insisted on creative control of its screen image. Only rarely, as when the newsreels were invited to cover the Berlin book burnings on May 10, 1933, did they obtain independent footage of events in Nazi Germany. From the Reichsfilmkammer, via the newsreels, Americans in 1932–33 first beheld the cinematic magnetism of Nazism, the "fascinating fascism" that seems likely to endure for the life of the motion picture medium.

Hollywood tracked the Nazi regime for reasons cultural and economic: cultural, because Jewish Americans in Hollywood were naturally alert to the persecution of their coreligionists in Germany; economic, because the takeover of the German film industry by the Nazis brought about two direct consequences. By purging Jews from German film production, the Nazis crippled Hollywood's only real competition in the European market (good). By purging "Jewish elements" from imported American films, they banned a goodly percentage of Hollywood product from German theaters (bad).

Shortly after Adolf Hitler consolidated power, the Reichsfilmkammer initiated strict censorship of imported American films. More ominous news circulated, although just how ominous no one could yet know: the "forced severance" of theatrical impresario Max Reinhardt from the Deutsches Theater in Berlin, the murder of musical comedy producer Alfred Rotter by Nazi thugs, and the elimination of Jewish and part-Jewish artists from stage and screen—an attention to genealogical detail so meticulous that German actress Kathe deNagy was dismissed from Ufa, Germany's premier film studio, because her grandmother was "non-Aryan." On June 19, 1934, *Variety* reporter Wolf Kaufman tallied up the final results of the purge in a front-page article with a German dateline and a blunt lead sentence, "The last German Jew is out of the film business in Berlin."

A year earlier in April 1933, the Nazi ban on Jews in the German motion picture industry had been extended to non-German employees from Hollywood when the Reichsfilmkammer demanded the removal of "every Jewish film man employed in all of the American film offices and branches." With Jews accounting for over 50 percent of Hollywood's representatives (Paramount's Gus Schaeffer being the only non-Jew heading an American film office in Germany), the Nazi edict meant reshuffling Hollywood's entire European workforce. A gentile on the studio payroll in Madrid might find himself transferred to Berlin while Jews in Berlin were sent anywhere German was not spoken. "American attitude on the matter is that American companies cannot afford to lose the German market no matter what the inconvenience of personnel shifts," shrugged *Variety*. Until the eve of World War II, the overseas distribution branches of the studios soldiered on in Germany with non-Jewish Americans or German representatives, a Faustian bargain justified as an "economic necessity."

Like the ethnicity of Hollywood personnel, the Nazis regulated the purity of Hollywood product. Of course, Jewishness in content or person qualified as prima facie justification for condemnation. *The Prizefighter and the Lady* (1933) was banned as a provocation to "national socialist feeling" because "a Jewish negroid type like [boxer Max] Baer is glorified as a Sports Hero" and "this Jew has love affairs with Aryan women, thereby endangering the continuity of a clean race." (As a contender for the heavyweight championship, Baer had also endangered racial continuity by defeating the German champion Max Schmelling.) *Grand Hotel* (1932) was pulled from circulation in Berlin because source novelist Vicki Baum was a "Jewess." The name above the title of a well-known Jewish American director was also sufficient reason to ban a film. Content notwithstanding, the Reichsfilmkammer deemed Ernst Lubitsch's *Trouble in Paradise* (1932) and Rouben Mamoulian's *Dr. Jekyll and Mr. Hyde* (1932) unfit for exhibition. Even the harmless Fox short subject *Hansel and Gretel* (1933) was banned for "contemptuousness of German folk songs and fairy tales."

Slowly, tentatively, opposition to the new Germany stirred in select provinces of America. By spring of 1933, antipathy to Hitler's regime, at least in metropolitan areas with sizable Jewish populations and among Jews in Hollywood, was already severe enough to scare producers away from German-themed material and to discourage distributors from importing German product. Boycotts and protests erupted against German films, even those produced before Hitler's ascension to power and opposed to the Nazi ethos. Tarred by their national origin, both Fritz Lang's *M* (1930, released in America in 1933) and *Maedchen in Uniform* (1931, released in America in 1932) were

Nazified Ufa product: Storm trooper Fritz Brand (Heinz Klingemberg) reassures the older generation in the German import *S.A.-Mann Brand* (1933). (Courtesy of the British Film Institute)

picketed and boycotted. With an estimated 70 percent of the patronage of German theaters being comprised of American Jews, and with sympathetic German Americans joining in, the boycotts killed a once-thriving domestic market. In 1932 one hundred theaters in America regularly played German language films. In 1933 the number had dropped to six "because of the situation in Hitlerland."

The deterioration of German cinema under the Nazis was so visible no political filter was needed to detect the aesthetic blight. So awful were the Nazi entertainment films that an embarrassed Goebbels assailed them as "thin and tasteless" and forbade their release abroad. After suffering through *Horst Wessel* (1933), a biopic extolling the young storm trooper and martyr to the Nazi cause, Goebbels personally banned it for "artistic inadequacy" and for imperiling the "vital interests of the State and the German international reputation."

A corrosive example of the Nazified Ufa product was the militarist melodrama *S.A.-Mann Brand* (1933). (*Variety* helpfully explained that the "S.A." in the title stood for "Sturm Abteilung" [storm trooper] not "Sex Appeal.") Released, though not widely circulated in the American marketplace in 1934, "the first 100% Nazi propaganda film to get a public showing in the United States" obtained a few playdates in select German enclaves, notably at the Yorkville Theater in New York City. The film chronicles the selfless efforts of SA trooper Fritz Brand to revive Germany despite the vile machinations of communist agitators who attack the amiable Nazis and conspire to subvert the Fatherland for Moscow. Brushing aside the misgivings of his old-fashioned parents, steadfastly opposing Soviet efforts to corrupt Germany, Fritz Brand is a tireless trooper and pure exemplar of the complete Aryan, the *Übermensch* as Everyman. Played by Heinz Klingemberg, whose very bone structure evokes Hitler, Fritz marches through the forests of the Fatherland at the head of a Hitler youth group and instills in the boys the tenets of the new faith. Next door to Fritz lives a Great War widow and her precocious teenage son, Eric, a budding Nazi whom Fritz takes under his wing. Eric is delighted by his birthday gifts: a brand new Hitler Youth uniform from mother and a framed picture of Hitler from Fritz.

Despite the fierce oppression of the Weimar regime (which outlaws the public wearing of the Nazi uniform) and the devious tactics of the communists (who incite street violence against the peaceful Nazis), Fritz remains stalwart in his commitment to the Nazi cause. When Hitler wins the election to the chancellorship, the nation is saved from the threat of Weimar degeneracy and Soviet infiltration. A huge torchlit parade celebrates the victory. Everybody sings.

Gauging the box office appeal of *S.A.-Mann Brand*, a British exhibitor expressed a widespread Anglo-American attitude, "I believe there is money [to be made on it] since people who would wish to hiss it would have to purchase tickets and come in to the theater to do so." Perhaps hoping to secure a beachhead in an antagonistic market, the Nazis tactfully reedited the American release print of *S.A.-Mann Brand* to purge the overt antisemitism in the German version. Similarly, when another Nazi propaganda film, *Hitlerjunge Quex* (1934), slightly penetrated the American market a few months later, distributors removed der Führer from the marquee and changed the title to *Our Flags Lead Us Forward*.

Other Nazi propaganda directed stateside did not lack the courage of its convictions. Much of the antisemitic venom was aimed squarely at the "nest of Jewry" that was Hollywood. In smuggled pamphlets and newspapers that began circulating stateside in 1933, motion pictures were branded as "fully Jewified," a force that "year in and year out consciously makes an attractive cult of crime and creates a load of Jew stars to sink and ruin the German cinematographic art."

Charles Chaplin was the favorite moving image target for Nazi vilification. The resemblance between the world's greatest comedian and the world's most notorious dictator was a doppelganger coincidence that made both men cringe. To the Nazis, Chaplin was "a repellent little yapping Jew." (In fact, Chaplin was not Jewish but almost alone among gentiles in the 1930s he relished the idea of being thought so. The persistent rumor of Chaplin's Jewish origins was first widely circulated in a column by Walter Winchell. A publicity agent hurriedly denied the report, but Chaplin rushed to deny the denial.) In 1933 the comedian announced that henceforth he would appear without his trademark moustache "for fear he might be mistaken for Hitler." Unamused, *Film Kurier*, the official organ of Reichsfilmkammer criticism, responded that "the creator and leader of new Germany, the war veteran and staunch friend of the new German film, stands much too high to even hear the barking dog from London's ghetto." (During World War II, the dog got his day with the anti-Nazi satire *The Great Dictator* [1940], in which Chaplin plays der Führer as the megalomaniacal buffoon "Adenoid Hynkel" and the Tramp as a persecuted Jewish barber.)

Hollywood's official response to the obstruction overseas and the slander at home was silence. Soon after the promulgation of Hitler's first antisemitic decrees in March 1933, anti-Nazi plays such as Leslie Reade's *The Shattered Lamp* and Harry Keller's *Madman* reached the stage, acts of protest as much as theater. None, however, reached the motion picture screen. The MPPDA discouraged even the mildest criticism of an overseas market for American cinema, no matter how unsavory the regime. An added disincentive was that the anti-Nazi plays flopped at the box office, even Yiddish-language productions such as playwright Ossip Dymov's *Germany in Flames* folding in a matter of days. Why venture into a white-hot controversy if there was no percentage in it?

So fearful were the studios of jeopardizing the export market to Germany that Nazi Germany came to exert a long-distance but real censorship power over American cinema. The Reichsfilmkammer held that any part of any Hollywood film deemed "repugnant from the German censor's standpoint, even if deleted for German consumption," tainted the whole motion picture. Unlike American censors, who could be placated with reediting and deletions, the Nazis banned a film forever on the basis of a single misstep. Given the predictability about what the Nazis found repugnant, the safest policy was to avoid anything to do with Jews or German culture. As a result, up until the outbreak of war in Europe, neither Jews nor Germans have much of a screen presence in Hollywood cinema.

Beneath the commercial considerations lurked a darker cultural worry. After all, antisemitism was a sentiment not exclusive to Nazi Germany. Fortified by a timely new slur, American bigots had long equated Hollywood's alleged penchant for salaciousness and sedition with the Jewish heritage of its producers. In 1930, when the notorious red-baiter Maj. Frank Pease spearheaded a noisy campaign to railroad the Soviet director Sergei Eisenstein out of Hollywood, the texture of his nativist bile vacillated between anticommunism and antisemitism. "If your Jewish clergy and scholars haven't enough courage to tell you, and you yourself haven't enough brains to know better or enough loyalty toward this land, which has given you more than you ever had in history, to prevent your importing a cutthroat red dog like Eisenstein, then let me inform you that we are behind every effort to have him deported," Pease telegrammed Paramount chief Jesse Lasky. He closed his jeremiad with two Old Testament references he thought appropriate for a man of Lasky's ethnic background: "It won't take any Samson to pull down the bolshevik temple you are starting and at this rate it won't be long now. *Mene tekel upharsin.*" The closing line invoked a divine threat from the Book of Daniel, the writing on the wall of Belshazzar's banquet hall: Thou art weighed in the balances, and art found wanting."

Focusing more on the threat from immorality than insurrection, another of Hollywood's fiercest critics employed like-minded rhetoric—though of necessity under his breath, not at the top of his lungs. In private correspondence to Catholic clergymen, Joseph Breen vented sentiments that might have been published unedited in the pages of *Der Stürmer.* "These Jews seem to think of nothing but money making and sexual indulgence," he stormed in a letter to a Jesuit friend. "The vilest kind of sin is a common indulgence hereabouts and the men and women who engage in this sort of business are the men and women who decide what the film fare of the nation is to be. . . . They are, probably, the scum of the earth." As film historian Gregory Black noted, the cardinals, bishops, and priests who received Breen's letters "made no effort to protest his anti-Semitic outbursts. They may not have shared his exact views, but all apparently saw some merit in placing a man with such views in Hollywood."

Notwithstanding the best efforts of the MPPDA and the worst insinuations of the antisemites, two anti-Nazi feature films reached the American screen in the pre-Code era. Significantly, both originated from independent outfits: one was a thinly veiled allegory, the other an unapologetic broadside.

Directed by Edwin Carewe and produced by Raspin Productions, *Are We Civilized?* (1934) was a low-budget exploitation film tied to the timely topic the major studios pretended did not exist. Although nowhere mentioned by name, the nation in question is never a question. *Are We Civilized?* is an accusation directed straight at Nazi Germany.

Returning to his native land after making a fortune in America, warm and tolerant newspaper publisher Paul Franklin (William Farnum) finds that the once civilized land of his birth has embraced totalitarian oppression. When government thugs break into his library and confiscate volumes by Freud and Darwin, Franklin finds his own freedoms threatened. Unbowed, Franklin condemns the "inhuman censorship bureau" which is even now "inciting racial hatred, bringing about religious intolerance, and ruthlessly destroying the liberty of the people."

To dissuade the brownshirts, Franklin delivers a long lecture about the evolutionary progress of man, from neanderthal savagery to upright enlightenment. The lesson in Western Civilization includes highlights from the past (Moses and the Ten Commandments, the crucifixion of Christ, and Columbus in the New World) depicted with footage lifted from silent-era spectacles. But the forward march of history backtracks with the stock market crash and the torments of the Great Depression. "Today the peoples of many nations are trembling on the brink of another Great War—a war more terrible, more horrible, more devastating than the last conflict."

As the pageant passes in review, outside the newspaper office, windows are broken and books are burned in a huge bonfire. The book-burning and the crowds encircling the bonfire evoke the already iconic newsreel footage of the Berlin book-burning of May 10, 1933. Speaking out to the mob, silhouetted against the flames fed by the records of humanity's struggle through the ages, the good publisher is beaned by a book and dies from the symbolic wound.

Eschewing the allegorical pretense of *Are We Civilized?*, *Hitler's Reign of Terror* (1934) put the dictator's name and the filmmakers' sentiment up on the marquee. Directed by Michael Mindlin, narrated by Edwin C. Hill, and photographed in Germany and Austria by Cornelius Vanderbilt, Jr., the film was part archival documentary, part dramatic reenactment. In addition to being the wealthy nephew of the nineteenth-century plutocrat, Vanderbilt Jr. was a sometime journalist who, during a 1932 tour of Europe, traded on his name to interview Hitler and the Kaiser. The home movies he took of his travels became the raw material for *Hitler's Reign of Terror*. Vanderbilt, screamed taglines, "brought to the screen authentic pictures smuggled out of Germany at the risk of his life!"

Hitler's Reign of Terror opens with condemnations of Nazism by historian Samuel Seabury, Rabbi Stephen S. Wise, and novelist Fannie Hurst. It then reviews the past with such newsreel footage of Nazi Germany as was available. Vanderbilt's interviews with the former Kaiser in Doron, Holland, and with Hitler himself are reenacted, with the parts of the Kaiser and Hitler played by actors who recite the lines of the originals (in English). "And what about the Jews, your excellency?" inquires Vanderbilt of the Hitler imposter in a reenacted moment of ambush journalism. Clearly identifying the special targets of Hitler's terror, newsreel footage unspools signs urging Germans to boycott Jewish stores ("Deutsche! Kauft nicht bein Juden") and flashes a ghastly image that soon became infamous: a primitively drawn death's head with the scrawled warning "Actung Juden!"

In New York, *Hitler's Reign of Terror* drew capacity crowds for two weeks, despite the fact that the state censor board refused the film a license. Mayor Fiorello LaGuardia ignored an appeal from the Steuben Society of America to ban the film on the grounds it stirred up racial hatred—against the Germans. In Chicago the film was initially banned in compliance with the wishes of the German counsel, but it was permitted to reopen after the title was truncated to the nonjudgmental *Hitler's Reign*. The publicity campaign for the film capitalized on the efforts to suppress it. "In spite of extraordinary caution to prevent these terrifying conditions to be shown to the outside world," *Hitler's Reign of Terror* exposes "the horrible Nazi truth." "See Hitler's brutalities with your own eyes! Atrocities that have been suppressed until now! Ripping aside the curtain on history's most shocking episode and exposing the Nazi menace in America!"

Critics were unimpressed and audience reaction outside of New York tepid. "Significant only in the sense that it is given over almost entirely to denunciation of Hitler and his works, this picture adds nothing to the knowledge of Nazism that is not already known," the *Film Daily* observed dryly about the most prescient American film of 1934. "It argues that Hitlerism is directed not only against the Jews, but against the Protestants and Catholics and that it menaces world peace."

The fate of an anti-Nazi project that never reached the screen offers the best case study of the anti-anti-Nazi forces at work in Hollywood during the early days of the Third Reich in Germany. In 1933 Herman J. Mankiewicz, one of Hollywood's most prolific screenwriters, quotable wits, and notorious boozers, and Sam Jaffe, an associate producer at RKO, worked on a project entitled *The Mad Dog of Europe*. It bid to be, but failed to become, the first motion picture assault on Nazism from Hollywood.

Jaffe took out full-page ads in the trade press announcing that he had resigned from his position at RKO to devote his entire attention to the project and to ask his competitors to respect his "priority rights" because he sincerely believed *The Mad Dog of Europe* was "the most valuable motion picture property I have ever possessed and because I wish to take sufficient time to prepare and film with the infinite care the subject merits." He described the project as "an anti-Hitler motion picture depicting the sacrifices of the Jews and Catholics in a Central Europe Nation and the indignities to which they are being subjected."

On July 17, 1933, Will Hays called Jaffe and Mankiewicz into his office and told them to cease and desist. Hays accused the pair of trying to make a quick profit on a "scarehead situation" and thereby create problems for the motion picture industry in Germany. Mankiewicz, a man who could never resist a defiant wisecrack in the presence of authority, replied that he always kept uppermost in mind the refined taste of the American public and had written *The Mad Dog of Europe* for the same noble motives Hollywood had produced *Baby Face*, *Melody Cruise*, and *So This Is Africa*.

Though Mankiewicz and Jaffe initially seemed willing to defy the MPPDA chief, the project never came to fruition. Jaffe was later "talked out of" producing the film by the Hays Office and sold the story rights to Al Rosen, a popular Hollywood agent. Rosen acquired several thousand feet of newsreel footage ("atrocity stuff") and at one point was scheduled to begin shooting the project with director Lowell Sherman. Hays later dispatched a representative to lean on Rosen and *The Mad Dog of Europe* was suppressed again.

Nonetheless, Rosen spent most of the 1930s trying to bring the anti-Nazi scenario to the screen, badgering everyone from Jewish philanthropists to the State Department for funding and cooperation, always tenacious, never successful. In 1936, responding to the latest flurry of activity by Rosen, Joseph Breen outlined the official MPPDA attitude toward *The Mad Dog of Europe* and anti-Nazi projects generally. Back in 1933, he recalled, "it was the consensus that such a picture ought *not* to be made," a judgment time had done nothing to change. "No official action has ever been taken on the proposal, but the *un*official judgment seems to be that such a picture should not be produced." In measured tones, Breen explained the cultural downside of anti-Nazi preachment yarns:

It is to be remembered that there is strong pro-German and anti-Semitic feeling in this country, and, while those who are likely to approve of an anti-Hitler picture may think well of such an enterprise, they should keep in mind that millions of Americans might think otherwise.

Choosing his words carefully, Breen hit a sensitive nerve:

Because of the large number of Jews active in the motion picture industry in this country, the charge is certain to be made that the Jews, as a class, are behind an anti-Hitler picture and using the entertainment screen for their own personal propaganda purposes. The entire industry, because of this, is likely to be indicted for a mere handful. It is certain to be inflammatory and might result in a boomerang.

Breen concluded his brief against *The Mad Dog of Europe* with the Haysian bromide that justified Hollywood's willful blindness to Nazism. "The purpose of the screen, primarily, *is to entertain* and *not to propagandize*." Not until World War II would Hollywood change the way it did business.

5

Vice Rewarded

The Wages of Cinematic Sin

Laughing Sinners, The Road to Ruin, Free Love, Merrily We Go to Hell, Laughter in Hell, Safe in Hell, The Devil Is Driving—the titles court not just disgrace but damnation, portending a realm of moral anarchy where reprobates run head-long into perdition, their reckless abandon leading inexorably, though gaily, to ruin. If paid out in the final reel, the wages of sin are less a warning about the costs of the unregenerate life than an advertisement for its compensations.

The censors called them "sex films," but the promiscuous embrace of sex was only the most commercial and carnal element of a broader assault on traditional values. The complete spectrum of vice, not sex alone, infest-ed the films in question, an epicurean spirit of enthusiastic indulgence in activities illegal, forbidden, and stimulating. Antiauthoritarian, adultery-driven, and pleasure-seeking, the vice films surrendered willingly to one or more of the seven deadly sins and discovered that succumbing wasn't nec-essarily fatal.

Both a cross-generic ingredient and a genre unto itself, vice energized compliant formats (notably gangster films and the backstage musicals) even as it fueled the whole body of the main attraction in "fallen women" and "bad girl" films. In 1932 Warner Brothers made both strategies official studio policy, ordering screenwriters to cultivate the vice film and to spice up the rest of the product line with vice additives on the theory "that an average of two out of five stories should be 'hot' " and that most other films could well be "pepped up a little by adding on something having to do with ginger." *Variety* estimated that during 1932–33 no fewer than 352 of 440 pictures possessed "some sex slant," with 145 having "questionable sequences" and 44 being "critically sexual" at feature length. "In other words," lectured the trade paper, "over 80% of the world's chief picture output was partly, partially, or completely flavored with the bedroom essence. And that flavoring, it is also admitted, has strongly favored the theme of perversion." By way of illustration, consider the immoral tonalities of three ripe and resonantly titled exemplars of vice on the pre-Code screen: *Call Her Savage* (1932), *Love Is a Racket* (1932), and *Unashamed* (1932).

Call Her Savage was conceived by Fox as a comeback vehicle for Clara Bow, lately dismissed by Paramount in the wake of nearly two years of sordid scandal and career mishaps. In 1930 Bow's private secretary Daisy De-Voe had sold the names and tallied up the numbers of Bow's myriad lovers to the New York tabloid *GraphiC*. Though Bow won a civil suit against De-Voe, the torrent of bad publicity led to her nervous breakdown and, worse, box office slowdown. Making the best of the tabloid headlines, *Call Her Savage* invited audiences to link the affairs of the actress with the antics of the lusty hellion she played on screen. As extravagantly profligate as Bow's private life, the film checked off a litany of Code violations: marital infidelity, interracial marital infidelity, sadomasochistic whipping, erotic frolicking with a Great Dane, prurient exposure of female flesh, kept women, femme-on-femme catfights, a demented husband who tries to rape his wife, prostitution, gigolos, and a pair of mincing homosexual waiters.

Yet beyond any single lapse into sin, the vice film projected an off-center world where the moral scaffolding was all out of joint. In *Love Is a Racket*, the ambitious aunt of a callow gold digger murders the gangster who threatens her niece's marriage to a wealthy suitor. A newspaperman in love with the gold digger covers up the crime and his best friend in turn covers up the first cover-up. In the end, the aunt gets away with the killing, the gold digger marries her meal ticket, and the two accessories to murder chuckle about the brush with homicide, wiser to the ways of women and the world.

Unashamed occupies the same moral dimension. Headstrong society girl Joan Ogden (Helen Twelvetrees) falls in love with a moneygrubbing louse named Harry Swift (Monroe Owsley). "Three million dollars and she's not bad looking," snorts the faithless Harry. After Harry seduces Joan, he is surprised to discover that both Joan's doting father and her very doting brother Dick (Robert Young) prefer Joan with a sullied reputation to him as a member of the family. When Harry threatens scandal, brother Dick's repressed incestuous desire for Joan boils over. He pulls out a pistol and shoots Harry dead.

Unashamed settles into an extended courtroom sequence, with a cynical defense attorney calculating that his guilty-as-sin client will be saved from the electric chair by the "unwritten law" that permits a man to kill when he defends a woman's honor. Despite the fact that the family maid and the defendant perjure themselves on the witness stand, things look bleak for young Dick until Joan decides to sacrifice her reputation. On the witness stand, she acts the part of a shameless hussy, unworthy of the chivalrous act of her stalwart brother. The jury's outrage at the tramp of a sister transfers as sympathy for her noble sibling and results in a verdict of not guilty. After murdering a middle-class social climber and lying under oath, the plutocrats with the slick lawyer get away with murder. "Hallelujah!" squeals the maid for the exit line.

Predictably, that exhilaration was not shared by state censor boards, women's groups, and editorialists. To the moral guardians, the vice films were a personal affront and cultural peril. If the lurid advertising oversold the vice-to-virtue ratio, enough of the film content lived up to the titles and taglines to confirm the impression that an unending stream of decadence flowed from Hollywood.

That the wards of the guardians seemed to prefer low entertainments to high-minded uplift only confirmed the infinite corruptibility of mankind. From the vantage of religious leaders and social reformers, the perverse output was a sorry legacy of the wanton excesses of the 1920s, the corrupt past lingering into the devastated present and preventing spiritual renewal. Not yet awakened to the shift to sterner times, Hollywood seduced the vulnerable with the behaviors and values of a discredited epoch.

Rallying to its own defense, Hollywood posed as a mere service industry willing to purvey whatever genre the public paid good money to see.

"Why should some studios follow out [the Code's] dictates and find themselves with a lot of sweet pictures that will not draw flies at any box office, while others, disregarding the Code, cash in on box office smashes?" asked the *Hollywood Reporter*, whose three-word headline summed up a review of *The Man Who Played God* (1932): "Clean, Wholesome, and Dull." Vice-drenched films might put the bluenoses out of joint, but moviegoers, often young couples, welcomed them with open arms. "As figures at the box office dwindled the boys underline the sex angle the more," *Variety* conceded in 1931. "And who's to blame them?" Not the producers, who considered the censors out of touch with moviegoers who flocked to the very films the censors condemned.

Fortunately for the souls of the majority, a discerning minority stood ready to make the right choices for them. In 1933 Mrs. Thomas G. Winters, a former national president of the General Federation of Women's Clubs and present associate director of public relations for the MPPDA, attempted to explain the virtue gap. "There are more oversexed pictures and more objectionable scenes in otherwise good pictures than the lovers of drama could wish, but the popular taste needs a good deal of education to register its dislike," declared Mrs. Winters. "The many-millioned audience is, after all, largely decent—more decent than the so-called intelligentsia." Mrs. Mildred Lewis Russell, chairwoman of the Better Films Committee of the Daughters of the American Revolution, agreed. "The more thoughtful among us must try to control with intelligence—to impress upon others the importance of selecting our entertainment. We can make unwholesome films so unpopular, so unremunerative, that a greater number of good films will be made." Taking extreme umbrage at what the DAR called the "going-to-have-a-baby cycle," Mrs. Russell abided "no excuse for such films as *Eight Girls in a Boat* [1934] and *Lessons in Making Love* [?]" and charged "such filth is suited for low dives and the people who frequent them." The same admixture of condemnation and self-justification animated the pronouncements from the Chicago Board of Censors. "Illicit relations between the sexes, illegitimacy, disrespect for or ridicule of the marriage state, and other forms of sex immorality" were bad enough, bewailed the Chicao censors in 1931, but more sinister still was the " 'modern' attitude with its elusive standards" that made it "impossible for the large majority of picture audiences to make any distinction between the rightness and the fallacy of that attitude."

As ever for the cultural elites, the common rung of mankind was all too susceptible to the lure of the unregenerate life. If, when tempted, weak-willed moviegoers lapsed into vice, then more was the responsibility of Hollywood to uplift and ennoble and more the duty of the moral guardian to be vigilant and ensure that Hollywood did what was right.

PACKAGING VICE

Pre-Code vice came in two packages—or rather, a wrapper and a package. Hollywood dangled the promise of salacious material with lurid advertising and then dodged around, and sometimes delivered on, the enticements of the marketing wraparound. The interplay between the advertising campaign and the motion picture was determined less by the content of the film than the wild imaginations of studio ballyhoo boys. The colorful ribbons and bows festooned about the project on the outside often made the dull prize on the inside a letdown.

Nominally, the major studios were signatories to the Advertising Code, an addendum to the Production Code that mandated decent copy and demure illustrations. "Every person of any competency in the advertising profession knows that the immorally suggestive twist in advertising copy leads to no good result," blustered Martin Quigley of *Motion Picture Herald*. "It is simply a confession of the writer's inability to prepare copy with attention-wrestling value without leaping over the borderline of good taste and common decency." Long experience had taught studio publicity flacks just the opposite: that the "immorally suggestive twist" led audiences in a straight line to the box office. As with the Production Code, then, the Advertising Code was stretched, sidestepped, and violated. Titles, taglines, poster art, and publicity photographs titillated with indiscretion and misdirection.

As the biggest words on the theater marquee, titles were the first and best advertising hook for the vice film. Studios regularly held in-house contests for employees to come up with the best title for a screenplay and orchestrated nationwide competitions for moviegoers to do the same. The practice is satirized in *Footlight Parade* (1933) when a fey fussbudget tries to obtain a showbiz job as a "title thinker-upper." The competition for timely and magnetic catch phrases was fierce enough to inspire the MPPDA to establish a Title Registration Bureau to file claims by member producers on surefire titles. The moral tone of the suggestions was low enough to warrant a separate section in the Production Code: "Salacious, indecent, or obscene titles shall not be used."

Merrily We Go to Hell (1932) defied the rule, passing muster with the Hays Office but not the editors of respectable newspapers who refused to print so gleeful an outlook on so unholy a destination. Likewise, producer Howard Hughes was deaf to pleas to change the virile title of his airborne adventure *Cock of the Air* (1932). *The Half-Naked Truth* (1932), a story of an exotic dancer and carnival hokum, also slipped by, probably because the title was not even half accurate. "For every person who is brought in by a borderline title, there are probably a couple of more who are kept away," insisted Martin Quigley uncertainly. Yet so widespread were the borderline titles that by 1931 the Hays Office was giving special scrutiny to "lurid, ultra-sexy, and misleading titles" with words such as "Hell," "Devil," "Hades," and "Damn" deemed the most troublesome vulgarities. In consequence, some of the most arousing title pitches never saw the light of a marquee. Fox floated the title *Sandy Hooker* for Clara Bow's follow-up to *Call Her Savage*, but the prostitutional pun was forbidden. One producer spent years unsuccessfully suggesting the title *Pink Chemise*, another the fetishistic *Virgins in Cellophane*.

Exclamatory advertising copy stretched the naked truth by more than half, spouting breathless exclamations and posing interrogatives for overactive imaginations. "Who are they? What are they?" badgered the copy for *Leftover Ladies* (1931). "Why are they called leftover ladies? A pulsating story of modern women's ruthless sacrifice for freedom—and what *is* this new freedom?" (*Answer:* divorced women who spurn alimony payments.) "Why do a million men leave home every year?" asked the copy for *Convention City* (1933), answering its own question. "Join in the daffy doings of one of those convulsing conventions where big business makes hey-hey—and farmer's daughters make hay! Make the rounds with the boys—make whoopie with those dazzling convention sweeties!" *What Men Want* (1930) clarified the declaration of the title with a tagline: "She gambled all—and lost all!"

An eyebrow-raising come-on might make even the blandest film fare sound tantalizing. "We could not have shown this picture ten years ago. We'd have been put in jail," claimed an ad for *Life in the Raw* (1933), not a nudie film but a fully clothed and very tame western. D. W. Griffith's reverent biopic *Abraham Lincoln* (1930) pledged a picture of Mary Todd unknown to history: "She taught Lincoln how to love—and to like it!"

Amazingly, a few taglines delivered on the promise. "If your Aunt Minnie from Duluth happens to be in town next week, don't invite her to *The Story of Temple Drake*," warned the ads for the most notorious vice film of 1933. "That is, if she happens to be an old-fashioned Aunt Minnie who shies from gin and sex." *Baby Face*, a close second to *The Story of Temple Drake* in

Violating the Advertising Code: a publicity still from *Tarzan and His Mate* (1934). (Courtesy of the Museum of Modern Art)

notoriety, traced its plot outline in first-person confessional prose: "I don't want to keep on living like a dumb animal! So I'm getting out. My father called me a tramp. And who is to blame? A swell start he gave me. Ever since I was 14 men have been trying to paw me!"

A vintage advertising ploy was a practice known in the trade as "pinking," that is, to advertise a film as "recommended for adults only!" or "no children under 16 admitted!" in order to send up a red flag about sexual content. *Baby Face* profited from the reverse psychology with "an ad campaign that's bringing in the kids by warning them to stay away; also the grown-ups in paying numbers," reported *Variety*. "It's the same old gag and it's working again." Besides luring in the prematurely mature, the "adults only" banner served as cover against charges of corrupting the young. "I played this to adults only and was glad I did on two counts," gloated an exhibitor done right by Mae West in *She Done Him Wrong* (1933). Ballyhoo boys for *Unguarded Girls* (1929) pulled another old gag, but along gender not generational lines, with "men only" and "women only" screenings.

If the images conjured by words left little to the imagination, pictures were a thousand times better. Lurid posters sketched orgiastic tableaux and degrees of décolletage exposed nowhere on screen. Pen-and-ink drawings filled in, or left out, material that no actual photograph could depict without being legally actionable. Throughout the 1930s and beyond, the non-photographic publicity picture remained popular in one-sheets and ad mats because illustrations could undrape actresses and flaunt cheesecake more explicitly than photographs.

Of course risqué photographs, distributed to the racier fan magazines and to markets overseas, delivered a higher-definition form of titillation. Besides the high-tone gloss of studio portraiture that bathed the stars in shimmering lights and strategic shadows, revealing photographs of lesser known actresses, presumably in featured sequences but in actuality nowhere to be seen on screen, were distributed by press agents and publicity departments. Though in clear violation of the Advertising Code, the practice was widespread and subsidized by the publicity departments of the major studios. A case of "considerable gravity" concerned the publicity stills of a near-naked Doleres Muray circulated by RKO to advertise *The Common Law* (1931), a film in which the actress seems not to have appeared either dressed or undressed. Such "pornographic stills," lectured *Motion Picture Herald*, damaged the good repute of the industry and offered disturbing evidence that the studios were "continuing to go merrily thumbing their noses at both the Production Code and the Advertising Code."

Along with the avid moviegoers who were the prime targets of motion picture advertising, a less susceptible audience monitored the billboards and newspaper ads. For the moral guardian, vice-drenched exploitation was a doubly convenient target of opportunity, presenting irrefutable evidence of Hollywood decadence while allowing the pure of heart to gather it without being sullied by direct exposure to impure cinema. In 1932, during an address to the Women of the First Presbyterian Church of Lancaster, Pennsylvania, the Reverend Clifford Gray Twombly had only to scan the pages

Leg artistry: Barbara Stanwyck poses for a cheesecake photograph and Jean Harlow reveals herself in pen and ink.

of the local paper to cull examples of shameless advertising copy. "Alluring, pursued by many men! Experimenting with love, wild passions, gay parties!" the reverend intoned to the—shocked?—Presbyterian ladies. "It tells who really pays for those ladies known as expensive."

In December 1933, Hays tried to extinguish the flash point of lurid advertising. In an emphatic memorandum whose anatomical precision well describes the kind of material being routinely circulated, he issued a set of twelve commandments to rein in the libidinous flow of pictures and words. Adopting the tones of a biblical command come down from Mount Sinai, *Variety* published the bans. The first seven regulated still photography:

I. Thou shalt not take or cause to be taken any photography in which girls are shown posed in underwear, fancy lingerie, teddies, scanties or drawers.

II. Thou shalt not photograph girls in scenes in which the femmes pull up their skirts to show a lengthy display of legs and the unfastening of a garter.

III. Thou shalt not photograph girls in salacious or bending over postures which show the legs above the knee or displaying a section of the thighs, whether covered or not, at which other persons in the photograph are pointing or making fun of.

IV. Thou shalt not photograph the so-called fan dance type of photograph in which delicate parts of the anatomy are covered by fans, feathers, lace, or other types of scanty or peek-a-boo material.

V. Thou shalt not photograph groups of chorus girls in scenes in which legs, thighs, or outline of body is shown through the transparency of the outer garment.

VI. Thou shalt not photograph scenes of a bawdy nature, in which the only appeal is to the salacious minded.

VII. Thou shalt not photograph kissing, necking, or any type of lovemaking scenes in which the principals are in a horizonal position. In any kissing scene the pose must be standing, or sitting.

The last five regulated the prose of advertising copy:

VIII. Thou shalt not cause to be written, photographed, or sketched any advertising that is a misrepresentation of facts.

IX. Thou shalt not use the word "courtesan" or words meaning the same in any advertising copy used for the exploitation of pictures.

X. Thou shalt not reprint sections of dialogue from a picture that would convey a different meaning to the picture than is contained in it.

XI. Thou shalt not suggest to exhibitors the use of salacious copy or the misrepresentations of facts in order that he might appeal in his advertising copy to persons seeking the unclean in pictures.

XII. Thou shalt not use adjectives in advertising description that will lead a reader to believe that one playing a sympathetic part in a picture is base, dishonest, profane, unholy or otherwise an undesirable person.

As soon as Hays issued the strict guidelines on the "leg art" and cleavage in studio publicity stills, the ad-pub departments figured out how to sidestep the restrictions. They simply told magazine editors to send around their own photographers and "we'll supply the girls."

Ultimately, the come-hither copy and lurid images that baited moviegoers proved to be hooks that caught the studios on their own lines. Scanning newspapers, handbills, and billboards, moral guardians were alerted to the awful doings in films they would never have been aware of otherwise. In 1934 a racy billboard so infuriated Philadelphia's Cardinal Dougherty that he launched the motion picture boycott that helped bring about the Production Code Administration. Outside his residence, a provocatively painted and leeringly taglined billboard for a Warner Bros. melodrama daily affronted his eyes. Finally, his Christian forbearance spent, the cardinal went to the pulpit and announced his crusade. If Hollywood had kept quieter about the vice quotient, real and imagined, and depended more on word of mouth to pass along the details, it would not have drawn as much attention to its jaunty detours from the path of morality.

MODELS OF IMMORALITY

Having lured audiences with the tonic of sin, vice films diluted the damnation with a dose of redemption. An end-reel restoration of official morality or the climactic revelation that a sordid suspicion was all a terrible misunderstanding atoned for eighty minutes of wanton mischief. The taglines for *Young Sinners* (1931) neatly summarized the arc from turpitude to rectitude: "Hot youth at its wildest . . . loving madly, living freely . . . tamed by life's realities—and coming through gloriously!" After sowing wild oats, reformed sinners reap the rewards of respectability, wiser but not necessarily sadder.

Yet if what was promised seldom matched what was seen, pre-Code Hollywood presented visions and upheld values that violated the laws of God and man without contrition or consequence. The trade press summed up Hollywood's variations on vice as "the eternal triangle" and "fallen woman and straying girl themes." The division singles out the sites of opportunity and the gender of the perpetrators: the institution of marriage and the character of woman.

The most sacred bond torn asunder was holy matrimony. Marriage was a contract open to redefinition, amenable to renegotiation, and easily terminated by mutual consent. In *The Prodigal* (1930), an unloved wife considers forsaking her virtue by running off with a smarmy suitor. Saved from dishonor by her brother-in-law, she and he fall hopelessly in love, but "there are some things one must not do," says he chastely after kissing his brother's wife. When the husband rejects a divorce, the lovers accept their fate—until the mother of the men intervenes to save the young lovers, not the institution of marriage. She orders her bad son to get a divorce and tells her good son and good daughter-in-law (present and future) that, having found true love, they deserve to keep it. "This is the twentieth century," she declares. "Go out into the world and get what happiness you can."

Adultery can be a normal enough, even salutary passage in a marriage that stands the test of time. In Frank Borzage's *Secrets* (1933) gubernatorial candidate Leslie Howard betrays his devoted wife (Mary Pickford) with a raven-haired signorina and, he confesses, a few others. The other woman publicizes the affair to ruin both his marriage and political career. But Mary knows that her man has never really stopped loving her. She withstands the bad patch in the marriage with wifely forbearance and forgives her serial adulterer husband, as do the voters who elect him governor.

Cecil B. DeMille's *Madame Satan* (1930) not only tolerates adultery but prescribes it as shock therapy for a marriage in trouble. "Love can't be kept in cold storage," says philandering husband (Reginald Denny). "It's a battery that's got to be recharged every day." Learning that an energetic jazz baby named Trixie is the new power source in her husband's life, his "below zero" wife resolves to win him back by adopting a sizzling new persona, the sexy "Madame Satan." At a bizarre costume ball aboard a zeppelin floating over Manhattan, the identity confusion and spousal straying works out as marriage counseling.

Outside of marriage, throngs of female libertines flirted and coupled for fun and profit. For an in-depth reading of the sexual contours of the extramarital vice film, the best template is Paramount's *The Story of Temple Drake*, the screen version of William Faulkner's sensational novel *Sanctuary*. Originally titled *The Shame of Temple Drake* and taglined as "a love story understandable to every woman . . . pulsing with all the emotional power of *A Farewell to Arms*," the film depicted rape, prostitution, and perversity among the lowest orders of stunted hicks and seedy patricians. Despite the attempt to link Faulkner's lurid tale with Hemingway's more conventional romance, the odor of sleaze hung over the project from the start. "What is the function of the Hays Office if it doesn't keep projects like this off the screen?" demanded the *New York News*. That a major studio undertook so disreputable an enterprise is an index both of Paramount's financial straits and the lure of the vice film as a quick fix in the early 1930s. George Raft was under contract to play the lead in the film but refused, saying it would be "screen suicide." This from an actor who built his career impersonating gangsters.

As overture to Temple Drake's story, stormy music fills the soundtrack and flashes of lightning illuminate a dilapidated house in the back country, its shattered exterior and busted windows shimmering eerily. After the cast takes

a curtain bow, the scene shifts to the bright interiors of the Dixon County
Courthouse, presided over by crusty old Judge Drake (Sir Guy Standing). In
chambers, he talks with Stephen Benbow (William Gargan), the idealistic
young defense attorney whom he wants to marry his wild daughter, Temple.
"She's a good girl, Steve."

The first glimpse of Temple (Miriam Hopkins) belies the old man's faith
in Southern womanhood. From the interior of her father's mansion, the unseen Temple is heard flirting with a beau, who entreats her for more than a
kiss as she teases and pouts ("I said no!"). Rushing inside, leaving the beau
frustrated on the front porch, she smiles at her talent to spark and then
smother his ardor. "What hour of the night is this to come home?" scolds
Judge Drake. Temple slinks her way out of the reprimand. "Darling," she
coos, turning her back to him, "won't you unhook me?"

A montage of small town commentary gives the backstory on the flighty
Temple. "The girl made a sucker of me," grouses the crestfallen beau. "You're
not the only one," chimes in a companion, another victim of Temple's temptations. Downstairs in the Drake mansion, a black maid fingers Temple's torn
chemise and shakes her head over the judge's naive trust in his daughter. "If
he done the laundry, he'd know more about that child." Spinsters cluck about
Temple's wild streak and the genetic predisposition of the Drake family to
spawn sexual renegades.

Stephen will listen to none of the town gossip, but Temple's modus operandi is all too clear. She teases the polite young men of the town, works them
into a tumescent lather, and then leaves them hot and bothered. "It ain't fair,"
whines a victim. "Fire a man all up then—poof!—put him out." "Do I do
that—sho' nuff?" warbles Temple. Later, with loyal Stephen, she confesses,
"I'm no good," but shows no interest in not being bad. In the men's bathroom, Stephen angrily erases some poetic graffiti that has it about right:
"Temple Drake is just a fake / She wants to eat and have her cake."

Driving through dark and dangerous back roads with a drunken boyfriend, Temple and the sloshed driver careen off the road. Shaken but un-
harmed, they regain consciousness as a scary figure with a flashlight shines
the beam on Temple's shapely figure. The lecher is a well-dressed gangster
named Trigger (Jack LaRue) who, according to his feeble-minded hillbilly
companion, shoots dogs for target practice. Trigger and the hillbilly escort
the frightened couple through the stormy woods to the ramshackle house
of the title sequence. A trembling Temple wants to leave, but the wind and
the rain make escape impossible. She must go inside where the backcountry trash are liquoring themselves up on moonshine. The men leer at Tem-

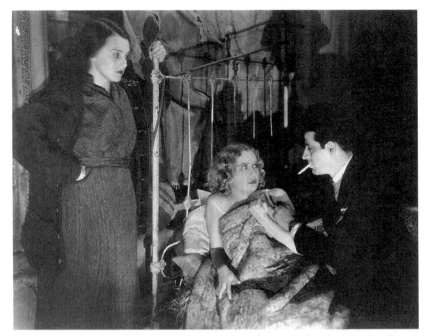

Just comeuppance: Ruby (Florence Eldridge) watches as Trigger (Jack LaRue) threatens Temple (Miriam Hopkins) in *The Story of Temple Drake* (1933). (Courtesy of the Museum of Modern Art)

ple and slur out suggestive remarks. "Sit here kid—right in my lap." The threat of sexual violation is thick in the air, from Trigger, from the drunken hicks, perhaps from them all.

Ruby Lemarr (Florence Eldridge), the lone woman in the shack, is initially gruff to Temple ("you pretty-faced little fool!"), but she offers comfort and protection from the crude males. "Take off those wet things," she orders, when the two are alone. Temple strips to her chemise and dons a man's overcoat, a layer of protection she must relinquish when the owner barges in and orders her to give him back his coat. Removing it, she cowers beneath a blanket. Ruby brings Temple to the safer regions of a barn to sleep, where the hillbilly boy pledges to guard her for the night.

At dawn Trigger creeps to the barn, the camera following his feet, implicating the spectator in the pursuit of the object of his desire. Looming over Temple from above, he spies her reclining figure crisscrossed with beams of light shining in from between the planks of the barn wall. Trigger shoots her hillbilly protector and inches forward, ablaze with lust, looming into the camera for a tight close-up. Temple screams.

In the next scene, Trigger is driving down a road with the traumatized Temple in the front seat of his convertible. "Fix yourself," he orders, and takes her to a brothel. "I spotted you the minute I seen you," Trigger sneers, moving in for another monstrous close-up. "You holler and you faint—[unspoken: but really you like what I do to you]."

While investigating the murder of the hillbilly boy, Stephen comes upon Temple in the brothel, apparently Trigger's prostitute. "Are you—[unspoken: working here]?" he sputters. "Did you—[unspoken: sleep with him]?" Temple sees Trigger going for his gun to kill Stephen, so she acts the part of the fallen woman to save him. She *wants* to be with Trigger, she insists, kissing her rapist and blowing cigarette smoke at Stephen. Yet when Stephen leaves, Temple musters the courage to walk out. "I got your number and you know it," insists Trigger, who prepares to assault her again. Grabbing his gun, Temple shoots him dead and flees back home.

Temple's ordeal is not over. Stephen must call her to testify in the murder case of the innocent backcountry man accused of the hillbilly's murder. "Leave me out of this," she pleads, suddenly sensitive to her reputation. "It'll all come out and I'll be disgraced." But though Stephen must put her on the stand, he cannot bring himself to ask her the question that will force her to confess her tainted status. So she sobs out the story of Temple Drake herself. "He attacked me—Trigger did," she cries. "I went to the city with Trigger and stayed with him until this week." "And stayed there a prisoner, you mean?" asks the court. "I killed him!" she shouts, and then faints, leaving the question unanswered. Stephen carries her from the courtroom and delivers the exit line: "Be proud of her, judge—I am."

The Story of Temple Drake is a model of pre-Code immorality in at least three ways. First, the open questions posed by the narrative would neither be raised nor answered under the Code. Did Temple enjoy the rape? Did she willingly prostitute herself for Trigger? The inquiries alone are invitations to profane thoughts, occasions for sin at the moment of utterance. Second, the questions are truly open, unanswered, not closed by the narrative. The degree of Temple's complicity in her rape and culpability for Trigger's murder is unresolved. Third, the one lesson taught by the story of Temple Drake is the poetic justice in unlawful vengeance. In being raped, Temple receives just comeuppance for her sexual teasing, for advertising promiscuity while being "just a fake." The rapist-murderer Trigger is the agent of an unholy but just retribution, an avenging angel who shows this girl that she can't have her cake and eat it too. If Temple doesn't enjoy her degradation, the audience should.

FIGURATIVE LITERALNESS

Though each sex might well partake of the cinematic sexual preferences of the other, the taste for vice films tended to split along gender lines. The lascivious male gaze focused on the sight of the female form laid bare and filled in the outlines with the offscreen suggestion of her nudity. The fertile imagination of women preferred a more cerebral kind of vice, conjuring violations of the marriage bed and the forbidden pleasures of sleeping in another without needing the details affronting their eyes.

Finding innovative ways to reveal women in states of undress and dishevelment was a creative challenge pre-Code Hollywood met unblushingly. Coeds pranced about in lingerie, chorines danced in translucent costumes, and society girls waltzed around in diaphanous gowns, low-cut dresses, and form-fitting silks. A scientific interest in female undergarments justified leering mise-en-scène and lavish montages of nylons and garters donned and cast off. *Night Nurse* (1931) concocts repeated occasions for Barbara Stanwyck and Joan Blondell to disrobe, slipping from civilian clothes into nurses uniforms and back again. In *Red Headed Woman* (1932) director Jack Conway choreographs a peek-a-boo sequence that pans back and forth between Jean Harlow and Una Merkel, from the bare legs of the one to the bare shoulders of the other, exposing a fleeting glimpse of Harlow's breast as the women undress and exchange pajamas.

The backstage musical ecstatically celebrated the female form—dozens of female forms actually—in production numbers showcasing geometric patterns and curvaceous figures while also affording ample opportunity to glimpse the girls changing between numbers and prancing up spiral staircases. As the financial backer of the stage show in *42nd Street* (1933), a wide-eyed Guy Kibbe relishes his role as audience surrogate, sitting front and center during rehearsal to inspect the chorus line. Jiggling, bouncing, and sashaying, pre-Code women flounced about with a freedom of movement that extended to all points on the body, fore and aft, port and starboard.

Occasionally, a naked woman might be spied in part or whole. Inspired by expeditionary films that exposed native girls in a state of nature, the studios sought to extend the custom to white women in exotic environments, often underwater. In *Bird of Paradise* (1932) the immovable Hawaiian lei adorning native girl Dolores Del Rio serves as a protective bodice, but a nude underwater swim sequence is more generous with dorsal exposure. Likewise, in *Tarzan and His Mate* (1934), an extended nude underwater swim sequence drapes Johnny Weismuller in a loincloth and a body double for Maureen O'Sullivan in nothing.

Before the Production Code put offscreen space under the same strict surveillance as onscreen images, mental pictures of what lay just beyond the edges of the film frame were vividly outlined. In *The Common Law* artist's model Constance Bennett stands before Joel McCrea in nothing but a towel. He tells her to drop the towel. She does. Bennett is shot from the shoulders up, but McCrea's appraising eye shows he sees what can be readily imagined. Similarly, in *Cabin in the Cotton* (1932) a purposeful Bette Davis doesn't wait to be told to expose her offscreen self to a shocked Richard Barthelmess.

Unlike the dull male spectator, who required the image (or most of it) before his eyes for erotic arousal, women preferred the exercise of imagination. Falling short of the overt teasing of the male gaze was a female-friendly diversionary tactic known as "figurative literalness." Where clumsily prurient directors might run afoul of even pre-Code strictures, stylishly sophisticated directors more cleverly tried to "exemplify in their work the teachings of the Code and yet inculcate in their finished releases risque matter, etc., possessed of all the emotion pep and range, without the Hays finger being able to descend on a single foot of their exposed film." That is, just as the edge of the film frame served as a beckoning "No Trespassing" sign (for the male gaze), a timely detour into offscreen space could infuse the onscreen narrative with otherwise censorable material for the female imagination.

In *Ann Vickers* (1933), director John Cromwell's version of the Sinclair Lewis novel about a feminist penologist, Ann (Irene Dunne) dines in the hotel room of the ardent Captain Resnick (Bruce Cabot), a Great War soldier with but one more week of furlough before transfer overseas. She must go, he gets her coat, and they embrace for a good-bye kiss. The camera frames the pair and then moves downward, catching the image of Ann's coat falling to the floor. In a continuous pan, the camera leaves the embracing couple and moves to the hotel window where, backframe, a neon sign outside advertises *Joan the Woman*. After a slow dissolve, the marquee title changes to *Shoulder Arms*. Ann has surrendered to her lover and spent the week with him in his hotel room, the amount of time it takes the motion picture program to change from Cecil B. DeMille's religious melodrama to Charles Chaplin's comedy.

Likewise, in John Ford's *Arrowsmith* (1931), the consummation of desire between the beautiful Joyce Lanyon (Myrna Loy) and the married Dr. Arrowsmith (Ronald Colman) is suggested through the subtlest of visual cues. Smitten with the doctor's dedication and matinee idol looks, Joyce proclaims her love for him, knowing it can never be. Arrowsmith retires alone to his room and sits at the foot of his bed, bathed in light, smoking a cigarette, thinking, and glancing sideways at the wall of her room. From an adjacent room, in crosscut action, Joyce fiddles with her nightgown. Her eyeline somehow seems to meet his gaze through the walls. Arrowsmith remains sitting, smoking, thinking. Backscreen, a small rectangular patch of light spills through the door to his room. A shadow flutters onto it. Fade out. When the couple encounters each other the next morning, the slightest of significant glances passes between them.

More literal was the figurativeness in *Laughing Sinners* (1931). On a windswept, rainy night Joan Crawford drives up to a train station to meet her traveling salesman boyfriend. Her face is ecstatic, ravenous with sexual passion: only the most naked lust could compel a woman out on a night like this. She leaps on the train, embraces him, and runs down the train corridor arm in arm with her lover.

According to MPPDA secretary Carl Milliken, the need for suggestive inventiveness spurred creative ingenuity. "The Code provides the laws of art for motion pictures and every art must have its laws," Milliken declared approvingly in 1931. "The Code is making dramatists out of writers." In other words, as long as the immoral intimations were subtle, tasteful, and mainly offscreen, they were cleared for release. After the imposition of the 1934 Code, "figurative literalness"—though now more figurative than literal— would be the preferred, often the only, way to smuggle impure thoughts and deeds onto the Hollywood screen.

Queer Flashes

The imputation of homosexuality, played usually for laughs, sometimes as threat, and most subversively as alternative, was the most scandalous vice element. When *Variety* spoke of strong flavorings of "the theme of perversion" in the "bedroom essence" of vice films, the homosexual hovered as the unnamed culprit.

Like so much else deemed culturally aberrant, the homosexual appears with greater frequency and readier acceptance in pre-Code Hollywood cinema. "The thirties were surprisingly full of fruity character comedians and gravel-voiced bulldyke character comediennes," film critic Andrew Sarris observed in his touchstone study *The American Cinema*, "but it was always played so straight that when [character actors] Franklin Pangborn or Cecil Cunningham went into their routines, it was possible to laugh without being too sophisticated." Maybe in the later thirties the homosexual was played straight, but in the pre-Code era, he, and she, was played queer. No sophistication was needed to read the same-sex orientations as gender disorientations.

The screen homosexual was called the nance, the poof, the fairy, or the queer. He was a flouncing twit, the supporting character whose mere presence sparked a snicker. Associated with the upper ranks of the British class system and the backstage worlds of theater and high fashion, the mincing gestures and perfumed wardrobe of the nance had been staples of vaudeville sketches, legitimate theater, and the silent screen in the 1920s. In *It* (1928), one of the running gags is that the second male lead is a gay flibbertigibbet. "You've got 'it,' old boy," he tweets to the mirror in intertitle.

Sound gave the nance a voice: a high-pitched trill, often British in inflection or vaguely foreign in accent. He was a butler, a waiter, a decorator, a choreographer, a tailor, the dowager's best friend or protégé. In 1932 a Pathé cameraman acted the part of a nance cooing over his precious pups at a dog show. Unlikely as it seems, his performance sparked a fad for nance impersonations onscreen. "Now the male magnolia is getting the play," *Variety* snapped in its trademark vernacular. "Effeminate boys crept occasionally into motion pictures before. Winked at, they are now apparently the stock comedy business easiest at hand." Though the Hays office would not stand for "more than a dash of lavender," as long as the imputation of homosexuality sped by quickly and tangentially, "pansy comedy" was tolerable in pre-Code Hollywood. "Despite the watchful eyes of the Hays Office, which is attempting to keep the dual-sex boys and lesbos out of films, producers are going heavy on the panz stuff in current pix," the trade paper continued. What were called "queer flashes" and "mauve characters" sashayed through *Cavalcade* (1933), *Our Betters* (1932), and *Sailor's Luck* (1932) in the figures of hand-holding girls, a flitty dance instructor, and a gay swimming pool attendant ("gay-zee ansy-pay," cracks a sailor in a winking aside missed by those not fluent in Pig Latin).

Though the male magnolias sprouted up with greater regularity, lesbians also walked arm-in-arm in the customary hangouts: prisons, all-girl schools,

Classical vice: the virtuous Christian girl (Elissa Landi) is tempted by the pagan lesbian (Joyzelle) as Roman prefect Marcus Superbus (Fredric March) eyes them both in Cecil B. DeMille's *The Sign of the Cross* (1932) (Courtesy of the British Film Institute)

and decadent nightclubs. In the prison film *Ladies They Talk About* (1933), Barbara Stanwyck is oriented to life behind bars by fellow inmate Lillian Roth. In the women's lavatory they come upon a stocky, cigar-smoking inmate. "Watch out for her," advises Roth. "She likes to wrestle." Later, the same butch lesbian exercises in her room, watched by her whiny femme partner. More sensual from either perspective were the lithe frauleins in *Maedchen in Uniform* (1932), a German import whose surprise success was mainly due to a "whispering campaign" insinuating the lesbian vibrations in an all-girl gymnasium. Probably the most notorious girl-on-girl tango of the pre-Code era occurred in the pagan chambers of Cecil B. DeMille's *The Sign of the Cross* (1932), when the dancer Joyzelle swirls temptingly around the pure Christian slave girl Mercia (Elissa Landi). Paramount's publicist Arch Reeve salivated over the Sapphic charms of classical antiquity. "Rome burns again!" he exulted. "The sets are marvelous and the costumes spell sex. There's Claudette Colbert in a milk bath. And Fredric March using the sensuous Joyzelle to break down the resistance of Elissa Landi—mentally, and how!"

Onscreen and off, the female attraction with the most candid attraction to females was Marlene Dietrich. Where Mae West's wisecracks challenged the image of the demure female, Dietrich's persona expanded the range of erotic alternatives. At least West was reliably male-directed. Dietrich was brazenly androgynous. In the early 1930s, she is often spoken of in the same breath as Garbo, the foreign stars thought to be feuding alley cats, there being limited space for two northern European females in the Hollywood firmament. But Garbo's remote and regal beauty, a beauty that never seemed to give her pleasure, contrasted with the whiff of Weimar decadence that always swirled about Dietrich. Where Garbo wanted to be alone, Dietrich was open for suggestions.

Dietrich first came to American consciousness as the mercenary man-killer Lola-Lola in Josef von Sternberg's *The Blue Angel* (1930), an international blockbuster in German- and English-language versions. Imported by Paramount, she and her Svengali collaborated on a series of smoky, lushly lit melodramas with Dietrich a soft-focused goddess crooning torch songs in fantastically ornate nightclubs: *Morocco* (1930), *Dishonored* (1931), *Shanghai Express* (1932), and *Blonde Venus* (1932). As the fallen woman in *Blonde Venus*, she shows that whatever the state of the economy a woman's assets give her collateral aplenty. While her impoverished and sickly husband cannot even sell his body to medical science, Dietrich has to beat back buyers. She glides up and down the socioeconomic ladder with an agility no male protagonist in the Great Depression can match: from a Berlin cabaret to tenement penury as an American housewife, from swank Manhattan apartments as a high-class mistress to Deep South flophouses as a low-down prostitute, and, in the space of a brisk thirty-second montage of neon signs, to the star attraction in the hottest stage act in France. Performing in sleek drag at a Paris nightclub, she waltzes on stage in white hat and tails, indiscriminately desirable.

Dietrich's gestures offscreen nourished her fluid sense of gender identity. When she took to wearing male suits, the act was more than a fashion risk. At the Hollywood premiere of *The Sign of the Cross*, appropriately enough, Dietrich upstaged DeMille's cast by striding down the red carpet wearing a tuxedo and black hat. Dietrich "has practically discarded women's attire in favor of the more sensational business and sport clothes of the opposite sex for street wear," ran a typical fashion report. "One of Hollywood's ace tailors has just completed six male suits for her, one a dinner suit she re-

Mannish girl: Marlene Dietrich makes a fashion statement.

cently wore at a formal affair. Miss Dietrich has picked up where Greta Garbo left off, and has gone a bit farther than the Swedish star, who confined her male attire to slacks." At first Paramount's publicity department played up her cross-dressing (great publicity), then played it down (backlash), and finally played it back up again (what the hell). When men's clothing stores approached the star to endorse their coats, vests, and pants, Dietrich pouted, "I am not trying to encourage other women to wear men's clothes. Male clothing is just what I want, but I don't say other women would be satisfied. I am not going to endorse hats, shoes, or trousers, so leave me alone."

Paramount finally decided, for good, not to encourage the publicity after Dietrich confided that she also wore men's underwear.

Like the gangster, another social threat and corrupting influence, the homosexual, male and female, felt the first chills of the cultural backlash. In 1933, a year before the vigilance of Joseph Breen pushed "the dual-sex boys and lesbos" firmly back into the celluloid closet, Will Hays ordered all "nance" characters eliminated from screenplays. The same year, in a scam to publicize both of its in-house blonde Venuses, Paramount filed for formal incorporation papers for the "Society for the Advancement of Feminism," a group formed "to discourage the wearing and usage of mannish clothes and habits among women." Mae West signed on as the first board member.

"Women Love Dirt"

Women and vice forged an inseparable link: they were its subject, they defined its limits, and, bewilderingly enough, they were its core audience. Reconciling the delicate manners of the gentler sex with their coarse tastes for vice was a mental task that perplexed the best masculine minds in the motion picture business. The nature of the appeal of naked flesh and fast women was evident enough for men, the unregenerate gender and weaker sex in matters of visual pleasure and biological compulsion. But women: what did they want on screen? Or rather, why did they seem to want such sordid scenarios?

Configured as the guardians of the moral fiber of the nation, matrons and mothers made up the foot soldiers and field officers of the censorship movement. In 1930, when Congressman Grant Hudson (D-Mich.) introduced legislation to establish a federal censorship commission for motion pictures, it was only natural that the bill specified that at least four of the nine members "would have to be women." The General Federation of Women's Clubs claimed some thirty million affiliated members whose notion of public-spirited citizenship was to monitor motion picture depravity. "No program should be lowered in tone to satisfy a moronic element," huffed the group's 1932 report. So troublesome and influential were the civic-minded women's groups that the studios hired permanent full-time liaisons to assuage them and put some of the ladies on the payroll.

Consequently, the taste for vice that was virulent among the gentler sex defied cultural expectations. The very same gender whose hand rocked the cradle and whose refined sensibilities warranted protection from crudeness and vulgarity consumed the most ribald material with relish. "Women are responsible for the ever-increasing public taste in sensationalism and sexy stuff. Women who make up the bulk of the picture audiences are also the majority readers of the tabloids, scandal sheets, flashy magazines, and erotic books," reported *Variety* in a perplexed front-page story in 1931. Next to the prurient mentality of women, "the mind of the average man seems most wholesome in comparison," declared the trade paper. "Women love dirt. Nothing shocks 'em."

Before the days of precision statistics and overnight movietracking, industry estimates on the composition of motion picture audiences were rough approximations, but by common consent women made up the better half of American moviegoers. Women "decide the fate of motion pictures," *Motion Picture Herald* stated flatly in 1930. "There can be no argument with the accepted fact that women patrons make or break a picture, because women make up the majority of the vast motion picture public, particularly at the matinee performances." "In making a picture it is always a case of women first," *Variety* agreed in 1931, asserting that "audiences are 75% female controlled." As the demographic group most devoted to films and most decisive in their box office impact, women were catered to as no other group of moviegoers—not children, not adolescents, certainly not men.

The separation of tastes along gender lines was also a piece of conventional wisdom seldom challenged by box office experience. Though squeamish about violence and gruesomeness, women were deemed to possess a propensity for imaginative suffering just short of masochism, a quality that made them especially prone to the machinations of heart-wrenching melodrama. Since the rise of the sentimental novel in the mid-eighteenth century, virtue beset had been the most reliable road to female readership and best-seller status. Apparently, women's tastes were of a kind in screen entertainment, with modern American courtship rituals adding a valuable dividend. "When properly maneuvered, the cry stuff for women always gives a picture an edge," *Variety* observed sagely, and "where there's a crying woman, there is usually a man for consolation."

Ruth Morris, *Variety*'s resident expert on the creature habits of American women, tried to explain to her male readers why "the wages of cinema sin" were "smash films." As Morris told it, women "fully endorsed heroines of easy virtue" because they liked the fantasy projection of "glamorous, shameful ladies, pampered by penthouses, coddled by limousines, clothed in couture smartness." Dubious about the intellectual faculties of both genders, Morris patiently expounded on her theories of "femme cinematurgy" and the contradictory impulses tugging at the heart of the female moviegoer. "The smug and contented housewife subconsciously envies the glamour that surrounds cinema mistresses. Luxury, excitement, dangerously stolen romance are an alluring opposition to her own conventional life. She experiences them vicariously in the film she patronizes." But subconscious yearnings always yield to the resurgence of super-ego conscience. "When the mistress is established in luxury, she must suffer the retribution and remorse that placates the housewife. When she happens, as in *Back Street* [1932], to represent the glamour of the mistress and the faithful sacrifice of the wife, she makes an unconquerable bid for the interest and sympathy of feminine audiences." And woe to the filmmaker who attempts to rehabilitate Anna Karenina or Emma Bovary. "The faithless wife is a heroine that women will not tolerate. However painstakingly devised, sympathy is not for her. She menaces the ideals that women have helped to build about the institution of marriage."

John Stahl, the director of the instructive *Back Street*, basically agreed, but added an important caveat. "The reality that women approve in fiction is not palatable to them on the screen. They edit as they read, eliminating from their imaginations the sordidness and squalor of modern fiction. The screen's reality cannot be glossed over. Harshness and bad taste must be blue-penciled by the director." Reviewing *The Story of Temple Drake*, the *Hollywood Reporter* picked up on Stahl's theory of the difference between vice in print and vice on screen. "It may do all right in literature where nauseating themes can be made less repellent by beautiful writing," asserted the distraught critic. "But there is no beauty in seeing a lovely girl stripped of all charm on the screen, standing before her audience a base and vile representative of all that is disenchanting in sex." If women were really shown on screen what their imaginations glossed over in literature, "they would run miles from the theater," joked Stahl.

In the end, the conflict between woman as moral guardian and woman as vice aficionado was chocked up to another unaccountable contradiction in a species defined by mutually exclusive desires. Undaunted, the motion picture trade papers scrutinized the mysterious ways of the American female in special "To the Ladies" pages and film reviews written with an eye to the "woman's angle." Thus, whereas the maudlin *The Sin of Madelon Claudet* (1931) was considered perfect for "those kind hearted matrons who just love a good cry," the Great War epic *The Battle of Gallipoli* (1931) was "one prolonged military battle" that would not interest women because "they're only interested in the battle of the sexes." Picturesque violence might divert boys of all ages, but women preferred their violence to be emotional, in the form of romantic suffering, maternal self-sacrifice, and, when necessary, suicide.

An exemplary combination of all three elements determined the star-crossed fate of aviatrix Lady Cynthia Darrington (Katharine Hepburn) in Dorothy Arzner's *Christopher Strong* (1933). Having committed adultery with the man of the title, consumed by guilt about breaking up his marriage to the angelic Mrs. Strong (Billie Burke), Lady Cynthia ascends to the sky in her biplane in a reckless attempt to break the world altitude record. As the plane soars into the clouds, her life flashes before her in double exposure on the altimeter. Upon breaking the record, she pulls the oxygen mask from her tear-stained face and slips into unconsciousness. The plane spirals to earth and explodes in a ball of flames.

No actress suffered with greater intensity, received more unmerited heartache, and caused more smitten suitors to jump to the wrong conclusion than Greta Garbo. Her spellbinding beauty cloaked a tragic interior life, the knowledge that the woman she was could never match the ideal female in the minds of enraptured men or win over the women who secretly wanted her punished for her otherworldly allure. A figure apart, a galaxy beyond even the biggest stars, she attracted more blithering expressions of purblind worship than the entire roster of down-to-earth ingenues at Warner Brothers. "Garbo talks!" screamed the ads for her first talkie, *Anna Christie* (1930), which mentioned nothing about the words she was speaking, by a playwright of some repute named Eugene O'Neill. A decade of melodramatic abuse later, an equally stunning exclamation announced another talent of the goddess on the pedestal. "Garbo laughs!" screamed the ads when she played against type in *Ninotchka* (1939). "What, when drunk, men see in other women, they see in Garbo sober," swooned the critic Kenneth Tynan, still reeling in 1954.

Like Chaplin, Garbo was not just a motion picture star but a universal referent. Her throaty contralto was imitated by Constance Bennett's star-struck waitress in *What Price Hollywood?* (1932) and her loyal demographic was personified by the reluctant male guest in *Dinner at Eight* (1933), a man who would much rather be watching the new Garbo movie than making small talk with an MGM ensemble that is minus the brightest star in its firmament.

In *Susan Lennox: Her Fall and Rise* (1931)—the subtitle is often transposed as "her rise and fall," the more usual trajectory for the fallen wo-

man—Garbo suffers, sins, and sacrifices for the sake of true love and generic convention. Like Dietrich in *Blonde Venus*, she moves easily up and
down the economic ladder while her man (Clark Gable) stays level. From
orphan runaway, to blissful fiancée, to circus performer, to fallen women,
to bad girl, she scales the ladder of success in the space of a montage and
then dives back down, dancing but not hustling in a seedy brothel-cum-
nightclub in the equatorial jungle. She speaks few lines, allowing her face
to mask and expose her emotions. When Clark Gable exits her room to
leave her alone for the night, her eyes say "No!" and her jaw goes slack
with desire, beckoning him to come back. He, if not the audience, misses
the moment.

Along with doomed love, a baby boom in unwed motherhood populated the regions of women's melodrama. Though the maternal devotion of
the girl often paid the moral debt for her brief but costly interlude of reckless romance, so great was the shame, so noble the mother, that such fallen
women typically conceal the birth of the child from the man who fathered
it and the identity of the father from the child. Though the act of procreation violated a stern commandment, the child was guiltless and the woman
redeemable after a suitable penance.

Sadly, the penance was often the death of the child. In *Born to Love* (1931)
Constance Bennett's love child is given legitimacy when she marries an understanding suitor, but when her former lover and (unbeknownst to him)
father of the child returns from his insensible convalescence in the Great
War, her husband is awarded custody of the baby in the divorce settlement.
Years later, reduced to penury, she is finally permitted to visit the boy: but
on the very day of the reunion, the child has died! The same awful blow is
visited upon *Mary Stevens, M.D.* (1933). The physician flees to Europe to
bear her love child, but on her cruise home to reunite with the father (unbeknownst to him), the child dies en route. More fortunate was the reform-
minded warden played by Irene Dunne in *Ann Vickers*, who bears a child out
of wedlock to a Great War soldier but winds up happy with the child and a
new husband in the last reel.

In fact, the Great War was a great background for melodramatic machinations. Fresh-faced doughboys impregnated good girls, then went off to the
trenches where the staggering incompetence of War Department recordkeeping reported them missing in No Man's Land or killed in action. The
Great War variant of the out-of-wedlock plot locked in three acts of in-
creasingly tearful momentum. First act: girl surrenders her virtue to doe-eyed

doughboy. Second act: the fog of war envelopes the doughboy as the girl bears out-of-wedlock baby alone and suffers accordingly. Third act: doughboy is resurrected and the couple is reunited.

James Whale's *Waterloo Bridge* (1931), the first of several film versions of Robert E. Sherwood's popular stage melodrama, played a variant on the theme of star-crossed, war-buffeted love. Impoverished prostitute Mae Clarke falls in love with a very dim doughboy who thinks she is merely a chorus girl down on her luck. She knows she cannot, must not, marry him, despite his kindly parents and English country estate. Moments before he must return to the front, he discovers the truth, but his love is unshakable. He presses her to agree to marry him and, sobbing joyfully, she agrees. After his troop truck rushes him away, she runs smack into an artillery shell dropped by a German zeppelin on Waterloo Bridge.

The Sin of Madelon Claudet was another hugely successful exemplar of the crime-and-punishment cryfests that shopgirls and housewives took to heart. Framed as a homily to wifely self-denial, the singular sin of the French mademoiselle Madelon Claudet (Helen Hayes) is to fall in love with a visiting American, to whom she bears an out-of-wedlock son. She sacrifices her honor to provide security for the boy, becoming the mistress to a kindly old aristocrat. In a slow, lifelong descent, she sinks to walking the streets to finance her son's medical education (unbeknownst to him). With her son a respected doctor, she ventures to visit him, merely to look upon the sturdy, good-hearted man whose own life has redeemed hers.

Written by Charles MacArthur, who with Ben Hecht was more likely to compose cynical comedies than women's weepies, *The Sin of Madelon Claudet* traded a transgression in the first reel for a purgatory of repentance until the closing credits. "Charlie didn't attempt to write a great American masterpiece," Helen Hayes said of her husband, a bit defensively. "He knew tragic meller hoke gets sympathy from picture audiences, so he wrote a sad part for me." Well he might: the rewards of slumming with sob stories paid out reliably, tear for tear, dollar for dollar. "Every infant torn from a sobbing mother brought a happy smile at the box office," read a synopsis of motion picture trends of 1931. "Saccharine on the screen means sugar in the box office."

But if sugary sweetness provided a profitable additive, the spice of vice also fueled the plot engines of women's melodrama. Along with tragic meller hoke, carefree sexy stuff attracted dry-eyed females of less masochistic appetites.

WORKING GIRLS

The aggressive, as opposed to the apologetic, vice film tended to involve a sex-for-hire female who fit two job descriptions: the fallen woman or the bad girl. In one, the woman is a victim of economic or romantic circumstances, forced to make a desperate choice when buffeted by hard times and bad men. In the other, the woman is a calculating agent of her moral decline and financial ascent who treats sex like any other business transaction. Where the fallen woman stumbled, the bad girl jumped.

Inspired by the real-life compromises working girls made to get and retain employment, a recurrent motif of women's melodrama in the Great Depression was the threat of sexual violation and the hard necessity of risking virtue to keep a paycheck. During the casting call for the chorus in *42nd Street*, the selection process favors contestants who are fast on more than their feet. "See what out of work girls are up against these days," read the ads for *Employee's Entrance* (1933), where women both succumb to ("Give me a job—at any price!") and resist ("All I want is my job!") marketplace forces.

In Busby Berkeley's nonmusical *She Had to Say Yes* (1933), the executives of a foundering department store decide to reverse a Great Depression job slump by offering their best customers "dates" with the girls in the stenographers pool. The rich buyers are bored with the "hard-boiled gold diggers" the store usually procures for them. Florence (Loretta Young), the prettiest girl in the office, is in love with her ambitious supervisor Tommy (Regis Toomey). When the two-timing Tommy tricks Florence into entertaining a rich customer (Lyle Talbot), her consort assumes the worst. However, once set straight by virtuous Florence, he falls in love, only to assume the worst again. Florence meanders toward compromising positions but her virtue, despite appearances, remains intact and she marries the richer guy in the end reel. Playing the "women love dirt" angle for laughs, *She Had to Say Yes* advertised itself with the teaser: "We apologize to the men for the many frank revelations made by this picture, but we had to show it just as it was filmed. The true story of a working girl."

For every working girl on the receiving end of an unwelcome sexual advance from a lecherous male employer, another was taking matters, and men, into her own hands. In distaff versions of the rake's progress, women of loose morals and mercenary motives prospered in stories of vice rewarded. In *The Common Law* nude model and kept woman Constance Bennett finds happiness and respectability in the arms of wealthy painter Joel Mc-Crea. In *Old Morals for New* (1932) a society girl turned kept woman lands her married lover and finds connubial bliss after he dumps his wife. In *Penthouse* (1933) call girl Myrna Loy lassos wealthy lawyer Warner Baxter.

The most cold-blooded and single-minded of the hustling sirens embodied a bad girl cycle, a crafty, proto-feminist series of films dedicated to the proposition that in one area of enterprise women were a little more equal than men. In *Red Headed Woman, Baby Face, Shopworn* (1932), *Bed of Roses* (1933), and *Beauty for Sale* (1933), cunning women worked their wiles on dimwitted men as a way to wealth. The bad girl film holds to a gendered code of human behavior: a determined female sexual predator can break down the resistance of any male no matter how outwardly moral his exterior. The two most colorful, conniving, and controversial bad girls gave fair warning with their featured attractions up on the marquee: *Red Headed Woman* and *Baby Face.*

Directed by Jack Conway from a screenplay by Anita Loos (*Gentlemen Prefer Blondes*), MGM's *Red Headed Woman* showed that gentlemen prefer platinum blonde Jean Harlow in any hair color. Harlow plays Lil Andrews, a scheming vixen who targets her rich married boss and any other male conduit to social and financial advancement. "He's a man, ain't he?" sneers Lil when her powers of persuasion are questioned. Virtually every diegetic ellipsis in the film is occupied by the certainty that Lil and the man she was with in the prior scene have spent the interim in an illicit sexual encounter. Subsequent dialogue fills in any imaginative gaps. "There we were like an uncensored movie!" gloats Lil self-reflexively.

Lil begins by wrecking the marriage of her rich employer Bill Legendre (Chester Morris), who cannot help but be flattered by the miniature portrait of himself that Lil wears on her garter. After an offscreen consummation ("Where's my shoe?" wonders Lil afterwards), Bill tries to regain his moorings, but Lil clings tight and reassures him that his wife Irene (Leila Hyams) "doesn't need to know about us." Irene returns home early, however, and comes upon the pair in flagrante delicto. A close-up of Irene in tearful heartbreak dissolves into the laughing face of a victorious Lil.

Cold-shouldering her husband, Irene moves into a separate bedroom, a prideful miscalculation in a battle with this scarlet woman. "If she wants to leave the barn door wide open, what's to keep a girl from going in?" figures Lil. Encountering Bill at a nightclub, she tricks him into a phone booth and wiggles close. Against her body, and his better judgment, Bill agrees to an assignation, but he reconciles with his wife and fails to meet

The bad girl on the make: Lil (Jean Harlow) exposes her pictorial garter to her first victim (Chester Morris) in *Red Headed Woman* (1932). (Courtesy of the Museum of Modern Art)

Lil. As long as the sheer physical proximity of the red-headed woman can be kept at arm's length, the red-blooded man has a fighting chance to heed the call of conscience.

Drunk, but knowing exactly what she is doing, Lil barges into Bill and Irene's home and blurts out the news of Bill's planned liaison with her. Irene is crushed. Enraged, Bill barges into Lil's apartment. Lil locks him into the bedroom, with her. Bill slaps Lil. "Go ahead, do it again! I like it!" she cackles wildly. From behind the door, Lil's roommate listens as Bill roughs up Lil. In the next shot, Lil is sobbing, crumpled on the floor. Taking pity, Bill lifts her onto her bed. He asks for the key to the room so he may leave. Smiling, she drops the key between her breasts.

Fade to divorce court, where a smirking Lil watches her homewrecking handiwork from the gallery. After the hearing, Irene's old aunt, wise in the ways of weak-willed men, counsels her against so self-defeating a course of action. Cold-fish wives who do not understand the uncontrollable urges of besotted men warrant a portion of the blame for the breakup of their marriage. The aunt likens Bill's adultery not to moral failing but hormonal poisoning. "He's sick or insane or whatever you call it," she lectures Irene. "Get dressed and go after him." Too late: Bill has married the hussy. "You caught him with sex," hisses Irene.

When Lil's social aspirations are blocked by the respectable elements of Bill's class, she sets her sights higher up the financial ladder, to the upright coal magnet Charles B. Gaerste (Henry Stephenson). Cut immediately to: a shot of Lil, legs outstretched, putting on nylons, perched on a couch, the pillow indented, her gloves off. The once-moral Charles B. Gaerste stands by a window, flummoxed that he has just made love to the wife of his business associate. Later, after trying repeatedly to resist her warm flesh rubbing against him, Gaerste surrenders with a weary, "What's the use?"

The logistics of Lil's two-timing ultimately catch up with her. She is not only betraying her husband with his boss but the boss with his chauffeur (Charles Boyer). Finally wised up, Bill exposes Lil's treachery to Gaerste and reunites with the very understanding Irene. Less understanding, Lil pulls a gun from her handbag and shoots Bill. A montage of tabloid headlines screams the sensational story, but Bill survives and refuses to press charges.

The coda to *Red Headed Woman* shows the payoff for the wages of sin. "In Paris, two years later," reads an intertitle. Lil is the toast of the town, winning the trophy at a horse race and what looks like the hearts of fifty million Frenchmen. Sliding into the back seat of a Rolls Royce, she rides off with a rich Gaelic sugar daddy. "To the house," she instructs the chauffeur in French. The camera pulls back to reveal the driver behind the wheel— Charles Boyer.

A woman's vertical movement up the economic ladder via horizontal means is also the plot of *Baby Face* (1933), the most notorious of the sex-in-the-workplace vice films of the pre-Code era. "She played the love game with everything she had," bragged the taglines, "and made 'it' pay." Conceived as a reply by Warner Brothers to MGM's *Red Headed Woman*, *Baby Face* is credited with, or blamed for, ending the career of Darryl Zanuck at the studio. With some justice, Zanuck felt that the Hays Office applied stricter standards to Warner Brothers than MGM, refusing to allow the working-class, financially strapped studio to do in *Baby Face* what the high-prestige, profitable studio had done in *Red Headed Woman*.

Lily (Barbara Stanwyck) is sassy, smart, and single-minded, a superwoman whose will to sexual power is encouraged by a Germanic mentor with a taste for Nietzschean philosophy. "You must be a master, not a slave," he tells Lily, urging her to get out of the speakeasy dive where she gets pawed by

The bad girl on the make, again: Lily (Barbara Stanwyck) twists another man around her finger in *Baby Face* (1933). (Courtesy of the Museum of Modern Art)

corrupt politicians and hairy laborers ("Aw, lay off, you big ape!"). After the explosion of a bootleg still kills her despicable father, Lily takes off to the big city with her partner in ambition, her black maid Chico (Theresa Harris). Arriving in front of the headquarters of the Gotham Trust Company, she scans the building bottom to top and resolves to leap to the executive suite two floors at a time.

Lily bats her eyes at the doorman, invites the personnel director to get personal, and rises floor by floor, flirtation by flirtation, into upper management. After breaking up the marriage of the fair-haired boy of the company, she seduces the bank president and secures fur coats, diamonds, and penthouse digs complete with a butler. Lily's career plans go awry when her previous suitor encounters the present one and, in a fit of jealous rage, kills his rival then himself. Lily calmly phones the cops. "I was a victim of circumstances," she later explains.

The resulting scandal threatens the reputation of the Gotham Trust Company, but new president Courtland Trenholm (George Brent) outmaneuvers

Lily's blackmail scheme. Lily takes a job in the company's Paris bureau and bides her time until Trenholm arrives for a visit. Drawn into her web, he surrenders like the rest of the male population. "I'd like to have a Mrs. on my tombstone," says Lily, upping the ante. When the news of their marriage reaches stateside, the bank is threatened with insolvency and Trenholm with indictment. He tells Lily he needs all the money and gifts he bestowed upon her. She refuses. Despondent, he shoots himself. Repentant and redeemed by love, Lily tearfully apologizes to her wounded husband. The final shot relegates the pair, working-class but happy, to life in a steel town. All of this happens in seventy minutes.

Baby Face doesn't just depict vice; it glories in it. A father who pimps his daughter, politicians who trade political patronage for sex, laborers who cheat on their wives, managers and workers at every level who betray the codes of the Bible and the workplace for sex—even in pre-Code Hollywood the package was too sordid to escape censorship and extensive reediting. The surviving print of *Baby Face* is a jerry-built mess, with the Nietzschean subtext obscured and the tacked-on morality lesson a thudding afterthought, due not least to the fact that Stanwyck was unavailable for exculpatory retakes. As a result, the indomitable Lily is never shown on screen reduced to straitened circumstances. The memory of her is untainted by punishment and penance. And behind Barbara Stanwyck's sly smile is the certain knowledge that even in an era of economic scarcity a determined woman always possesses one sure means of ascent.

6

Criminal Codes
Gangsters Unbound, Felons in Custody

On March 20, 1934, Will H. Hays fired off a cablegram to his subordinates decreeing that "no picture based on the life or exploits of John Dillinger will be produced, distributed, or exhibited by any member of the Motion Picture Producers and Distributors of America, Inc." Hays had determined that "such a picture would be detrimental to the best public interest" and warned that "action supporting the decision has been taken by the executive committee of the association. Please advise all studio heads." Like J. Edgar Hoover and the FBI, Hays and the MPPDA had decided it was high time to take John Dillinger seriously.

John Dillinger was Public Enemy Number One, front page news, and the most mythically resonant American outlaw since Jesse James. Hays's broadside came on the heels of Dillinger's sensational escape three weeks earlier from his jail cell in Crown Point, Indiana, an act of personal liberation that thrilled more law-abiding citizens than it appalled. Motion picture audiences

"Scarface" Al Capone, 1931: the face that launched the gangster genre. (Courtesy of the Associated Press)

chortled when a slow-talking garage attendant named Edwin J. Saager went before Pathé News cameras to tell how Dillinger took him hostage during the brazen jailbreak. Inspiring "more laughs than chills" with his droll account, Saager recalled he thought Dillinger was kidding at first, but when it became clear the outlaw was dead serious, he "went right with him." Once across state lines, Dillinger gave Saager some money, shook his hand, and went driving merrily down the road.

Dillinger's name was so famous then and so enduring now that the brevity of his criminal life span and nationwide notoriety comes as a surprise. From May 22, 1933, when he crashed out of his first Indiana prison and embarked on a spectacular series of bank robberies, shoot-outs, and hairbreadth escapes, until July 22, 1934, when he was gunned down outside Chicago's

Biograph Theater after watching the pre-Code gangster film *Manhattan Melodrama* (1934), Dillinger flashed across Depression America like a comet, fiery and luminous even in his fateful flame-out.

Dillinger's opposite number was not FBI agent Melvin Purvis, the man who devised his sidewalk execution, but Al Capone, alias "Big Al," "the Big Fellow," "Snorkey," and most of all "Scarface," in the tabloids if not to his face. With his broad-shouldered henchmen and short-lived enemies, Capone gave Chicago its durable reputation as the locus classicus of American gangster-dom, a cityscape where bullet-proof roadsters with tommygun-toting hoodlums on running boards careened around State Street, spraying fusillades of slugs into flower shop windows and mowing down the competition in blood-spattered garages. In 1930 he became the first authentic gangster to make the cover of *Time* magazine.

Between them, Capone and Dillinger cornered most of the market on the morphology of American criminality. Each embodied a distinct criminal type. Capone was a man of the 1920s in his vocation (bootlegging), style (managerial), and situation (sedentary). Dillinger was a man of the 1930s in his targets of opportunity (banks), modus operandi (independent and improvisational) and mobility (on the road). Capone was the kingpin, Dillinger the outlaw. By 1931, Capone was caught and confined, neutered by the Internal Revenue Service, of all federal agencies, for tax evasion, sentenced to prison and soon withered in mind and body from syphilis. Dillinger was merely killed and thereby became the richer folk legend.

As timely as today's headlines and ready-made for screen appropriation, the charismatic gangsters of the Roaring Twenties and desperate thirties muscled onto the American screen as inspirations for a kinetic new motion picture genre, the gangster film. With Capone as the supreme model and dozens of less magnetic thugs filling out the picture, the gangster was stolen from the streets, the tabloids, and the courts and remade as a motion picture star. By 1948 the critic Robert Warshow could rightly presume that while few people had actually seen a gangster, "the gangster *as an experience of art* is universal to Americans." Hollywood performed that cultural work over the period of a few short months between 1930 and 1931.

No motion picture genre of the pre-Code era was more incendiary than the gangster film: neither preachment yarns nor vice films so outraged the moral guardians or unnerved the city fathers as the high-caliber scenarios that made screen heroes out of stone killers. Even before 1934, much of the pre-Code license that let the gangster run wild was revoked under pressure from state censorship boards and law enforcement agencies. The speed and efficiency of the clampdown indicates that the gangster was never exclusively a criminal threat to civil society. On screen, if not on the street, he was also a political agent.

RUSHING TOWARD DEATH: THE GANGSTER FILM

Born in the Great Depression, enduringly popular as the crooked alternative to the straight and narrow way to wealth, the Hollywood gangster was more parts Capone than Dillinger, at least in his first incarnations. As bearers of cultural meaning, each figure represented a distinct criminal type, a face-off that pitted the ethnic, metropolitan gangster against the sturdy frontier stock of the Midwest desperado, the geneology of the Chicago-based hoods Al Capone (Italian), Dion O'Banion (Irish), and Hymie Weiss (Jewish) versus the Anglo-Saxon and Teutonic heritage of John Dillinger, "Baby Face" Nelson, Bonnie Parker, Clyde Barrow, and the Barker Gang, imported thieves of lower European origin against men related to a longer lineage in American lawlessness. As a communist critic in *The New Masses* gloated, "It must be a point of some concern to the professional patriots to realize that the crooks of the Middle West are not Wops, Pollacks, or Jews. There are the Barrows and Barkers and Pretty Boy Floyds of Texas and Oklahoma, the Twohys of Minnesota, the Dillingers and Pierpoints of Indiana—all native-born." Like most organs of American popular culture, Hollywood preferred to portray the gangster as a foreign infestation rather than a homegrown plague. In the city, from immigrant blood, he sprang from alien sources and perverse impulses. Though a pure product of America, the gangster was demonized as a swarthy stranger whose name ended in a vowel.

Rumors that Capone himself was being courted for a starring role reinforced the kinship between the Chicago gangster and his Hollywood incarnations. Los Angeles prosecutor Buron Fitts decried reports that an unnamed Hollywood producer had promised Capone $1,000,000 to get shot in the final reel of a gangster film, a slur on his character that Capone laughingly denied. "I wouldn't go into a picture for all the money in the world," he claimed. "It doesn't interest me and I've never considered the thought even." Despite a Hays Office prohibition against casting the gangster to type, Capone was asked on two occasions to star in the pictures—one offer for $200,000, the other for $350,000, both from major studios. Capone was reportedly receptive, pledging to turn over his salary to charity.

Capone's other brush with the motion picture camera was a near miss in the sound newsreels. "I've never willingly posed for any of them," he declared in 1931. "If they sneak in a picture of me, I can't help it, nor do I resent it, but I won't stand in front of any camera. Most of the boys understand my prejudice." Coaxed by Fox Movietone to say a few words before the sound camera, Capone did once travel with his lawyer from Chicago to the newsreel offices in New York. After some pleasantries in an outer anteroom, the newsreel editor joked, "If you gentlemen will park your guns here, we'll go into the recording room." Capone's lawyer jumped to his feet and shouted, "My client did not come here to be insulted!" Both men then stormed out of the office. So at least went one version. Perhaps the vain Scarface Al, ashamed of the gash on his left cheek, simply reconsidered showing his bad side to the camera.

Unlike the accessible Capone, Dillinger was constantly on the lam and thus unable to meet the press and negotiate his screen appearances. However, before Hays's edict cut short the bidding wars, Dillinger-themed scripts circulated throughout the major studios. RKO, Fox, and Warner Brothers were all said to be interested in a story treatment that anticipated Dillinger's crash-out at Crown Point. "To save the rest of the industry its valuable time and money," Paramount thoughtfully published a full page ad in the *Hollywood Reporter* warning rivals that it had already staked claim to the Dillinger franchise. Based on an original screenplay by Bartlett Cormack, author of Cecil B. DeMille's vigilante teenpic *This Day and Age* (1933), the project was "derived entirely from 'the Dillinger story'" and described as "a comment and reflection on this day and age—in which Dillinger, rank individualist that he is, is both hero and heavy." Already typecast, George Raft was slated to play the lead. That a major Hollywood studio would brag about an upcoming portrayal of an escaped prisoner, serial bankrobber, and accused murderer as "both hero and heavy" reveals the depth of the private admiration behind the public condemnations for Dillinger's brand of lawlessness. Few harbored such tender illusions about Al Capone.

The star power of Dillinger's presence in the newsreels certainly augured well for the film career of a surrogate. Within weeks of his escape at Crown Point, federal agents ambushed the Dillinger gang at a remote summer lodge in Little Bohemia, Wisconsin, a raid that turned into a bloody fiasco. When the smoke cleared, Dillinger had once again evaded the law and once again had left behind delighted eyewitnesses. The Pathé News postmortem on the Little Bohemia raid showed the innkeeper, whose lodge was riddled with bullets, calling Dillinger "very congenial" and a housewife who considered him "very kind." The upbeat coverage by Hearst Metrotone News featured a smiling resident of Little Bohemia mugging for the camera behind the shattered window pane "through which the bandit Dillinger, under cover of darkness made another of his remarkable escapes." Universal Newspaper Newsreel interviewed Dillinger's weather-beaten father, a laconic farmer who reduced audiences to helpless laughter (the police, he opined, were "making a mountain out of a mole hill") and inspired raucous applause (his boy "would have made a good cop"). Noting the crowd reactions, *Variety* wisecracked that "if Dillinger remains at large much longer and more such interviews are obtained, there may be some petitions circulated to make him President." Outflanked in the court of public opinion by Public Enemy Number One, the FBI was "incensed" at the flippant newsreel coverage of Dillinger, a glorification of gangsterdom that the bureau considered "inimical to public interest."

At the height of Dillinger-mania, Midland Film Corporation released *Dillinger—Public Enemy No. 1* (1934), a short biopic that feverishly recounts the criminal's escapades. The quickie short subject is a good overview of the official version of Dillinger's life, where the frowning face can't help but break into a toothy grin.

Newsreel clips of Dillinger's capture in Tucson, Arizona, on January 30, 1934, and his airplane flight back to Indiana serve as overture to what is, after all, one of the very few documentaries devoted to a living American released in the 1930s. "A shudder of relief thrilled the country for the entire nation had hoped for the capture of this gunman," the narrator intones, a disingenuous reading of popular attitudes toward a man "who from petty obscurity had leaped to shameful notoriety as public enemy number one within a few brief weeks."

The film chronicles Dillinger's early years growing up near the quiet farm community of Mooreshead, Indiana, where he was a "selfish, sullen, stubborn brat" who "slighted his studies" by "idling about poolrooms." Having no "moral backbone," he robs a grocery store and lands in a reformatory. An incorrigible juvenile, he is transferred to an adult institution, "where prison severities might teach him the futilities and folly of crime as a career." The commentary insists that "John Dillinger is not smart. Only a fool thinks that crime pays." Yet the tale is so rich in thrills and twists, the antihero so audacious and stylish, that a tone of giddy exhilaration cannot be suppressed. "Crime's hyenas were on the loose!" "Cars mean nothing to Dillinger—he never pays for them!"

Captured in Tucson, Dillinger is flown back to Indiana to stand trial for the murder of a patrolman. The airplane flight itself certifies his celestial

Public Enemy Number One: On March 3, 1934, a little over a month after irreverently leaning on prosecutor Robert Estill, John Dillinger crashed out of jail at Crown Point, Indiana. (Courtesy of the Associated Press)

status as a one-man crime wave; even Capone was taken away to jail by train. During stopovers, hordes of onlookers and journalists crowd the airfields, surging in hungrily for a look, as if the gangster were a movie star. At Crown Point, Dillinger poses for two instantly iconic newsreel clips. In one, a crisp medium shot, he is caught like a panther behind bars; in the other, he lines up with Sheriff Lillian Holley and Prosecutor Robert Estill. Clad in white shirt and black vest, Dillinger stands between them, in the privileged position, grinning broadly for the newsreel boys and still photographers, his right arm insolently resting on Estill's shoulder. He seems untouchable and immortal, already a figure of myth. Transmitted to every newspaper in the country via wirephoto, screened incessantly in the newsreels, this "happy family picture" alone would have destroyed the careers of Sheriff Holley and Prosecutor Estill. What happened next guaranteed their lifelong humiliation.

At 8:30 A.M. on the morning of March 3, 1934, while "the sheriff busied herself making pies," Dillinger crashed out of the Crown Point jail, stole

Sheriff Holley's car, and drove off into American folklore. He had escaped in the time-honored tradition of deceiving his jailer with a wooden gun. (Historical consensus now holds that Dillinger brandished a real gun, smuggled in to him by a bribed guard.) Crown Point "had become the laughing stock of the world and John Dillinger the most wanted man in America." While speeding away though the backroads of Indiana in the sheriff's stolen automobile, Dillinger voiced his allegiance to the frontier outlaws of yore by singing "The Last Roundup" at the top of his lungs, "Git along, little doggies, git along."

Teamed with his machine gun–wielding sidekick Homer Van Meter, "he and Homer write a new Iliad of crime." In yet another sensational shoot-out, Dillinger and his gang eluded the FBI at Little Bohemia, though three innocent civilians, shot by panicked federal agents, were not so lucky. "Dillinger is going to accidentally get with some innocent bystanders some time, then he will be shot," predicted Will Rogers. FBI director J. Edgar Hoover did not partake of the general hilarity. On June 22, 1934, he officially conferred on Dillinger a criminal appellation ready-made for tabloid headlines and motion picture marquees: Public Enemy Number One.

Still speaking of Dillinger in the present tense, the film seems to be winding to a finish with a close-up of his ordained final seating place and a last admonition. "Here lies the inevitable end of criminals like Dillinger. The electric chair yawns for its fodder of calloused human beasts whose warped minds prompt evil deeds. The wages of sin is death." And again: "Crime never pays."

But events overtake *Dillinger—Public Enemy No. 1*. Edited and released in late June 1934, the film became outdated on July 22, 1934, and required a hasty reedit for a timely rerelease. After fourteen months of "wild crime and carnage," "the long arm of the law got him" in front of the Biograph Theater in Chicago. The newsreel obituaries served as both graphic anatomy lesson and moral closure. Morgue shots of Dillinger show the corpse in several different poses, in medium shot and tight close-up, with arms carelessly tossed above his head, bare chested, shrouded in a white sheet, his face puffed up and scarred by plastic surgery, unnatural and waxen. (The Dillinger morgue shots printed in the metropolitan dailies were more grotesque. Admitted into the Cook County morgue by the coroner, drunken revelers congregate around the still blood-spattered corpse, with Dillinger the guest of honor at a macabre party.)

"Perhaps in death he has learned what he never learned in life—that the federal government always gets its man," concludes *Dillinger—Public Enemy No. 1*. The last line is repeated and emphasized: "the federal government *al-*

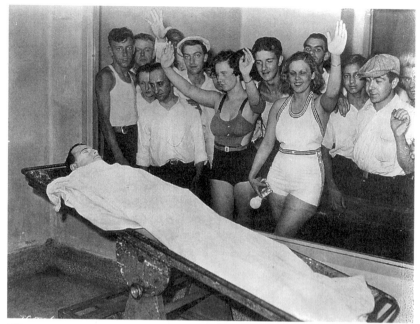

Dillinger in death: the macabre festivities at the Chicago morgue on the evening of July 22, 1934.

ways gets its man"—not the local cops, or the state jailers, but the feds. In New Deal America, with J. Edgar Hoover's FBI patrolling the beat from coast to coast, the lethal police authority emanates from Washington, D.C.

If Dillinger and Capone shared equal billing in the criminal pantheon, Capone ruled as the backstory star in the movies. Besides the foreign lineage that made the Italian-American a safer target, two accidents of historical timing gave him the edge. Capone's long reign from 1925 to 1931 climaxed with the perfection of the sound film and the furthest reaches of pre-Code license. Dillinger's crime spree lasted just over a year, from May 1933 to July 1934, by which time the censorship battles over the gangster film had mainly been settled. Not until 1941 would Dillinger earn a screen treatment in Raoul Walsh's *High Sierra*, where lookalike Humphrey Bogart plays paroled convict Roy "Mad Dog" Earle, a version of Dillinger as allegorically transparent as Paul Muni's impersonation of Al Capone in *Scarface* (1932). "Remember what Johnnie Dillinger said about guys like us?" a career criminal muses to Roy. "That we were just rushing towards death." Had Dillinger been sent to jail in 1933 and served the same eight-year stretch given to Roy Earle, he would have been released in 1941, just like *High Sierra.*

The three pre-Dillinger, post-Capone films that cast the mold for the gangster genre were *Little Caesar* (1930), *The Public Enemy* (1931), and *Scarface.* Precursors to the triad wander aimlessly, without a narrative road map or thematic blueprint, unatuned to the tragic dimensions of the criminal. Archie Mayo's *Doorway to Hell* (1930), with Lew Ayres miscast as an underworld boss and James Cagney as his lieutenant, looks like a rough first draft. Champing at the bit in his sidekick role, Cagney seems ready to eat pretty boy Ayres for breakfast.

Moreover, just as the gangster arrived on the crime scene with the new technology of personal artillery (tommy guns) and mobility (automobiles), the gangster genre was born not in the noisy gang wars of Chicago in the 1920s but with the consolidation of sound technology in 1930. Despite the silent era antecedents (notably Josef von Sternberg's *Underworld* [1928], scripted by Ben Hecht), the gangster film is unimaginable without the sense of sound. Tommy guns rat-tat-tat, tires screech, windows crash, women scream, newsboys shout, crowds murmur, jazz blares, and the ambient noise of the street assaults the ears or percolates just under the edge of consciousness. Above all, the patois of the city murmured a melodic leitmotif—laden with slang and cynicism, clipped dialogue spat out rapid-fire, mouthed by fast-talking hoods and hard-bitten molls.

In the merging of actor and persona, the three classic gangster films calibrated a demographically precise balance in their ethnic bloodlines: Edward G. Robinson/"Rico" Bandello (Jewish/Italian) in *Little Caesar*, James Cagney/Thomas Powers (Irish/Irish) in *The Public Enemy*, and Paul Muni/Tony Camonte (Jewish/Italian) in *Scarface*, together adding up to equal portions of Irish, Jewish, and Italian, America's dominant immigrant groups. The three films also evenhandedly parcel out social pathology and sexual aberration: homosexuality (*Little Caesar*), misogyny (*The Public Enemy*), and incest (*Scarface*).

Directed by Mervyn LeRoy from the novel by W. R. Burnett, *Little Caesar* was first out of the gate and an immediate sensation. A diminutive bandit whose single-minded ambition compensates less for his stature than his repressed homosexual desire, Caesar Enrico Bandello is compact, swarthy, and tightly wound; his golden boy pal Joe (played by the scion of Hollywood royalty, Douglas Fairbanks, Jr.) is tall, patrician, and easygoing. When Joe finds a female dance partner and show business success, the jilted Caesar, unhinged by a jealousy that dare not speak its name even to himself, makes his first mis-

A creature of the imagination: gangster Rico Bandello (Edward G. Robinson) in the eyes of himself and his gunsel (George E. Stone) in *Little Caesar* (1930). (Courtesy of the Museum of Modern Art)

takes in judgment. The male triangle is completed by Caesar's worshipful lap-dog, Otera (George E. Stone), who gazes up at Rico with a rapturous desire that, unlike Rico, he barely bothers to sublimate. Doubly deviant, Rico dies for his social and sexual sins, asking in tight close-up and choked-up tones, "Mother of Mercy, is this the end of Rico?" The famous last words inspired an incisive remark from Robert Warshow on gangster psychology: "Even to himself he is a creature of the imagination."

In William Wellman's *The Public Enemy*, Tom Powers embodies an utter ruthlessness almost without redemption, save for a sudden epiphany ("I ain't so tough") before he crumples into a rainswept gutter. Formed in equal parts by social environment (as a kid, he hangs around poolrooms) and dys-functional nuclear family (his mother is too weak, his father is too strict), Tom hones his native cunning and frenetic style. His strict Irish brother Mike, the elder good son, takes the Ben Franklin road to lace-curtain respectability, working on a streetcar by day, going to school in the evenings ("learning to be poor," scoffs Tom).

Unlike the ascetic Rico, Tom luxuriates in his success, hungrily consuming clothes, cars, and dames. He is also more multifaceted and complex, motivated by lust, loyalty, and revenge. Among his murder victims are the Faginesque figure who put him on the path to crime, the mobsters who gunned down his buddy, and the horse that killed his mentor. If Rico attracted appalled fascination, Tom Powers invited emulation. No exculpatory preface could deflect admiration from so magnetic a screen presence. To make identification easier, before *The Public Enemy* begins, Cagney takes a precredit bow, smiling and friendly, the actor not the persona.

Of all the gangster films, *Scarface* was the most controversial and violent. Patterned on the life of Capone, it teased audiences to connect the dots between the Chicago mobster and his Hollywood double. Like Capone, Camonte has a scar on his left check acquired in a fight back in Brooklyn (though Tony's is in the shape of an X, a sign that foreshadows murder). Like Capone, Camonte aspires to middlebrow culture and attends a Broadway production of Somerset Maugham's *Rain* with a phalanx of burly bodyguards. Both Capone and Camonte hail from the Five Points Gang in Brooklyn; both own a custom-built, bullet-proof sedan; both remodel their living quarters with steel-plated shutters and secret passageways.

Most boldly, the killings in *Scarface* reenact Capone-ordered executions with a forensic attention to detail. Like Dion O'Banion, murdered in his Chicago flower shop by a gunman who shook his hand and wouldn't let go, an Irish hood is murdered in a flower shop on Camonte's orders. The tableau that receives the most artful and precise depiction is the St. Valentine's Day Massacre of 1929, in which seven hoods were lured into a Southside garage by mobsters disguised as cops, lined up against a wall, and machine-gunned down execution style.

In his less homicidal moments, Tony evokes another figure from the 1920s whose American dream went bad. The imagery and backstory of F. Scott Fitzgerald's *The Great Gatsby* informs Ben Hecht's literate script, the sense that the fresh green breast of the New World has rotted on the vine, the cultural metaphor of 1925 having become the economic report of 1932. Outside Tony's window is a billboard with a sign that beckons with the promise of the frontier, "The World Is Yours." In a gesture lifted directly from Fitzgerald's novel, Tony reenacts the moment when Gatsby caresses his silk shirts, tangible proof of his successful self-made man-ness.

Lovers unto death: Tony Camonte (Paul Muni) and sister Cesca (Ann Dvorak) in *Scarface: The Shame of the Nation* (1932). (Courtesy of the Museum of Modern Art)

Like Rico, however, Tony's unrequitable passions derange his solid head for the business of crime. His incestuous obsession with his slutty sister Cesca (Ann Dvorak), who shimmies lasciviously before right-hand man Guino (a coin-flipping George Raft), compels him to kill his loyal aide. Reunited in a death pact with Cesca, he plunges into dementia before dying in the final shoot-out.

Unprecedented in the context of the times, the violence in *Scarface* shocked and outraged editorialists, politicians, and, it seemed, anyone within reach of a pen or typewriter. A vitriolic front-page commentary by Jack Alicoate in the *Film Daily*, a trade paper that was more often an industry shill than critic, said *Scarface* generated a "distinct feeling of nausea," the action was "so compellingly forceful as to leave one limp," the only suspense lying in "the additional brutal methods employed in each new massacre." "There are certain things that simply do not belong on the screen," declared Alicoate. "The subject matter of *Scarface* is one of them. To show it indiscriminately on the screens of America will do more harm to the motion picture industry and every one connected with it than any picture ever shown." He added firmly: "It should never have been made."

The tonal shifts in *Scarface*, the carefree blend of brutal violence and light comedy, particularly disturbed critics. During a fusillade of machine gun fire into a cafe (again, based on an assassination attempt on Capone), Tony is undaunted by the bullets whizzing by but exudes boyish exuberance in discovering the latest innovation in handheld artillery, a tommy gun.

To outmaneuver the outraged, producer Howard Hughes sent prints of *Scarface* to state censor boards "to gain the cooperation of state authorities in putting down the gangster menace" and vowed "to show *Scarface* in its original, unaltered, version in every state in the United States, including New York, where opposition to the film is most persistent." Hughes claimed that "ulterior and political motives" lay behind the opposition to *Scarface* and that corrupt politicians resented the film for its "unpleasant political truths." Dr. James Wingate, then chief New York censor, soon to helm the Studio Relations Committee for the MPPDA, discerned Hughes's own ulterior motive when he said that the whole affair smacked of "box office publicity."

The criticism from churches, civic groups, and politicians intensified any time an incident of juvenile crime could be attributed to the baleful influence of a gangster film. After an adolescent killer in East Orange, New Jersey, claimed incitement from Hollywood, the town's mayor called on Hays to ban the entire gangster genre. In Worcester, Massachusetts, the chief of police took matters into his own hands, sending a written directive to exhibitors informing them "that henceforth gangster films will not be approved by me for showing in local theaters."

What went largely unremarked was the vicious nature of the relationships between men and women in the gangster genre. The grapefruit James Cagney squashes in the face of Mae Clarke in *The Public Enemy* is the least of the physical assaults by tough guys on doormat dames. In *The Picture Snatcher* (1933), Cagney forcefully beats back the sexual aggressions of a moll by knocking her cold and tossing her roughly in the back seat of a car. On their own turf, the sassy women of the bad girl cycle took no guff, but in the masculine environs of the gangster film the dames, molls, and dishes are pushed around and cast aside.

The motion picture industry responded to the furor by denying evil intent, crying foul, and pointing fingers elsewhere. The motion picture screen had done much to "debunk" and "ridicule" the gangster, Hays asserted. "The insistent message flashed upon the screen is: you can't get away with it." During a rowdy public debate between famed defense attorney Clarence Darrow and censor John S. Sumner ("the pious Pope of the Society for the Suppression of Vice," as Mae West tagged him), Darrow brought down the house by thundering, "This talk about glorifying or making heroes of crooks is silly piffle. Right always triumphs over wrong in the movies and that is more than we can say in real life!" *Variety* pointed out that the tabloid press purveyed "more crime and sex in one issue than the entire picture industry could in an entire season." Besides, "gang pictures are action pictures. The screen has played them for years. It called them westerns when they stole horses instead of booze."

One group of critics took a perverse pleasure in the crime wave from Hollywood. For Marxists, gangsterism was only a slightly cruder version of the dog-eat-dog capitalist marketplace, the ruthless self-interest and aggressive materialism of the criminal enterprise a mirror image of the legal business of America. The Great Depression had merely forced the acquisitive speculator to channel his energies into a more direct mode of thievery. With the corrupt industrial engine of the exploitative system sputtering, with economic conditions foreclosing legitimate means of ascent, the only possible stage on which to act out the American dream of material success and upward mobility was crime. The *New York Post* recognized the bent success ethic of the gangster, dubbing *Little Caesar* "an Horatio Alger tale transferred to the underworld." In 1930, *Chicago Daily News* reporter Fred D. Pasley published a best-selling study of Al Capone, with the only slightly ironic subtitle, "The Biography of a Self-Made Man."

The moral equivalence between crime boss and capitalist executive is schematic in *Success at Any Price* (1934), directed by J. Walter Ruben from the play by John Howard Lawson. The narrative follows a heartless money-grubber from 1927 to 1934, the Jazz Age to the Great Depression. Go-getter Joe Martin (Douglas Fairbanks, Jr.) works for an advertising company whose main client is "Glamour Cream," an expendable consumer product of the 1920s rendered extravagant in the 1930s. The communist screenwriter Lawson laces the play with a venomous hatred for his antihero and the system he prospers under. Compared to Joe Martin, even Rico Bandello enjoys a warm personal life.

The film opens with a Jazz Age prelude, a headline from 1927: Joe has just buried his gangster brother before setting out on a parallel career track in business. He is a dynamic workaholic, but a pathological one, betraying mentor, girlfriend, and business partners. In the last unpersuasive seconds of the film, the likable Fairbanks reveals the kind heart under his sinister skin, but Joe Martin has been a witting tool of capitalism too long to pull off a deathbed conversion.

Less dialectical variations on the gangster film also proliferated in the pre-Code era. Designed to deflect criticism while still retaining the core elements of the genre, adroit screenwriters wedged gangsters into newspaper films, courtroom dramas, and women's melodramas.

Consider, for example, William Wellman's *The Star Witness* (1931), a multiple hybrid, a gangster-cum-courtroom-cum-domestic melodrama. When the family dinner is interrupted by gunshots from the street, the folks go to the window and witness a gangland murder. The killer escapes through the house in plain sight of everyone and assaults the aged grandfather. Asked by the district attorney to testify against the murderer, the family agrees to perform its civic duty, but the spirit of good citizenship wilts when the gangsters brutalize the father and kidnap the child. The one unbowed member of the clan is Grandpa (character actor Chic Sale), a crotchety old Civil War veteran. As the voice of patriotism and xenophobia, Grandpa delivers two shrill harangues against "yellow-bellied back-stabbing foreigners" and insists upon the un-American origins of the gangster menace. "I'll tell you," he wheezes during the climactic trial scene, "a danged, dirty foreigner can crowd an American just so far—*just so far!*" The courtroom bursts into applause.

The inevitable distaff version of the gangster film was *Blondie Johnson* (1933), featuring Joan Blondell in the Rico Bandello role. Almost always, good girls gone bad have been forced to sin by extreme circumstances. Whereas Little Caesar is congenitally bad, period, women go wrong for a reason, usually one in trousers, or in Blondie's case, judicial robes.

When the spunky but penniless Blondie appears before a magistrate, pleading for help on behalf of her sick mother, she seems a nice enough girl. Blondie has tried to find work, but the scarcity of jobs and the paws of brute men foreclose her options. Unmoved, the stern government official brushes aside her pleas. When Blondie returns home, her mother has died of pneumonia. The same fate, she resolves, will not befall her.

Unlike the scheming minx of the bad girl cycle, Blondie relies on her smarts not her body, trading on her looks but not offering sexual favors. She cons men to get ahead, but finally she is a self-made not man-made woman. "I got plans—big plans," she tells a would-be suitor. "And the one thing that don't fit in with them is pants." Like Rico Bandello and Tony Camonte, Blondie Johnson is a criminal visionary with the grit to grab for her dream. Like Rico and Tony too, she is brought down by a romantic fixation. The man she loves has married another and perhaps betrayed her to the police. She assents to his murder, but reconsiders and runs to his rescue. Despite the mayhem and murder each has caused, they are sentenced to a token term of imprisonment of six years. As a woman, Blondie can be redeemed and domesticated by true love. A man would have been gunned down in the last reel.

The violent edge and hard profile of the gangster genre was polished by its wraparound publicity. Even by the elastic standards of motion picture exploitation, the advertising for the "alky and artillery" films ran to lurid excess. Theater lobbies displayed tommy guns and blackjacks. Machine gun fire printed out the ad copy and cast credits on screen trailers. *Little Caesar* bragged of action scenes peppered by real bullets, dodged by an extra glad to risk his life for $25 a day. For a better salary, James Cagney did likewise in *The Public Enemy*, ducking behind a building as a machine gunner trained in the Great War blasted the facade to bits. A quick-thinking exhibitor in Pittsburgh keyed his advertising campaign to the timely triple homicide of the city's bootlegging Volpe brothers—John, James, and Arthur—who had been gunned down hours before the local premiere of *Scarface*. Fearful of rousing the ire of censors, studio ad-pub departments actually had to rein in overzealous exhibitors. "Please don't let the characters in newspaper ads and lobby ballyhoo tote personal artillery," the front office warned Fox Theaters.

Scarface also exploited what was surely the quintessential criminal tie-in of the entire gangster genre. As photography on the film was winding up in 1931, director Howard Hawks engaged in some bracing dialogue with a man described as "a western representative of Capone."

> "The Big Fellow wants to look over your picture. How's chances of arranging it?"
>
> "The Big Shot will have to lay down his money at the box office if he wants to see *Scarface*," replied Hawks levelly.
>
> "Well," said Capone's emissary, "we just wanted to let you know what the Big Fellow said."

Hughes's publicity office gleefully circulated the story and added a calculating embellishment: that Capone vehemently opposed gangster films that depicted underworld characters as "rats" and not "heroes," that indeed Hollywood's courageous exposés of gangsterdom had helped to bring about his downfall. Little wonder, said the publicity release, that Capone was financing agitation against gangster films and maintaining expensive lobbies in state capitals to ban them. Taglines worked the same theme for *The Doorway*

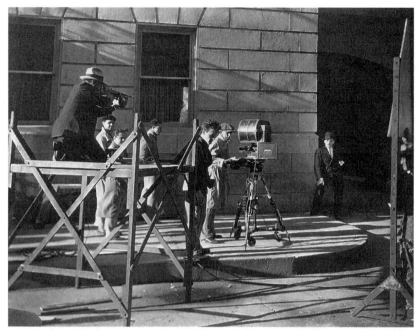

The "alky and artillery" cycle: James Cagney prepares to dodge real bullets in *The Public Enemy* (1931). Director William Wellman appears foreground. (Courtesy of the Museum of Modern Art)

---

to Hell ("the picture Gangland dared Hollywood to make!"), *Little Caesar* ("the picture Gangland defied Hollywood to make!"), and *The Last Parade* (1931) ("the most terrific indictment of racketeering ever presented!"). According to this line of defense, the moral guardians were giving aid and comfort to the gangsters by joining the opposition to gangster films.

To further deflect political heat, the gangster film made fulsome use of the exculpatory preface. Usually in the form of an inscription or precredit epigraph affirming the social import and theological worth of the forthcoming motion picture photoplay, sometimes articulated from the screen by a Voice of Morality cloaked in judicial robes or wrapped in clerical collar, it was a sorrowful admission that, in certain regions of America, picturesque violence erupts and unregenerate criminals reign. As a public service and cautionary notice, it is the sad but necessary duty of the motion picture industry to portray a tale of violence and immorality, with as much tact as possible given the need to be faithful to the sordid facts of the case. *Scarface* sought instant exculpation with its official subtitle "The Shame of the Nation." Taking no chances, *The Public Enemy* posted a double warning, bracketing the film with an exculpatory preface ("It is the ambition of the authors of "The Public Enemy" to honestly depict an environment that exists today in a certain strata of American life, rather than glorify the hoodlum or the criminal") *and* an exculpatory afterword (" 'The Public Enemy' is not a man, nor is it a character—it is a problem that sooner or later WE, the public, must face").

The simple expedient of splashing a crime-does-not-pay homily onto seventy-five minutes of blazing mayhem was the most reliable alibi: Rico Bandello is machine-gunned by the police, Tom Powers is killed by rivals, and Tony Camonte is cut down on the steps of his fortress. "It is the function of the dramatist to show the futility and peril of wrong doing and the triumph of good," declared Warner Bros. director Roy Del Ruth before directing *Larceny Lane* (1931). "The point is that criminal types should not be glorified. The relentless fate which comes to him as a logical result of his career should be emphatically pointed out, and if that is done there can be no bad effects." "I have no excuse for a film glorifying a gangster," declared Will Hays, denying Hollywood did any such thing. "The proper treatment of crime as a social fact or dramatic motive is the inalienable right of a free press or an unshackled stage or screen. Success of self-regulation is shown on many screens in the words: 'Crime does not pay.' "

Not even the censors fell for so transparent a ploy. Few commentators were able to resist some variation on the line that although crime might not pay in the gangster film, it surely paid at the box office window. In truth, compared to more law-abiding enterprises, the gangster genre was dependably and sometimes astonishingly profitable. In 1930 gangster themes accounted for an estimated 11 percent of studio output, with the figure jumping to 20 percent in early 1931 on the strength of *Little Caesar* and *The Public Enemy*. *The Public Enemy*, *Little Caesar*, *Smart Money* (1931), *City Streets* (1931), *Scarface*—these were some of the few bright spots in a bleak season. At Warner Brothers' Strand Theater in New York, *Little Caesar* played eleven performances on a nineteen-hour grind, daily from 9:30 A.M. to 4:30 A.M. the following morning. "Taken all in all," *Variety* estimated, "the gang cycle has been more productive commercially than any other so-called cycle in years." Under the circumstances, confirmed the *Hollywood Reporter*, "exhibitors throughout the country are ready to take their chances with the small minority of their patrons who have squawked the loudest when shown anything with a gangster element in it."

However, in the wake of the furor over *Scarface* and a glut of less worthy product, two forces converged to cut short the first life of the gangster film, at least in its pure form as a tale built around an urban, ethnic outlaw shooting his way to the top of the criminal heap. First, the protests against gangster films emanated not just from a culturally isolated cadre of moral guardians and state censors but from a wide range of public opinion and editorial commentary. Widespread outrage and "newspaper tirades against gangster features" compelled Will Hays in the summer of 1932 to inveigh against the genre publicly and to communicate same to studio chieftains privately. The result was a tacit agreement that "there would be no more sawed off shotgun stuff." Second, the cycle had run its course. "The major industry quit gangster themes because the public just tired of them," *Variety* asserted in 1933. "There was never any real dictum against underworld material properly handled. Commercial more than the moral angle was responsible for sudden gangster surcease." Moreover, it was mainly a domestic taste; overseas, the bent version of the American dream tended to flop.

In the pre-Code era, an edict from Hays alone might have been circumvented or ignored had the gangster cycle continued to be artistically vital and commercially profitable. But when vociferous opposition from politicians, newspaper editors, and large segments of the public combined with a sharp downturn in the box office mandate, the gangster film became more trouble than it was worth.

Nonetheless, not until the creation of the Production Code Administration would the gangster genre be effectively rounded up and neutered. In 1934, two years after the production hiatus wrought by *Scarface*, the classic gangster triad and myriad hybrid crime films still remained at large, playing in small towns and second-run theaters, a continuing presence constituting "a definite menace" in the eyes of law enforcement. Days before the MPPDA met to revamp the enforcement mechanism for the Code on June 13, 1934, an ominous front-page article in *Variety* helped spur studio executives to action. "Infuriated federal officials" were "getting ready to move in much more militantly" on Hollywood. The Labor Department thought gangster films bred criminality in children; the Justice Department believed gangster films "encouraged general disrespect for police and [a] lenient attitude toward thugs." Though acknowledging that the genre opened with an exculpatory preface and closed with a crime-does-not-pay warning,

> Government psychologists and criminologists maintain that American youth isn't concerned with such abstract ideas and principles, but is primarily interested in seeing the big-shot toughies have wads of dough, swell apartments, fast cars, and plenty of girl friends. . . . [The] feeling is

that Hollywood's efforts to conceal [the] technique of murderers, gangsters, and other villains are essentially minor and that youth with criminal tendencies will supply the details themselves if they are inspired with the basic idea that crime is entertaining, glamorous, and at least temporarily profitable.

Moreover, in the lineup of sinister influences in American popular culture, Hollywood had been named Media Enemy Number One:

> The Federal reaction is nothing to be trifled with, judging from the passion displayed by officials concerned about the film matter. Instead of merely regarding pictures as *one* of the influences to be combated in the crime situation, they are practically in a frenzy in condemning films. [They] admit newspapers are to blame in part, but are hesitant about tackling the press and hopeful of more willing cooperation than has been forthcoming from pix.

The ad hoc censorship of the gangster film that became systematic in 1934 culminated a long, prohibitionist campaign from a broad spectrum of government officials, academics, and opinion leaders. Criticism from one expert source indicated just how widespread the consensus was. On the eve of his sentencing for tax evasion in 1931, Al Capone weighed in against the deleterious influence of the genre he had done so much to inspire. "These gang pictures—that's terrible kid stuff. Why, they ought to take all of them and throw them in the lake," Capone told newsmen. "They're doing nothing but harm to the younger element of the country. I don't blame the censors for trying to bar them. Now, you take all these youngsters who go to the movies. Well, these gang movies are making a lot of kids want to be tough guys and they don't serve any useful purpose." Clad in black silk pajamas, holding forth from his plush Chicago hotel suite, Capone was the very image of the screen image he condemned.

Men Behind Bars: The Prison Film

Where the gangster was mobile, the convict was trapped; where the gangster was rushing toward death, the prisoner was digging his way to freedom. Escape over the wall and riot in the cellblock were his fated destinations, either one being an end-reel burst of liberating violence. In some ways, the prisoner in stripes was more unnerving than the gangster in pinstripes, for his crim-inality, though caged, was not subdued. He did his stretch with a stoic digni-ty and existential élan. In the final reel, before the long march to the electric chair, the condemned killer ate a hearty last meal, bid a brusque farewell to his cell mates, cracked wise at the warden, brushed aside support from the guards, and exited leaving a clean smell. "If I can't live the way I want, then at least let me die when I want," snarls Clark Gable before striding into eter-nity at the end of *Manhattan Melodrama.* "C'mon, warden—let's go."

Like the gangster film, the prison film bespoke insurrection, under the eyes of guards and closed in by concrete architecture, but never quite suppressed. During the worst years of the Great Depression, life behind bars seemed to exert a certain perverse appeal for free men facing an open-ended term of economic entrapment. Viewed from outside the big house, an environment with commodious shelter, three squares, and no breadwinner responsibilities might be worth going over the wall *into.*

In a nation on the brink of chaos, the prison genre also reflected a wary attention to the mechanisms of social control. The expedient death sen-tences meted out on screen accurately mirrored a conveyer-belt justice system that brooked no undue consideration of due process. In *The Star Witness* the prosecuting attorney allows ninety days from indictment of suspect to execution of same. It was a conservative estimate. On February 15, 1933, a nihilist immigrant named Giuseppe Zangara shot Chicago may-or Anton Cermak in an attempt on FDR's life in Miami, Florida. When the mayor died on March 6, the assassin was indicted for first degree mur-der within ten hours. On March 20, he was electrocuted. The prison films were cautionary reminders that the state retained its power to move with alacrity on the domestic tranquillity front if not on the economic pros-perity front.

From the other side of the social contract, the quality of modern penol-ogy fostered public concern, even outrage, over the methods of crime and punishment in America, reviving an interest in prison reform and life behind bars that had lapsed since the Progressive era. On April 21, 1930, a fire broke out at the Ohio State Penitentiary. Fearing a mass escape, guards refused to unlock the cellblocks and over three hundred inmates died in the blaze, most from suffocation, some burned alive. That same year, two commercially suc-cessful and critically acclaimed prison-set melodramas played on Broadway, *The Last Mile* by John Wexley and *Criminal Code* by Martin Falvin. Thus cued, no fewer than seven studios soon had prison melodramas in the pro-duction pipeline, a list that included MGM's *The Big House,* Warner Broth-

Domestic tranquillity: the convicts line up in the urban prison film *The Big House* (1930). (Courtesy of the Museum of Modern Art)

ers' *Numbered Men*, Paramount's *Shadow of the Law*, Columbia's *The Criminal Code*, and Raystone's *Convict's Code*.

The prison genre served time in two types of correctional facilities and visual landscapes. Prisoners were either caged or chained, placed in the confines of the big house, a stern bureaucratic institution sterile and modern, or on the chain gang, a medieval system in the open air, with straw bosses, mules, and bloodhounds, in the rural South. If the former institution might boast a paternal, reform-minded warden, the latter was a hellhole under a blistering sun and an overseer brandishing a whip.

In the first type of prison film, the orchestration of masses of men recalls the choreography and mise-en-scène of *Metropolis* (1926), Fritz Lang's Weimar vision of an industrial dystopia. All attired in identical gray prison uniforms, soulless automatons march in lockstep, their metronomic footsteps trudging on the soundtrack. In long shot, even the star actors are impossible to discern. In close-up, though, the inmates are regular fellows, almost affable while walking the prison yard or chewing the fat in the cell ("What are you in for, kid?"). The moral perspective frankly accepts the codes of prison life, above all the schoolyard injunction never to rat out a comrade to the forces of authority.

MGM's *The Big House* (1930) is the first true prison film and the genre prototype. The frightened perspective of Ken Marlowe (Robert Montgomery), a rabbity young man serving six years for manslaughter in a drunk-driving case, serves as orientation to life inside the walls. After a lecture from the warden (Lewis Stone, MGM's in-house fount of patriarchal sagacity), the regimentation begins: fingerprinting, mug shot, the surrender of civilian clothes and personal tokens, and the issuing of an ill-fitting prison uniform, a ritualistic cleansing before immersion into the world behind bars.

Marlowe's cell mates are Butch (Wallace Beery), a personable if hot-tempered murderer, and John Morgan (Chester Morris), a stand-up inmate inured to the ways of the joint and imprisoned for the nonviolent crime of forgery. The film surprises by making young Marlowe the villain of the piece. He will not learn the codes of confinement and reform himself but will become the most despicable of prisoners: an informer, a coward, a man who betrays his friends and turns hysterical in the final crash-out.

Double-crossed by Marlowe, Morgan is thrown into solitary confinement, where sound and image work in concert to render his isolation. A long take on the dungeon corridor measures the passage of time. After prison guards toss Morgan into the cell, the camera stays locked on the stark tableau, a hall with cells on each side. The lights dim and the soundtrack falls silent. And the image remains as still as a photograph—no cutaways, no pull-in, just a stationary and unchanging view of the prison corridor. After what seems an eternity, Butch's voice rings out and a conversation ensues between Butch and Morgan, with the image still locked and stationary, their voices mixed in with the maddened screams of less stoical inmates.

To ventilate the stifling atmosphere and break up the single-sex monotony, exterior locations and visits from women must enliven the claustrophobia of the prison film. Thus Morgan escapes and drops in on Marlowe's sister, who cannot find it in her heart to turn him in. Courting the girl and recapture, the fugitive sticks around more than he should. During their goodbye scene, the pair embraces while, backscreen, a squad of detectives swoops in.

Back in the big house, Morgan resolves to go straight, but he remains quiet about Butch's plans for a huge prison break ("I'm no rat"). Marlowe is the rat; he squeals to the warden. When the inmates overpower the guards and rush through the gate, the warden greets them with withering machine gun fire. The prisoners retreat into the prison and make a desperate stand against superior firepower. Butch threatens to "bump off every screw," but the warden will not negotiate. "I'll see them in hell first. Let 'em have it." The machine gun barks and Butch retaliates by shooting a guard. The nearly nonstop gunfire on the soundtrack subsides after army tanks break through the gate and the inmates are beaten back amidst a cloud of tear gas. In a final showdown, Butch and Morgan shoot each other but reconcile before Butch expires. Morgan receives a pardon and plans to take off for "the islands" and start a new life on "government land." Outside the big house, the land of opportunity offers none.

In addition to freedom from wage-earner worries, open-minded male bonding was a singular compensation of life behind bars. In *20,000 Years in Sing Sing* (1933), based on the marvelously titled 1932 memoir by warden Lewis E. Lawes and directed by Michael Curtiz, the multiethnic camaraderie and egalitarian ethos of cellblock life flourishes within an institution dispensing firm but fair treatment. The death row companions of Tom Connors (Spencer Tracy) sound off like a protean World War II platoon. As a dim-witted southern boy grabs his harmonica for the long march to the chair, he passes an Irishman, an African-American, and an Italian ("Bon giorno!"). The integration of African-Americans occurs with relative ease in prison, an aberrant environment beyond the bonds of Jim Crow. As the warden tells Connors's shyster lawyer, "People on the outside are supposed to be created free and equal, but they aren't. In here, they really are. One inmate is just as good as another inmate but no better."

Not every Hollywood prison was an oasis from the barren vistas of the Great Depression. If the big house offered a kind of security against the cold winds on the outside, the chain gang system of penology warned of lower circles of hell within America. Sensational and all too true reports of brutality and torture in the rural prison system of the Deep South splashed across the headlines of tabloid papers in the North throughout the 1930s, especially when some unfortunate inmate died in a sweat box or from a beating. Given the stark barbarism of the chain gang system, the penal preachment yarn could afford to be uncompromising and outspoken. *I Am a Fugitive from a Chain Gang* (1932) "will make us some enemies," admitted an unapologetic Jack Warner, but he stood behind the taglines ("Warner Bros.' defiant masterpiece will have conscience-stricken America talking in its sleep!"). Preaching the abolition of the chain gang system was a safe sentiment, not a controversial position.

Medieval conditions: hardcore con Richard Dix defies the screws while his brother bakes in the sweatbox in *Hell's Highway* (1932). (Courtesy of the Museum of Modern Art)

Three chain gang films—RKO's *Hell's Highway* (1932), Warner Brothers' *I Am a Fugitive from a Chain Gang*, and Universal's *Laughter in Hell* (1933)— competed for a piece of the prison reform movement. Even before FDR's New Deal, Hollywood's depiction of the two types of institutions—the rural prison of the southern states and the federal or reformed state prison of the North—foretold the shift in power and sympathy away from state autonomy and toward national authority. In the rural prison film, police thugs in the employ of a corrupt state overturned the moral hierarchy of guard and inmate. Convicted murderers were ennobled and the right of insurrection upheld.

RKO's *Hell's Highway* inaugurated the convict film cycle. A soundtrack of black voices moans a chain gang tune over a montage of tabloid headlines ("Prison Guards Accused of Murder as Tortured Youth Dies in Sweat Box"; "Convicts Describe Brutality Like Dark Ages"). For once, the printed preface seeks no exculpation: "Dedicated to the early end of the conditions portrayed here—which though a throwback to the Middle Ages actually exist today." Along *Hell's Highway* are chains, whippings, sweat boxes, sadistic guards, corrupt wardens, and a fashion innovation in convict attire: a bull's eye target painted on the back of each prisoner's uniform. Hardcore con Duke Ellis (Richard Dix) leads a convict ensemble that includes a would-be Romeo who adorns his bunk with pictures of his girlfriends Bette Davis and Greta Garbo ("Sure, I know 'em!"), a "nance" cook who bats his eyes at the guards, and a Bible-quoting polygamist, Matthew the Hermit. "It takes a lot of nerve to rob a bank," Matthew says to Duke. "It takes a lot of backbone to keep three wives happy," replies Duke slyly. The inventory of men and equipment, and the rough hierarchy of importance, is scrawled on a blackboard:

93   Men—white
21   Negroes
32   Mules
 4   Wagons

Segregated in their own barracks, a gang of black convicts acts as a Greek chorus, commenting on the action with work tunes and wisecracks ("Yes, suh, boss—mules cost $40 a head and convicts don't cost nothin' "). In a striking montage sequence, director John Cromwell employs still illustrations, sketched in charcoal by a black hand, to render a funeral scene.

As an unscrupulous country road constructor exploits convict labor, the guards cover up two murders (of a young prisoner in a sweat box and an adulterous wife). After a long train of abuses, the prisoners exert their rights of revolution, grabbing rifles from the prison storehouse, shooting up the guards, and setting the hated camp ablaze. Going soft in the last reel, *Hell's Highway* bows to state power in the person of a reformist governor and references to "state laws passed to stop this kind of thing [abuse of prisoners]." But in the survival of the hard-nosed con Duke and the imminent parole of his brother Johnny, the fires of insurrection have been justified. The original version of *Hell's Highway* ended with Duke turning his back to escape, knowing full well he would be shot. When preview audiences in Los Angeles frowned, RKO permitted the convict hero to survive.

The most famous of the rural prison farm films is a certifiable classic that retains its power to grip audiences by the throat, *I Am a Fugitive from a Chain Gang*, directed by Mervyn LeRoy from the true-life memoir by Robert E. Burns. With the first-person title stressing the present-tense experience of a living hell, the film rewinds the 1920s from the perspective of the early 1930s, looking back, only yesterday, as it tells a tale of unjust imprisonment and official malice, before closing with one of the bleakest wrap-ups in Hollywood history.

Transformed by the crucible of combat, returning veteran James Allen (Paul Muni) finds the Great War has changed his vision of the American dream. The drab routine of a "stupid insignificant job" holds no allure for him, so he takes to the open road. The camera pans a map of the United States and follows his search for work through Boston, New Orleans, Oshkosh, riding the rails to St. Louis, walking down dusty tracks, a montage that speaks more to the present reality than popular memory of the 1920s. On the bum in a flophouse, Allen follows a hobo into a diner to mooch a meal, but the man pulls a gun and forces Allen to assist him in the robbery. Captured on the spot, he is swiftly sentenced to ten years on a chain gang, speed and callousness being the defining qualities of the criminal justice system.

On Allen's first day on the chain gang, the men are awakened before dawn, fed rancid slop, and mustered out into trucks. Allen scans the faces of his fellow white convicts and of the black prisoners segregated in another truck, and then looks over at a line of mules yoked together. All are dumb brutes in a naturalistic equality—white men and black men, men and mules, all alike chained to the same fate. At the end of the backbreaking day, the system inflicts more punishment. Rendered through shadow and sound (the silhouette of the overseer, the coiled crack of the leather strap, and the pathetic whimper of the victim), director LeRoy's image of torture conceals the worst of it but reveals enough for the picture to be indelible in the mind's eye. When Allen is punished, the strap cracks but Allen doesn't, a silent sign of his determination and grit.

With the help of a sympathetic "big buck" of a black convict, Allen escapes and makes his way to Chicago, the epicenter of gangsterdom, now a site for the lawful pursuit of happiness in a civil society. Here, like Tom Holmes in *Heroes for Sale* (1933), Allen prospers via the traditional American blueprint, a slow and steady progress up the economic ladder. Blotting out the memory of Harold Lloyd and other instant successes of the 1920s, the 1930s recast the past decade as a zone where, through dint of hard work and rigorous self-improvement, a man can get ahead incrementally but surely. A montage sequence tracks his upward mobility, showing a succession of pay raises as Allen ascends year by year—1925, 1926, 1927—from $4 to $8 to $12 a day. A business associate tries to coax Allen to relax a little. "All work and no play—" "Makes Jack," interrupts the apostle of the self-made man.

When Allen's past catches up with him, he decides to waive extradition, trusting in the word of the state to grant him a pardon. But the state reneges

The rural prison film: Paul Muni in a publicity shot from *I Am a Fugitive from a Chain Gang* (1932). (Courtesy of the Museum of Modern Art)

on the deal and Allen is thrown back into the living hell of the chain gang. "The state's promise didn't mean anything—it was all lies!" Allen shouts to the sanctimonious cleric who is also his brother. "They're the ones who should be in chains—not we!"

The second time around, chain gang life is worse—not because of any escalation in institutional brutality but because of the calculated betrayal of the state and the open-ended nature of the new sentence. Told he will not receive his promised pardon, Allen cracks. The camera focuses on Muni's stricken face and his clenched fists as he collapses back on his cot. The prisoner of 1932 is more beaten down than the prisoner of 1922: what was merely a tragic misunderstanding has become state-sanctioned malice.

Allen escapes again, nearly deranged and beyond caring. This time, the camera doesn't follow him in his journey through what is now Depression America, but a flurry of newspaper headlines registers the passage of time ("What Has Become of James Allen—Is He Too Just Another Forgotten Man?"). The montage dissolves into the sleek environs of his fiancée's carport where, like an apparition, Allen emerges from the shadows to bid a last goodbye. Haunted, feverish, his face shows no trace of the other incarnations of James Allen, the hopeful war veteran, the determined prisoner, or the prosperous businessman. "How do you live?" asks his girl. Allen's parting shot signals a shocking blackout. "I steal!" he rasps from the pitch darkness. The sound of his frightened footsteps scampers away on a black screen. The End.

The jolting blackout that closed *I Am a Fugitive from a Chain Gang* rattled audiences more forcefully than any film ending of its time. In his 1974 autobiography, director LeRoy claimed the idea came to him when a fuse blew on the set and plunged the soundstage into darkness. During an interview in 1933, however, LeRoy told another story, saying he filmed no fewer than three different endings. The first version showed James Allen crossing over the border between the United States and Canada and, looking over his shoulder back toward America, muttering, "Nuts to you!" In the second version, the "I steal!" line was shot with the lights full up. Finally, LeRoy remembered "how an audience loves a black out, how the words a scene blacks out on linger in their memory." In truth, LeRoy and Warner Brothers probably never considered so unpatriotic a kiss-off as "Nuts to you!" But neither did they compromise the dark trajectory of the tale with a picture of James Allen happy, sane, and free of chains. The last words and final darkness portended no hope, no future, and no morality for this unforgettable man swallowed by the abyss of Great Depression America, just a brutal logic in the only career path left open: "I steal!"

So as not to indict the state of Georgia by name and thereby shield the studio from lawsuits from Georgia prison officials, Warner Brothers changed the title of Burns's book, *I Am a Fugitive from a Georgia Chain Gang*. However, everyone knew that Georgia was the unnamed location, and the film coyly reveals as much. When Allen surrenders to a state official with a southern drawl, the camera traces his movement southward by scanning down over a map of the United States and fading out before hitting the Georgia state line. The lack of specificity actually expanded the reach of the political indictment beyond a single regional site and onto the whole overarching system.

The last of the chain gang troika, Universal's *Laughter in Hell*, directed by Edward L. Cahn from a script by Tom Reed, sounds provocative, but unfortunately no print of the film seems extant. Descriptions in the trade press are tantalizing. The normally upright Pat O'Brien plays a railroad engineer who kills his unfaithful wife and her lover. Justly condemned to life on the chain gang, he meets up with the dead man's brother, the prison warden, who turns his life into a living hell short on laughter. Besides floggings and lynchings, the prisoners are forced to dig graves for the victims of a yellow fever outbreak in a neighboring town. One night, they revolt, kill the warden, and launch a mass escape. While on the run, O'Brien picks up the beautiful Gloria Stuart, "orphaned by the plague, and the two make their way to safety and the film's happy ending."

Laughter in Hell contained one inflammatory sequence that was singled out for special comment. Noting that "little has been glossed over in attempting a graphic picture of [chain gang] conditions [and] methods," *Motion Picture Herald* zeroed in on what it termed "rather strong medicine for certain audiences," namely the moment "when four Negroes are seen taken from their box-like cells and hanged from the limb of a tree while other convicts look on." The "certain audience" referred to was that segment of American moviegoers for whom lynching was more a palpable physical threat than a motion picture fantasy. Yet Vere E. Johns, the film critic for the African-American weekly the *New Age*, argued that the "strong medicine" of the depiction was salutary, not so much for blacks who knew the score but for whites who didn't. Disagreeing with a friend who condemned the sequence as an incitement to anti-Negro violence, he praised *Laughter in Hell* for exposing and condemning the practice of lynching in the states of the former Confederacy. "Any picture that will tend to lessen the brutality of these savages in the South should be encouraged," he asserted. Interestingly, the *New Age* saw the scene differently from *Motion Picture Herald*. According to Johns, black *and* white prisoners were lynched together in *Laughter in Hell*. Moreover, he counted not four but nine lynch victims, an echo perhaps of the nine Scottsboro boys then facing execution in Alabama. Johns also noted the popularity of the chain gang films with Harlem audiences, the resonance of chains and liberation for African-Americans being too transparent to need elaboration.

Like the gangster genre, the prison film spawned offshoots on the convention: distaff prison movies (*Ladies of the Big House*, 1931), juvenile prison movies (*The Mayor of Hell*, 1933), and loony parodies (Wheeler and Woolsey's *Hold 'Em Jail* [1932], where the comedy duo "turn the Big House into the Bug House"). Though the women-behind-bars films exude an undeniable prurient appeal (trademark scenes: girls in showers, girls in scanty prisonwear, and girls fighting), the juvenile prison film better reflects the cultural moment. It exposes the fears of a bewildered society no longer able to guide and restrain the next generation.

The juvenile prison film tackled what was perceived to be the burgeoning crisis of underage criminality. Whereas the problem of the younger generation during the Jazz Age was cultural, a youth rebellion against Victorian rigidity, the problem of the younger generation in the 1930s was economic, a protest against dead-end options that exploded in disruptive, sometimes lawless behavior. By modern standards for teenage predators, the juvenile delinquents nurtured most devotedly by Warner Brothers seem more like scalawags than sociopaths. If not paid twenty-five cents in protection money, they vandalize cars.

Being in the vanguard of dysfunction, the young sent out early warning signs of the deeper illness in American culture. In the 1930s, experts offered two explanations for adolescent social pathology: the streets or the home. If the latter, it was typically the weak father who warranted the blame, mothers being sacrosanct in an age where Mom was still a goddess not an "-ism." More often, though, a youngster was led astray by the bad influences and stunted circumstances of his environment. The mean streets and the tenement stairs bred disrespect, despair, and deviance. In this, the fault lay not in the younger generation but in the older generation for making such a mess of things. Unlike later generations of juvenile delinquents and youth rebels, whose psychological maladies and cultural alienation perplexed and enraged their elders, adults of the Great Depression understood perfectly why their children were acting up. Given the present, who could blame them for behaving as if they had no future?

In lowering the age of consent for the prison film, Archie Mayo's *The Mayor of Hell* showed that the real problem of the younger generation was the adult world. When a shoplifting heist goes wrong for a gang of street toughs, a kindly magistrate has no alternative but to sentence them to a Dickensian hellhole of a reform school, overseen by the malevolent Mr. Thompson (Dudley Digges, the designated sadist in the Warner Bros. stock company). He beats the boys senseless and feeds them slop despite the social reform sympathies of pretty young nurse Dorothy Griffith (Madge Evans). During the first night in juvenile stir, the boys stare blankly at their spartan bunks. Skinny, the tubercular runt of the group, lies in bed next to his hungry African-American companion, Smoke. "I'm scared," Skinny moans. Smoke's black hand reaches over from offscreen and clasps the white hand in comfort.

James Cagney enters as racketeer Patsy Gargan, a ward heeler who as a lark takes the job of reform school commissioner. Bitten by the reform impulse, he ejects Thompson and institutes Miss Griffith's progressive program of nutritious food, self-government, and personal hygiene. The underage polis proves its maturity when a Jewish youth tries to finagle a candy bar from the boys' commissary. "Ich bin ein Yid ["I'm a Jew"]," the lad says fraternally in Yiddish to the Jewish boy behind the counter, Izzy (Sidney Miller, the designated Jewish kid in the Warner Bros. stock company). But Izzy rebuffs the appeal to religious solidarity. Undeterred, the boy grabs the chocolate and runs off. Izzy shouts after him, "I'll get you, you *goniff* [thief]!" Later, with Smoke acting as defense attorney, the boys' judicial system convicts the candy bar crook.

Having neglected his ward heeling back home for his juvenile wards in the home, Patsy Gargan must leave the reform school, whereupon Thompson returns things to status quo ante. In an act of premeditated murder, he locks the sickly Skinny in the cooler. On his deathbed, Skinny opens his eyes, whispers "Mom," and expires.

With Gargan and nurse Griffith gone, the boys erupt into an insurrection worthy of the denizens of *The Big House*. Bearing torches, they attack the guards, overpower Thompson, and haul him before their juvenile justice system. The courtroom howls for vengeance. Terrified, Thompson crashes through a window and tries vainly to escape over a barn roof. The youth mob sets fire to the barn and Thompson falls to his death, onto barbed wire and into a pig sty. Gargan restores order but exacts no retribution on the boys: the murder of Thompson is forgotten, written off as rough justice.

For adult cons and juvenile delinquents alike, the prison film presumed institutional injustice as a matter of course and redress by insurrection as an inalienable right. The advertising campaigns underscored the tyranny of the system and the raw brutality inflicted upon the inmates. "Sugar coated? Hell, no! It's real!" screamed the ads for *Hell's Highway*. "Brutal and true! The clank of leg irons! The swish of the snake whip! The crack of rifle shots aimed at the men with targets on their backs! You will ask, 'Can this be America?' " A Dallas theater owner playing *I Am a Fugitive from a Chain Gang* splashed his marquee with the logo "Ten years ago we'd be jailed for showing this picture—Now nobody fears the unvarnished truth!" He also placed torture implements on display in the lobby, including a whipping post, sweat box, perforated lash, and regulation ball and chain.

During the production of *I Am a Fugitive from a Chain Gang*, Warner Brothers tantalized Georgia law enforcement with reports that Robert

Burns was prowling around the Burbank studio, "literally a fugitive and a wanderer" and "living in constant terror of extradition to the state from whose chain gang he escaped some years ago." When Burns was captured in Newark, New Jersey, an event that received front-page coverage as *I Am a Fugitive from a Chain Gang* went into wide release, Warner Brothers was not displeased.

Faced with such criminal uprisings, nervous sentries of law and order censored prison films on the grounds that the incendiary riots on the cellblock and the thrilling flights from baying bloodhounds seemed to justify a kindred spirit of insurrection outside the walls. The state of Ohio, site of the era's most horrific inmate massacre, banned *The Big House*. Elsewhere, state censorship boards responded with typical idiosyncrasy. The prison riot in *Numbered Men* (1930) caused considerable controversy, but not the uprising in *The Bad One* (1930) because "although vividly presented [it] takes place on an island in a foreign country" and was thus too distant to be taken as domestic incitement.

In their resistance to the prison film, fearful wardens of civil authority found an ally in the most influential segment of the motion picture audience. As the only Hollywood genre aimed almost exclusively at men, the prison film targeted a fickle audience. Not even gangster films or war films were so relentlessly male-dominated, so casually cruel, so bereft of boy-girl romance. The prison film "does not interest or please women at all," reported an exhibitor, "the rough and brutal stuff only makes women talk about a poor show." *Motion Picture Herald* cautioned producers against overdoing "the gruesomeness of certain of the chain gang methods and devices for fear of alienating the feminine portion of the patronage in particular." Downbeat by definition, preachy by temperament, masculine by necessity, the prison genre helped persuade Hollywood that social conscience cinema didn't pay the bills as handily as social forgetfulness cinema. "My personal opinion is that *I Am a Fugitive from a Chain Gang* would do 25% more business if it had a happy ending," complained a theater owner. "Everyone knows that Burns has been pardoned and outside of Georgia is a free man. Exhibitors should be given a choice of having a happy or unhappy ending."

7

Comic Timing

Cracking Wise and Wising Up

In 1933, the year that Mae West pursed her lips in *She Done Him Wrong* ("I'm one of the finest women that ever walked the streets") and Groucho Marx raised eyebrows in *Duck Soup* ("Remember, you're fighting for this woman's honor—which is probably more than she ever did"), the word *wisecrack* first entered the Oxford English Dictionary. Though the deployment of the sly one-liner in vaudeville routines, radio byplay, and legitimate theater well predated its formal induction by the OED, the wisecrack thrived in the talk-mad environs of pre-Code Hollywood. Cracking wise become the domi-nant verbal inflection and conversational style in voice-over commentary, screen dialogue, and advertising taglines. A refugee from Nazi Germany, the aspiring screenwriter Billy Wilder listened with a second-language ear for puns, patter, and vernacular that would make all his Hollywood films a veri-table dictionary of American slang.

At its best, the wisecrack was a bright volley besotted with language, the streetsmart American cousin to the droll British witticisms dropped through clenched teeth by Oscar Wilde and Noel Coward. With so many screen voices still tremulous and tongue-tied, the sharp retorts, surreal nonsequiturs, and loony wordplay provided a unique pleasure of the talking, as opposed to the musical, cinema. For every moviegoer still grieving for the quiet reveries of the silent screen, many more welcomed the loquacious jabbering of the articulate motion picture. "It's hard to make clear to people who didn't live through the transition how sickly and unpleasant many of those 'artistic' silent pictures were—how you wanted to scrape off all the dust and sentiment," recalled film critic Pauline Kael. "Filmed plays without the actors' voices, and with the deadening delays for the heterogeneous audience to read the dialogue, were an abomination." Sound, Kael continued, made it possible for a generation of fast-talking playwrights and fast-typing journalists to "liberate the movies into a new kind of contemporaneity."

That new kind of contemporaneity was actually an echo of the past. In the 1920s flippant flappers and an incivil "younger generation" looked askance at the Jazz Age, fashioning an ironic, cutting-edge style new to the comic spirit in America. On the highbrow end, the self-conscious wits of the Algonquin Round Table unfurled killer bon mots at each other and anyone else who wandered into the crossfire. Among the lower orders too, the snappy exchanges and leering prattle of burlesque and vaudeville skits trained ears to prick up for double meanings and unexpected twists.

Especially on the legitimate stage and in the pages of the *New Yorker*, the stance was smug, self-satisfied, and fashionably alienated, itself a word that entered discourse around the same time as the wisecrack. In this linguistic atmosphere, the most countercultural literary character of the 1920s was F. Scott Fitzgerald's romantic dreamer Jay Gatsby, the idealist among a generation of hardened ironists, a man out of his time and doomed by his innocence. The 1920s wordsmiths who came to the screen with sound—Ben Hecht, Gene Fowler, Charles MacArthur, Herman J. Mankiewicz, Mae West—specialized in the modern attitude of distancing oneself from experience with a glib line and stabbing the enemy with a verbal dagger.

Throughout the early 1930s, the wisecracking protagonist, male and female, was everywhere in American cinema. Yet behind the smirking commentary was a forced, frightened edge, less serenely contented and above it all than seriously vitriolic and frazzled, just this side of blasphemy and breakdown. Informed in 1933 that former president Calvin Coolidge had suddenly died, Alice Roosevelt Longworth didn't miss a beat: "How can they tell?" Whether muttered under the breath or spat out angrily, an undercurrent of anxiety seeped into the wisecrack. Humor has always done double duty as both shield and sword, a defense against misfortune and an assault on the fortunate, but in the early years of the Great Depression, it voiced a resentment that barely cloaked the fear between the lines.

In *American Humor*, a study of the national temper and the comic mind published in the very unfunny year of 1931, the critic Constance Rourke argued that the deepest wellsprings of American comedy had always been unifying and conciliatory. "Humor has been a fashioning instrument in America, cleaving its way through the national life, holding tenaciously to the spread elements in that life," Rourke asserted. "Its objective—the unconscious objective of a disunited people—has seemed to be that of creating fresh bounds, a new unity, the semblance of a society and the rounded complexion of an American type." As a partisan of the better humored strains of American humor, Rourke looked upon the shift in temperament as no laughing matter. "The solvent of humor has often become a jaded formula, the comic rebound automatic—'laff that off'—so that only the uneasy habit of laughter appears, with an acute sensitivity and insecurity beneath it as though too much had been laughed away." Or perhaps too much could not be laughed away. "Whole phases of comedy have become empty," bemoaned Rourke. "The comic rejoinder has become every man's tool." But the wisecrack phase was not empty of meaning. In such times, not only could every man use a good laugh, he could get it by fighting back with a weapon at the tip of his tongue.

After the election of FDR, after the enforcement of the Code, the dangerous wisecrack diminished in frequency and potency, exiled to the provinces of screwball comedy and backstage musicals. Emblematic was the career move by short story writer, drama critic, and raconteur Robert Benchley. A humorist who had more than held his own during the razor-sharp dueling at the Algonquin Round Table, Benchley starred in a series of popular short subjects that recast him as warmly likeable, befuddled everyman, winning an Academy Award for the instructively titled *How to Sleep* (1935). Frank Capra's heroes in *Mr. Deeds Goes to Town* (1936) and *Mr. Smith Goes to Washington* (1939) personify the same transition in verbal taste. As wisecracking cynics swirl around them, Longfellow Deeds and Jefferson Smith drawl deliberately and sincerely, innocent of irony. Under Hoover, cynicism was a way of life; under FDR, idealism was the watchword. Hollywood still talked a good game, but it was a new game, where the honored players were less apt to crack wise than to "wise up": to drop the sophisticated guise and smart-mouth babble and embrace a misty-eyed faith in New Deal America and old-fashioned verities.

COMMENTATORS ON THE ACTION

In the cacophony of voices that competed for attention in American culture in the early 1930s, two of the loudest were heard but not seen. One emanated from the atmosphere itself, the other from the offscreen space of the motion picture. For radio and screen wits, quick and dull alike, filling the dead air became the main objective and shooting off wisecracks the ammunition with the highest caliber. On radio, talk was the coin of the realm, cheaper than music, so the aural medium nourished the verbal shenanigans of solo monologists, comedy duos, and babbling ensembles. On screen, talkers worked in junior partnership with images as voice-over narration. Competing against what was before the eye, they had to speak up boldly to get attention.

Though the wisecrack might break out in any format, it was pandemic in newsreels, sports shorts, and travelogues. An allegedly wry commentary on the action, the flippant, nasal, and pun-laden wisecrack always seemed to be trying too hard to be offhand and witty. Rather than gently amusing auditors, the labored and lame attempts at mirth whacked them over the head.

Newsreel commentators (dubbed "talking reporters") fancied a vocal stance in tune with the report. Since most of what passed for news in the newsreels was transient nonsense anyway, the smirking attitude well fit the action on screen. From clip to clip, the voice-over switched over blithely from tones of somber oration to cheeky irreverence, hoary bombast to sophomoric drivel. "It won't be long before the world's most notorious gangster is only an offensive memory," brays Graham McNamee in a Universal Newspaper Newsreel clip on the conviction of Al Capone for income tax evasion. As a train transporting the gangster to the federal penitentiary in Atlanta pulls out of Chicago, McNamee can't resist cracking "now for a change they're taking *him* for a ride. Let that be a good lesson to you—always be sure and pay your income tax!" Unamused, Martin Quigley at *Motion Picture Herald* suggested that the commentator hold his fire, wisecrack-wise. "McNamee's lines are inclined at times to labor and strain rather seriously after a far-fetched witticism." Warily anticipating the much-ballyhooed newsreel coverage of the solar eclipse of 1932 ("the first important cosmic spectacle since the coming of the sound camera"), Quigley's colleague Terry Ramsaye also pleaded for mercy. "Let us hope that it will not reveal that the music of the spheres is a carillon of dumbbells. We like our eclipses silent, but they'll all be lectured and probably wisecracked."

Other segments of the audience also heard nothing to laugh about. Covering a raucous exhibition match staged by a group of African-American boxers, Pathé News offered the kind of ringside commentary that made 10 percent of its listeners seethe: "It's a case of every darkie for himself! Look at that big buck swinging!" "The talk of these newsreels is no haphazard stuff but a script carefully prepared for synchronization with the film," protested the African-American weekly the *New Age*. "It must be put down as deliberate and studied calumny perpetrated by impertinent fools and countenanced by a careless and inconsiderate executive."

Often the wisecrackers punned to more painful than mirthful effect. Narrators of travelogues and expeditionary films were incorrigible perpetrators of loose talk. Adventurer John Medbury must have searched the world over for the right shot of a native artist to justify the observation that "three months ago, she didn't have a pot to paint on." In *Congorilla* (1932) Martin Johnson scatters tortured banter throughout his lectures on African wildlife. A crocodile yawns. "Gee, what a place to throw old razor blades." Ostriches prance. "This old bird is long on legs, short on brains. I don't know why, but they always remind me of chorus girls." And so on. Contrasting the modesty of the girls who turn away from the camera with those who frolic naked along the rocks at the seashore, the narrator of the expeditionary film *Virgins of Bali* (1932) points out that "some are a little timid; others somewhat bolder among the boulders." It gets worse. As a parade of ducks scatters out of the way of an automobile, it seems that "since motor cars came to Bali, even a duck has had to learn to duck all over again!" Speaking of ducks, not even Groucho Marx was above tossing off a pun to wince at, as when a duck bleats over the last syllables of a song Groucho croons in *Duck Soup* and Groucho berates the bird for his "wise-quack."

The "all talking" feature film expended the most breath on wisecracks, with few genres escaping a verbal fusillade of marginal utility to the plot. Separate credits went to "dialogue directors" and "dialogue writers" who staged and composed self-contained bits of verbal business that might with no damage, or contribution to, the course of the narrative or the depth of the character be inserted into any film.

Sexual innuendo was the standard punchline to wisecrack mano à mano, or more often mano à femo or femo à femo, duels. The boy-girl jousting in *No More Women* (1934) catches the singsong quality of the sparring:

BOY: You know, I always like to take an experienced girl home.

GIRL: I ain't "experienced."

BOY: Well, you ain't home yet.

In *Employee's Entrance* (1933) a pretty blonde struts into the office of her rakish employer, who gives her a quick once-over and remarks, "Oh, it's you—I didn't recognize you with all your clothes on." In *Skyscraper Souls* (1932) a man turns to the floozy next to him and brags, "I'm established. I'm in a very old business." "So I am," cracks the veteran of the oldest profession.

Giving as good as they got in the war of words, women took no lip. Chorines and working girls deflated would-be romeos with a comeback line that hit him right between the eyes or, more painfully, below the belt. When a shady male customer propositions saucy waitress Constance Bennett in *What Price Hollywood?* (1932), she douses his ardor with a streetsmart jab: "Why don't you stick to blackmailing?" In *Other Men's Women* (1931) waitress Joan Blondell has no trouble putting down a randy male customer.

BLONDELL: Anything else you guys want?

MALE CUSTOMER [*eyeing her hind quarters*]: Yeh, give me a big slice of you—and some French fried potatoes on the side.

BLONDELL: Listen, baby, I'm A.P.O.

MALE CUSTOMER [*to his pal*]: What does she mean, A.P.O.?

BLONDELL: Ain't Putting Out.

Among themselves, women dished the dirt with unladylike wit. In the ribald, same-sex environs of *Finishing School* (1934), a girl tells her underdeveloped sorority sister that to try on a brassiere would be "like putting a saddle on a Pekinese." In *Footlight Parade* (1933) Joan Blondell bids good riddance to a gold-digging minx with the reassurance, "As long as they have sidewalks, you've got a job."

Finally, a visual wisecrack spliced together in the editing room juxtaposed innocuous dialogue for leering effect. In the medicinal melodrama *Men in White* (1934), an intern enjoins his pals to "eat, drink, and make merry." Cut to a girl at the telephone: "This is Mary speaking." Similarly, a lowcut comeback in *Dinner at Eight* (1933) featured a begowned Jean Harlow declaring her modesty and then turning her bare back to the camera to sashay away.

Next to sex, ethnic insults fueled the motormouths of wisecracking comedy. Pre-Code Hollywood luxuriated in crude, offensive, and often

Unladylike wit: saucy waitress Constance Bennett deflates a male customer in *What Price Holly-wood?* (1932).

quite hilarious ethnic stereotyping, a shameless immersion in vaudeville-derived smears on national origins, usually played by members of the ethnic group under derision: drunken Irishmen, sputtering Italians, hot-blooded Latins, cheapskate Jews, and shuffling African-Americans. In *They Learned About Women* (1930) a Jew and an Irishman exchange barbs. When the Irishman tells his partner he doesn't understand the value of money, the insulted Jew laughs and presents his nose as proof of his economic/ethnic credentials. "Take a look at my profile."

At its best, the rich diversity of American life rubbed shoulder to shoulder in a house of babble ringing with equal-opportunity insults. At its worst, as was usually the case with African-Americans, it was loathsome. Where Jews and Irish were anointed with the gift of gab, African-Americans were struck dumb. Afflicted by slow drawls, chattering teeth, and tongue-tied sputtering, blacks seldom got a word in edgewise, the lack of verbal agility being audible proof of the lack of mental facility. "Baffled and bewildered by the mere thought of moving fast, shuffling and mumbling his way to resounding laughter at every appearance," read the taglines describing Stepin Fetchit, the most successful black comedian of his day. Though unable to think fast or crack wise, Stepin Fetchit was "the very incarnation of humor." The punchline spoken by the black man was unintentionally funny, understood by everyone but him. (Backtalk by the servant class was almost unheard of in Hollywood cinema in the 1930s—hence the cultural significance of the radio wisecracks fired at Jack Benny by his quick-witted valet, Eddie "Rochester" Anderson, beginning in 1937.)

Though the wisecrack punctured the puffed up and self-important, it also demeaned political reformers who took things too seriously. The anticapitalist sentiments declaimed from soap boxes and at labor meetings got little hearing save as comic relief. If not downright sinister, communists and others of radical stripe were portrayed as eccentric kooks, spouting party rhetoric that their hipper comrades knew was so much "hooey." In *Hold Your Man* (1933) Jean Harlow is introduced to her roommates in a women's reformatory, one of whom, named Sadie Kline, the Jewish moniker alone being a red flag for social activism, welcomes her to prison in New Pioneer spirit. "I salute you, comrade, in the name of—" "She's a communist," interrupts one of the girls. "I am not! I'm a socialist!" objects Sadie. "Save your breath sister," sneers Harlow. "I don't care what the difference is—I'm a Democrat."

After weathering years of steady bombardment, some audiences became adept enough at wisecrack technique to fill in the blanks. In the wisecrack-laden *Footlight Parade*, a dowager with an off-key voice auditions for a singing role. Theater manager James Cagney quickly rejects her. "I've sung before crowned heads!" she blusters. "You've laid yourself open for a crack," cracks Cagney, but decides against taking so easy a shot. "We'll let it go." Inundated by barbs to the point of breakdown in *42nd Street* (1933), a genuinely distraught Bebe Daniels screams, "Enough of the wisecracks!"

In truth, the wisecrack was wearing thin to many ears. In 1933, when Harold Lloyd sought to update the antiquated "glasses character" from his silent thrill comedies, he contemplated concocting a "wiser hero" but one who would nonetheless "steer clear of the wisecracking, off-color brand of sophistication." Especially resistant to the sometimes harsh edge of the wisecrack were women, who were also thought to be slower on the uptake. *Variety*'s expert on the "woman's angle" judged the "rapid fire farce" of *Convention City* (1933) as "too fast, wise, and irreverent of women for average femme comprehension and approval." Children shared the dimness of their mothers, "the talker emphasis on sophisticated dialogue" having had an adverse "effect on kid patronage throughout the country."

Another drawback with wisecracking in the early sound film was the difficulty in timing the dialogue track. The nonstop play of witticism and half witticisms came so fast and furious that any given motion picture audience kept alert or floundered in confusion. On the Broadway stage, where virtuosi wisecrackers like Mae West and the Marx Brothers honed their technique, the live audience response, whether bursts of hilarity or the dreaded dead air, cued performers on how long to "hold" a line. If laughter threatened to drown out the next setup or punchline, the actor paused. If the line was a dud, he quickly moved to the next pass. Onscreen, however, no matter how many times a film was previewed, the reactions of audiences varied, especially since the preview audiences in southern California tended to be more languid in reaction than the audiences back East, the natural constituency for Groucho's asides and Mae's come-ons. Some lines went over the heads of an audience, other lines were smothered by laughter. Of course, a lot of the dialogue just wasn't funny. "There aren't enough brains in Hollywood to write enough clever lines to fill 600 scripts each year," Paramount director Richard Wallace pointed out in 1931, not trying to be funny.

The wisecrack also tended to travel poorly, whether to overseas markets, where the best lines were impossible to translate (not least to the British), or to the American heartland, where the clever chatter seemed so much inane city prattle. Complaining about the hard sell of "the essentially American 'wisecrack' " to essentially non-American audiences, film distributor Sherwin A. Kane asserted that foreign exhibitors were more likely to be the "inspired enemies" of wisecracking comedy than "censor boards or Parent-Teacher Associations." "The screen, once a universal language, has become too American for its own good," declared Carl Laemmle in 1932. "Pictures have become too chattery, too much 'talkie,' and we have catered too much to American slang, wisecracks, and local subjects even for American audiences, which insist on a wide variety of subjects and locales."

What Laemmle referred to was not just how non-American speakers overseas were bewildered by the wisecracking talkfests but how language comprehension problems beset some of the indigenous population. "We need more effortless entertainment and less of the type that makes intellectual demands on our patrons," pleaded a Kansas City exhibitor. "With large audiences the motion picture has come near to talking itself out of a job. Words are too smart." He had a point. The early talkies were urban, ethnic, and polyglot, written and spoken by glib Jews and mordant Irishmen, men and women who relished wit, irony, and verbal dueling. It made for the kind of slang-driven, head-spinning banter that in regions west of New York City—sometimes in regions a few blocks beyond the Lower East Side—sounded like a foreign tongue.

Occasionally, the language spoken from the American screen was literally foreign. Imported vernacular, understood widely in the melting-pot metropolis, registered not at all in the hinterlands. In 1927, programs to *The Jazz Singer* included a glossary to help gentiles with the Yiddish vocabulary of the intertitles ("Maybe he's fallen in love with a *shiksa*," worries Jack Robin's Jewish mother when she learns the whitebread name of her boy's girlfriend). No guidebooks accompanied the talkies. In *Wild Boys of the Road* (1933), a kid snarls "*khazar* [pig]" at a public official. *The Mayor of Hell* (1933) introduced rural hamlets to useful urban vocabulary ("I'll fix you—you *goniff!*") and challenged even city dwellers with an extended conversation in untranslated Yiddish between a Jewish father and his wayward son.

Irish-American actor James Cagney mastered enough of the lingua franca of the Lower East Side to wink verbally at his bilingual fans. In *Taxi!* (1931) cabbie Matt Nolan (Cagney) overhears a communications problem between an irrepressible Yiddish speaker and a befuddled Irish policeman. Nolan smirks knowingly from the seat of his cab and breaks into the conversation—in Yiddish. When the Jew expresses surprise at Nolan's fluency, Cagney jokes, "Nu, was denn, a shaygetz? [You expected maybe a gentile?]" The cop does a double take. "Nolan," he drawls in a broad brogue, "what part of Ireland did your folks come from?" "Delancy Street, thank you," trills Cagney in the accents of a Lower East Side *yenta*. Not a word of the Yiddish, from the immigrant or Cagney, is translated. Likewise, in *The Picture Snatcher* (1933), reformed hoodlum Danny Keene (Cagney again) gets fitted for a new suit by a Jewish tailor. The tailor assures him, "Don't worry—you'll be the best dressed *goniff* in America." Cagney pauses a beat. "I heard it when you said it, Maxie," he grins, signaling that he understood the mild insult, that a streetsmart Irish hood (and an Irish actor bred in Hell's Kitchen) would know the Yiddish word for "thief."

All the lightning-quick talk and inside-dopester slang gave a new set of headaches to censors whose lips moved when they read intertitles. "There has been a marked tendency in recent productions to use the wisecrack and phrase of double meaning to convey filth," warned Dr. James Wingate, head of the New York Censor Board, in 1931. "This has brought about a situation as serious in its offensiveness as anything achieved during the silent picture era [because] offensive dialogue is being used to take the place of risqué situations." A small town exhibitor agreed with the big city censor. "The theater patron as a whole in the United States does not talk smut in his or her home and does not want it spoken from the talking screen. All the complaints I have had during the year I have been showing talking pictures have been on this one thing, smut lines and smut gags placed in there by some nitwit who thought it would get a laugh, and it always does from the roughnecks and morons." Like most of Hollywood's moral failings, the salacious language was attributed to the baleful influence of the sophisticated metropolis. "When in 1927 sound came to the movies, they went to the [New York stage] drama to get words to say on the screen and a lot of the words have turned out to be naughty, too naughty for the masses," Terry Ramsaye declared in a speech to the Rotary Club of New York in 1934. "The cracks of Broadway are not for Main Street."

The inability of slow-witted censors to keep up with the implications of fast talk from "ultra-modern slanguists" made for a fun game of hide-and-seek between the hip and the hapless. "Are you trying to 'weekend' me, darling?" asks a man suspicious of the true whereabouts of his two-timing mistress in *Call Her Savage* (1932). "Well, if you must know, I'm going out for a Chinese singing lesson," jokes a society girl in *The Last Flight* (1931), a line that flew over heads unacquainted with opium pipes.

For a few actors, the wisecrack lay not in the words but in the delivery. A consistent source of trouble for tone-deaf censors was the remark that read innocent on the page but sounded suggestive to the ear, notably in the insinuating octaves of Mae West, Groucho Marx, and Jean Harlow. *Photoplay* editor James Quirk was not referring to her body alone when he said of Jean Harlow: "When she appears in a picture, sex rears its ugly head."

Another exotic kind of communication—physical gestures and body movements—had to be seen to be censored. Unlike silent film where the eyes were always attentive, the soundtrack might distract censors from vulgar gestures that were as eloquent as any proscribed word. In *Registered Nurse* (1933) a man sidles up behind a woman, who jumps, pop-eyed, into the air, goosed. In *The Miracle Woman* (1931) a man who has a door closed in his face quickly thrusts his middle index finger upward, flashing a hand sign either too fast or too Sicilian to be spotted by a Midwest Presbyterian like Will Hays.

In 1933, to guard against the cursing, innuendo, and gestures that came in under its cultural radar, the Hays Office demanded translations of all foreign language communications, no matter how obscure the tribal dialect. Keeping an ear out for vulgarities from the native inhabitants of Skull Island in *King Kong* (1933), Hays requested a translation of the savage vernacular—which was, of course, total gibberish.

Story, Screenplay, and All Dialogue by Mae West

Just as the mighty King Kong helped restore RKO to solvency in 1933, Paramount retained under contract its own larger-than-life force of nature, a creature who almost single-handedly and double-entendre-ly rescued the studio from bankruptcy. "Paramount's gift to a jaded world" was Mae West. For the studio, she was a life preserver, which is what her name would mean to American sailors during World War II.

Motion picture actresses had always sold sex. Mae West was the first motion picture actress to sell sex talk. Though she had been a national scandal since April 26, 1926, when her Broadway show *Sex* delivered on the title, only with sound on film could Mae West make the transition from stage to screen. Intertitles wouldn't have carried the lilt in her voice. "Mae West couldn't sing a lullaby without making it sound sexy," commented more than one critic, not without admiration. Or as the New York district attorney who successfully prosecuted her for indecency in *Sex* argued, "Mae West's personality, looks, walk, manner and gestures made the lines and situations suggestive." Sentenced to ten days in the cooler, she served eight—two off for "good behavior."

More imposing than attractive, West was no conventional beauty. Unlike Garbo or Dietrich, she seldom figured as the luminous object of worshipful male desire. In physique and attire she embodied a fin-de-siècle physical ideal: big-breasted and curvaceous, the antithesis of the trim and athletic females of the 1920s and 1930s. In 1933, West's break-out year in Hollywood, the admiring eye of columnist Cecelia Ager took the full measure of the woman: "Upholstered in the costumes of the 1890s, Miss West photographs a series of good fancy pictures for brewery calendars. Ostrich feathers to stagger a wench less stalwart, waistlines to choke a belle a whit less conscientious. Billowing bosom, expressive derriere, just miss bursting their eloquent seaming." Any chorine in a Warner Bros. musical showed more flesh, Constance Bennett and Joan Crawford strayed more explicitly from social mores, and Jean Harlow wallowed in the pleasures of her flesh more wantonly. Mae West did wrong by speaking, the vice lodged deep in her voice.

In truth Mae West didn't utter many double entendres; her specialty was the single entendre, the blunt come-on and right-between-the-eyes proposition. The invitation that became her signature line ("Come up and see me some time") did not solicit social intercourse. Having enjoyed a lot of sex, craving more, she was a woman for whom men held no secrets and only one pleasure. In world-weary, seen-it-all tones, she flirted, baited, and savored the power of language to arouse and enflame. She was less concerned with a particular suitor than what he was best suited for. The two kinds of men she liked? Foreign and domestic. "I see a man in your life," predicts the fortune teller in *I'm No Angel* (1933). Mae arches her eyebrows skeptically: "What? Only one?"

West was already a succés de scandal by the time Hollywood beckoned in 1932. Playing the wisecracking slattern in a scene-stealing turn in *Night after Night* (1932), she transferred her stage shtick to the talking screen without missing a beat. "Hollywood has a sweetening and cleansing effect upon one's views of life," she winked in a Paramount press release. In offstage interviews too, she stayed in character as Broadway's most experienced broad. "Personally I admire good women." she claimed, "but you never hear about good women in history. The only good girl to make history was Betsy Ross and she had to sew up a flag to do it."

Of course the character "Mae West" was a calculated construction of Mae West, who played Svengali to her own Trilby. West knew precisely the nature of her appeal and calibrated exactly how far she could go in mocking morality. "I've developed a different way of selling my sex," she explained to a reporter in 1933. "I laugh them into it. I cover it with comedy. If you laugh with a sinner, you like her. You grow fond of her, feel sympathy for her." She continued: "There are some people who can get away with anything yet always come out on top. The worse they are the better you like them. They happen to have something different that wins you no matter what they do. No, the wages of sin in all cases is not death."

Certainly not in Mae West's case. The screen version of her notorious 1928 stage play *Diamond Lil* was so inflammatory that the Hays Office demanded that the studio change the title and the plot. In *She Done Him Wrong* (1933) Paramount met them halfway. Diamond Lil was rechristened Lady Lou, but her personality and wisecracks remained intact. (By way of compensation, the two most brazen bad girls of pre-Code Hollywood, Jean Harlow in *Red Headed Woman* and Barbara Stanwyck in *Baby Face*, are named Lil and Lily.) "Nothing much changed except the title, but don't tell that to Mr. Hays," *Variety* joked.

Set in the Gay Nineties of New York City, the title card to *She Done Him Wrong* coyly evokes a nostalgic era both ribald and innocent: "A lusty brawling florid decade when there were handlebars on lip and wheel—and legs were confidential." The expository montage is confidential about legs but not much else: a streetcleaner eyes the hind quarters of a horse and the task of shoveling below him, two lesbians stroll arm in arm, and a woman buys a buggy whip from a Jewish peddler for reasons obscure (a cop catches the peddler's eye and the peddler just shrugs). A picture of a naked woman, languidly supine, adorns the wall above a rollicking barroom, the full frontal view concealed by a customer's derby strategically jutting up at her waistline.

The plot concerns a white slavery ring, but the real story is the sexual rapaciousness of Lady Lou, the model for the oil painting over the bar. At age forty-one, West struts like a Ziegfeld girl, but already the dialogue overcompensates with insistent reminders of how beautiful and desirable she is. The risqué wisecracks ("When women go wrong, men go right after them," she assures a fallen chick under her wing) and salacious inferences ("a little bit spicy but not too raw," she says of a photo session) infuse an atmosphere of guiltless sex for barter. The songs suit the mood: "I Wonder Where My Easy Rider's Gone," a plaintive lament for a jockey no longer in the saddle, and "A Guy What Takes His Time," a lyric to foreplay and stamina.

As Lady Lou jiggles and jousts, she juggles the pressing attentions of no fewer than five earnest suitors. The top of the line is Cary Grant, playing hard to get. Swiveling up to her boudoir, Lady Lou nails him with a statement of fact: "You can be had." After luring Grant onto a swan-handled divan, West demonstrates the difficulty with censoring Mae West on paper. "That's it. Loosen up, unbend," she purrs, pushing Grant affectionately. "You'll feel better." Then the pair exchange the classic volley and return:

GRANT: Haven't you ever met a man who can make you happy?

WEST: Sure, lots of times.

At the box office, in decadent metropolis and pure-hearted hamlet alike, *She Done Him Wrong* was a surprise, spontaneous sensation. Cued by the persona of their meal ticket, Paramount began "spicing up the ads as much as the traffic will bear with hot punch lines and still hotter art." Screen trailers teased imaginations with silent scenes of Mae West and Cary Grant and the voice-over challenge, "If you can read lips, you can read what Mae is saying." Exhibitors advertised it as "adults only," a sure-fire lure for males above and below the legal age. "A man's picture, it will restore grandpa's boyhood and age the sophomores," smirked the *New York Mirror*, in an accurate demographic reading. West was the major exception to Hollywood's ironclad "women first" rule of box office priority.

With West the hottest item in show business, Paramount rushed a sequel into the market within nine months. *I'm No Angel* opens with a Blue Eagle NRA title card and dissolves to the bustle and con artistry of a carnival

Svengali to her own Trilby: Mae West as Mae West in *She Done Him Wrong* (1933).

sideshow, a self-reflexive gloss on the ballyhoo surrounding the star attraction of *I'm No Angel*. Like moviegoers urged to "go West" and see Mae, hordes of men crowd around eagerly as a barker plies his carny patter, exhorting the boys to take a gander at the "supreme flower of female pulchritude." Poured into a form-fitting gown, West prances down the catwalk preening before the dumbstruck male sheep. "No wisecracks, now," she wisecracks, but an on-looker can't resist remarking that "next to her a wiggly worm looks para-lyzed." Like the scandalous wiggler of another generation, Elvis Presley on *The Ed Sullivan Show*, West is shot mainly from the waist up when she sings, the area of locomotion hidden from view, though not from the imagination.

Referring to her arrest for hip-shaking lasciviousness during the run of *Sex*, the barker describes her as the woman who proved "you didn't need feet to be a dancer." Like Paramount, the sideshow promises more of West than it delivers, there being less raw content in either act than meets the eye. "Suckers," West sneers as she walks offstage. But for the men in the carnival crowd, happy to get their pockets picked, the tease is as tantalizing as the payoff.

West was no fallen woman, not even a bad girl. Her eyes were never downcast, her demeanor never shamed, nor was her interest in the male sex ever truly mercenary: the diamonds and furs she regally accepts from the platoons of smitten suitors are but baubles, to be given away to maids and casual friends. No wonder she has become a beacon for feminist and queer studies. Not only is she a rank independent and auteur ("Story, screenplay, and all dialogue by Mae West," asserts the credit line to *I'm No Angel*), but her warmest moments are with her maids and girlfriends. In the trial scene that concludes *I'm No Angel*, when West launches into a brief for the defense, the double meaning was lost on no one. Just as the sideshow scene in the first reel doubled for Paramount's ad-pub efforts, the end reel testimony and cross-examinations are West's own summation to the court of American opinion. When confronted by a lineup of men from her checkered past, she shrugs, "All right, I'm the sweetheart of Sigma Chi. So what?" Blindsided, her own attorney demands, "Why didn't you tell me there were so many men in your life?" Unabashed, she shoots back, "Why shouldn't I know guys? I've been around. I travel from coast to coast. A dame like me can't make trips like that without meeting some of the male population."

Needless to say, the verdict on *I'm No Angel* was resoundingly in favor of the defendant. "This is dandy entertainment and our patrons had a good time, although a few wouldn't admit it," chuckled a small town exhibitor. "Plenty of hot cracks that will get rises out of your audiences," reported another "nabe" outpost, giving the lie to hinterland prudery. "Good old Mae makes your tickets unroll." "I cleaned up on the picture," said yet another grateful exhibitor, concluding his thanks to Paramount with an anticipation of wartime slang: "Mae West was a life saver for an anemic box office."

Before the Production Code Administration sealed her lips, West claimed to be able to function quite well between the lines of screen censorship, preferring the clear limits of Hollywood to the ambiguous standards of Broadway. "Why in pictures, you don't have to worry about censorship—much— once you learn the rules," West declared in 1934. "Here they tell you what not to do before you do it. In New York they let you go ahead and do it and then break in and arrest you." Unbowed in the face of bluenose outrage, she baited the matrons and clerics mercilessly. "Yes," she admitted, "I wrote the story of *I'm No Angel* myself. It's all about a girl who lost her reputation and never missed it." When asked what she thought of the censors, West wise-cracked. "Tell them they made me what I am today. I hope they're satisfied."

NEWSPAPER PATTER

Screen characters of all stripes and denominations cracked wise, and in Warner Bros. melodramas, they usually did. But though the practice crossed class lines and career choices, one category of wisecrackers worked at wit for a living. Lean language and staccato prose being their stock and trade, newspapermen, and the stray women too, were the glibbest mouthpieces for the wisecracking talkies.

The proliferation of journalists in pre-Code Hollywood reflected two intersecting cultural forces. First, the heightened profile of media messengers in the pioneer decade of mass communications made them figures of prestige and charisma fit for screen celebration, the 1930s nourishing not only the prime of Hollywood cinema but of radio broadcasting and mass circulation weeklies. Second, the refugees from Park Row and the Loop who came to Hollywood with the sound revolution ("doing a Horace Greeley" in the lingo) invested their screenplays with a wisecracking conviviality that aggrandized the profession they abandoned. Recruited for screenwriting service and transplanted West, a generation of New York and Chicago newsmen met their studio deadlines with an ink-stained cycle that included *Gentlemen of the Press* (1929), *The Front Page* (1931), *Scandal Sheet* (1931), *Five Star Final* (1931), and *The Great Edition* (1932).

Fueling the onscreen cynicism was the offscreen disorientation of the transplanted newspapermen whose income soared in the California sun even as their self-respect sank in the studio system. "Schmucks with Underwoods," Jack Warner called screenwriters, low men on the studio totem pole. Resentful writers returned the contempt in kind and got the last word in the epigrams if not the higher tax brackets. "They outrank you in salary two to one," griped Ben Hecht in 1933. "It's like giving the printer $2000 a week for setting the type for the Great American novel."

Like the gangster, another fast-talking, disreputable denizen of the urban underworld, the newspaperman was ethnic and déclassé, chatty and cynical, hard-drinking and insubordinate. Trafficking on his Bodini-bold byline, he gained access to all levels of society, from lowlife snitches to

high-class debutantes. Not that the tedious job of fact-gathering and com-
posing copy ever made Hollywood's final cut. The most popular of the pre-
Code newspapermen, Clark Gable in Frank Capra's *It Happened One Night*
(1934), is not once shown actually pounding the keys of a typewriter, with
or without his undershirt.

The two films that typeset the conceits and conventions for the Hollywood newsroom were *The Front Page* and *Five Star Final*, both adapted from
popular Broadway plays. Cynical but noble newshounds pounded typewrit-
ers with two fingers, cranky editors kept whiskey close at hand, and hook-
ers, hustlers, and sundry hangers-on waltzed through with hot tips and spicy
talk. The gentlemen of the press were inured to the ways of the world,
where a gulled electorate got the political hacks it deserved and a barely literate readership feasted on a diet of sex and scandal they only pretended to
be appalled by.

The stop-the-presses exuberance of the newspaper film sprang almost
fully formed from *The Front Page* (1931), the less-remembered version of the
hit Broadway play by Charles MacArthur and Ben Hecht, today known best
from Howard Hawks's gender-switch remake *His Girl Friday* (1940). Directed by Lewis Milestone, fresh from his masterpiece *All Quiet on the Western Front* (1930), the early talkie is a stagebound play-on-film whose rapid-
fire wordplay outruns its slow-moving camerawork. Hecht's memory of his
cub reporter days on the *Chicago Daily Journal*, circa 1910, served as the
shooting script for a tale of journalistic larceny up against City Hall chicanery, mixed in with a love triangle between unscrupulous editor, ace reporter, and ace reporter's mousy fiancée. By the 1930s the tabloid high jinks
of the Hollywood newsrooms were already an anachronism, a re-creation of
a bygone era of printer's deviltry perpetrated and witnessed by a young
Bennie Hecht a generation before ("Earthquake Rips Chicago" may have
been Hecht's most bald-faced deception in boldface, a front-page headline
about an earth-moving event that never happened).

The newspaper subculture was defined not by what the gentlemen of
the press covered (executions, corruption, scandal) but by how they wrote
it up and talked it over (clipped, laconic, streetwise). Notably short on boy-
girl stuff, the true romance of the newspaper film was in the delirious love
of talk. "And I heard language," rhapsodized Hecht in his classic memoir *A
Child of the Century*. "It was the language of wandering scholars, of wit that
found no paper, of genius with wings of alcohol. It was the language of
Dickens, Twain, Carlyle and Rabelais come out of book covers and glad-
dening bars, city rooms and whore houses." Hecht wrapped up his revery

Newspaper patter: Edward G. Robinson beset by tabloid headlines in a publicity shot for *Five Star Final* (1931). (Courtesy of the British Film Institute)

with a better definition of the wisecrack than the OED: "the whiplash phrase, the flashing and explosive sentence, the sonorous syntax, and bull's-eye epithet."

In Warner Brothers' *Five Star Final*, the pace of the camerawork matched the velocity of the wordplay. Based on the hit Broadway play by Louis Weltzenkorn and directed by Mervyn LeRoy, it opens with a montage of rolling presses, banner headlines, and newsboy shouts of "Extra!" Since the *Evening Gazette* specializes in mudslinging not muckraking, guilt-stricken editor Joseph Randall (Edward G. Robinson) compulsively washes his hands while the paper's front pages, tossed on street corners and blown into gutters, are splattered with mud. When the greedy publisher asks his secretary her opinion about a scandalous story, she coolly responds, "I think the part about the illegitimate child is not made quite clear enough." The stakes in the big city newspaper wars are high and the tactics nasty: thugs attack street-corner newsies and brass-knuckled goon squads beat up the competition.

The tabloid's eye view of life is softened by the rough-edged but warm-hearted camaraderie of the newsroom. Cub reporter Arthur Goldberg flirts with Randall's smart-mouthed stenographer (Aline MacMahon) and utters a mild blasphemy, "Suffering Moses!" "Mr. Goldberg," she says in mock shock (inflecting the "berg" into an East Side "boig"), "ain't you got no religion?" "Gee," says the crestfallen pup, "the way you say that I ought to change my name." "Don't you do it, kid," she laughs. "New York's full of Christians as it is." Reporter Ziggie Fienstein (George E. Stone) strolls in with a bottle of bootleg booze and greets his ethnic kinsman Goldberg with a friendly, "Hey, schlemiel." As the contest editor for the *Evening Gazette*, Ziggy plans to stage a wild taxi race across the city. "I'm going to let an Irishman, a Jew, and a Wop win," he announces open-mindedly. Kitty Carmody (Ona Munson), a woman whose credentials are not journalistic, flounces in looking for a position as "girl reporter." The previous employee was fired for being flat-chested, an area in which Kitty possesses ample qualifications. She is hired to "vamp stories out of shyster lawyers."

Demanding larger circulation and more titillating tales ("Why are we printing tables from the League of Nations?"), the publisher decides to resurrect the famous Nancy Voorhis murder case of twenty years past, a sensational story in which a pregnant secretary shot her scoundrel boss. Initially reluctant, editor Randall goes along with the scheme, but soon gets fully caught up in the scandalmongering.

Of course, Nancy (Frances Starr) is now a respectable married woman with a loving husband and a daughter engaged to a rich and respectable scion of society. To see the sordid past splashed again across the tabloids would ruin her child's life. Director LeRoy stages Nancy's frantic efforts to stop the presses in a triptych split screen: on the telephone, Nancy is at the center of the frame, getting the switchboard runaround from both ends of the screen. As her hopes to connect fade, the left and right sides of the frame go dark, trapping her between two black borders.

All was for naught, anyway: the paper is already on the streets. When the future in-laws demand the wedding be stopped, Nancy walks into her bathroom and takes a bottle of poison from the medicine shelf. The door closes, she moans, and a body falls. Her husband finds her body and follows her lead: door closes, he moans, and a body falls. The enterprising Kitty Carmody comes through the window with a photographer and stumbles upon the two bodies in the bathroom. In a flash, without the slightest hesitation, she orders the photographer to get the picture and then rushes to phone in the scoop of her life.

Though the bridegroom remains true despite being disinherited by his wealthy parents, Nancy's hysterical daughter runs to the offices of the *Evening Gazette* to confront the vultures of the press. "Why did you kill my mother?" she shrieks in turn to reporter, editor, and publisher. She raises a gun to fire but her fiancé stops her before she can pull the trigger. He delivers a screed at the fourth estate whose class-based anger applies as well to the other three. "You'll go on hunting down little people who can't fight back. You'll go on with your filthy newspaper, pulling the clothing off women and selling their naked souls," he shouts. "You've grown rich off filth—and no one's ever dared rise up and crush you out." He raises the gun and points. "But remember this—if you ever mention my wife's name in your rotten paper again, I'll hunt you down and kill you!" He pauses a beat, a space for audience applause. Randall then delivers his own tirade at the publisher. As in *The Front Page*, the dialogue ends with an unspoken obscenity. "Tell him to shove it up his—," he bellows as he tosses a phone through a glass door, the crash drowning out the forbidden word.

Though the intoxication with language breathed life into the newspaper film, the intensity of class antagonisms—sometimes rubbed raw, sometimes smoothed over—was the other front-page news of the genre. Bouncing between the upper classes and the lower orders, the newspaperman acted as a kind of reconnaissance agent, penetrating the walls of the aristocracy to satisfy the curiosity of the peasants lurking outside the gates. His ability to reconcile the two worlds is a good index of the social cohesion of the American body politic. The most famous commingling of classes occurred in Frank Capra's *It Happened One Night*, the classic screwball comedy that united the rich and the rough in the persons of Claudette Colbert and Clark Gable. By the mid-1930s, the dynamic relationships in the screwball comedy expressed the renewed social equilibrium under FDR, with the lower orders injecting warmth and humanity into the cold but salvageable upper class. They may have the penthouse apartments and trust funds, but we have the heart and the happiness.

Three years earlier, however, another Frank Capra film of like-minded content (class warfare, the battle of the sexes, and newsroom backgrounds) expressed no faith in a common ground between the classes, romantic or otherwise. *Platinum Blonde* (1931) begins where *It Happened One Night* ends, with the marriage of a newspaper reporter to a society girl. However, where the later film reconciles class antagonisms, the earlier one reasserts them.

Stu Smith (Robert Williams) infiltrates high society via his native moxie and press credentials, but soon surrenders the power of the press to the charms of the decidedly un-madcap heiress Ann Schyler (Jean Harlow). Despite warnings ("Ann Schyler's in the blue book. You're not even in the phone book"), Stu elopes with Ann and moves into her mansion. He soon finds himself dubbed "Mr. Ann Schyler" and the butt of humiliating newspaper headlines ("Cinderella Man Grows Hair on Chest"). He hates her crowd, she can't abide his. When his motley friends arrive for a drunken visit, Ann erupts at their boorish behavior and Stu finally reasserts his manhood. Granting Ann an alimony-free divorce, he returns to the arms of his real love, his fellow reporter and lateral-class relationship Gallagher (Loretta Young).

In *Platinum Blonde*, the rich corrupt the working class; in *It Happened One Night*, the working class redeems the rich. In *Platinum Blonde*, the virility of the man is sapped by the heiress; in *It Happened One Night*, the man trumpets his cocksure superiority by breaking down class barriers and the resistance of the heiress.

In the years to come, Frank Capra refined the political edge of his wisecracking social satires, an impulse that would take his skeptical eye from newsrooms to courtrooms, to the very chambers of the U.S. Senate. "The man in the street has had so many dogmas crammed down his throat that he is prepared to revolt against the current underestimation of his intelligence. He's fed up," Capra declared in 1932. "Politics, prohibition, patriotism, big business, high powered advertising, are ripe subjects for ridicule." Capra predicted that "someone is going to evolve a great film out of the Depression," perhaps aware even than that he would be responsible for a half dozen of them.

THE BLUE EAGLE AND *Duck Soup* (1933)

Although usually silent on political matters, actually all matters, Harpo Marx confided during a visit to the Soviet Union in 1933 that, well, yes, he and his brothers *were* descendants of that other famous Marx. Harpo's rare foray into speech partook of the traditional prerogatives of the court jester in the presence of power. Sheltered within the zone of comedy, seditious and salacious backtalk banished from the realms of the preachment yarns and vice films might percolate wildly, without fear of retaliation. In the outrageous satire and anarchic insults of the Marx Brothers, Olsen and Johnson, Wheeler and Woolsey, and Laurel and Hardy, the bleakest critiques and most shocking sentiments could be uttered, albeit with a grin. After all, it was only a joke.

Of all the comedy teams of the 1930s, the Marx Brothers are the longest lived, an artistic longevity often linked to the timeless appeal of the shambles they made of normality. Skulking about the mansions of the rich and spraying insults and seltzer at officials in formal wear, they become guerilla comedians, subversive forces of disorder bent on overturning a stifling status quo. So at least goes one Marxist critique. Against such romantic conceptions of the Marx Brothers as the vanguard elite of "an American comedy of radical discontent," film historian Henry Jenkins cautions that "it is not clear in what meaningful sense the Marx Brothers films may be read as a political reaction against any particular social system or as reflecting a coherent ideological position (anarchistic or otherwise)."

Fair enough: coherence is not a word that fits comfortably into any sentence with the Marx Brothers as subject. The absence of a programmatic platform, however, does not mean that the comedy of the Marx Brothers, and of early sound comedy generally, lacks a political dimension and cultural edge. Tellingly, for example, the comedy stars of the early 1930s tended to come in pairs or teams, almost as if the denial of individual achievement in the nadir of the Great Depression extended to solo acts no less than entrepreneurs. Only the indomitable Mae West stood alone as a superstar comedy performer, and she was selling more than laughter.

In the search for alignments between film and history, moreover, the trajectory of the Marx Brothers' career in the 1930s spans a series of suggestive parallels: from Paramount to MGM, from pre-Code Hollywood to Hollywood under the Code, from Hoover to FDR. The arc from the first sound films at Paramount (*Cocoanuts*, 1929; *Animal Crackers*, 1930; *Horse Feathers*, 1932; and *Duck Soup*, 1933) to the midcareer revival at MGM (*A Night at the Opera* [1935] and *A Day at the Races* [1937]) trace a course from chaos to cohesion. In the pre-Code films for Paramount the quartet is a unit unto themselves, a four-pillared bulwark (or three, minus the mutant normal brother, Zeppo) against the rest of the world, whose population serves as straight men and women to their zany antics and non sequitur comebacks. The connection of the pre-Code Marx Brothers to normality is to disrupt it linguistically, logically, and hierarchically. Groucho, Chico, and Harpo are grotesques, not really humans. After 1934, the brothers join the family of man—as oddball cousins, to be sure, but as recognizable blood relatives. The difference between *Duck Soup*, the classic in retrospect and box office disaster in 1933, and *A Night at the Opera*, their comeback blockbuster, is the difference between anarchy and zaniness, subversive comedy and good-natured burlesque.

Duck Soup opens not with a joke, or the musical theme and animated credit sequence that usually heralded the entrance of the Four Marx Brothers, but with a full-screen title card of the Blue Eagle, symbol of the New Deal, and the printed slogan, "We Do Our Part." For the antiwar, antiestablishment critique of corrupt and feckless leadership, the genuflection to the New Deal order seems a prestrike apology for the insults and bedlam in the wings. Only then does the soundtrack theme chime in over an image of four ducks, birds of a feather, in hot soup.

Though a plot synopsis of a Marx Brothers film is a sucker's bet, *Duck Soup* is a lucid enough political allegory. The Middle European nation of Freedonia teeters on the brink of bankruptcy because "the government has been mismanaged." To address the "present emergency" and secure a bank loan from the rich dowager Mrs. Teasdale (Margaret Dumont), the nation's leaders agree to appoint "the progressive fearless fighter" Rufus T. Firefly (Groucho) to helm the ship of state. This is a mistake. Before rushing off to a session with the House of Representatives, Firefly sings "I'm Against It," his program of paralysis and austerity. The lyrics tweak the administrations both of Will Hays ("No one's allowed to smoke / or tell a dirty joke") and Herbert Hoover ("The last man nearly ruined this place / He didn't know what to do with it / If you think this country's bad off now / just wait till I get through with it").

As innocent of the art of diplomacy as the logic of English-language communication, Firefly leads Freedonia to war with the neighboring state of Sylvania. The news calls for a song. Crossing the martial zeal of George M. Cohan and the plantation sentimentality of Stephen Foster ("They got guns / We got guns / All God's children got guns"), the musical extravaganza "We're Going to War" features cast and chorus celebrating the hostilities in a manner queasily reminiscent of the blithe jingoism of Great War propaganda.

The last act is an extended battle royal, with echoes of trench warfare, artillery bombardment, machine gun fire, rear-screen newsreels of tanks barreling across No Man's Land, and gas attacks (Groucho's defense against a gas attack is "a teaspoon of bicarbonate of soda and half a glass of water"). When Harpo draws short straw for a suicide mission ("the rare privilege of sacrificing his life for his country"), Groucho bids farewell with a wisecrack that sums up the Great War cynicism toward all things patriotic: "And remember—while you're out there risking life and limb through shot and shell, we'll be in here thinking what a sucker you are."

Groucho's personal favorite among all the Marx Brothers movies, revived and beloved in the 1960s, a certified classic of comedy on the list of the National Film Registry, *Duck Soup* was a dud in its day. The surreal comedy inspired an unusually vitriolic reaction from exhibitors angry about the box office terms Paramount demanded and the paltry drawing power of the suddenly repellent quartet. "Talk about your unmitigated gall," protested an independent theater owner. "This picture was sold with a heavy grab off of the gross [that is, a percentage deal favoring the studio not the exhibitor] and the running time is exactly 67 minutes, which means the 'Exi-bitter' must furnish almost half of the balance of the show with his own dough for the 'Wisecrack Brothers' and Paramount to share on. As for the music," he went on disgustedly, "Harpo don't harp and Chico don't tickle the ivories. Just a lot of gags and chatter that did not appeal to the masses." Another embittered exhibitor asserted that "each picture they make gets worse. Means nothing at the box office and following nice business on *Little Women* [1933] one wonders why the producers wish such trash off on poor unsuspecting exhibitors."

Duck Soup contained two badly timed themes that help explain why the film left such a sour taste in 1933. First, the Firefly regime, an apt enough travesty of government during the Hoover trough, came across as blasphemy during the revival of faith under FDR, a "progressive fearless fighter" in all seriousness. Second, with a renascent militarist Germany dredging up war jitters dormant since 1918, the flashbacks to the Great War played as a portent of things to come. Already America was looking to the past as preview to a future conflagration.

After the commercial debacle of *Duck Soup*, the Marx Brothers did not make another film for two years. In the interim, the motion picture industry had become prosperous and moral. Dropping the misfit Zeppo, they began a successful streak at MGM, a studio that restrained their worst, or maybe best, impulses.

The rushed almost hysterical quality of the early films for Paramount yields to a calmer, more deliberate style of comedic byplay at MGM, controlled not unhinged zaniness. Besides the strictness in censorship surveillance (though the shifty-eyed Groucho manages to slip the odd inference past Joseph Breen's blue pencil), the Marx Brothers under the Production Code do not run riot. *A Night at the Opera* pauses for extended interludes of sheer lyricism, with Chico delighting a group of adoring children with his nimble piano playing and Harpo doing the same at his stringed instrument.

Groucho serves as a romantic go-between and delivers extended lines of non-wisecrack dialogue to advance the plot and the course of true love. The Marxes disrupt opera houses and race tracks, not university systems or whole governments. They tweak, but do not trash, the social and moral order.

In *A Night at the Opera* Chico voices the aesthetic of the Marx Brothers. "You can't fool me," he tells Groucho. "There ain't no sanity clause." Of course, there is a sanity clause, and after 1934 the rest of the film universe abided by it. The irreverent opening of *Duck Soup*—where the stationary Blue Eagle dissolves into four ducks swirling in a kettle of soup—failed to reckon on which bird was more powerful in FDR's America.

8

News on Screen

The Vividness of Mechanical Immortality

With the advent of sound on film, American history became a motion picture pageant apprehended mainly through the compilation and reediting of moving images. The most readily retrievable and comprehensive source for history on film is the screen format that first wedded journalism to the moving image, the newsreels. Whether to conjure the broad strokes of a decadal zeitgeist or to paint the backdrop to a private memory, the newsreels trace the main currents of an American past unimaginable without their images. They remain the prime documentary legacy of Hollywood cinema.

Initiated in 1904 when anything recorded on screen was news, terminated in 1967, when television finally snuffed out the moribund format, the newsreels were an integral, privileged item on the motion picture program, a selected short subject whose profile was higher than its profit margin. Issued twice weekly, running about eight minutes in length, five commercial newsreels (Universal Newspaper Newsreel, Pathé News, Fox Movietone News,

Hearst Metrotone News, and Paramount Sound News) played subservient accompaniment to the Hollywood feature film in over three-quarters of the nation's theaters. More a headline service than a comprehensive summary, part journalism and part hokum, the newsreel provided an eclectic and erratic overview of current events, a lineup of madcap stunts, bathing beauties, and sports highlights alongside glimpses of the more serious stuff of history, such as political affairs, social crises, and crime sprees.

Like the entertainment film, the newsreels began in silence and turned loquacious with sound. Between 1927 and 1930, the sound newsreel erased its mute antecedent with the same dispatch that the sound feature film terminated the silent film. By the early 1930s two decisive aural innovations had enhanced the impact of news on screen: voice-over narration and commentative music. In January 1930 Universal Newspaper Newsreel first devised "an ingenious and sure-fire tie-up between a big name and a good idea" when it hired Graham McNamee, a popular radio commentator for NBC radio, to be the "talking reporter" for their biweekly newsreel issues. Initially, McNamee didn't comment on the news; he merely read the intertitles aloud. In time, however, the newsreel narrator evolved into a voice independent of intertitles and eventually supplanted them. By September 1930 Fox, Paramount, Pathé, and Hearst all followed suit with "off stage" voices of their own.

Through deployment in the newsreel, and concurrently in archival documentaries and expeditionary films, the narrative voice-over, an omniscient speaker floating above the film text as articulate guide, became an integral part of motion picture grammar. At first bombastic and portentous, he gradually modulated his Olympian declamations with a more common, conversational touch. Just as radio announcers set aside vocal inflections learned at the stage or the bandstand and adapted to the atmospherics of the living room medium, screen commentators perfected a more intimate style: less like a man before a microphone at a big show working a live crowd, more like a close friend or gentle mentor sidling up to the auditor for a chat, no longer the Voice of God but a neighbor at the back porch.

In March 1930, two months after the talking reporter first spoke, Universal initiated the second news on screen innovation, commentative music. The musical strains of a mini-overture opened the newsreel, McNamee narrated, and as soon as he finished, the music segued into the next subject, eliminating the dead air between talk and successive sequences. As in feature films, commentative music set the scene and encouraged an emotional response: somber, sprightly, or sporty depending on the clip, working with the voice-over and intertitles as editorial comment. The trademark musical themes of the newsreels, trumpeted at the top of each issue at each screening, soon had regular moviegoers wincing on cue.

Like the studios, each of the newsreels sought to establish a distinct identity, reinforced by the vocal personality of the talking reporter. Distributed by MGM, Hearst Metrotone News marketed itself as one pillar in a transmedia troika comprised of newspaper, radio, and newsreel ("the voice of news and the visual reproduction of news on the talking screen"). The company's "Globe Trotter" column appeared in Hearst chain newspapers, while Hearst-affiliated radio stations broadcast the audio version, and Hearst Metrotone News screened motion picture verification to spectators in Loews-MGM theaters. The Hearst organization thus constructed an ideal news-awareness process for the informed citizen: first, radio broadcast the news headlines, then the newspaper expanded on the radio reports with extensive print coverage and wirephotos, and finally, the newsreel closed out the process with sound moving pictures of the story. "The world of news in the newspaper" and "the voice of news over the radio" thereby metamorphosed into "the voice and sound of news of the talking screen."

The contents of a Fox Movietone issue from August 18, 1932, provide a fair sampling of the scope and priorities of the early sound newsreel:

1. President Herbert Hoover speaking before an auditorium of supporters during his reelection campaign

2. An extended and respectful obituary of canine star Rin Tin Tin

3. A speedboat race

4. An interview with the Crown Prince of Germany

5. A few casual remarks from Democratic challenger Franklin Delano Roosevelt and vice presidential candidate John Nance Garner

6. A static long shot of a West Point parade

Designed to showcase live sound recording (speedboat motors, martial music, and the accents of European royalty), the newsreel packages six discrete segments, only two of which bear any relation to each other (the 1932 presidential contest between Hoover and FDR). The arrangement of the segments indicates little hierarchy or logical order: the FDR segment does not immediately follow the Hoover segment and the death of Rin Tin Tin precedes European royalty and the Democratic opposition. The eulogy for the dog also warrants the longest running time of any segment.

As a theatrical attraction, the newsreels were popular enough to sustain about a dozen specialty "newsreel theaters" located in big cities, whose programming was devoted exclusively to newsreel and documentary material. On November 1, 1929, the Embassy Newsreel Theater opened on Broadway in New York and remained a local fixture until 1949. Culling its programs from Fox Movietone News and Hearst Metrotone News, the Embassy played a 45–50-minute program with fourteen showings daily, from 10:00 A.M. to midnight. The 578-seat house was an immediate success, attracting a cosmopolitan audience described by *Variety* as "strollers along Broadway, the impatient date makers, the train waiters, the time killers," as well as "the untold thousands who think the newsreel is the best single feature, now that it is in sound, ever devised in the film industry, as it was also in the silent era." For a while the Embassy was the only theater of its kind in the country, but the concept soon expanded to other metropolitan markets domestically and overseas (newsreel theaters in London, Berlin, and Paris being particularly successful). Adhering to regional stereotypes, however, a sister venture on the West Coast, the Los Angeles Newsreel Theater, closed its doors after three weeks of poor business in 1930.

Competing with the Embassy chain was a circuit of newsreel theaters begun by Trans-Lux in 1931, which culled its shows from Pathé, Universal, and Paramount newsreels for 50-minute programs at the top of each hour. Trans-Lux ran a cost-efficient operation, employing an automatic turnstile instead of a box office window, into which patrons deposited twenty-five cents for admission.

Like the Hollywood feature film, the newsreel showcased the new dimension of sound, delighting equally in the music of nature (crickets chirping, canaries singing, animals howling) and the discordant metropolis (horns blowing, streetcars clanging, crowds roaring). Just as spectators watching the first motion pictures eagerly attended to anything that moved, anything that moved and sounded warranted newsreel coverage.

Of course the sweetest sound was the human voice. Thirty years previously, at the dawn of cinema, to be photographed in moving images was to attain a kind of celluloid immortality. Now men and women in full animation and locution offered themselves to the ages. A parade of politicians, aristocrats, inventors, sports heroes, adventurers, writers, and artists marched dutifully before the cameras to stand stiffly and enunciate clearly. They comprise a generation of public figures not yet media-savvy, still ill at ease talking to a camera lens, nervously eyeing cue cards off camera or spouting memorized lines. Apparently, the uncertainty about proper newsreel deportment worked both ways. In 1928 in London, when Fox Movietone screened the first talking pictures of King George, his respectful British subjects rose to their feet and remained standing until His Majesty's address came to an end.

Royalty at home or in exile made regular newsreel appearances, but more forbidding if no less colorful leadership attracted the better portion of coverage. One of the first to present himself to the sound newsreels was Italian dictator Benito Mussolini. Never camera shy, Il Duce was a ham on film and a microphone hog. Mussolini debuted speaking Italian and later tried his hand at semicomprehensible English utterances read from cue cards off camera. "Italy's Duce," wisecracked *Variety* in 1930, "seems to crash the newsreels every week." Another signature politician of the twentieth century, Leon Trotsky, also spoke to the American masses in his sound-on-film debut in 1932. Although his "diction was hard to follow," Trotsky flattered the hometown crowd by remarking that "New York is the best spot from which to get a perspective on the world."

Not to be outdone, novelists, inventors, and businessmen rushed to get their wisdom and faces on screen. In 1930 George Bernard Shaw made the first of many appearances for Fox Movietone and awarded the outfit a nice plug in the bargain. "Here I am enjoying myself at Malvern, and there you are enjoying yourself by allowing a photograph to talk to you. That, you see, is one of the marvels of Movietone." Not all literary artists were as popular as Shaw, whose presentation of self perfectly accorded with American preconceptions about eccentric British playwrights. The sound newsreel also rendered a few eminent Victorians ridiculous. "It is hard for audiences to take H. G. Wells seriously in a camera interview on the economic situation," observed *Variety*, because "H. G., in addition to possessing a voice that reproduces notes in the highest pitch, has wrinkles around the eyes which causes him to register chronic mirth on film." Likewise, the nonprint version of Theodore Dreiser suffered by comparison. "As an actor he is an amateur compared to George Bernard Shaw. The poise is not there."

Greeting the New Year in 1930, John D. Rockefeller made an eccentric sound-on-film debut. Upon landing at an airfield, he hands out dimes to a crowd of welcomers, saying "bless you" to his pilot, to children, and to the newsreel cameramen, capping the loony character turn by looking straight into the camera and bestowing a more heartfelt benediction: "God Bless Standard Oil." On the other end of the materialist spectrum, Mahatma Ghandi broke a twenty-five-year resolution never to be photographed and consented in 1931 to speak before the Fox Movietone cameras. Ghandi was adjudged an uncooperative subject by newsreel standards, meaning that unlike American politicians or Hollywood personalities, he refused to take direction or speak up for the microphone. "He is temperamental and conceited, a hopeless case for sound pix," Fox's crew reported back to headquarters. "But if, in the future, he loses his conceit and egotism and becomes normal, he will possibly make a good subject." More warmly received was the "foreign flavor" of the gemütlichkeit professor Albert Einstein, even when he recited his lines in German. "Neat human interest touch here was that Frau Einstein followed her husband with a greeting to the Americans spoken in English," beamed *Variety*, grateful to encounter a pair of congenial newsreel subjects.

The "ear entertainment afforded by the talking news has created greater interest in newsreels than ever before," declared Fox chief Winfield Sheehan in 1930. "Theater patrons have become more intimately acquainted with the personalities of the world, and they in turn have become a part of the motion picture family. The Prince of Wales, Lindbergh, Mussolini, John D. Rockefeller, and the political idols of the world have taken rank with Charles Farrell, Janet Gaynor, and Mary Pickford." Note the hierarchy: with the sound newsreel, the leaders of nations and the titans of industry attained equal billing with Hollywood stars.

The newsreels not only confirmed public stature; they conferred a kind of immortality. In 1931 Tom Waller, *Variety*'s man at the Embassy Newsreel Theater, first observed the life-giving quality of sound on film during what he considered "the most unusual audience reaction in the history of newsreel theaters." Waller's comments are worth quoting at length as a vivid evocation of what was then still a new experience, the vitality of a photographic image made flesh by sound on film.

The newsreel item reported the death of Sir Thomas Lipton, a well-known and beloved British sportsman. "There is deep silence while a funeral dirge accompanies the lettering telling of nations mourning the great sportsman's death," Waller relates, referring to the printed intertitle that preceded the newsreel clip. "But when an old Fox interview, showing him in all his vigor and joviality and [wise]cracking about how he'd swap all of his [trophy] collection just to bring the America's Cup home for a week—there's laughter." What did the abrupt shift from solemn silence to bright laughter mean? "Probably no single piece of film with a sound track has had such an opportunity to establish such a precedent: the vividness of mechanical immortality, as reflected in the strip of celluloid hurriedly retrieved from the newsreel archives, over the factfulness of the printed word and mortality." Against the animated reality of Sir Thomas Lipton's sound-on-film image, his printed obituary faded from memory.

As in the case of Sir Thomas, screen obituaries were most invigorating when the subject had been in the newsreel eye long enough to provide background clips to animate his life. With an inventiveness the decedent might have admired, the death of Thomas Edison early Sunday morning on October 18, 1931, inspired an exemplary death knell. By noon that same day, Pathé News was screening a four-minute special issue in theaters across the nation. Sensing the imminent death of the eighty-four-year-old giant of their industry, Pathé had prepared an obituary in advance, including a pre-posthumous tribute from RCA chairman David Sarnoff. The company then sent the reels to theaters and green-lighted their release by telegram upon news of Edison's death.

But if the sound newsreel animated even the dead, it might also render the record of reality lifeless. The tethering of the newsreel camera to sound equipment thwarted the mobility and spontaneity of silent photography. Sound equipment was cumbersome, delicate, and expensive (outfitting a mobile sound news wagon cost nearly $35,000). "I suspect we've sacrificed news for sound," lamented H. E. Jameyson, a prominent Midwest exhibitor. "There's no news in hearing Margaret Sanger discuss birth control via the sound track. She was doing it before the photo electric cell was invented." Universal Newspaper Newsreel ultimately abandoned most live sound recording and shot silent in the field, adding music, sound effects, and commentary in the studio. "Sound made the newsreel articulate," continued Jameyson, "but it made it slow, cumbersome, immobile. It was not a fair exchange. The newsreel lost its potency."

It also lost some of its accuracy as a record of history. Virtually every public event or formal ceremony witnessed by the early sound newsreel was staged or reenacted for the benefit of the cameras and microphones. Common practice was to rehearse an event beforehand or to repeat the event afterwards, with the newsreel cameraman and sound man acting as directors of a playlet featuring politicians and businessmen who compliantly recited lines and repeated gestures. "OK for sound?" was the incessant question. If not, the deed was done again.

Whether a political address, a formal signing, or a ceremonial announcement, the newsreel record tends to preserve a secondhand, one-step-removed version of American history. Newsreel events are not quite "pseudo events" as the cultural historian Daniel Boorstin defined the term, "synthetic happenings" that would not have happened were not the cameras present. However, they are *skewed* events, happenings that would have occurred differently without newsreel coverage or whose newsreel reenactment was slightly

'START YOUR DIALOGUE OVER AGAIN, WILL YOU BOYS? ———— WE JUST ARRIVED."

Not OK for sound: a cartoon from Motion Picture Herald satires the mediated newsreel, 1931.

different from the original performance. In 1937 the critic Gilbert Seldes cited a worrisome instance of newsreel revisionism. In the presence of his cabinet, President Roosevelt signed a bill into law. One of the cabinet members was called away and the event was reenacted in his absence for the newsreels. Thus, the man who had attended the real signing was absent from the newsreel record of the signing, erased on screen from an occurrence he was present for in reality.

LIBRARY STOCK

The blips in time in the newsreel record of reality were minor annoyances when weighed against the historical significance of the new motion picture genre born of the format, the archival documentary. Unlike the expeditionary film or travelogue shot in the field, the archival documentary drew on the newsreel backlog ("library stock" in the jargon of the day) to fashion a motion picture replay of the past. Although sporadically preserved and selectively resurrected, some thirty years of motion picture footage could be reedited and repackaged. For the first time in history, history might be writ large on the motion picture screen.

Fittingly, the pioneering archival documentaries of the early 1930s drew on the historical event best documented by motion pictures and most worth remembering: the Great War. Tapping into the war jitters incited by a resurgent, militarist Germany, a documentary film cycle comprised of *The Big Drive* (1933), *This Is America* (1933), *Hell's Holiday* (1933), *World in Revolt* (1933), and *The First World War* (1934) reveals that some Americans had already sensed that the Nazis were busy planning a sequel.

The archival documentaries of the Great War share a sense of elegiac despair for the past and uneasy foreboding about the future. Like most interwar recollections of the misbilled "war to end all wars," the spirit is pacifist and relativist. War is a fruitless, murderous business; all of the combatants, from whatever nation, are morally equivalent, friend and foe alike, the memory of the Mad Hun blotted out by common suffering in No Man's Land for no discernable reason. *The Big Drive* dedicates itself impartially to "the memory of millions of victims, friend and foe, whose noble convictions and fearless devotion enabled them to give *their all* in 'A War to End All Wars.'" Looking forward, the films evince a premonition that the Great War was not to be the last world war. The premature title of *The First World War* assumed that numbering would sooner or later become necessary.

Narrated and compiled by A. J. Rule, *The Big Drive* expresses the emergent sense of film as a historical treasure, proudly presenting "in their natural sequence scenes from the world's greatest human conflict—the World War." Taglines ratcheted up the lure of motion picture history. "Real! Actual! Secret archives of eight nations in the world war give up their truth at last!" promised ads, with a homicidal hyperbole that outdid any competition: "Five cameramen and ten million soldiers killed to make it!" Despite such pledges, *The Big Drive* casually mixed authentic newsreel footage with silent-era melodrama and faked wartime newsreels, most evidently in a staged bayonet fight between two soldiers in a trench. (Motion picture imagery of the Great War is notoriously unreliable because of the cumbersome camera equipment and restrictions on filming at the front.)

Besides the past, *The Big Drive* teaches germane lessons for the present. Tracing the course of the Bolshevik Revolution, narrator Rule admonishes like-minded Americans to learn from the turbulent Russian experience. "Little did they realize what it means to overthrow a government and try to establish a new one." More than fears of civil disorder, however, the dread

The birth of the archival documentary: a staged sequence from *The Big Drive* (1933). (Courtesy of the Museum of Modern Art)

of another war in Europe permeates the retrospective Great War documentaries. "Airplanes played a very important part in the World War but nothing to what they will play in the next one, if there is a next one," narrator Rule predicts. "And in another war the civilians in all probability will suffer as much if not more than the soldiers." Rule pessimistically concludes that "another war will in all probability stain the pages of our world history" and closes with a benediction: "The big drive that we called the World War ended, but the big drive for eternal peace shall never end."

The most successful and prestigious of the Great War documentaries was *The First World War*. Produced by Truman Talley and written by Laurence Stallings, it demonstrated a new smoothness in the integration of sound and image, with the narrative voice-over supplementing images, not stepping on them or describing what was before the eyes anyway. "The Stallings comments drip on this monstrous kaleidoscope of human imbecility with the subtle, dark, and murderous bite of acid," noted the *New York Times*, which placed the film on its Ten Best List for 1934. *The First World War* expertly orchestrated the core elements of the archival documentary, a genre no longer being born but now in early adulthood: library stock, voice-over narration, commentative music, intertitles, subtitles, slow-motion photography, newspaper headlines panned by the camera, still photos telescoped in on, and (the surest sign of the arrival of generic maturity) the confidence to remain silent and let the images speak for themselves.

The film's first intertitle defines the genre it exemplifies: "an authentic motion picture record reaching back to the turn of the twentieth century, collected from official sources and the archives of the great nations, and presented by Fox Film Corporation in association with Simon and Schuster." The last line referred to the book published in tandem with the film, a marketing device that underscored the new turn of current events: the parity between history from books and history from film. Thus too the prefatory tribute: "Dedicated to the soldiers and sailors, known and unknown, who fought in the Great War, and to the cameramen, known and unknown, whose work made this record possible," a sentiment that links in honor the actors on the stage of history with those who photograph the drama.

Like a history book, the film is organized into eleven chapters, but the arid task of reading words cannot compete with the wonder of watching action on screen. "With the turn of the century, cameras begin their turning," begins the voice-over self-reflexively. The images recapture a past already remote for the 1930s spectator, a courtly realm of kings, heraldry, and horses, "the panoply of a world that was . . . a world soon to perish under the fire of thunder and guns." Repudiating the bombast of the Voice of God style then current, the narration delivered by stage actor Pedro de Cordoba is both sardonic ("America, in the midst of a world sharpening its swords, indulges in a few mild reforms") and daring ("Lenin—the seer, the incorruptible prophet, the founder of Bolshevism"). Frequent references to the camarawork remind spectators they are privileged eyewitnesses to history: de Cordoba points out that "this is perhaps the only film ever made from a balloon while under fire" and that the submarine-eye-view shots of British frigates come from cameras placed aboard German U-boats.

Foreshadowing not just the Great War but the next war, the early chapters of *The First World War* chronicle "the Teutonic war machine" gearing up for action with goose-stepping soldiers cheered on by a people hypnotized by martial ceremony. Aerial bombing, another fear that haunted the 1930s, is introduced with the flat declaration, "Here is a foretaste of wars to come." The penultimate sequence is a florid montage, without voice-over narration, set to music, and indebted to the KINO eye of Soviet director Sergei Eisenstein. A symphonic score acts as contrapuntal beat for the visual rhythm of artillery barrages, belching flamethrowers, maimed soldiers writhing on the battlefield, and corpses dangling in concertina wire. Nothing marks the end of the early sound era so sharply as the fluid cascade of music and image, articulate without speech.

The final chapter ("ARMISTICE!") inspires another innovative sequence, a kaleidoscope of newsreel images and multiple dissolves. "The war that was to end wars is dead," concludes de Cordoba, with no sense of victory or finality, with the intimation rather that the drama is to be continued, for "today there is another generation." The images that swirl about the screen—of global turmoil and armies on the march, of Mussolini and Ghandi, Stalin and the Pope, Hirohito and FDR—prove that the past really is prologue. The one face missing from the dizzying pageant, conspicuous and inexplicable in its absence, belongs to Adolf Hitler. The decision to edit him out of *The First World War* serves only to make his presence more palpable. Even Americans in 1934 must have known that he was not to be erased so easily from history.

As landmark efforts in what became one of the most influential motion picture genres of the twentieth century, the Great War documentaries showed how easily old motion pictures might breed new motion pictures, how smoothly the currents of the past flowed with deft editing and eloquent narration. "Into the short space of seventy minutes," *This Is America* had packed "more history than might be learned from dozens of textbooks," proclaimed the *New York News*, which defined the genre as it praised it: "Although the pictures have been taken from the newsreels, they have been carefully selected and strung together in continuity to form an exciting historical pageant."

THE NEWSREEL ETHOS

Within the media matrix of the 1930s, the newsreels occupied a unique niche. As both news bearers and items on the motion picture program, they were caught between the journalistic impulse to cover the news of the day and the commercial pressure to avoid any unpleasantness that might disturb a mood conducive to a good night out at the movies. The muddled ethos had the predictable consequence of placing the newsreel version of American life in the Great Depression at serious variance with offscreen reality.

Like the promethean cameraman of the expeditionary film, the newsreel cameraman assumed the guise of an intrepid daredevil, not a working journalist. "I say there is more of adventure and romance in world newsreel gathering than in most any other occupation I can think of," declared Harry

Lawrenceson, foreign editor for Fox Movietone News. To celebrate the exploits of the dauntless brotherhood, Universal edited a two-reel compilation entitled *The World's Greatest Thrills* (1933), comprised of twenty-six sequences of fires, hurricanes, stunt flying, and fiery crashes of cars, locomotives, and planes. "The picture is primarily exciting entertainment and is intended as a tribute to newsreel cameramen of all countries and companies," said Universal Newspaper Newsreel editor Allyn Butterfield. "Wherever one finds a man risking his life in some sort of stunt, or wherever human beings face danger, there one will find a cameraman, frequently staking his life too in order to get pictures of the event." Ads promised "the biggest thrills in newsreel history just as they happened—not faked but so real as to bowl you over."

The reassurance that the newsreel history was not faked was a tacit admission that manipulations were accepted practice and fabrications a shameful secret. Though the brazen duplicities of the tawdry expeditionary film were rare, newsreel editors regularly took a bait-and-switch approach to screen imagery. When real coverage of an event was unavailable, the substitution of stock footage of a similar event filled the gap and the voice-over commentary continued as if nothing were amiss. Unable to obtain footage of the king of England opening the World Economic Conference in 1933, the newsreels substituted a decade-old shot of the king visiting the British Museum. Sensational sports footage also tended to illustrate more than one game, as long as the action on the field and the uniforms of the players matched the voice-over commentary.

As viewers became more alert and knowledgeable, such bald-faced deceptions diminished in frequency. In 1932, to encourage competition and professionalism, *Variety* inaugurated a monthly listing of "newsreel scoops" that sternly lectured newsreel editors on journalistic standards. "This chart will not classify as a scoop any clip, no matter how spectacular, which is a misrepresentation or strictly a phoney. For that reason a reel which ordinarily would be credited with a scoop in the Lindbergh case is not getting the credit in this count." The last line referred to a well-known and widely condemned example of duplicity in which a newsreel cameraman had falsely claimed to be filming at the site of the discovery of the body of the kidnapped Lindbergh baby.

Working against efforts to elevate professional standards was the manner of newsreel production and distribution. Rented as part of a studio-designed package of shorts and features, the newsreels had little incentive to be aggressive and upright, save for company pride. "Under current methods of distribution and selling," complained *Motion Picture Herald*, "a newsreel fifty per cent the best in the field would not enjoy a two per cent advantage" in rentals.

One advantage the newsreels did enjoy was relative freedom from official censorship. Neither the Studio Relations Committee nor the Production Code Administration ever subjected newsreel content to the systematic scrutiny given the Hollywood feature film, always the prime target of Hays Office interest in both the pre-Code and Code eras. "Efforts to establish a censor formula for newsreels similar to that of the Hays Code for features and shorts have been abandoned," *Variety* reported in 1932. "Judgment of news matters has been relegated solely to the newsreel editor." The location of the newsreel operations (in New York, not Los Angeles, a coast away from the Studio Relations Committee's office and, after 1934, the hawk eyes of Joseph Breen) and the fast pace of production of the twice-weekly issues (in special cases, a news event shot at 9:00 P.M. in the evening could be edited and shipped to New York exhibitors by 3:00 A.M. the next morning) militated against a meticulous review process. Moreover, the newsreels possessed some special status as screen journalism. In 1931, New York exempted newsreels from state censorship laws and in 1933 Ohio followed suit, leaving only the state censorship boards of Maryland and Virginia vetting newsreel content. By 1934, Chicago, Illinois, was deemed "the only situation in the country where newsreels may be clipped by censors."

By and large, then, internal editorial policies, not interference from the government, shaped the boundaries for the coverage of hard news, forcing hard choices for newsreel editors and exhibitors. In 1932 the *Akron*, a Navy dirigible, was docking near San Diego when a gust of wind unexpectedly blew it skyward. Three sailors were holding tether lines. The men froze, held the lines tight, and went aloft with the ship some sixty feet in the air. Two lost their grip and plunged to the earth before the *Akron* descended. Though the newsreels captured the entire scene, all save Hearst Movietone edited the plunging bodies from the clips and even Hearst pulled the clip after adverse audience reaction. "Scenes of actual death are rarely shown in this country," reported *Variety*, before passing along an intriguing sidebar: "Cameramen from force of habit keep grinding, but superstition often makes them open up their boxes and pull out the tragedy, exposing it to the light and fogging the film."

That even the jaundiced eye of *Variety*'s Tom Waller almost blinked before the grisly exhumation of a corpse verifies the rarity of such images. According to Waller, "the all-time shocker of newsreel history" to date was being screened by Universal Newspaper Newsreel in its April 10, 1934, issue. "It's a clear view of an exhumed male corpse. Universal for some time has been getting nearer and nearer to the real thing, first smudgy views of wounded and dead in train wrecks and now straight from the shoulder views." Waller dubbed the scene "almost like a [Boris] Karloff terrorizer" and described the real-life nightmare picture:

> It starts on a dark day outside the dreary Stavisky home [scene of a notorious murder in Paris]. The gendarmes are in search of evidence that the lender was murdered. It travels naturally enough to the cemetery. Men begin to open a grave. Suddenly the audience is looking at a coffin in the bottom of a pit. And then—bang—the lid opens and there is the body of a man who has been in the earth for weeks.

Waller speculated that "criticism will probably pile upon the reel because in the screen news field there's a silent understanding among the editors, or at least so some of them aver, that subjects of violent death will be treated with the greatest delicacy." In fact, any newsreel venture into gruesomeness met with audience resistance, especially from female patrons. Even Universal tended to limit its horror films to the backlot.

Terry Ramsaye, documentary filmmaker and author in 1926 of the pioneer compendium *A Million and One Nights: A History of the Motion Picture*, reflected the prevalent schizophrenia about the role of the newsreels in his commentary in *Motion Picture Herald*, the influential trade journal for exhibitors he edited from 1931 to 1949. Ramsaye's contradictory observations remain some of the best-informed analysis of the content and character of the newsreels for the simple reason he was one of the few critics who paid them regular attention. As a former documentarian himself, Ramsaye felt a proprietary interest in a format he helped shape, and he was never reluctant to share his advice.

Sometimes Ramsaye condemned the newsreels for their timorousness and vacillation, their craven willingness to knuckle under to authority. Unlike the print press, which defended its own and enjoyed protections under the First Amendment, the newsreels "in the eyes of the law and the tradition of the courts, are merely a part of the amusement business." Ramsaye placed the blame for the low status squarely on the medium. "Newsreels have been issued in the United States since 1910. They have not in the subsequent twenty years ever shown any teeth. They have never taken a good, first class editorial wallop at anybody or anything," he grumbled in 1931. By bowing before power, the newsreel sycophants deserved to be treated like lapdogs.

Yet at other times Ramsaye criticized the newsreels for trying to be *too* journalistic and hard-hitting, for somehow being under the "impression that they are in the news business, that they purvey news, and that they are to be classified as publications." Offended by the "views at all angles of the stark body of the exceedingly dead John Dillinger on a slab in the Chicago morgue," Ramsaye argued that "the newsreels are just in the show business, or they should by all means get into it." Perhaps a place existed for the aggressive newsreel in newsreel theaters like the Embassy and Trans-Lux, but as long as the newsreel was part of the balanced program it "ought to be an entertaining and amusing derivative."

The newsreels were certainly a profitable derivative. In the late 1940s, boxed in by television and with expenses rising as profits plunged, the newsreels would be "loss leaders" well before they were officially closed down. In the Great Depression, however, they were solid profit makers for the studios. In 1933 the estimated cost for 104 issues of a newsreel, a complete year's run, was a little in excess of $1.4 million, or about the price of a single expensive A feature. The total costs for the five newsreels was estimated at a little under $10 million, with box office revenues yearly at $19.5 million.

Revenues aside, the newsreel paid back other kinds of tangible dividends to Hollywood. More so even than feature films derived from literary classics, the newsreel was valued for prestige and respect, "the one product of the screen which, to a highly important portion of the audience, is especially laden with responsibility for establishing and maintaining the status of the motion picture as a medium," as Ramsaye expressed it, lending American cinema "some part of the status and prerogatives of the art of publication." The Embassy Newsreel Theater is "drawing the best, the class and the intellectuals of New York into its seats every week," *Variety* noted in 1930. "Probably there are numberless citizens of Manhattan who go to the Embassy and no other picture theater—perhaps no other theater." On the newsreel, then, weighed the burden of elevating the motion picture medium in the eyes of elite opinion makers and thereby gaining it some of the First Amendment protections granted the print media.

Unlike newspapers, however, and to a lesser extent radio, the newsreels tended to tremble before authority and turn a blind eye to the urgent issues of the day. At times, the deference to politicians was abject, the avoidance of the Great Depression stupefying. In September 1931, when President Hoover spoke before the American Legion in Detroit, the Prohibition-weary veterans interrupted his speech with shouts of "Beer! Beer! We Want Beer!" a demand edited out of the newsreel coverage. No wonder government officials pushed the newsreels around with a high-handedness they would never have ventured to show the print press. They denied access, restricted photography, confiscated cameras, and destroyed footage. In 1931, when Paramount Sound News attempted to cover a prison break at Leavenworth Federal Prison, prison officials detained the cameraman, confiscated his equipment, and exposed his footage. From the warden, no apologies; from the newsreels, no protest. "If not for their own sake, then for the motion picture, the newsreels might well develop a backbone," pleaded Ramsaye in disgust.

RKO's *Headline Shooter* (1933), a newspaper film transferred to the world of screen journalism, offers a glimpse into the offscreen pressures on the newsreel. Armed with "a pint of scotch and a camera," an intrepid newsreel photographer is sent into the Deep South to cover the raging floods along the Mississippi. Learning of shoddy construction work in the levees, he sneaks his way into the flood site to photograph the evidence ("I think my public would like to see it on the screen"). After obtaining a picture-perfect scoop, he is accosted by local authorities who lean on him to surrender the incriminating footage. They first try persuasion (the local judge who oversaw the construction of the defective levees was himself the victim of chicanery) and then force ("That film's not going to leave here"). Under threat of violence, he removes the film from his camera and tosses it into a fire. The celluloid flares up in the flames and the image match cuts to a lit match. Back in New York, the cameraman sits in a bar chatting with other newsreel boys. He had destroyed only unexposed film, he assures them, not his footage of the scoop. "The clip's playing in theaters now," he brags. He has done the right thing, his colleagues agree. "That's the trouble with this country— there's been too much covering up of things that ought to come out in the open. News is news and belongs to the public." That sentiment, however, was Hollywood pretense, not newsreel policy.

Covering Up the Great Depression

The most conspicuous absence in the newsreel coverage of the 1930s was the small matter of the Great Depression. Hunger, unemployment, social disorder, political ferment, protest marches, seditious speeches, the full fury of a time of radical discontent and anger in the streets—though some of this was captured by the newsreel cameras, little of it reached newsreel screens that always managed to make time for stunts, sports, and cheesecake. Motion picture images of the breadlines and dust bowls of the Great Depression tend to be ex post facto visual tricks of memory: that is, recalled from post-Depression archival documentaries utilizing outtakes and censored material, pictures that went unscreened and unseen in the 1930s themselves.

The decision to play down the Great Depression was seldom the result of a formal edict from government officials or even the Hays Office. It was mainly an informal policy of censorship by omission from studio executives who embraced an ethos of "100% entertainment." Fox theater managers were instructed not to give "excess influence to unemployment in newsreels and other film matter" because "too much talk and publicity serves to accentuate the adverse side of the unemployment situation and detract from the program's entertainment value." The unscreenable material encompassed the most urgent issues of the day, specifically:

> Subjects of a controversial nature on Prohibition.
> All subjects that may be construed as Bolshevik propaganda.
> All political speeches that take sides on matters of public interest.
> Clips showing breadlines.
> Economic discussions on which patronage reaction may be divided.

In 1934 *Variety* surveyed newsreel content and concluded that self-censorship originating from *within* the newsreel ranks was as confining as any restrictions imposed from without. "Fear instilled by that censorship within . . . has had an observable tendency to intimidate otherwise imaginative and daring editorial brains," charged the trade journal. "It's safer for the reels to pad their spools with amusing but innocuous freak tidbits." Scenes of labor strikes, hunger marches, and other threatening gatherings were routinely cut as an exercise of "editorial judgement." No wonder that a prime motivation for the creation of the communist-backed Film Forum in 1933 was to produce and screen "newsreels that reflect social events such as are customarily suppressed by commercial newsreel organizations."

In 1932 Universal Newspaper Newsreel perpetrated an emblematic instance of suppression with a series of cheerful economic forecasts under the title "The Tide Turns." "Renewed manufacturing activity throughout the nation recalls thousands of workers as industry forges steadily upward," was the official news of the day. "Nation's business continues upward trend as industry adds thousands to swelling payrolls." Courtland Smith, president of Pathé News, actually bragged about the "camera campaign to relieve unemployment" by featuring optimistic outlooks from industrial leaders and job tips for the unemployed. "By preaching a doctrine of optimism during the time of depression," editorialized *The Billboard*, the newsreel can "make one realize that nothing is as black as it's painted. Every cloud has a silver lining, and the screen can reflect and emphasize points that government leaders are trying to bring out." An upbeat newsreel did "a world of good toward correcting present business conditions."

Particularly under Hoover, the chirpy tone of the newsreels could seem like glad tidings from never-never land. In 1930 Fox Movietone News created two characters called "Mr. Fear" and "Mr. Courage" to depict the proper response to hard times. In one vignette, a man enters a restaurant and orders a small meal. He is advised by a fellow customer to order a larger meal. The first man protests he cannot afford a larger meal because of the Depression. This, he is told, is the wrong way to look at things. In times of Depression, each American should spend *more*, should in fact commit himself to spending an additional dollar a week and thus pump more money into circulation. The first man concedes the point and orders a much larger dinner. Outside, on the street, the sage economist suggests they walk to their destination. "No," says his convert. "We'll take a cab." That kind of bonehead boosterism—advising Americans to squander money they did not have—discredited the newsreel among audiences even as official voices praised its cluelessness.

Another reason the newsreels avoided controversial figures and divisive issues was the boisterous response from audiences. Looking at the newsreel images of politicians, businessmen, experts, and evangelists, moviegoers registered support or contempt much as they cheered on the cavalry in a western or hissed the cad in a melodrama. From many a disgruntled Depression crowd, the reaction to the rosy scenarios and disengaged personalities was rancorous and sarcastic. In extreme cases, arguments and fights broke out between patrons, cracking the orb of serene theatrical space exhibitors sought so avidly to cultivate. Bouncy forecasts and blithe commentary in the newsreels inspired snorts of disbelief and muttered expletives. Embittered laughter and venomous hissing greeted the pronouncements of more than one national leader, up to and including President Hoover. Throughout the Great Depression, *Variety* reporter Tom Waller heard "a riot of catcalls and wails which drowned out most of the dialogue" when one or another self-righteous face spoke up for a discredited dogma. If the target was ripe for ridicule, the newsreels might cue the crowd's contempt. In 1933 Paramount Sound News set up a segment on evangelist Aimee Semple McPherson with a caption revealing her salary for saving souls was $5,000 a week. When McPherson launched into a spirited call for converts, audiences hooted in derision.

By 1930, defenders of Prohibition were being enthusiastically razzed by motion picture audiences. When Col. Amos Walter Wright Woodcock, the new Prohibition head, appeared in a Fox Movietone newsreel to explain government policy, his remarks were "roundly hissed" at the Embassy Theater. Confronted with effete teetotalers such as Dr. Clarence True Wilson, spokesman for a Dry America, and O. S. Poland of the Anti-Saloon League, thirsty patrons reacted with "resentful guffaws," "catcalls," and "Bronx cheers" (a new coinage, an act executed by using the tongue as a reed and blowing outward). The changing political winds were registered when a dry speaker was "as usual joshed and hissed" and "the wet eloquence" of Congressman Fiorello LaGuardia (R-N.Y.) was cheered and applauded.

One of the few public figures who retained affection and grew in popular esteem in the early 1930s was Will Rogers. Rogers' status was unique: in his stage show, radio commentaries, motion pictures, and newspaper columns, the beloved humorist uttered seditious remarks under the cover of homespun innocence, the aw-shucks bumpkin pose not for a minute concealing his razor sharp wit and populist sentiments. Though a registered Democrat (not being a member of an organized political party, he explained), Rogers specialized in nonpartisan expressions of the vox populi. "The returns are just coming in from the Virgin Islands," he joked on the night of the 1932 election. "Clark Gable is leading Hoover and Roosevelt both." Until his death in 1935, Rogers's Oklahoma drawl spoke to a reality before which other, more refined accents remained oblivious. In 1932 Rogers sparked rueful laughter with one of the few unscripted exchanges in the early sound newsreel. John Nance Garner (D-Tex.) is welcoming Rogers back to America after his return from a trip abroad. The pair exchange pleasantries and a crowd laughs affably at Rogers' remarks. "You've got them eating out of your hand," says Garner admiringly. "Yeh," cracks Rogers. "The ones that *are* eating."

Gentle laughter aside, the vociferous reactions to controversial personalities and topics unsettled theater managers. Some exhibitors concluded that any newsreel clip with the potential to incite any portion of the audience was best left unscreened. "We will not run on the screen of our theater any talks on 'depression' or any picture pertaining to the subjects and I think it is time the newsreels realized that what we want is one hundred per cent entertainment," declared a New York exhibitor, who personally deleted any newsreel clips that dared to broach the subject. At the 5th Avenue Playhouse in New York, violence nearly erupted when a newsreel showed Congressman Hamilton Fish (R-N.Y.) reading a speech against communism and telling foreigners who "don't like this country" to "get out." The crowd that hissed Fish was surely unrepresentative (the rest of the motion picture program consisted of three Soviet films), but with audience sympathies varying so widely from theater to theater, why court trouble by showcasing controversy?

Images from overseas could be no less inflammatory. As Hitler's campaign of terror against German Jews gained momentum, newsreel editors anguished over how to cover Nazism and the man who was its public face. For a time, Universal Newspaper Newsreel deleted clips of Hitler to avoid inciting altercations between patrons. Unlike Mussolini, a strutting martinet hard to take seriously onscreen, Hitler was a controversial and feared presence from his first noteworthy appearances in American newsreels in 1932, despite wisecracks about the Charlie Chaplin moustache.

Domestic crimes were safer territory. If the criminal and his exploits were sensational enough, and if a crime-does-not-pay lesson could be solemnly appended to the mayhem, newsreels might blend tabloid thrills with moral opprobrium. Gangsters alive or dead, behind bars or laid out in morgues, ranked with starlets and sportsmen in screen appeal. The coverage of the death of John Dillinger, so upsetting to Terry Ramsaye, offered a graphic example of how the newsreels worked the crime beat. Dillinger's body, served up on a slab in the jubilant environs of the Cook County morgue, was shown in the newsreels within days of the gangster's death on July 22, 1934, a gruesome tableau that would never have been allowed in the entertainment feature. That the portrait of Dillinger in death was a departure from normative newsreel content, and that exhibitors might have reason to be wary of such morbid scenes, was confirmed by Tom Waller in *Variety*: "Death of Dillinger has established another precedent for the newsreels and assignments for cameramen. After this the boys will have to add the morgue to their coverage. A genuine semi-close-up of the dead gunman's face is graphic to say the least." Waller then warned about the lingering aftereffect of the dead man's image: "It will stay with an audience of any imagination for a long time. And the immediate memory might even distract them from the rest of the program."

Graphic images did upset susceptible viewers. During one grisly week in November 1934, the newsreels unspooled the death tableaux of Baby Face Nelson ("seventeen slugs in his body") and the bodies of three little girls found murdered in the Blue Ridge Mountains. "What should be shown in the newsreels?" inquired a roundtable discussion in *Motion Picture Herald*. "Do shots of slain bandits and murdered children bring money to the box office window or do they shoo away the more sensitive customers?" The consensus from exhibitors was that "harrowing scenes make an indelible impression that even a light, enjoyable feature cannot erase," particularly on women and children, to the detriment of box office revenues and moviehouse reputation. "I remember just a few years back that a corpse was rarely exposed to public view," observed an exhibitor in 1934 after witnessing the morgue shots of Dillinger and Baby Face Nelson and glimpses of the three dead children. The decision to show such faces of death would rebound against the theater, for moviegoers come "to be refreshed mentally" but "leave feeling as though they have attended a wake!" Against his better judgment the exhibitor had shown the scenes of the murdered children and found himself bombarded with angry calls from "prominent well meaning friends" in the community "condemning me for showing such a scene." "It not only upset them," he reported pathetically, "but it had a terrifying effect on the children they brought to see *A Girl of the Limberlost* [1934]."

The most dramatic instance of the early sound newsreel in action was the coverage of a crime that nearly warranted its centennial superlative: the kidnap-murder of the Lindbergh baby, the "Crime of the Century." The kidnapping of the twenty-month-old son of Charles and Anne Morrow Lindbergh from their home in Hopewell, New Jersey, on the evening of March 1, 1932, was not just a personal tragedy but a cultural shockwave. "The world's most famous baby has been kidnapped, and the attention of literally the whole world has been aroused," announced NBC radio's Lowell Thomas the next evening. Amid an atmosphere of national outrage, President Hoover ordered nearly five thousand federal agents mobilized to crack the case, with J. Edgar Hoover's FBI leading the posse.

Already, however, more journalists than detectives were working the Lindbergh beat, including a huge contingent from the newsreels. In what a Paramount Sound News editor described as "the greatest concentration of men and equipment for newsreel coverage since the war," the five newsreel companies dispatched more than one hundred men, fifty cameras, and thirty-five sound trucks to Hopewell and chartered planes to obtain aerial shots of the Lindbergh grounds. Paramount Sound News kept seven crews on duty in the vicinity, with the men in each unit sleeping in three shifts to keep watch.

Though Lindbergh balked at going before the sound cameras to record a personal appeal to the kidnapper, the family released 16mm home movies of the child, which were then bumped up to 35mm for release prints, reportedly the first time private pictures were "conscripted for public service" in the newsreels. Processed and distributed with unprecedented speed, the first

Watch for him everywhere: an all points bulletin in the newsreels for the kidnapped Lindbergh baby. (Courtesy of the Associated Press)

pictures of the Lindbergh baby appeared in New York theaters the next day. Just as the newspapers printed extras and increased circulation of regular editions, the newsreels made up approximately a thousand additional prints. They functioned as a kind of all points bulletin to moviegoers, reviewing what was known of the crime and disseminating the baby's picture in hopes he might be spotted. "Watch for him everywhere," urged commentators. "Bring him back to his mother's arms." In Universal's clips, talking reporter Graham McNamee voiced both the anger ("I'd sure like to have that kidnapper alone for just about four minutes," he growled) and wishes of a nation ("Well, come back soon, little Lindy, our hearts are with you").

When the child's body was found ten weeks later less than five miles from the Hopewell estate, half buried in underbrush, his skull crushed, convulsions of shock, grief, and righteous fury rippled across the nation. Radio bulletins broke into regular programming and two-word headlines ("BABY DEAD") filled the tabloid extras. The newsreels released special issues reporting the death, but spared audiences still photographs of the child's decayed corpse. So disturbing was the news that some theater managers pulled the newsreels from their program for fear of upsetting patrons before the main attraction.

Under that kind of box office pressure, it is not surprising that the most popular newsreel story of the Great Depression concerned neither dismal conditions at home nor war clouds overseas, neither criminal activity nor civil disturbance. The birth of the Dionne Quintuplets on May 28, 1934, in Corbeil, Ontario, was a statistical anomaly that became the longest-running and most widely covered diversion of the 1930s. No politics, no crime, no depression—just a pure human interest story of extraordinary appeal.

The birth of the five girls was also, blared taglines, "a box office feature unparalleled in the history of news reels!" Exploiting its international contacts, Pathé News acquired exclusive rights to the quintuplets from the Ontario government which, in an act of legal kidnapping, had conscripted the girls as wards of the state and a national treasure. "The biggest scoop in the history of Pathé News! First time on any screen!" trumpeted full-page ads in the trade press. "Exclusive and comprehensive pictures of the FIVE BABIES that all the world wants to see! How they live, how they eat, how they bathe, intimate glimpses of their home, their mother, their father, their nurses, guardians, and themselves." For most of the next decade, the newsreels never forgot an anniversary or childhood milestone: through birthdays, first steps, first day of school, first communion, public outings, and private moments, the Dionne Quintuplets were documented with obsessive and oppressive thoroughness.

In the choice between hard news and soft human interest, distressing sights and soothing images, the newsreels usually opted to meld into, not shake up, the rest of the motion picture program. Better a segment on couples getting married in strange places, bathing beauties parading around swimming pools, or an update on how a potential calamity—five new mouths to feed in hard times—had turned into a gold mine.

9

Remote Kinships

The Geography of the Expeditionary Film

Published in 1899, when the deepest interiors of equatorial Africa were still blank spaces on the European atlas, Joseph Conrad's *Heart of Darkness* conjured the unholy lure of the jungle and the horrible attraction of the black savage for the civilized white imagination. The laconic narrator is a former steamer pilot named Marlowe, a colonial trader who summons up the ghastly story of Kurtz, a refined Belgian "gone native" up river in the Congo. "We were wanderers on a prehistoric earth, on an earth that wore the aspect of an unknown planet," he intones. What terrified Marlowe was not the prospect of being speared and eaten by his business partners but the bond he felt with the natives lurking along the riverbank, the cannibals crooning a neanderthal chorus apprehended only in "a whirl of black limbs, a mass of hands clapping, of feet stamping, of bodies swaying, of eyes rolling, under the droop of heavy and motionless foliage." Not just listening but responding to the music, Marlowe comes to an epiphany. "What thrilled you was the thought of their humanity—like yours—the thought of your remote kinship with this wild and passionate uproar."

The remote kinship with primitive peoples sustained a forgotten motion picture genre, the expeditionary film. Immensely popular throughout the 1920s and early 1930s, still fascinating as a Westward look at what were not then called Third World peoples, the expeditionary film gained new life in the pre-Code era with the invigoration of sound technology and the relative freedom from censorship. At its best, the genre opened a window on wondrous worlds with remarkable folk whom Americans might delight in and come to know as blood relations. At its worst, the expeditionary film shut out the possibility of kinship with a narrow focus both cultural and cinematic, framing strange people from strange lands with glib condescension and racist perspectives, pinning them like insects under glass for the paid customers to stare at.

As with any variant of documentary cinema, the expeditionary film defies neat categorization and raises questions of authenticity. Where does the "docu" end and the "drama" begin? What is reality in film? Isn't anything photographed mediated and falsified? A skeptical eye knows that rehearsals, retakes, and the very presence of the camera filter the authenticity of the image, that the search for the pure expeditionary film is a trek after fool's gold. Best to take it as it is: a bastardized, hybrid form, promiscuous in its coupling of fiction and fact, merging the fabricated and found, born on the backlot and in the field.

The expeditionary film should not be confused with its lightweight cousin, the travelogue. A travelogue is the cinematic equivalent of the act of tourism, a film that provides a comfortable berth for seeing the sights and gawking at the natives. Wedged between Silly Symphony cartoon and big-budget A feature on the motion picture program, it took a photo album excursion through safely exotic ports of call where smiling dancers in native dress undulated before overfed, guffawing tourists. A short subject of modest goals, the travelogue blended static cinematography with the probing ethnographical insights of a Baedeker guide. Pallid pans of overexposed horizons alternated with voice-over disinformation enunciated in a zesty baritone. "As the sun sets into the azure Atlantic, we bid a fond farewell to the cheerful people of sunny Montserrat, jewel of the Caribbean . . ."

In contrast, the expeditionary film demands hard traveling. No packaged tour but an adventure in cinema at feature length, it possesses the immediacy and intensity of on-location shooting and spontaneous action, a sense of wonder mixed with the adrenaline rush of fear. The expeditionary film promised a true voyage of discovery for filmmaker and spectator alike. Embracing duress and danger, presuming priority, it seemed to say: "These motion pictures unspooling before you are the first to photograph this virgin land, to capture on film this tribe untouched by civilization, and to eavesdrop on the song of the savage and the roar of the beast. Watch in security from your cushy seats for I have risked much for your entertainment."

Some expeditionary films are lucid magnifying glasses on primitive lives, almost scholarly in their impulse for thick description and interior access. Others are working definitions of cultural myopia in their refusal to perceive the folks in the frame, documents that reveal more about America in the 1930s than their putative subjects. All have the fascination of a rear window peek at lost worlds, relatively untouched civilizations, and untrammeled locations, when the motion picture medium captured glimpses of life on the brink of extinction. Any sense of outrage at the violations done to nature and humanity is liable to be softened by a gratitude that the moments were preserved at all.

Besides, in subject matter if not in outlook, expeditionary films are models of multicultural diversity and global inclusiveness. A fashionable roll call of indigenous peoples (Native Americans, Inuits, Africans, Asians, Pacific Islanders) and environmentally privileged landscapes (jungles, forests, rivers, and tundra) checks off a rainbow coalition of ethnic and earthly exotica. Despite all the condescension and callousness, the expeditionary film expressed an eager curiosity about alternative worlds and primitive lives. "The way of the world is West," reads the opening intertitle to Ernest B. Schoedsack and Merian C. Cooper's *Grass* (1925), but the perspective of the film faces in the opposite direction. The way of the expeditionary film is any which way but West.

In this, the genre reflects broader cultural impulses. The great age of expeditionary films coincided with the great rage for Jungian psychology and Boazian anthropology. It was a time sympathetic to notions like the psychic unity of mankind and the cultural relativism of Margaret Mead's *Coming of Age in Samoa* (1928) and Ruth Benedict's *Patterns of Culture* (1934). After the carnage of the Great War, few Westerners could speak with straight faces about the intrinsic superiority of Greco-Roman, Judeo-Christian culture. Marlowe's intimations of "remote kinships" with African cannibals, shocking to Victorian England, had become conventional wisdom after November 11, 1918. "When all was over," ruminated Winston Churchill, "Torture and Cannibalism were the only two expedients that the civilized, scientific, Christian States had been able to deny themselves: and they were of doubtful utility." The poet T. S. Eliot picked up on the theme of Europe, not Africa, eating its own when he scrawled "Mistah Kurtz—he dead" as the epigraph for "The Hollow Men" in 1925, the title of which summed up the vacuum in Western Civ in the wake of the Great War.

The Great Depression exacerbated the collapse of faith in the Western world, the spiritual void of the 1920s now matched by the material emptiness of the 1930s. On the most obvious level, the infatuation with vistas beyond American shores is a projection of frontier visions onto new worlds in an age of territorial limitations and economic dead ends. On another, it is an intimation of cultural uncertainty, a gnawing realization that the West is not the only place to look, the only way to be. In 1931 director John Ford tried to persuade Fox to option Pearl S. Buck's novel *The Good Earth*, but studio chief Winfield Sheehan nixed the project. "Not a chance," he snapped. "Who the hell is interested in the Chinese?"

Lots of people, actually. *The Good Earth* was a literary sensation and a phenomenal bestseller. Like the gangster films, Buck's novel recast the American myth of upward mobility, though not by twisting the career path into a criminal course but by changing the gender of the protagonist and shifting the environment of endeavor. The former slave girl O-lan is a female Ben Franklin whose way to wealth is Calvinist self-denial and frontier fortitude (after giving birth to her baby, she bites off the umbilical cord and returns to the rice field). Buck's Chinese characters fight the old-fashioned, biblical plagues of famine, drought, and earthquake, not the complexities of a failed economic system that allowed children to starve when milk was being dumped on roads by farmers. Hunger, a physical condition formerly reserved for primitive savages, was a pang felt by a sizable portion of America in the 1930s, the most famous rough estimate being that one-third of the nation was ill-fed, ill-clothed, and ill-housed. No longer sheltered and sustained by a roaring economy and modern technology, learning how thin the veneer of civilization might be, many Americans were thrown back on their basic animal instincts for day-to-day survival, foraging for food and seeking shelter from the elements. The early years of the Great Depression conjured the prospect of a return to a state of nature with all its Hobbesian terrors.

At the same time, Americans might take comfort that no matter how dreadful their condition, some folks had it worse. Measured against the lot in life of the impoverished Indian, Asian, or African, American-style poverty seemed less catastrophic, more endurable. The expeditionary films offered a sense of global scale and taught the old compensatory lesson, "there but for the grace of God go I." In a review of *Around the World with Douglas Fairbanks*

(1931), a critic rebuked his fellow Americans by describing Chinese stoicism in the face of deprivation, how "that ancient country's toiling millions fight starvation with a complacency that shames our own belly-aching about 'depression.'" Nonetheless, "belly aching" was a resonant theme of American cinema in the Great Depression and nowhere more so than in the expeditionary film. The title of *The Silent Enemy* (1930), H. P. Carver's docudrama about the Ojibwa Indians, refers not to a rival tribe but to hunger and the daily struggle to keep starvation at bay.

Another appeal of the genre was frankly prurient. Just as *National Geographic* magazine provided a respectable forum for the exposure of native peoples in states of natural nudity that would be unnatural for straitlaced Americans, expeditionary films were granted wider latitude than entertainment features in the exposure of naked flesh, ostensibly because they were educational documents and definitely because they unveiled a lower order of humanity. The New York Board of Motion Pictures set its own patterns of culture by forbidding "any scene showing an infant at the breast of its mother" but only "where the mother is civilized." Similarly, outbreaks of violence and gruesomeness were less provocative in the South Seas than on the south side of Chicago. *Around the World* (1931), a 20-minute short by explorers Martin and Osa Johnson, offers detailed instruction on the care and preservation of human heads from a tribe of cannibals.

Doubtless too for alienated denizens of the modern metropolis, a battle with something as tangible as the elements must have had an almost nostalgic appeal. If few Americans questioned a natural order that placed Euro-Caucasians at the top of the racial taxonomy, the heralded "decline of the West" predisposed others to attend warily to the state of the competition, even to embrace tentatively their remote kinship with strange folk in distant lands. A heritage at once cinematic and cultural, the expeditionary film chronicled worlds and peoples whose time was running out even as the cameras were cranking. The visions were not unspoiled, surely not unmediated, but they were close enough to the original for Western eyes of discovery to see more than their own reflections.

POINTS ON THE COMPASS

A tour of the expeditionary genre organizes itself naturally into geographical spheres of influences—to equatorial jungles and polar icecaps, through tropical heat and arctic cold, over whitewater rapids and sunbaked deserts.

Beginning at the poles and working toward the equator, the genre encompasses the known universe of places and people. But whatever the location, the expeditionary film shares some common points of reference.

The first point is not them but us. Whatever the nominal cover story for the expeditionary film (a fight for survival against uncaring Nature, a Romeo and Juliet romance in tribal dress) and whoever the star native (the great hunter, the struggling farmer, the beautiful maiden), the real story is always: Great White Photographer Brings Back Movies from Savage Land for American Moviegoers.

The dominant figure in the expeditionary film was not the happy native or fearsome tribesman, but the promethean cameraman: the bold photographer who ventures into unknown interiors, plucks precious images of primitive peoples and man-eating animals at risk of life and limb, and returns to the Western world to project his treasure before wide-eyed acolytes. Glimpses of the cameraman in the act of photography appear incessantly in the expeditionary genre—if not framed onscreen in intrepid poses then as a felt offscreen presence and, after the arrival of sound, as personal tour guide narrating the action. He (and in one fascinating case, she) serves as diegetic witness and audience surrogate, never letting faint-hearted spectators, secure in their seats, forget the deprivations and dangers withstood in service to their entertainment.

Second, while out in the field, the first thing the expeditionary filmmaker stumbles upon is a story. All journeys recorded on film congeal into a narrative, the forward march of the moving image leading inexorably to a drama of sorts, some quite conventional and rigorously structured, others offbeat and meandering. The Homeric outline of an odyssey lends itself naturally to three-act dramaturgy—departure, adventure, and return—and provides ample room for diverting detours, character actors (human and animal), and comic relief.

Third, the overt instructional value of the expeditionary film in man, beast, and nature bolstered covert lessons in the process of moviemaking and the grammar of cinema. Where Hollywood feature films embraced an aesthetic of full immersion into the fabula (dubbed the "invisible style"), the impulse to inspect and analyze that was at the heart of the expeditionary film conspired to expose the tricks of the film trade. Like selected short subjects and the sports clips from the newsreels, expeditionary films pioneered the use of slow motion, reverse motion, and freeze frames. Moreover, unlike the Hollywood feature, the genre showcased these devices, taking the spectator into its confidence to get a better look at the wondrous pictures and peculiar people.

No film technique was highlighted more than the latest innovation in cinema. With the introduction of sound in 1927, the expeditionary genre acquired a second life and fresh appeal. Many of the classic expeditionary films of the 1920s were rereleased with synchronized musical scores and voice-overs, but the real action unleashed new adventures into the unknown. For the first time in film history, the songs of exotic natives and beasts beckoned like sirens. Praising MGM's African-set epic *Trader Horn* (1930), the *Hollywood Reporter* was as enchanted with the sound of the picture as the look: "The hiss of the panther, the snort of the hippo and the rhino, the roar of the lions, the snarl of the crocodile . . . every living thing that has voice they have caught with the microphone." Like images, sounds of all kinds might now be brought back from afar for Americans to hear in motion pictures.

Sound also cemented the bond between the filmmaker and the spectator, for now a human voice accompanied the images. As if brought into the confidence of a marvelous raconteur, the moviegoer entered the private club of an old Africa hand, sharing cigars and cordials as the crusty adventurer reminisced about his exploits. The implied conceit became explicit in the framing device for *Explorers of the World* (1931), a compilation of the exploits of six expeditionary filmmakers. It opens with a formal dinner honoring the hardy voyagers, now safely repatriated in tuxedos at the Explorers Club of New York. Each in turn adopts the guise of a cinematic tour guide and takes the audience with him to the Amazon, the Arctic, and so on. Now articulate, the photographer moves out from behind the camera to take his place center screen, to comment on the action, to share behind-the-scenes anecdotes, and to show off not just his courage and marksmanship but his rapier wit and poetic soul.

Whatever the global destination, the "where" of the expeditionary film is a good index to the "what" the journey is really about. To begin at the furthest outposts, the frozen wastes of the North and South Poles exerted a magnetic pull that was as philosophical as geographical—as if, with cartography and exploration having reached their earthly limits, all that remained was to contemplate a blank, existential void. *With Byrd at the South Pole* (1930) and *90° South* (1933) voyage to Antarctica. In the former, Paramount newsreel cameramen Joseph Rucker and Willard Van der Veer spent a year documenting Rear Admiral Richard E. Byrd's mission to fly over the South Pole. In the latter, Herbert Ponting recalls his experience photographing the

The promethean cameraman: a Paramount newsreel photographer braves the ice in *With Byrd at the South Pole* (1930). (Courtesy of the Museum of Modern Art)

storied efforts of Capt. Robert Scott to reach the South Pole, a drama twenty years past but still vivid in his film and memory.

As befits his priority in the billing, Admiral Byrd appears in a sound prologue to *With Byrd at the South Pole*, rigid and ill at ease, his eyes darting to cue cards off camera. No-nonsense and informative, the film confirms a consistent trait of the expeditionary genre: the tangential human and animal vignettes linger in the mind longer than the hard news story of Byrd's historic flight. The most dramatic moment is the death sentence imposed upon an aged husky, whom one of Byrd's men (his identity discreetly left unrevealed) is forced to shoot rather than abandon to the elements. "*With Byrd at the South Pole* is an invigorating tonic for all mankind at a time when we need it most," read the taglines in an oblique reference to the present crisis. "It is a renewal of faith in humanity, an inspiration for men, women, and especially children."

Ponting's *90° South* is a documentary memoir of Capt. Robert Scott's disastrous expedition to the South Pole in 1911-12. This is the third time around for Ponting's priceless footage, it being the sound version of material released episodically in 1912 and later compiled for a silent version, *The Great White Silence* (1924). Ponting's celluloid hagiography was an integral part of the mythmaking machinery that installed Captain Scott as a dauntless hero for generations or British schoolboys, rather than exposing him for the reckless dolt he was.

After addressing the camera stiffly in a sound prologue, Ponting assumes voice-over duties while his past unspools onscreen. At first glance, "Ponty" evokes the kind of addled upper-crust clubman played by C. Aubrey Smith for MGM, but Ponting's British rectitude and heartfelt affection for his men, his misty recollections of a peak experience twenty years after the fact, are cumulatively quite moving. Still vivid in memory, the men of the expedition, as well as the horses and dogs, whom Ponting names and bestows close-ups on, appear like apparitions before him on the screen. Integrated into the moving imagery, Ponting's still photography is starkly beautiful and eerily appropriate for a horizon that itself seems inert and motionless. One image makes for grim foreshadowing. Looming over the men from atop a mountain near their base camp, a cross marks the burial site of a fallen explorer, a symbol more warning than solace. When Ponting shows a brief shot of himself, fighting frostbite while cranking his motion picture camera, he has earned his moment in the polar sun, a Prometheus taking fire from the ice.

Neither Byrd nor Scott was concerned with ethnography; their expeditions were to the uninhabitable terrain of an abstract point on the compass. On the opposite end of the earth, however, in the inhabited regions of Alaska and Canada, the Eskimo dominated the landscape of the expeditionary film. Of course, the prototype is Robert Flaherty's majestic *Nanook of the North* (1922), the most admired and popular film of the entire expeditionary genre. Measured against *Nanook of the North*, the others pale, not just in cinematic but in human terms. Flaherty alone granted his native subject due billing on the marquee. The frigid titles of three fusions of on-location shooting and soundstage re-creation—*Igloo* (1932), *Eskimo* (1933), and *S.O.S. Iceberg* (1933)—all celebrate the scenery or the type over the individual.

Igloo is carefully defined in precredit prose as "an authentic story based upon incidents in the life of the Primitive Eskimo in the Arctic Circle." Director Ewing Scott managed to "faithfully record the courageous struggle for existence of these forgotten people" by "living with the people as a member of the tribe." He thanks the cooperative "Eskimo villagers and huntsmen of the Nuwak tribe in the Arctic" and promptly imposes a romantic melodrama on Inuit life. An American narrator lends false authori-

ty ("a gentle happy folk" are the Eskimo) and frames the love story ("whoever is the greatest hunter is the most desirable husband in the eyes of the
Eskimo maidens").

Making the sham ethnography tolerable is the stunning location photography. Panoramic shots of polar wastes, ice packs, and fissures in the ice
render a harsh environment that requires cruel choices. Twin babies cannot
both survive. One must be sacrificed. After the baby is placed lovingly in the
snow ("the tiny one has returned to the great snow god"), ravenous huskies
dig up the gravesite.

To distinguish itself from *Igloo*, *Eskimo* showcased the most intriguing aspect of Inuit folkways. "Eskimo Wife Traders! Weird Tale of the Arctic!"
blared electric signs on Broadway, and in smaller print on lobby cards: "The
strangest moral code on the face of the earth—men who share their wives
but kill if one is stolen!" Though *Eskimo* was shot on location with a partly
native cast, director W. S. Van Dyke brought back several Inuit players to
Hollywood for interior shots and publicity appearances.

The last of the Arctic trio, *S. O.S. Iceberg* (1933), opens with a fulsome list
of acknowledgments. Producer Carl Laemmle tenders thanks to (1) "the directorial staff who devoted a year to the making of this picture," (2) "the
cameramen who risked their lives in the Arctic so that a new star, Nature,
might be presented," (3) "the courageous leaders who guided the expedition past mountainous glaciers where the slightest mis-step meant instant
death," and (4) "the artists who bravely faced incomparable hardships in the
Polar outposts of the world." The direction is credited to Tay Garnett, but
the film bears the style and stamp of the director of record in the German
release print, Dr. Arnold Fanck, the airy auteur of the German "mountain
film" genre of the 1920s and the first Svengali to actress Leni Riefenstahl.
Their teaming in the popular import *The White Hell of Pitz Palleu* (1929)
persuaded Universal that an English-language depiction of German Alpine
fever might play in the U.S. market.

Unfortunately, the pace of *S. O.S. Iceberg* is as glacial as the location, and
the intertitles read as if translated verbatim from the German ("Terrifying
days pass swiftly in the barren wasteland where there is no nighttime").
While on an expedition for the International Society for Polar Research, a
team of flinty adventurers is stranded on a drifting iceberg from which they
send the title distress signal. Again, the plot is tangential to the astonishing
polar vistas. To better inspect the most spectacular sequences, the action is
projected in slow motion: sixty tons of ice cascading from the side of a gla-
cier roiling into the ocean, an iceberg tossing in the polar sea, and avalanch-

On location: cast and crew travel to Point Barrow, Alaska, to bring verisimilitude to the hybrid expeditionary film *Eskimo* (1933). (Courtesy of Quigley Photo Archive)

es displacing mountains of snow. Beholding the birth of the iceberg, a character utters a line heard repeatedly and nearly word-for-word throughout the expeditionary genre: "You're going to witness something few white men have ever seen." In whatever locale, before whatever sight, only when beheld by white eyes, in the field and in the theater at home, is a natural vision truly discovered and verified. For modern audiences, however, the most stunning image in *S. O. S. Iceberg* is apt to be Leni Riefenstahl playing a faithful wife and near-victim of sexual assault. Two years later, the actress turned director to create a more chilling spectacle in her paean to Nazism, *Triumph of the Will* (1935).

Further south, a familiar tribe of American aborigines found a hospitable habitat in the expeditionary genre, the once savage Indian elevated to star attraction as noble savage. Ojibwa Indian life "long before Columbus" set the scene for H. P. Carver's *The Silent Enemy*, an off-putting title for a film released in the midst of the sound revolution. Silhouetted against a black background and tinted a color-coordinated yellow, the authentic Indian and featured player Chief Yellow Cloud testifies to the film's verisimilitude ("Everything you see is as it always has been—our buckskin clothes, our birch bark canoes, our wigwams, and our bows and arrows") and offers exculpation for white-eye spectators ("Your civilization will destroy us, but by your magic we shall live forever. We thank the white man who help us to make this picture"). Seeing and hearing the aged warrior, whose life span stretches back across time to the Indian wars of the post-Civil War era, is like watching a frontier ghost rider made flesh.

Closer to the equator, the bold team of Ernest B. Schoedsack and Merian C. Cooper dominated the expeditionary franchise for the Far East and the Orient. Throughout the 1920s, the pair scoured the globe, shooting exteriors for Hollywood studio films and creating full-length features, such as *Grass* and *Chang* (1927). A few years later at RKO, Schoedsack and Cooper culled their personal backstories for an epic tale of an explorer-impresario who brings back "the eighth wonder of the world" in *King Kong* (1933).

Set in the jungle of Sumatra, Schoedsack's *Rango* (1931) mixes ethnography and zoology in a tale of two father-son relationships, a hunter and his son and an ape and his son. *Rango* is all native peoples and local animals, with no intrusive cameraman. "No shots of anyone 'making pictures,'" noted a reviewer, thankful *not* to see the promethean cameraman. A child's tale, framed by a conversation between a reminiscing adventurer and his grandson, it makes a serious miscalculation by portraying the cruelty of nature all too faithfully. In the final reel, the cuddly little baby orangutan gets eaten by the tiger! In the jungle, this may happen, but in the movies the parent animal, not the child animal, should die, a rule always adhered to by a future wild kingdom filmmaker with better box office instincts, Walt Disney.

As the expeditionary film moved south, the erotic temperature warmed up. In the sensuous tropics languished a surplus of bare-breasted women whose skin color was light enough to make them permissible objects of desire and dark enough to stimulate forbidden lusts. The title of F. W. Murnau and Robert Flaherty's *Tabu* (1930) illuminates the sexual lure of the South Sea archipelago, a dreamy landscape where the contours of Hawaii, Polynesia, the East Indies, and Bali blended into a single island vista of sun-drenched beaches, swaying palm trees, and compliant, seminaked women. Two epics devoted to the females and the folkways of the same "rare tropical jewel in the South Seas" uncovered the secrets of the Pacific atoll, *Goona-Goona* (1932) and *Virgins of Bali* (1932).

Released during a fallow period for major studio product and riding a crest of "titillating exploitation and smart salesmanship," *Goona-Goona* was the most profitable of the exotic island excursions. It was billed as "an authentic melodrama of the Isle of Bali," and the phrase well captures the fusion of documentary detail and Hollywood melodrama. A title card introduces Monsieur André Roosevelt, shown with notepad in hand intently listening to local informants so he might "reconstruct this Balinese story as it was told to him by the natives." It is a tale of tragic, star-crossed love in the "last paradise" on earth.

The edenic Bali hides a serpent in the form of the Western-educated Prince Nonga, back from Europe and imbued with notions of personal happiness and individual rights. Prince Nonga is clearly caught between two worlds: he wears a business suit on the top half of his body and a Balinese skirt on the bottom half. When the prince rejects his chosen mate, the lovely Princess Maday, and sets his eyes on the fetching Dasnee, the betrothed of the handsome coolie Wyan, trouble in paradise looms. "Is it from Europe that you have brought such notions?" ask his outraged parents. "Will Nonga, with the advantages of his European education, have the courage to protest? Or will he submit to his father's will?" hectors the narrator.

The most visible evidence of the paradisal state of nature in Bali is the undraped state of its women. When the lovely Princess Maday first appears topless, the narrator explains that "in Bali, women wear ordinarily but a skirt and cover the rest of their handsome bodies only on ceremonial occasions." Like Princess Maday, Dasnee and her future sister-in-law Seronee are beautiful teenagers seldom seen engaged in ceremonial occasions.

Between visions of Maday, Dasnee, and Seronee and interludes of Balinese ethnography (cock fight, marriage ritual, fan dancing), a Shakespearean sense of doom pervades interpersonal relations. Nonga's evil sister acquires a dose of "goona goona" from a shaman, it being "a strange potion which acts as both an hypnotic and emotional stimulant." Goona-goona is not quite a drug but a belief that "embraces a variety of unpleasant magics which actually work in Bali, whether or not they sound credible to you." Drugging the innocent Dasnee, now the faithful wife of the steadfast Wyan, the prince invades her room at night, leans over her insensible form, and consummates his desire. Enraged, Wyan finds the prince bathing nude in a river. A terrible fight ensues, the outcome of which finds the lifeless prince washed downstream. In turn, the villagers run down Wyan, who is stabbed to death by the prince's father.

If *Goona-Goona* ranks as the classiest entry in the South Seas cycle, *Virgins of Bali*, also known as *Jungle Virgins*, held lower aspirations. Barely covered by the pretense of ethnography, it is an unblushing showcase for the

Erotic ethnography: the featured attractions of *Virgins of Bali* (1932). (Courtesy of the Museum of Modern Art)

winsome frolicking of Balinese girls. Produced and narrated by Deane H. Dickason, it blends elements of fairy tale romance ("Dawn in the tropics is romance. Dawn in the tropics is enchantment. But dawn in Bali is utopia!"), cornball lyricism ("as we approach this tiny isle, the peak of Bali shining like a silver pyramid . . ."), and wide-eyed voyeurism ("Observe the grace and suppleness of each slender, sun-brown figure").

The plot of *Virgins of Bali* is to flaunt the bodies of a pair of beautiful Balinese teenagers. They represent "two of the fairest flowers of a handsome race," but "there are hundreds, yes, thousands of others. Yes, Bali is the land of beautiful women." Narrator Dickason is tireless in his scrutiny of the female figure and generous with illustrative images. The girls are "firmly and harmoniously developed and walk with a swinging, easy, rhythmic movement" and "they have fine features and well-rounded, slender bodies." Fortunately, the camera happens to be on hand to record "the first act of what is to be a busy day" for the girls, namely "to bathe their shamelessly nude bronze bodies in the refreshing though murky waters." Dickason cannot avert his eyes: "They wade in with such grace and nonchalance as belong to true daughters of Eve. There is no false modesty here." Leering high-angle shots reveal the naked girls splashing in the water while Dickason highlights points of special interest: "This faultless specimen is in her 40s, yet she retains the figure and complexion of a schoolgirl."

At the New York premiere of *Virgins of Bali*, the reviewer for *Variety* managed to look away from the screen long enough to notice that "the house was nearly full and not a score of women in the 300-seater." Initially nervous about the native nudity, exhibitors found that ethnography served as a profitable cover story. "This simple little nature story slipped into my program with fear and trembling," related a theater owner. "Sold as entertainment it would be highly questionable, but it went over beautifully sold as highbrow. I made a month's salary trying it." Travel agents reported an abrupt upswing in passages to Bali from men inspired to explore personally the sights of the expeditionary film.

FAKING IT: PHONEY EXPEDITIONS AND REAL DEATHS

Virgins of Bali notwithstanding, expeditionary films tended to traffic in reality, not fantasy, the documentary aura being a singular selling point. Authentic pictures, or pictures that could credibly be advertised as such, gained enhanced market value from the vicarious thrill of imminent danger. "And it is REAL," trumpeted the ads for *With Byrd at the South Pole*. "Everything actually happened, making it ten times more moving than fiction!" The authenticity of *Eskimo* was purchased "at the risk of human life," asserted taglines that also bold-faced the rigors of location shooting in Point Barrow, Alaska, and Greenland. "The heroic company of men and women fearlessly braved the Arctic for more than a year," boasted full-page ads in the trade press. "Thank God, they're safely back!" Not least, authentic but salacious ethnography more easily circumvented censorship under the pretense of educational value.

Filmmakers who played it straight naturally resented those who staged things crooked. "Misrepresentations in expedition pictures not only deceive the public, but are unfair to those who risk their lives and capital to obtain genuine films of this kind," declared the Better Business Bureau, in launching an investigation into *Ubangi* (1931), a quasi-documentary record of a 1924 safari into the Belgian Congo that claimed its director had been killed by a charging hippopotamus. Despite attempts to bring better business practices to the motion picture business, however, the ratio of reality to reinvention in the expeditionary genre remained highly unstable from film to film.

In 1930 an independent release from Congo Pictures entitled *Ingagi* (allegedly meaning "gorilla") sparked an uproar that raised questions of documentary metaphysics and studio system monopoly. To the consternation of the major studios and authentic adventurers, it hijacked the reputation of the genre for exploitation purposes. As an expeditionary film, *Ingagi* was a pioneering con job. Like not a few con rackets it exudes a certain charm and, in the tradition of P.T. Barnum's humbug, the suckers at the ticket window were mainly in on the joke.

Released both in silent and sound versions, *Ingagi* opens with a lengthy title card avowing it portrays "the thrilling adventures of Sir Hubert Winstead, F.A.S., during his two years' expedition into the hitherto unknown regions of darkness" in Africa. But it is the racially and sexually charged promise of a carnal union between African women and jungle apes that is at the dark heart of *Ingagi*:

> In the Ingagi country there exists a tribe who annually give one of their women to the Gorillas (Ingagi). This sacrifice seems to be part of a tradition which, in the superstitious minds of these natives, protects them from raids of these beasts.
>
> The legend says that years ago the tribe ostracized its barren women, and when these women discovered their weakness, they visited the nests of the gorilla offering food, with the hope of acquiring prolificness and being granted the boon of motherhood.

Before proceeding to the expedition proper, *Ingagi* pays tribute to the sacrifices of the heroic cameramen, praising

> their cold grit in the face of danger; their unflinching nerve in the tightest places; supported solely by their faith in our ability to shoot straight, enabled them to carry on with but one thought in mind—The Picture.

What follows is a hilariously bogus, counterfeit expeditionary film. The patchwork creation stitches together stolen footage from authentic expeditions to Africa with staged scenes of "Sir Hubert" wandering through the wilds of Southern California. The real footage is faded and splotchy, exposed over a decade earlier than the sharper film grain of the fake footage showing Sir Hubert, pipe in hand, pretending to hunt. Remedial cinematic grammar links the two grains of celluloid side by side: Sir Hubert looks right; insert stock footage of rhino charging; Sir Hubert shoots; insert stock footage of rhino falling, and so on. *Ingagi* didn't bother to match the shots or even match the white hunters, for Sir Hubert is visibly *not* the pith-helmeted hero in the original, authentic footage. True to generic conventions, however, a cameraman cranks away as a lion attacks him, another cameraman being conveniently on hand to film the first cameraman under attack.

Ingagi meanders for six bizarre reels through the flora and fauna of darkest Africa and sunniest California before the exploitation hook—insinuated in the advertising copy, whispered by word of mouth—reels in the spectator. "Could these tales be true?" asks the narrator breathlessly. "Tales we regarded as mere legends, of a native tribe lowest of all on the scale of humanity. Stories of their strange traffic with the great apes—creatures scarcely less intelligent than themselves."

The "strange traffic" starts with the sight of several naked African women on the prowl for a gorilla mate. Elsewhere, in what appears to be a ritual sacrifice, a topless maiden awaits her fate. Cameras ready, the intrepid explorers watch from the brush. The gorilla arrives on cue and drags the maiden away, but the white hunters intervene, rescue the girl, and kill the gorilla. A coda then shows a naked African woman emerging from the jungle brush and approaching the gorilla's corpse, in mourning for her dead mate. "After the sight of this vision," reads the final intertitle, "our boys fled in terror, and we quickly made our way back to civilization."

Back in civilization, *Ingagi* was a box office sensation, grossing in excess of $1,000,000 from a "stag population" of men drawn to the combination of "native women and apes." Newspaper ads, theater fronts, and sound trucks stressed the sensationalism of roving bands of gorillas in cross-species cohabitation with African women. Though the film itself was clumsy, jerry-built, and transparently fraudulent, the devious audacity of the racist exploitation hook paid off in theater after theater.

When Nat H. Spitzer, president of Congo Pictures, publicly admitted that 85 percent of *Ingagi* was made in Hollywood, he sparked a nationwide uproar over documentary authenticity. Spitzer later claimed he had been misquoted—that what he had actually said was that 85 percent of the picture was authentic footage and the remaining 15 percent was fabricated. But jealous competitors seized the opening. At the behest of Will Hays, members of the MPPDA agreed not to distribute the film because of "false representation and objectionable aspects." *Variety* commented that "there are a lot of ifs-and-buts in connection with *Ingagi*. Some say it suggests indecency in its last reel, with the gorilla carrying a native woman into a thicket. But the main squawks are about the phoney aspects." Unable to avoid smirking as it drew the moral distinction, the trade paper explained that "out in Hollywood they do phoney things, but they don't misrepresent them."

An investigation by the Hays Office revealed that the only location shooting done expressly for *Ingagi* occurred in Luna Park and the Selig Zoo in Los Angeles. Moreover, reported the MPPDA detective in a private memorandum to Will Hays, "After long efforts covering a long period I have finally been able to induce the man who took the part of the gorilla in *Ingagi* to come into the office and have him tied down by affidavit to certain facts." Among the facts stipulated in the affidavit by one Charles Gemora was the revelation that "deponent owns his own gorilla suit and furnishes these for his troupe."

Spitzer claimed *Ingagi* was being held to a double standard. "If we are forced to expose the film industry, let us expose all producers' methods which permit the use of doubles both in action and voice, miniatures and 'glass shots' upon the screen, and the employment of many studio-made foreign scenes and other trick and so-called travel pictures, and not confine it only to the independent [producer]," Spitzer argued, not unreasonably. "The criticism of representative film reviewers, naturalists, explorers, and lay folk with jungle experience" attested to "the authenticity of 85% of *Ingagi*."

Though Spitzer argued for authenticity, he knew box office returns were the real stakes. The success of *Ingagi* had distressed what he termed "the Trust," namely, the Motion Picture Producers and Distributors of America. "Behind the walls of their combine," the Hollywood studios "have been disseminating contrary libels designed to clear the decks for the presentation of their own jungle gorilla product in 'trust' controlled theaters," he asserted. "I claim *Ingagi* to be clean and extraordinary entertainment and instructive as well."

Spitzer had a point—not about the wholesome education in *Ingagi*, but about the monopolistic practices of the MPPDA, which was using the Production Code not to clean up the movies but to clean out the competition. The studio consortium was a private club that locked out independent producers and distributors from the best venues. The most controversial device was the practice known as block booking, wherein exhibitors were forced to book a whole slate of films from a studio in order to get a crack at the choice product. The subject of a twelve-year court battle between exhibitors and distributors finally resolved in favor of the practice in 1932, block booking had the quite intended consequence of squeezing out independents from choice venues and prime screen time.

Lacking stars and beset with inferior production values, independent features sold themselves on the strength of sensational material hysterically advertised. Typically, the low-budget and lowbrow product was relegated to a circuit of grungy, borderline theaters that kept one step ahead of a police raid with venereal disease films, nudist camp documentaries, and sundry sub-Monogram knock-offs. Tempted by quick bucks, upscale venues—or at least semi-upscale venues—sometimes allowed independent producers to break into a market the majors considered sewn up. When Hays banned *Ingagi* from studio-owned theaters, independent exhibitors were delighted because it left the field free for them to book a profitable film. "At last the Hays office has done something for the independent exhibitor," exulted one. Spitzer's publicists capitalized on the controversy by screening special trailers explaining the dispute and then handing out ballots for audiences to vote on whether the local theater should book the film. Audiences were unanimous: play *Ingagi*.

No less than the studio-owned theaters, however, independent exhibitors depended on the major studios for the bulk of their programming. If they defied the MPPDA's edicts over the likes of *Ingagi*, the studios locked them out of future deals. The Code thus functioned as a "velvet hammer" to beat the really independent "indies" into line. "The MPPDA gently reminds these exhibs that Hollywood supplies them with 99% of their screen material and that Hollywood accordingly expects them to regard the business of pictures in an ethical light," *Variety* explained. "Interpreted, the dictum means nothing less than that indies who continue to be naughty with their remaining 1% may legally find themselves without the good codified 99%." That is, play ball with the studios or don't play studio films.

As if to prove Spitzer's point, the selective eye of the MPPDA in the surveillance of documentary reality overlooked *Africa Speaks* (1930). Billed as the first sound film to be shot on location in Africa, it purported to chronicle a fifteen-month trek through some 18,000 miles of jungle by "noted explorers" Paul L. Hoeffler and Walter Futter under the sponsorship of the Colorado Africa Expedition. "*Africa Speaks* is an authentic and rare record of hitherto undiscovered monsters, disfigured folk, and customs of odd humans," assured Columbia Pictures. "Its authenticity has been endorsed by members of the Smithsonian Institution." Audiences were invited to attend special premieres with "leading scientific men, educators, travellers, and literati." Where *Ingagi* insinuated depraved sex, *Africa Speaks* bluntly advertised horrible death. "See Kiga, the king's son, torn to pieces by a lion in front of the sound camera!" urged ads.

Like *Ingagi*, *Africa Speaks* was accused of subterfuge, though not by the MPPDA but by Talking Picture Epics, the company releasing the authentic expeditionary films of Martin and Osa Johnson. In an affidavit paraphrased by the *Hollywood Reporter*, the company contended "that the big thrill in the Columbia picture, the scene showing a native being killed by a lion, is fake, same being staged in the local Selig Zoo by the use of a Los Angeles darkey and a toothless lion from the zoo." The Hays Office was caught in a double standard: having banned the independently produced *Ingagi*, on the grounds of fakery, it ignored the identical con job in *Africa Speaks*, produced by MPPDA member Columbia Pictures, on the false grounds that "Columbia is not advertising as genuine the Hollywood touches in *Africa Speaks*." (In 1933 an investigation by the Federal Trade Commission confirmed the charges of deception, but by then the film had already run a very profitable theatrical course. At a cost of less than $50,000, *Africa Speaks* was "one of the best films ever released at the box office by Columbia.")

Meanwhile, the MPPDA's campaign against Nat Spitzer and Congo Pictures was joined by two formidable combatants. Byron P. Mackenzie, a famous and quite real African game hunter, claimed that fully half of the authentic footage in *Ingagi* had been lifted from a duped negative of *The Heart of Africa* (1914), a documentary record of his mother's expedition to British East Africa. In an out-of-court settlement Mackenzie was awarded $150,000. Worse, in 1931 the Federal Trade Commission filed a complaint against Congo Pictures for "false, fraudulent, deceptive, and misleading advertising."

Two years later, the FTC issued a report on *Ingagi* that exhaustively tallied up its duplicities:

> The commission found that "Sir Hubert Winstead, F.A.S, F.R.G.S.," who was represented in advertising as having led the expedition into Africa, and "Capt. Daniel Swayne," billed as an American hunter and collector of museum specimens, who accompanied Winstead, were both fictitious persons not existing in fact. No expedition headed by such person on which pictures were made ever took place.

The animals and the Africans alike were fake:

> An animal proclaimed to be "new to science" and designated in the film as "Torradillo," because of its resemblance to a tortoise and armadillo, was

a turtle with wings, scales, and a long tail glued to it, while the so-called "pygmies" said to be shown in their native environment were not pygmies at all, but colored children of from five to ten years old, living in Los Angeles. The native woman represented as being sacrificed by her tribe to the gorillas was a Los Angeles colored woman, while the people represented as "strange creatures apparently half-human and half-ape" were actually colored people living in Los Angeles and made up for the purpose of the picture.

The cameraman was exposed as an imposter prometheus:

A lion shown in the film as attacking a cameraman and being killed was a trained lion in Hollywood, often used in moving pictures. Many jungle scenes of the film were taken in a Los Angeles zoo.

Even the etymology was bogus:

While the word "Ingagi" was represented as meaning "gorilla" in the African language, it was found that there was no such word in any written dictionary of any African language, the word for "gorilla" as given in such dictionary being entirely different from the word "Ingagi."

As a denouement to the farce, the gorilla star of *Ingagi*, or rather the actor who played him, appealed to the California Labor Bureau to force the producers to pay him twenty dollars in back wages. The cheating of performers who impersonated animals, natives, and explorers in the bogus expeditionary film was a common practice that commonly boomeranged back on the skinflint producers. In 1931 the Better Business Bureau condemned *Jungle Hazards* (1931) as a retread of a fake expeditionary film released in 1930 under the title *Jango: Exposing the Terrors of Africa in the Land of Trader Horn*. Filmed in the Bronx with a small animal circus, *Jango* had been exposed when the "cannibal" in the film, a Harlem janitor named Firpo Jacko, sued for back wages.

Where *Ingagi* was a bogus expeditionary film, *Around the World with Douglas Fairbanks* (1931) is an authentic expeditionary parody. Also known as *Around the World in Eighty Minutes*, this big-budget home movie of the actor's trip around the world in 1930 mocks the conventions of the expeditionary film and its own cinematic artifice with a devilish élan worthy of the premiere swashbuckler of the silent era. Accompanied by director Victor

Fleming, sound and cameraman Henry Sharp, and factotum Chuck Lewis, Fairbanks merrily jaunts his way from Hollywood to Hawaii, Japan, the Philippines, Cambodia, Thailand, and India. Hosted by the most genial and handsome of ugly Americans, the film wreaks havoc on the expeditionary genre, not to say the dignity of various host country nationals. At once admirable in his sincere warmth toward all peoples and appalling in his regal condescension, superstar Fairbanks lives a sheltered existence all over the globe. "The world is essentially funny," he announces blithely to Depression moviegoers, "a great place for laughs." The main ethnographic impulse behind *Around the World with Douglas Fairbanks* is the actor's desire to tee off on the best golf courses in each port of call.

Fairbanks begins his sojourn in the center of the expeditionary film universe, Hollywood. Addressing the audience, he stands astride a huge map of Asia, painted on a soundstage floor. To segue from country to country, he hits a golf ball from one place on the soundstage map to another. Atop the Philippines section of the map, he expertly lobs the golf ball from Manila and lands in Angor, the next stop.

In Japan, Fairbanks ridicules what had already become travelogue clichés. "Now I'm going to muscle in on Burt Holmes' racket," he declares over a Tokyo street scene, referring to a well-known producer of travelogue short subjects. "Every travelogue lecture has got to mention these things. Here they are: the contrast between the old and new Japan: rickshaws—elevated trains." Cut to images of rickshaws and trains. "The ability of the Japanese to adapt modern ideas from Europe and America while retaining at the same time everything that is beautiful in their own infinitely older civilization." Cut to images of Japanese attired in traditional garb and Western business suits. Finally, the tourist photo of Mount Fuji: "Here's another required scene of the travelogue—Fujiyama—world's largest bald spot." Later, in India, Fairbanks dutifully obliges with another visual cliché. "Every travelogue of the Orient must have the Taj Mahal at moonlight." Cut to the Taj Mahal at moonlight.

In a nod toward the likes of *Ingagi* and *Africa Speaks*, a slapstick sequence begins with the tongue-in-cheek assurance that "by great good luck" the cameras have come across a thrilling scene. A tiger attacks an Indian villager and carries him off into the jungle. The fearless Fairbanks dashes to rescue the man and do battle with the beast. The crosscut action depicting the pursuit delights in its own transparent fraudulence. Shot of tiger running right to left; shot of Doug running right to left in mock pursuit; shot of tiger; shot of Doug. Doug catches the tiger (now a stuffed doll) and behind a clump of bushes fur flies in a hand-to-paw struggle to the death. The cat fight fades to a shot of Doug in his tent, awakening from a deep sleep, wrestling a tiger skin rug. "I had the most terrible nightmare," he tells Victor Fleming. "I dreamt I was in *Trader Horn!*"

In the final reel, the Fairbanks touring party realizes it has scant seconds to get back to Hollywood before the film's allotted eighty minutes runs out. Commandeering the preferred mode of transport from Fairbanks's silent classic *Thief of Baghdad* (1925), they board a flying carpet and soar over newsreel shots of European capitals, the Atlantic Ocean, New York, and westward across the United States. Suddenly, a fusillade of gunfire erupts from below: "Chicago!" Over Hollywood, the artifice of the flying carpetry is exposed when the camera pulls back to reveal a motion picture set. Visible onscreen are the behind-the-curtain methods of studio magic-making: the rear screen projection, the wires holding up the flying carpet, and the soundstage crew recording the scene. Limited not to the golf courses of the world, Fairbanks's sportsmanship extends to the wry demolition of Hollywood's "invisible style."

Though few pre-Code expeditionary films were as wildly phoney as *Ingagi* or parodically sophisticated as *Around the World with Douglas Fairbanks*, many favored an elastic attitude to documentary reality. Generally the rule is the more hysterically advertised the film, the less authentic the images.

Frank Buck's *Bring 'Em Back Alive* (1932) is probably the best known of the expeditionary films that occupy a middle ground between outright *Ingagi*-style fakery and *90° South*–style fidelity. Buck, a preening self-promotor whose best-selling book of the same name was serialized in *Collier's* and the Hearst newspaper chain, incarnated every inch the popular image of the Great White Hunter. During the Great Depression, he was one of the few rugged individuals engaged in a lucrative and exciting trade, of necessity on a frontier far from American shores. An adventure in animal choreography, *Bring 'Em Back Alive* was sold on the strength of a remarkable sequence in which a tiger and a python tangled to the death. Cool and unruffled, Buck narrates the action and appears on screen as hunter and sometime cameraman. Of his faithful native companion Ali, Buck allows, "Even though his body was brown, he was pure white inside."

Watching "breathlessly," Buck has "wonderful luck" as a series of animal battles unfold. The creatures happen to duel in awesome combinations and Buck always gets a "box seat" for matchups pitting radically different weight classes against each other: leopard and python, leopard and tiger, python and crocodile, and tiger and python. "I didn't want to butt in," he explains. "I was just a spectator."

Native props: a publicity shot from Frank Buck's *Bring 'Em Back Alive* (1932). (Courtesy of the Museum of Modern Art)

"Every foot of this picture was actually photographed in the Malayan jungle country," a title card for *Bring 'Em Back Alive* pledges. True enough: the scenes of authentic jungle action were staged in a compound outside of Singapore, where animal trappers from Malaysia sold consignments to circus buyers. Eventually, the cat was let out of the bag by director Clyde Elliot, who to refute charges of cruelty to animals revealed that the battles had been supervised by professionals. *Wild Cargo* (1934), Buck's follow-up to *Bring 'Em Back Alive*, repeated the formula. "Why does Nature save her biggest thrills for Frank Buck?" asked the taglines. Maybe because she followed the shooting script.

Sharp-eyed critics spotted the tricks of the faithless expeditionary film and bemoaned the violation of the documentary contract. Terry Ramsaye dryly dissected the Hollywood technique in *Eskimo*, whose alleged Inuit amateurs "presented histrionic ability which was never nurtured on whale blubber." (The female lead was played by Lulu Wong, sister of actress Anna Mae Wong, and the Eskimo hunter was played by Ray Wise, a former Hollywood cameraman of half-Eskimo, half-Jewish heritage.) The outbursts of animal violence and native nudity also seemed to occur with unnatural frequency. "It would seem reasonable to ask the makers of pictures in alleged natural settings, pictures of animals and natives, to seek to be at least as authentic as the ordinary Sunday supplement," Ramsaye editorialized. "It is, after all, not true that Eskimos spend their lives trading wives, or that tigers, lions, and other jungle brutes, do nothing but fight." Once wholesome entertainment for the entire family, the expeditionary film had turned salacious and sadistic. "Today the expedition to anywhere is sure to come back full of gore and more likely than not a lot of titillating Goona-Goonas."

The fakery that marred the reputation of the expeditionary film fostered by way of response a kind of certificate of authenticity, a visible sign that something real was happening onscreen. Staged fights between exotic pairs of animals—some natural enemies, others unlikely opponents—was a hardened convention of the genre. *Eat 'Em Alive* (1933) delivered on the promise of its title with a duel to the death between a sidewinder and a king snake, ending with the king snake devouring his opponent alive and whole. *Igloo* highlights a startling death scene, filmed without a cutaway, of the Eskimo hunter Che-ak spearing a polar bear. The spear penetrates the bear's side and blood gushes from the wound, dark splotches on white fur. Later, when walrus are killed, blood flows in rivers from the beasts and steam hisses from their wounds. Sometimes, by way of justification, the cameraman is portrayed as under threat of attack from the big game. Via first-person point-of-view shots, lions lunge into frame and rhinos charge the camera. Even so, the modern spectator may well be rooting for the tormented beasts to devour the photographer.

The unfaked and explicit killing of animals vouched that at least some moments in the expeditionary film were undeniably real. A procession of future endangered species (rhinos, elephants, hippopotami, tigers, lions, mountain goats, polar bears, and whales) are shot and speared with a remorseless zeal. Nature may be red in tooth and claw, but the animal slaughter was a staged sacrifice for the delectation of the spectator, a kind of morbid "money shot" ensuring something real was being documented—death.

THE DARK CONTINENT

As a geographical and psychic landscape, Africa is always a special case in the American mind. The generous embrace extended to American Indians, Eskimos, Asians, and sallow-skinned peoples the world over was withheld from

Africans and thus, by easy extension, from their sable kinsmen on native soil. Yet the shunning of the black population at home lent the "dark continent" of the white imagination a hypnotic attraction. While flinching from the touch of African-Americans close at hand, white Americans expressed obsessive curiosity about their nature and lineage. Black and white relationships, the American dilemma since 1609, were cast in stark relief in the Africa-bound expeditionary film, a site for the unfettered expression of impulses too dark to be released stateside. Warner Brothers' *Adventures in Africa* (1931), a series of twelve two-reel shorts produced over two years under the supervision of Wyant D. Hubbard, laid its race card on the table. "Nothing like it ever filmed before," ran the ads, "because no white man has ever dared penetrate so deep in the African wilderness."

No filmmakers penetrated deeper into the African wilderness than the husband and wife team of Martin and Osa Johnson. Almost forgotten today, the Johnsons were a tagteam duo of motion picture adventurers who from 1910 until Martin's death in 1937 traveled the world in search of exhilarating images. A pioneering power couple, they produced a steady stream of shorts and full-length features, gaining enough celebrity to become regulars in the gossip columns and heroes of a syndicated comic strip. Sixteen-year-old Osa met Martin in 1909 when he passed through her Kansas hometown to present a slide show of his "Trip through the South Seas with Jack London." Smitten with the rakish adventurer and aching for a ticket out of the plains, she married him six weeks later.

Osa became a full partner in a lifetime of motion picture adventuring. It is she who holds the gun while Martin angles to get a shot of a charging elephant or roaring lion in *Simba* (1928). The very model of the emancipated 1920s woman, Osa was attractive, able, and energetic, in her way as appealing a feminist soldier of fortune as the aviatrix Amelia Earheart. Her suitability for role-model duty today is undercut by her politically incorrect attitudes toward her native bearers (whom she disdains), her animal prey (whom she shoots), and her husband (whom she worships).

Sound technology inspired *Congorilla* (1932), a record of the Johnsons' most elaborate safari into Africa. The subtitle, "Big Apes and Little People of Central Africa," links the two tribes in simian identity. The ad copy promised "fearsome sounds never caught before—amazing scenes never photographed before. The fabulous race of grotesque pygmies face the sound camera for the first time in motion picture history, as they practice weird rites hitherto unknown to civilization." Though the photography is crisp and the line of sight unobstructed, neither Martin nor Osa possessed a sense of visual storytelling

The morbid "money shot": Douglas Fairbanks bags a leopard in *Around the World with Douglas Fairbanks* (1931) and Osa Johnson brings down a rhino in *Congorilla* (1932). (Courtesy of the Museum of Modern Art)

Real expeditionary filmmakers: Martin and Osa Johnson in a publicity shot for *Congorilla* (1932). (Courtesy Quigley Photo Archive)

or a talent for narrative drive. What they delivered instead was priority, authenticity, and a genuine sense of wonder.

Billed as "the one and only talking picture shot *entirely* in Africa," and "the most thrilling adventure of their renowned career with gun and camera," *Congorilla* is a time-capsule glimpse of an Africa that safaris like the Johnsons' helped to destroy. The film's allure lay not in heretofore unseen images of Africa but in unheard images, the union of spectacle and sounds, natural, animal, and native. *Congorilla* records a jungle symphony. "You are going to hear the first pictures in natural sound ever made in the jungle of Central Africa," promises Martin over an introductory montage, "the next best thing to being on the Dark Continent itself." Listen:

> The natives will sing for you
> And dance to the beat of the tom tom.
> You will see and hear the wild life on the plains, great herds of wildebeests and of zebra, and our old friend the giraffe.

There will be the roar of the lion
And the ugly snort of the charging rhino . . .
You will hear the angry grunt of the hippo
And the roar of the beautiful Murchison Falls.

Besides the above, the human sounds of Africa accompany the safari: Martin narrating the action, Martin and Osa speaking to the natives in dialect, and the natives singing and talking. A strange music to the American ear, the native tongues fill the soundtrack without translation, the thrill of hearing an unknown tongue sufficient unto itself.

Throughout the sound-on-film voyage into the interior, the intertitles and Martin's voice-over reinforce the myth of the virgin land, casting Africa as an edenic landscape connected across time with the Old Testament dawn of creation (the rhino is "the worst-tempered brute that came out of the Ark" and the hippo is "the behemoth of Scripture"). In language that might have been written by James Fenimore Cooper or Meriwether Lewis, Martin evokes the other mythic resonance at the heart of the expeditionary genre, the projection of American frontier vision onto fresh horizons. "Before our eyes lies an animal paradise," he observes as images that match his words unspool in panoramic long shots. "We stand watching them in wonder—zebra in the tens of thousands, wildebeests roaming the plains in hundreds of thousands as buffalo once roamed the plains of western America."

In truth the Johnsons' scenes of the wildlife are some of the most spectacular images of Africa ever recorded. In awesome long shot, millions of flamingos take off from a lake bed, filling the sky in flight, every inch of screen space covered with birds. To better observe the movement of the animals, shots of oryx, giraffes, and vultures are screened in slow motion with no advance cues to the audience. By 1932 spectators realized that the slow motion was not a problem in the projection booth but an observational assist. For closer inspection of the flight of the flamingos, "Osa went down to frighten the birds so I could get a picture in slow motion," explains Martin. "Notice the takeoff—just like an airplane."

In her first sound incarnation, Osa is vivacious and lively. Sometimes Martin speaks brusquely to her; more often he is solicitous, playfully carrying her across a stream. Shooting over the heads of rhino, pursuing three bull elephants on foot, and getting bitten by a baby gorilla, Osa ("with a woman's curiosity") is a fearless female prometheus.

To their credit, the Johnsons treat the animals with more regard than most Great White Hunters. "In all our exploring we deplored the killing of animals," Martin says. "Our object was to get pictures. When possible we shot above and under and all around to frighten them away." Sometimes the nasty business is unavoidable, though, as when threatening rhinos block the path of the safari. With Osa behind the camera, a rhino charges within feet of Martin, who brings the beast down with one well-aimed shot.

The consideration extended to African wildlife did not extend to the African inhabitants. The Johnsons look upon the natives as hired help or children and treat them as bewildered straight men for snide remarks. Handing a pygmy a cigar, Martin wisecracks, "I hope you get sick." After spending seven months among the pygmies, they convince their hosts to call together other tribes. "An old pygmy of seventy years is still a child of ten both mentally and physically," Martin lectures, and immediately contradicts himself by showing the tribal elders conferring about the threat posed by unsprung elephant traps.

In chronicling the marriage of two Ituri, Martin fabricates a love story between the pair, whom he names Adeni and Phillipo. Over a full body shot of a nubile pygmy girl, Martin describes Adeni as "a shy young thing who had African 'It,' " though unlike Clara Bow she can be exposed naked onscreen. During the marriage ceremony, Phillipo's pent-up sexual desire for the girl almost boils over. After the wedding, the newlyweds are shown retreating into a hut for their honeymoon night. Next morning, Adeni is carrying Phillipo's goods on her back. The honeymoon is over.

The most revelatory moment of interracial connection and ethnocentric separation in *Congorilla* is a staged musical interlude, a sequence that combines all the elements of the Johnsons at their best and worst, of the open-mindedness and myopia dueling within the expeditionary genre. Ever the cultural missionary, Martin decides to give "the boys and girls some modern jazz." In long shot, fronting a lineup of pygmies, Osa sways in time as a hand-cranked phonograph plays a sprightly tune. She claps her hands, taps her feet, and shakes her hips, rhythmically bopping to the music, having the time of her life. In tune with the beat, the pygmies match her in a choral backup, rocking to the African roots of the American beat. "It was remarkable the way they quickly caught the rhythm of our modern music," comments Martin, presuming the possessive pronoun. "Sometimes they got out of time, but they quickly came back to it again."

Harkening to another "mass of hands clapping, of feet stamping, of bodies swaying," the wiser narrator of *Heart of Darkness* picked up a different undertone in the harmonic convergence between the races. Said Marlowe: "If you were man enough you would admit to yourself that there was in you just the faintest trace of a response to the terrible frankness of that noise, a dim suspicion of there being a meaning in it which you—you so remote from the night of first ages—could comprehend." Alas, the Johnsons were not man or woman enough to admit that the "remote kinship" might travel in the other direction, that the Ituri pygmies recognized in the wild and passionate uproar of the modern jazz the sounds of their shared humanity with the American intruders.

10

Primitive Mating Rituals

The Color Wheel of the Racial Adventure Film

Bored with the vanilla diversions of a downtown nightclub, an intoxicated party girl in *Strange Justice* (1933) suggests an expedition uptown, to Harlem, "where there are no Ten Commandments and the hat check girls are boys!" In Hollywood fantasy no less than expeditionary fact, the excursions to foreign lands inhabited by dark-skinned natives did double duty as safaris into the white subconscious, symbolic journeys to forbidden zones where the pallid rules of Anglo-American Christianity might be overturned with impunity. If the African-Americans uptown in Harlem were too close to home to raise to the level of conscious desire, all kinds of unspeakable interracial sexual liberties might be inflicted upon white maidens and dangled before white men (and vice versa) outside American shores. "Hot country! Hot love! Treacherous natives! They were HELL on the whites," drooled the ads for Monogram's *West of Singapore* (1933). Was it a warning or a guarantee?

The blonde captive?: as Mutia Omoolu stands sentry, Duncan Renaldo and Harry Carey try to rescue Edwina Booth from savagery in *Trader Horn* (1930). (Courtesy of the British Film Institute)

The seething currents of white racism propel a hefty percentage of the escapist fantasies of pre-Code Hollywood. Historical epics, horror movies, expeditionary films, and action-adventure escapades are all shaded by the American dilemma of race. Given how fast the generic bloodlines get mixed, a serviceable label for the cascade of color-coded narratives might be the racial adventure film. No matter where the white travelers purportedly voyage—to darkest Africa, exotic Asia, or uncharted islands of unspecified longitude and latitude—the movement into unknown territory is less geographic than psychic. Shot mainly on backlots, the racial adventure film is laughable as ethnography but indispensable as cartography—that is, as a map into the murky regions of American race relations.

At the psychic core of the genre is the shiver of sexual attraction, the threat and promise of miscegenation. Forbidden by Jim Crow, desired darkly by the id, the dread and the allure of racial mixing, cultural and sexual, is the thread that binds together the divergent motion picture styles of the racial adventure film. Reviewing the quasi-documentary *The Blonde Captive*

(1932), *Variety* connected the dots by noting the "number of known in-stances of white women who drift into the [Australian outback] just as white women consort with the Negro element in Harlem." The expeditionary film *Africa Speaks* (1930) publicized its interracial prurience by distributing small packets with a printed inscription on the outside reading, "Secrets." In-side were nude pictures of African women. "It's a pity some of these dames are saucer lipped and off-color," complained a male customer, aroused de-spite himself.

The lure of miscegenation was dangled most starkly in the violation of the blonde by the black, of the purest of white women threatened with de-filement by ebony savages. Columbia's lurid ads for *The Blonde Captive* show a misshapen, simian aborigine dragging off a beautiful, bare-breasted blonde. Based on adventurer Paul Withington's travels in Northern Australia, it was "sold on the strength of its being absolutely authentic," bragged the studio's ad-pub chief. "Stranger than fiction—you travel 10,000 miles, penetrate deep jungles, and discover there a White Woman living with her Caveman Mate—and refusing to be rescued!" In *Trader Horn* (1930) a missionary's daughter, kidnapped in infancy, rules as a princess over the cannibal Orsogi tribe, her waist-length blonde mane both a makeshift blouse and a totem of white power. In *Blonde Venus* (1932) Germanic goddess Marlene Dietrich dons a gorilla suit to front a chorus line of undulating blackface Nubians, peels off her apeskin, and sings "Hot Voodoo," whose lyrics voice the same dark desire:

> *Hot voodoo—black as mud*
> *Hot voodoo—in my blood*
> *That African tempo has made me a slave*
> *Hot voodoo—dance of sin*
> *Hot voodoo—worse than gin*
> *I'd follow a cave man right into his cave*

In the early 1930s, when terrorism against African-Americans was still normative recreational activity for white men in the rural South, when nine youths, the Scottsboro boys, faced legal execution for consorting with a pair of white prostitutes, when the most vicious caricatures slouched and sim-pered across all the popular arts, onscreen expressions of American racism are virulent and inescapable. Yet the most common projection was not an offensive stereotype but an empty frame. The erasure of African-Americans from American life was the first rule in Hollywood cinema. Despite census

figures (blacks comprised roughly 10 percent of the population) and geographical distribution (since the 1920s, a shift from the remote regions of the
rural South to the media centers of the urban North), African-Americans
remained a conspicuous absence more than a discernable presence: on the
edge of visibility, spied in background shots or servants quarters, awarded no
speaking lines, standing as mute witnesses amid the Art Deco ambiance.

No less than other expressions of American popular culture in the early
1930s, pre-Code Hollywood is tainted by and complicit with that other
more strictly enforced Code, Jim Crow. In fact, the freedom of the pre-Code
years liberated some of the worst images and impulses, nakedly revealing an
America twisted by racism, exposing the fears and desires deliriously with
no subtextual subtlety or textured nuances. George Lincoln Washington, the
performer whose stage name Stepin Fetchit became a synonym for the demeaning portraits of the African-American onscreen, thrived in pre-Code
Hollywood: eyes wide, mouth agape, a notch above a four-legged creature
in mental agility.

At the same time, on the same screens, the sheer number of relatively un-
regulated presentations of racial groups vented a multiplicity of complex
images. If the portraits of African-Americans in pre-Code Hollywood range
in frequency from the appalling, to the condescending, to the innocuous, a
few, a very few, are warmly humanistic. One is singular in its celebration of
a black man with nerve and brains.

Just as the expeditionary film follows the points of the compass, the
racial adventure film circumnavigates the color wheel. The purist vessel for
subliminal interracial attraction was the white body with black qualities under the skin. Elsewhere, mixing it up with nonwhite races traces a spectrum
of pigmentation in a descending order of acceptability: red, yellow, and
black, Indian, Asian, and African. Finally, most weirdly, the desire for human
beings deemed less than human was projected onto a shared relative on the
evolutionary scale, the gorilla.

"He's White": *Tarzan, the Ape Man* (1932) and
Tarzan and His Mate (1934)

The preeminent figure of the racial adventure film is Tarzan, the noble savage sprung from the imagination of Edgar Rice Burroughs on the eve of
the Great War, prior to the close of colonial frontiers and the collapse of
European confidence. Though Tarzan leapt almost immediately to the silent

screen and into numerous features and serials, MGM's twin pre-Code blockbusters, *Tarzan, the Ape Man* (1932) and *Tarzan and His Mate* (1934), bequeathed the definitive incarnations, images, and catchphrases ("Tarzan—Jane, Jane—Tarzan"). Throughout his reign over the jungle and the studio franchise, this Tarzan displays more kinship toward Cheetah and the other apes in his entourage than toward the black Africans whom he swings so regally above.

Tarzan's nom de plume, "King of the Jungle," presumes that his minions include not only the animals but the bestial humans of Africa. Whether Pygmy or Watusi, Masai or Orsogi, all black natives fear and worship the white divinity. Smooth shaven, muscular, alabaster, the "Adonis swimming champion" Johnny Weismuller is a Greek statue come to life, a true Olympian. He embodies a white physical ideal that seems lifted from a Wehrmacht poster or Leni Riefenstahl documentary. In publicity portraits, Tarzan raises his right arm upward, palm outward, like the ancient Romans, like the Nazis.

Tarzan is a white man with the sexual energies and jungle-wise ways of the black man, hence the repeated reminders that despite his formulative environment, Tarzan is to the manor born, sprung from the purest royal bloodlines of British aristocracy. At the same time he is rough, elemental, and primitive, a grunting caveman. Given Tarzan's remedial English and difficulty with intransitive verbs ("I love you—happy"), Jane exerts the controlling intelligence. Tarzan serves as her sex toy, a congenial stud who protects his mate from a menagerie of animal threats (lion, rhino, alligator, leopard, and lion again, in the first film alone). For the most sexually potent romantic lead of the talkative pre-Code era, conversation is not his strong point.

As told by MGM, the Tarzan story begins with a British safari led by crusty old Africa hand James Parker (C. Aubrey Smith) and callow Harry Holt (Neil Hamilton). They seek the mythical graveyard of the elephants, over the forbidden Mutier escarpment, a huge cliff protecting a hidden valley where one million tons of ivory lie waiting for export (the only things of value in African being pure white). In tow is Parker's vivacious daughter Jane (Maureen O'Sullivan), just arrived in country with a half dozen steamer trunks and the modern woman's dependence on facial cream and stylish footwear. "I'm through with civilization," she chirps to her father. "I'm going to be a savage, just like you."

Even for the early 1930s, the cutaway shots to stock travelogue footage and the rear screen projection are patently fake. No matter: the eyes of spectators were fixed upon the lithe bodies in loin cloth and less. Tarzan's entry

"He's white": civilization cannot compete for Jane's affections in *Tarzan and His Mate* (1934). (Courtesy of the Museum of Modern Art)

is wisely delayed until the second act, when an offscreen yodel, the trademark cri de coeur heard here for the first time, harkens his presence. Seized with an urge the man does not comprehend but the woman does, Tarzan spirits Jane off to his tree house among the apes. He tears her clothes and manhandles her. She squeals, fearing the worst, or hoping for it, but the primitive gentleman leaves her unmolested. Later, reunited with her father, she discusses Tarzan's creature habits. "He's not like us," says her father. "He's white," Jane responds defensively.

In a lush lagoon Jane is flirtatious and loquacious before her silent and good-natured suitor. They splash around, get wet, and send out white-hot romantic sparks. The sexually experienced partner, Jane insinuates what is on her mind with come-hither looks her consort seems too dense to fathom. Tarzan compares their hands, hers small and feminine, his big and strong. He lifts her into his arms. Consenting, she lies her head on his shoulders. Next morning, spent and satiated, Jane and Tarzan glow with postcoital satisfaction. "Tarzan, what I am doing here—alone—with you?" Jane asks dreamily, and very rhetorically.

Authentic pygmies being rare around Culver City, Parker's safari is captured and tormented by a genetically implausible tribe of black dwarfs who toss the adventurers into a pit with a raging gorilla. Tarzan kills the gorilla, rescues the white folk, and commands his elephants to rampage through the village of the black dwarfs. An elephant wraps a native in his trunk, flings him to the ground, and stomps him into the dirt.

Wounded in the stampede, a dying elephant leads the survivors to the graveyard of his species. "Solemn and beautiful," observes Jane. "We shouldn't be here." Her lines express the ecological pastoralism that coexists with the desire to penetrate the virgin land, the racial adventure film condemning the selfsame impulse to explore and exploit that propelled the expeditionary film. Ivory hunters, gold seekers, and meddling archaeologists are punished for intruding into the same areas the expeditionary cameramen violated without fear of retribution.

The finale to *Tarzan, the Ape Man* left open the possibility of a sequel and the scale of the film's box office returns assured it. In the brilliance of its suggestive title, *Tarzan and His Mate* shifted the focus from the single man to the activity of the biological pair: not "Tarzan and Jane," an equal partnership, or "Tarzan and His Wife," a conjugal union blessed by church and state, but a blunt commingling, "mate" being a verb as well as a noun.

The sequel finds Harry Holt, Jane's former fiancé, returning to Africa to try to lure the smitten Lady back to civilization with silk dresses, nylons, and perfume. "Where there's clothes, there's hope with a woman," he figures. Announced by the offscreen sound of his famous yell, Tarzan swings in screen left, followed by a soprano cry that can only belong to Jane.

Clad in a scanty jungle bikini, Jane performs a reverse striptease: donning nylons and, in silhouette, slipping into an evening gown as the Englishmen get an eyeful. Harry's partner Martin Arlington (Paul Cavanagh) lusts after Jane ("You're a fascinating little savage!"), who flirts with him brazenly. Tarzan swoops down, his knife poised erect, and seems about to attack the interloper, but he is distracted by the music blaring from a portable phonograph. He touches Jane's strange clothes, strokes her nyloned legs, and sniffs her perfumed scent. Inflamed, Tarzan carries his mate off to the bushes with one purpose in mind.

Like Captain Parker before them, Harry and the dastardly Arlington seek the priceless ivory of the elephant graveyard. As the safari penetrates into the

260 / PRIMITIVE MATING RITUALS

African interior, however, the whiteness of the ivory is stained by two visions of black Africans: the savage cannibals lurking in the jungle and the domesticated natives pressed into service as guides and bearers. An antebellum portrait of American race relations unfolds in the treatment of the jet-black Africans: forced labor, brutal whipping, and, when one of the natives balks at going forward, summary execution. Native bearers plummet from mountains or perish on the trail, their death meaning only a lost pack of medicine or one man fewer to carry 150 pounds of ivory. Only the black overseer Saidi (Nathan Curry) is granted a name and personality. Little more than a shriek echoing on the soundtrack, the native extras are fodder for sadistic variations in killing: shot, speared, torn apart, devoured by lions, crushed by elephants, chomped by alligators, and flung from cliffs. More emotional weight is given to the death of the courageous ape Cheetah, who stands in front of a charging rhino to protect his mistress, than to any of the African humans.

In the film's most scandalous scene, Tarzan grabs Jane and tosses her into a lagoon, ripping her dress off in midair. The underwater sequence shows a nude body double (Olympic swimmer Josephine McKim) swimming with Weismuller, a prolonged pas de deux that gives the clearest and most prolonged view of female nudity in any major studio production of the pre-Code era, not stolen glimpses of flesh but an eye-opening unblushing exposure, front and back.

Pre-Code era or not, MGM must have known it would never get away with so extended and explicit a display of white female nudity. In April 1934, Joseph Breen, then head of the Studio Relations Committee, not yet empowered with the bludgeon of the Production Code Administration, rejected *Tarzan and His Mate* for its quite visible violation of the prohibition against nudity. MGM appealed the decision, and, in accordance with the procedures then in place, a jury was convened to mediate the dispute. Representing the Code were Breen, his assistant Geoffrey Shurlock, and MPPDA vice president Frederick W. Beetson. For the plaintiffs, MGM sent in its biggest guns, production executives Bernard Hyman and Eddie Mannix, studio mastermind Irving Thalberg, and Louis B. Mayer himself. The allegedly disinterested jury was comprised of the chief executives from RKO, Universal, and Fox, B. B. Kahane, Carl Laemmle Jr., and Winfield Sheehan, respectively. The assembly of firepower on all sides portended a major showdown, a dress rehearsal for the final battle between the regulators and the studios that summer.

On April 9, 1934, *Tarzan and His Mate* was shown in its entirety in a screening room on the MGM lot, the diligent assembly rewinding the underwater ballet "several times" for inspection. As Breen later reported in a memorandum to Hays, "The offending sequence was an underwater shot of a man and woman going through a series of movements. The man in the shot wore a loin cloth, but a critical examination of the shot indicated that the woman was stark naked. There were four or five shots of the woman, which the jury referred to as 'frontal' shots, which showed the front of the woman's body. These, the jury remarked several times, were particularly offensive." Thalberg argued that the Studio Relations Committee had previously permitted nudity in *White Shadows of the South Sea* (1928) and *The Common Law* (1931). Breen responded that both films had actually employed "suggestive nudity." (Thalberg should have mentioned a better example, the nude swim sequence in RKO's 1932 *Bird of Paradise*. B. B. Kahane kept quiet about his own studio's precedent.)

Breen knew his position was unassailable on the merits of the case. As anyone could see, the swim sequence clearly violated the letter of the Code ("COMPLETE NUDITY is never permitted"). More importantly, however, he knew that the motion picture industry, in the spring of 1934, was under intense pressure from Catholics, congressmen, and social scientists to turn away from profligacy. In the present atmosphere, the MPPDA might be inclined to cut down one of its own, MGM, for the greater good.

"After a rather animated discussion between the jurors, the representatives of Metro, and Mr. Breen," Mr. Breen recorded in a memo to Will Hays, "the verdict of this office was sustained by the jury." The decision marked the first time that an MPPDA panel had upheld the Studio Relations Committee at the expense of one of its own members. By April 19, 1934, with the sequence cut, the film was judged "all right" and granted a Code seal. In retrospect, Breen's victory in *Tarzan and His Mate* presaged the new regulatory regime around the corner, one that would be a jury unto itself.

Surely less surprised than it pretended, the MGM hierarchy may well have fashioned the sequence as a negotiable offering to the censors. Knowing the scene violated the Code, knowing that Breen was no Wingate, the studio figured that once the self-contained nude scene was deleted the many scenes of Weissmuller and O'Sullivan prancing about in their revealing jungle togs could be retained in trade. Besides, despite the Code edict, trailers containing the nude scene and a few uncensored prints continued to circulate, with MGM's defiant complicity. Although under a misapprehension about the identity of the female, an appreciative critic for the *Hollywood Reporter* called the pas de deux "one of the most beautiful sequences ever filmed where Johnny Weismuller and Maureen O'Sullivan swim underwater, their swift white bodies carving intricate and lovely designs in the depths."

With or without the lovely designs of swift white bodies, *Tarzan and His Mate* ends with the invasive white men dead and Tarzan and Jane herding the ivory back to the elephants' graveyard, undisturbed. MGM, however, returned to harvest the Tarzan franchise for further profit in six more sequels.

Unlike expeditionary films, the two Tarzan films were aimed straight at the female audience, always Hollywood's target of choice. Weismuller, not O'Sullivan, is the privileged, strutting sex object. Posing a "question to the ladies," MGM's ad copy was both biologically urgent and gender-specific:

> Girls! Would you live like Eve if you found the right Adam?
>
> Modern marriages could learn plenty from this drama of primitive jungle mating!
>
> If all marriages were based on the primitive mating instinct, it would be a better world.

Other inquiries unfavorably compared the modern man in America to his primitive cousin in Africa. "Could you ever be interested only in 'men of business' after you heard HIS love call?" queried the taglines. "Could you ever be coaxed back to civilization as long as you had a bronzed mate like this to kiss you awake at every dawn?" A bronzed mate? But he's white.

RED SKIN, RED LIPS: *Massacre* (1934)

Safely restricted to the reservation of the mythic past, romanticized in the national literature since the *Leatherstocking Tales* of James Fenimore Cooper, the American Indian enjoyed high ranking along the color wheel. More often a figure of attraction and affection than fear and loathing, his demonization on the Hollywood screen has always been overstated. Even in the western genre, the war-whooping, horseback-riding savage, scattered by the bugle call of the U.S. cavalry, ceded territory to a more guilt-stricken and nostalgic vision, the noble savage not the savage redskin. In the B western, the need for action attacks on horseback and flaming arrows kept Indians alive as a moveable menace, but as early as *The Iron Horse* (1925) the red man was as likely to be the victim of white-eye depredations as a perpetrator of frontier terrorism. Will Rogers, the most beloved entertainer of the era, bragged of his Cherokee blood, the "one drop rule" that defined and denigrated the African-American not being applicable to Indians. At the end of *Call Her Savage* (1932), when the hellion played by Clara Bow learns the genetic reason for her lifelong affinity for red-blooded physicality, she prefers her new identity as an illegitimate half-breed to her old one as the lawful daughter of a cold Anglo-Saxon millionaire. In limited quantities, Indian blood added a sexually potent spice to pioneer stock.

The best example of the privileged racial status of American Indians in pre-Code Hollywood is Warner Brothers' *Massacre* (1934), directed by Alan Crosland, who inaugurated the sound era with the ethnic impostor film *The Jazz Singer* (1927). The title promises covered wagons and cavalry charges, but it disguises a preachment yarn set in a modern frontier.

Newsreel footage of the 1933 Chicago World's Fair ("A Century of Progress" was the billing for the boondoggle that lost $44 million) sets the scene. Chief Joe Thunder Horse (Richard Barthelmess) is a full-blooded Sioux Indian and the most popular attraction of a galloping Wild West Show. While performing tricks on horseback and feats of incredible marksmanship, he bares his chest for the sighing maidens in the stands. The eyes of a starstruck female spectator dart from his 8-by-10 souvenir photo to the figure in the flesh. "I'd be that big chief's squaw any time!" she swoons. With a clump of feathers adorning a flowing mane of jet black hair, a bronzed muscular form bared for inspection, and minimal command of English ("heap much pretty girls" he grunts to a gaggle of squealing fans), Thunder Horse is every inch the primitive, sexually potent Red Man.

After the show, the mask is quickly tossed aside. "Get this junk off me," he snaps at his valet, ripping away the Indian headdress and long-haired wig. In fact Thunder Horse (everyone calls him Joe) is a thoroughly assimilated Indian who left the reservation long ago. Fluent in slang and streetsmart, he basks in the trappings of white-eye success: a black manservant, Sam (Clarence Muse); a custom-made convertible with his picture on the spare tire; and a beautiful blonde socialite girlfriend. "It's a long way from the wigwam to her," cracks an onlooker. Like the Indians in the original Wild West Show of Buffalo Bill Cody, Thunder Horse puts on his warpaint to play the stereotype of the Indian in the white imagination—or in his case, the female white imagination. The owner of the Wild West show understands perfectly the erotic dimension in Thunder Horse's appeal. "A picture of you and a swell dish like that would be worth a thousand seats a day," he says when he spies a portrait of the girlfriend. Seeing the true face behind the mass marketing of the Indian mask, Depression moviegoers know that the donning of ethnic attire might conceal more than an ethnic stereotype.

Dressed in a sharp double-breasted suit and cowboy hat, Joe enters the cocktail party of the swell dish. "It's an Indian this time," says a guest, bemused by the latest masculine diversion of the woman of the house. The society girl lures him upstairs to a private room stocked full of blankets, headdresses, and assorted Indian regalia. "Feast your redskin eyes on this," she tells him. None of it makes an impression on Joe who confesses he "wouldn't know a medicine man from a bootlegger." Not wanting to barter over trinkets, she spreads herself down languidly on a couch. "Red skin," she coos. "Red lips," he replies and moves down on her.

As a savage attraction for the social set, the character of Thunder Horse seems inspired by the real-life case of Chief Buffalo Child Long Lance, a fake Indian of the 1920s and costar of *The Silent Enemy* (1930). As the toast of Park Avenue, Long Lance rode the erotic wave of desire for the authentic Red Man to social prominence and romantic conquests. In fact he was not a full-blooded Blackfoot Indian chief but an African-American from North Carolina, trading his real identity for a step up the ethnic ladder.

Massacre moves from eros to civilization when Joe gets news that his father back at the reservation is near death. Joe and Sam drive the gaudy convertible westward, passing through a montage of road signs by way of directional orientation. With Sam behind the wheel, black man and red man pull up to the entrance of the desert wasteland that is the Indian reservation. "Sure is dry," remarks Sam. "White folks didn't give the Indians much of a break."

With the help of pretty Indian secretary Lydia (Ann Dvorak), Joe uncovers pervasive corruption on the reservation. The tribal undertaker, lawyer, doctor, even the Christian minister, all conspire to steal from the Indian. "They always lie," a reservation Indian tells Joe. "White man is government. Government never change." His tongue is not forked: the official representatives of the state are all loathsome exploiters. The undertaker rapes Joe's sister during their father's funeral. The doctor refuses to treat tubercular children. The lawyer cheats Indians out of their inheritance. The head Indian agent wants only to milk the tribe dry.

As Joe reconnects with his Indian roots and reclaims his birthright as Thunder Horse, he experiences a change of heart and identity. Soon Joe, reborn as Thunder Horse, is beating up the quack doctor and breaking up a mock Indian ceremony. Disgusted by the hypocrisy of the Christian mis-

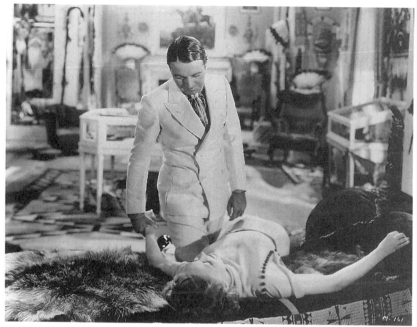

Savage love: a blonde socialite gives herself to "Big Chief" Thunder Horse (Richard Barthelmess) in *Massacre* (1934). (Courtesy of the Museum of Modern Art)

sionary, Thunder Horse orders the burial of his father according to Indian tradition. When he discovers his sister has been raped (a ripped shoulder strap being a sure sign of sexual violation in pre-Code Hollywood), he chases down the undertaker in his convertible, lassos him out from behind the wheel of his car, drags him along the road, and leaves him for dead. The Indian agent is furious at the uppity redskin. "I'll show this—" he gropes for the right word—"*Bolshevik* that he can't defy the regulations and authority of the government."

Strikingly, the indictment of American authority extends to the Christian religion, the theft of the Indian birthright being not just economic but cultural. The hypocritical minister colludes in the exploitation and speaks contemptuously of his congregation. "You know how superstitious they are," he complains when Thunder Horse tempts his "pagan flock back to the ways of sin." As the Indian agent rails at Thunder Horse, he implicates Christianity in the web of oppression. "You listen to me," he yells. "We got missionaries around here to give the Indians Christian religion. And what's good enough for us ought to be plenty good enough for you." Reservation justice is as corrupt as reservation religion. Presiding over a kangaroo court of wooden Indians, the agent railroads Thunder Horse on "assault, disorderly conduct, and attempting to demoralize the tribes by reverting to savage customs." When the rapist undertaker dies from his wounds, Thunder Horse escapes from prison and becomes a fugitive from the law.

Thunder Horse should be easy to spot in his custom-made convertible, but as the police zero in on the speeding car it is the black valet Sam behind the wheel acting as decoy. To the police, Sam plays Sambo, assuming the wide-eyed stance of the dumb black retainer he clearly is not. "Ain't he in jail?" he shuffles when asked Thunder Horse's whereabouts. Again, behind a racial mask resides a sly intelligence.

Meanwhile, Thunder Horse is riding the rails to Washington, D.C. He disembarks before a fence festooned with the Blue Eagle of the New Deal, the Capitol Dome looming in the background. Firmly in line with the New Deal–Warner Bros. axis, *Massacre* blames the social problems of blighted Indian reservations not on the white father in Washington but on malefactors at the local level. Leaping over the heads of municipal and state officials, the rewritten social contract of 1933 is between the citizen and the federal government. Separating them as obstructions to reform are venal local authorities and big money interests.

In the corridors of reform-minded Washington, Thunder Horse finds a sympathetic ear in the New Deal Commissioner for Indian Affairs. The commissioner cautions that "every move I make is blocked by the same organized groups that have been bleeding the Indian for years—water power, oil rights, cattle rangers, timber—whatever the Indian happens to own they manage to get away from him." But though the Good People and the New Deal confront the same Old Deal, together they can make a stand against local injustice.

As tabloid headlines scream ("Sioux Indian Becomes American Dreyfus"), a Senate committee investigates Thunder Horse's sensational charges. The politicians are not all advocates for this "renegade Indian," but Thunder Horse asserts that "a white man can violate an Indian girl and get away with it" and names his fifteen-year-old sister as proof. "You used to shoot the Indian down. Now you cheat him and starve him and kill him off by dirt and disease," he thunders. "It's a massacre any way you take it!" The New Dealers in the room applaud vigorously, including the Indian commissioner and an Eleanor Roosevelt stand-in wearing the First Lady's trademark fur-lined wrap.

But the Indian story is not over yet. Thunder Horse returns to the reservation to stand trial for his crime, with a New Deal–appointed attorney confident that the "unwritten law" permitting a man to kill in defense of a woman assures a verdict of justifiable homicide. However, upon learning that the perfidious Indian agents have kidnapped Joe's sister, the Indians go on the warpath. Though the sounds of war whoops and high-pitched keening evoke a B western raid on the covered wagons of pioneers, this time the audience rides with the Indians. Descending upon the town, they torch the courthouse and liberate Thunder Horse. As the building is consumed in flames, the Indians stand before the conflagration, their shovels, picks, and pitchforks silhouetted against the fire, a proletarian insurrection not a savage uprising. With his sister rescued and "federal indictments" assured against the perpetrators, Thunder Horse accepts a true test of his native talents—a job in Washington to reform the "accursed system," by which is meant more than the Bureau of Indian Affairs.

Despite a mediocre performance at the box office, the critical response to *Massacre* reflected the warm feelings toward the American Indian as mythic presence if not social reality. "*Massacre* proves that there is still material in the West and that large scale injustice is still the most inflammatory and exciting story material," commented the *New York Mirror*. "The most vigorous assault upon American injustice that the films have produced since *I Am a Fugitive from a Chain Gang*," claimed the *New York Herald Tribune*. "As entertainment the work can perhaps be recommended only with reservations [*sic*], but as a good, hearty social document it has fine and striking merit." *Variety* demurred with a wisecrack about the ethnic imposter Richard Barthelmess. "When surrounded by other big chiefs who are Indians on the up and up, he doesn't look an Indian any more than Jimmy Durante looks like a Chinaman."

EAST MATES WEST

Where Africans were savage subhumans whose threatened violations of white womanhood were akin to bestiality, the Asian moved up and down on the white man's sliding evolutionary scale. The vocabulary used to describe the Asian mingled respect with contempt. Male and female alike were inscrutable, sinister, wily, and seductive. American racism was tinged with the knowledge that within the mind of the Asian dwelt intelligence and within Asia untold millions stood ready to hasten the decline of the West. A credible and imminent challenge to the nation state and the hegemony of white civilization, Asians posed a menace that lent a geopolitical dimension to the psychological panic.

Of course, erotically charged orientalism had been a venerable Hollywood tradition since the silent era when authentic Asian objects of desire like Sesue Hayakawa and Anna May Wong floated in the ethereal realm of pantomime. More commonly, the taboo lust for the Asian was projected onto a white matinee idol encrusted under slanted eyes and yellow skin, as in D. W. Griffith's *Broken Blossoms* (1920), where the chaste interracial couple comprised of Richard Barthelmess ("Chinky") and Lillian Gish gaze longingly at each other in soft focus.

Sound cinema diminished the authentic Asian presence on the American screen even further. The heightened realism of the medium worked as a kind of exclusionary act in two ways. First, it made the romantic attraction toward the Asian less of a theatrical conceit aimed at an imaginary object and more of a tangible sexual attraction to a full-blooded sexual figure. Second, when a white actor played an Asian role in pancake yellowface makeup, the disguise looked freakish set against the faces of authentic Asian players. Originally slated to appear in the lead role of *The Son-Daughter* (1933), Anna May Wong was dropped in favor of Helen Hayes, whose casting then necessitated the firing of all other Chinese in the cast "with the possible exception of some Chinese as extras in long shots." Moreover, "in order to avoid comparisons between the principals in make-up and Orientals, even the bit parts will be filled with Occidentals." In lighthearted film fare, Occidental actors better withstood the proximity of authentic Asian-American actors in subordinate roles, notably in Warner Oland's impersonation of Charlie Chan alongside his number one son (Keye Luke) in the popular detective series of the 1930s.

A typical example of pre-Code Hollywood Orientalism is William Wellman's *The Hatchet Man* (1932), where the Chinese are both exotic other and proximate kindred. In San Francisco's Chinatown, Wong Low Get (Edward G. Robinson) is "the honorable hatchet man" for the Tong syndicate. Forced to kill his best friend, Wong pledges to take care of the man's young daughter and marry her when she comes of age. Fifteen years later, the process of American assimilation seems complete. Toya San (Loretta Young) is a thoroughly modern girl dressed in gossamer and dancing to jazz ("Boy, is this keen!"). Wong has cut his hair, donned a conservative business suit, and otherwise blended in to his adopted country. "Chinese girls have legs here just like their white sisters," he observes to an Old World friend shocked at a flash of ankle.

When years of peace between the two rival Tongs threaten to end, the former hatchet man, now a dedicated peacemaker, seeks to negotiate a settlement. The only recalcitrant at the meeting is the sole Caucasian gangster. "Cut out this Chink lingo," he demands. "Talk United States." Wong lets his hatchet do the talking and kills the rude Occidental. When Toya San runs off with Wong's no-good bodyguard Harry (Leslie Fenton), the hatchet man is ostracized by his fellow Tong members for refusing to exact revenge on the couple. Wong descends into poverty, but revives to return to China, rescue Toya San from prostitution, and regain his potency by plunging his hatchet into the back of Harry's head.

Occidentals playing Oriental in an all-Asian world submerged the erotic tension behind the interracial makeup, but an Occidental cast doing double duty as Asian *and* American could not disguise the desire for East to meet, and mate, West. In films where white actors romanced white actors in yellowface, the yellow peril was also an erotic possibility.

Just as the brushstrokes of Edgar Rice Burroughs colored the African racial adventure film, Sax Rohmer shaded in the outlines of yellow-peril imagery for the Asian variant. In an ouevre of delirious pulp fiction written from 1913 to 1955, Rohmer went East with a vengeance. His trademark creation was the unkillable Dr. Fu Manchu, mad scientist, master of the occult, and sexual predator. No African equivalent existed for Fu Manchu: a black man might have one or two of the attributes but never all three in combination.

The thrills and enticements of the yellow menace radiated hysterically in the first and best known of the incarnations of Rohmer's villain, MGM's *The Mask of Fu Manchu* (1932), directed by Charles Brabin. In yet another expeditionary setup, a team of British anthropologists must find the legendary sword and mask of Genghis Khan before Fu Manchu can use them for his own nefarious ends, namely to lead the "countless hordes" of Asia in an uprising against the West. Actually, the real mission is an exploration into the pornography of interracial sadomasochism.

The linkage between inhuman monsters and human monsters of un-American racial type is embodied in the person of Boris Karloff, lately Dr. Frankenstein's monster, now Dr. Fu Manchu. "You hideous yellow monster!" the female ingenue yells at him. The first look at Fu's face comes via a wide-angle, distended close-up in a mirror. As Fu reminds his British captives, he is a graduate of three Western universities. Both sorcerer and scientist, the

Chinese blends the mysticism of the East with the rationalism of the West, a double whammy of supernatural and scientific power. Fittingly, the set design of Fu's work station is a cross between Merlin's cave and an MIT laboratory: snakes, spiders, and crocodiles alongside test tubes, Bunsen burners, and electromagnetic gadgetry. "Will we ever understand these Eastern races?" muses the stalwart expedition leader Nayland Smith (Lewis Stone).

Smith understands all too well that Fu has more in mind than the extension of Chinese political hegemony. "Do you suppose for a minute Fu Manchu doesn't know we have a beautiful white girl here?" he asks darkly. Not at all one-sided, however, the erotic energy leaps across gender lines and racial barriers. The girl Fu modestly refers to as his "ugly and insignificant daughter" is the beautiful and sexually rapacious Fah Lo See (Myrna Loy), who desires the buff male hero Terrence Granville (Charles Starrett). Sublimating fiercely in a lather of sexual excitement, she orders him whipped by her Nubian slaves ("Faster! Faster!"). Supine, bare-chested, and trussed to an operating table, Granville writhes as Fu injects a serum designed to deaden his Anglo-Saxon free will. Fortunately, Englishwoman Sheila Barton (Karen Morley) manages to break through the wily Oriental drug with an injection of virginal Occidental love.

In the finale, Fu clutches the sword and mask of Genghis Khan while the Europeans cringe before an innovative lineup of inscrutable tortures: Smith is tied to a pendulum for slow descent into a pit of ravenous crocodiles; his colleague Dr. Van Berg (Jean Hersholt) is trapped between two walls of metal spikes slowly closing in; Granville is dragged back to Fu's laboratory to be trussed and drugged again; and Morley is dressed in a slinky white nightgown and paraded supine on a slab for sacrifice to the heathen gods of the Chinese. Wearing Khan's mask and brandishing his sword, Fu exhorts his obedient hordes to "wipe out the whole accursed white race" and tantalizes them with the likes of Karen Morley as the fruits of war. "Would you have maidens like this for your wives?" screams Fu. "Then conquer and breed! Kill the white man and take his women!"

Faced with an alluring enough Chinese gentleman, some of the white women were willing to be taken. Frank Capra's *The Bitter Tea of General Yen* (1933), the best of the Asian-looking racial adventure films, conceded that the East-West attraction worked in the other direction. Columbia's costliest production to that date, the war-torn melodrama is a wily treatise on the erotic attraction/repulsion of the Asian in the American mind.

Amidst the chaos of a Chinese civil war, while panicked refugees flood the cluttered streets of Shanghai, a privileged enclave of Westerners pre-

Yellow perils: as Dr. Fu Manchu (Boris Karloff) holds Nayland Smith (Lewis Stone) at gunpoint, his "ugly and insignificant" daughter (Myrna Loy) prepares to extract erotic pleasure from Terrence Granville (Charles Starrett) in *The Mask of Fu Manchu* (1932). (Courtesy of the Museum of Modern Art)

pares for a wedding ceremony. The bride to be is Megan Davis (Barbara Stanwyck), daughter of one of "the finest old Puritan families in New England." As the wedding party awaits her, a crusty old China hand recalls how he once explained the crucifixion of Christ to a gang of Mongolian bandits and learned to his sorrow the lesson the heathen gleaned from his missionary work: merchants who venture into the territory are now robbed and crucified.

Outside in the din and chaos, Megan moves through the streets of a city in anarchy. When her rickshaw boy is struck and killed by a car, the accident seems to bother no one but her. "Human life is the cheapest thing in China," she is informed. The Chinese are a "tricky, treacherous, and immoral" people, a dowager missionary hisses. "I can't tell one from the other—they're all Chinamen." Capra's camera pans to and holds on the face of a Chinese servant, blank and inscrutable. Already, however, one Chinese stands out from the faceless hordes: a legendary military leader, General Yen (Nils Asther), the man whose vehicle killed Megan's rickshaw boy.

Megan's fiancé must delay their wedding to bring a group of orphans to safety. As the couple rush through the streets by car and on foot, Capra unfurls a harrowing vision of urban warfare: armored vehicles barrel through the city streets with soldiers firing machine guns, killing civilians at random in a murderous turkey shoot, and planes zoom in for aerial bombardment. This is a new kind of war, not on battlefields but in the metropolis, not against warriors but against civilians. It is the first vivid sound-on-film depiction of what would soon become a newsreel commonplace.

Trapped in the terrified mob and buffeted from all sides, Megan is knocked unconscious. She wakes up on a troop train, the guest of the mysterious General Yen. A series of eyeline matches, from the general to his consort Mah-Li (Toshia Nori) and back to Megan, insinuates that the general's purpose is not chivalric.

Yen takes Megan to his sumptuous summer palace and military headquarters. When the gunfire from Yen's firing squads outside Megan's ornate bedroom rattles her, the general graciously orders the executions be taken out of earshot. "There is a famine," he explains serenely. Gradually, his motives emerge. "You yellow swine, you think that you can—" she protests, leaving the thought unfinished. General Yen's financial adviser, an American named Jones (Walter Connolly), cautions him. "Don't forget, this is a white woman." "That's all right," replies Yen. "I have no prejudice against color." Jones responds with a shrug and an apt metaphor. "It's no skin off my nose."

At night, Megan dreams up a Freudian montage sequence to express her conflicted emotions toward the alien and exotic general. Yen appears as a vampiric monster threatening her, fingernails bared, swooping in like Nosferatu. She is rescued from the monster by an attractive masked figure and behind the mask is—General Yen.

Megan alternately recoils from and moves toward the general, a state of emotional and racial confusion whose outward manifestation is the clothes she wears, either the stern garb of the female missionary or the florid patterns of the Chinese consort. Preaching the missionary party line, she tells him, "We're all one flesh and blood." Taking her at her word, Yen replies, "Do you really mean that?"

Early on in the production of *The Bitter Tea of General Yen*, the Studio Relations Committee flagged the blunt dialogue and blunter imagery as potential flash points. Though anticipating protests from both domestic guardians of Occidental superiority (over the interracial love story and the depiction of unctuous missionaries) and the Chinese foreign office (over the offhand cruelties and summary executions of everyday life in China), the internal censors supported Capra's audacious project and readily waived the

Interracial eroticism: Jones (Walter Connolly) offers to take Megan (Barbara Stanwyck) from her missionary work with General Yen (Nils Asther) in Frank Capra's *The Bitter Tea of General Yen* (1933). (Courtesy of the Museum of Modern Art)

Code's rules against derogatory portrayals of foreign peoples. "The whole purpose of the story *is* the convincing refutation of the foreign opinion of the Chinese characters and for that reason it is essential that the seeming derogatory remarks be used in the first part of the story in order to serve the chief purpose," explained John V. Wilson in a memo to a worried Will Hays. "The story is in fact a eulogy of the Chinese philosophy, fair dealing, morality, and graciousness. The audience, following the conduct of the Chinese General, who is the hero of the story, gradually becomes ashamed of the Americans who are placed in contact with him. They see that he really excels in all of the virtues which the first part of the story denied him."

An extraordinary film, *The Bitter Tea of General Yen* is perfectly aware of the racism at its own heart, but also perfectly persuaded that the twain can meet as friends and lovers. Yen is inviolably alien, beyond Western imagination, yet genuinely in love with Megan and as warmly attached to his comrade Jones as Jones is to him. In the end his empire collapses about him, done in not by the white woman but by his own passion for her, his own generosity of heart. With his servants gone, his palace vacant, his love unrequitable, General Yen prepares to drink his bitter draught. Before he downs the poison, however, Megan finally comes to him, not worn down but redeemed in the knowledge that "we're all one flesh and blood." She dons the clothes of the Chinese courtesan, applies her makeup, and goes to the general. "I had to come back," she confesses tearfully. "I couldn't leave you, I'll never leave you." The daughter of the Puritans falls at the feet of the Chinese warlord and he drinks the bitter tea.

"THE ETHIOPIAN TRADE"

Like every other man-made blight, the Great Depression hit African-Americans harder than their white countrymen. Relegated to service work as maids, cooks, valets, and chauffeurs, they were the first to be fired as middle-class whites moved downward on the economic ladder, the last to be hired in a workforce now crowded with white competition who had once considered service work beneath their dignity.

For the few black filmmakers and exhibitors catering to the African-American audience, the consequences were disastrous. Along the circuit of all-black "race houses," business fell off more than 65 percent in some districts and dozens of theaters folded. Save for a pitifully small independent market of "race films," notably by the pioneer independent producer-director Oscar Micheaux, African-Americans were a captive market for the same Hollywood fare as the rest of nation. "Negro houses seem to draw best with white pictures with white casts," observed *Variety* in 1931, as if they had much of a choice. Often the race houses were at the very terminus of the distribution line, recipients of beat-up prints in circulation for years.

Hollywood cinema might also reach the estimated fourteen million black moviegoers in segregated sections of white theaters (usually in the balcony, the "Jim Crow roost") or during special all-black evenings in white theaters. Ironically, hard times improved the climate for mixed moviegoing. By the early 1930s, many white theater owners were so desperate for customers that they could no longer afford to be particular about whom they sold tickets to. With mercenary egalitarianism, *Variety* explained how showmen "anxious for the extra revenue from the dusky section of America's melting pot" now wanted back the "extra shekels" from an audience they had earlier scorned. Seeing a profit margin in marginal integration, "those that have balconies are dusting 'em off and them that hasn't are turning to midnight matinees, giving the cottongrabbers the whole house."

On screen as before it, African-Americans inhabited restricted space. In 1933, Vere E. Johns, film critic for the African-American weekly the *New Age*, undertook a bitter survey of the limited options for black actors in American cinema. Though a "few get a chance now and then as extras in some mob scene that calls for people of color, with few exceptions their roles have been those of menials." Menials or worse: an all too typical denigration was the role played by the black character actor "Blue" Washington in the John Wayne western *Haunted Gold* (1932), a part Johns characterized as "an unreal frightful monkey, jumping at his shadow and bursting through walls and doors with his eyes popping from his head, teeth chattering, et al." Exaggerating only somewhat, a disgusted Johns claimed that "in the case of the Negro 95% of the parts are of this nature."

From the evidence of memoirs and commentary in the Negro press, the African-American audience watched with a conflicted admixture of identification and resentment. Attending a screening of *Trader Horn* at a segregated race house, an African-American critic for *The Crisis* was chagrined to find the black audience immersed totally in the white milieu of the racial adventure film. "One scene depicts the 'beautiful'—of course, blond—heroine in the clutches of 'savage' Africans," he recalled. "In typical Hollywood thriller style the girl is saved just as all hope is ebbing away. At this particular showing the audience burst into wild applause when the rescue scene flashed on screen. I looked around. Those who were applauding were ordinary Negro working people and middle class folk. Hollywood's movie makers had made the theme so commonplace and glorious that it seemed quite natural white virtue should triumph over black vice."

On the other hand, the growing importance of the African-American audience and that audience's growing resistance to Hollywood's moral color scheme is indicated by a cautionary note sounded in *Motion Picture Herald*'s review of a *Trader Horn*-like sequence in Columbia's racial adventure film *Black Moon* (1934). "In that the colored natives involved in the film are rather harshly pictured as bloodthirsty worshippers of black gods who indulge in sacrificial orgies," the trade paper warned, "the film may meet with objection in those situations where colored people make up a portion of the patronage." Either way, Hollywood insiders readily linked the domestic population to its African roots in the flippant label applied to African-American moviegoers, "the Ethiopian trade."

By whatever name, African-Americans saw few reflections to identify with on screen. Seldom in front of the camera, almost never behind it, they have so slight a presence in Hollywood cinema that cultural historians sometimes settle for substitutes one step removed. That is, just as most of the roles for Asians and Indians went to white actors coated with pancake makeup, the black face on screen sometimes covered a white man underneath. Yet the operative conceit for depictions of Asians and Indians, where audiences suspended disbelief to embrace white actors in ethnic disguise, collapsed in the case of African-Americans. With the heightened realism of the sound moving image, the silent era pretense of *The Birth of a Nation* (1915), in which whites in blackface played African-Americans in straight drama, was unsustainable. For portraits of African-Americans on the Hollywood screen, two quite different kinds of depictions emerge: the real item, where African-Americans appear as dramatis personae, frequently in the most demeaning of roles, and the fake item, namely the conceit of blackface minstrelsy, where the actor's essential whiteness beneath burnt cork makeup is never forgotten.

Nonetheless, pre-Code Hollywood was more casual about the enforcement of Jim Crow codes of segregation and hierarchy than Hollywood under the Code. Especially in exotic settings (prisons, foreign outposts, and the mythic past), the breakdown of white civilization might mean a relaxation of racial boundaries. Beyond the racist law of the land, blacks and whites might, briefly and conditionally, share screen space and the human condition in a relation approaching equality. In *Hold Your Man* (1933), Jean Harlow is tossed into a women's reformatory where she pines for her fugitive lover Clark Gable. As in the all-male prison film, a singular compensation of prison life for females is multiracial camaraderie. A montage of the women singing "Onward Christian Soldiers" in the prison chapel flashes close-ups from the congregation, including a Jewish girl in profile and an Asian-American woman, each belting out the Anglo-Protestant hymn. Though in residence "across the hall," presumably in segregated quarters, a black woman named Lily Mae (Theresa Harris) is smoothly integrated into the sisterhood of the reformatory. The film is nonchalant about the race of Lily Mae and her preacher father. Neither Harlow nor Gable, neither the inmates nor the matrons, blinks an eye at their black skin. Gable pleads with the preacher to marry him to Harlow in a secret ceremony, a power reversal—a white star begging a black character actor for a favor—unimaginable after 1934.

Sisters under the skin: the otherwise unscrupulous Lily (Barbara Stanwyck) remains loyal to her black maid Chico (Theresa Harris) in *Baby Face* (1933). (Courtesy of the Museum of Modern Art)

In more civilized quarters, the byplay between master and servant or mistress and maid often breached boundaries of race and rank with an affectionate informality, notably in the sisterly bond between Mae West and her black entourage. Likewise, the one redeeming quality of the ruthless Lily in *Baby Face* (1933) is her loyalty to her black companion Chico (Theresa Harris). When a wealthy male suitor suggests Lily should really get rid of "that woman," Lily says flatly, "Chico stays."

The most bucolic realm for racial equality was the prelapsarian world of children, little rascals yet too young to know the adult codes of segregation. In *The Champ* (1931), Jackie Cooper and his black playmate are boon companions and their color blindness is contagious. No one objects to interracial bonding in the very young because Jim Crow swoops in with puberty, a double loss of innocence.

Sometimes, though, the racism that fed Jim Crow was exposed for the fiction it was in pre-Code Hollywood. *This Day and Age* (1933), Cecil B.

DeMille's otherwise deranged preachment yarn, executes a sharp about-face on a racial stereotype. In a daily ritual, a gangster gets his shoes shined by a typical Hollywood bootblack, a man who taps to the Stepin Fetchit rhythm. However, a student at the local high school, an African-American lad named George Harris (Onest Conley), marches to a different beat. He will participate as the linchpin in a scheme to abduct the gangster. "Is George Harris in on it?" asks one of the student masterminds. "I think so," says his companion, who approaches George with a meaningful question: "Do you shine shoes?" "I shine my own," replies George levelly. Putting his arm around George's shoulder, he explains George's assigned role in the plot.

After the boys divert the real bootblack, George dons the man's apron and assumes his place at the shoeshine stand. The well-spoken student will act the slow-witted Sambo to lull the gangster into a false sense of security. George shuffles, grins, and prattles on nonsensically to distract the white man. At the right moment, the boys strike in unison, binding the gangster's legs, hands, and mouth and carrying his struggling form into a waiting car. As the vehicle speeds off, a startled passerby wonders, "What was that?" Still in character, walking toward the screen so the audience but not the passerby can see his face, George laughs, "That's a high school fraternity initiation! Yes, M'am!" George then takes off the bootblack apron, tosses it aside, and smiles knowingly to himself, a Sambo no longer.

Another glaring exception to the rules of avoidance, subservience, and exile occurs in the remarkable second half of *Arrowsmith* (1931), John Ford's adaptation of the Sinclair Lewis novel. The film chronicles the medical and melodramatic travails of noble physician Martin Arrowsmith (Ronald Colman) and his spunky wife Leora (Helen Hayes). Inspired by his stern mentor Professor Max Gottlief (A. E. Anson) and the colorful old Swede Dr. Sondelius (Richard Bennett), Arrowsmith is determined to be a hero of medicine, a soldier scientist who makes a permanent contribution to the betterment of mankind.

The temperature of the medical bildungsroman heats up as Gottlief dispatches Arrowsmith and Dr. Sondelius to the West Indies to test a serum. The medieval scourge of bubonic plague has broken out in the islands, and the sight of rats scurrying up ropes onto ships from foreign ports portends a wider epidemic. Employing the scientific protocols he has previously used on cattle, Arrowsmith will treat one half of the infected population and withhold treatment from the other half. In the interest of science and future generations, he must close his heart to human sympathy and "sternly defy" pleas to treat all of the afflicted. "I've done that sort of thing with cattle—

but, Good Lordy, chief, these are human beings," he protests to Dr. Gottlief. With the West Indies an epidemiological fire wall, however, sentiment must be shunted aside. If the black plague is not stopped offshore, it will infect the white mainland.

The governors of the islands, graybeard Englishmen in white plantation dress, are repulsed by Arrowsmith's cold-blooded scheme. "You actually propose using the inhabitants of this island as you use guinea pigs in your laboratory?" they ask, shocked. "That is precisely what I *do* propose!" he rejoins.

Watching the debate from a balcony above, off to the side in a Jim Crow roost mirroring the situation of African-American moviegoers, is a black man, well dressed, alert, obviously intelligent, mulling over the proposal. The black man is himself a medical doctor, Dr. Oliver Marchand (Clarence Brooks), a graduate of Howard University. As a man of science, he understands the harsh necessity in Arrowsmith's medical experiment. "If you succeed, it will be a privilege for my people to serve the world," he declares. The men shake hands and Arrowsmith invites Dr. Marchand to his home. "Come in, doctor," says Leora respectfully.

When Arrowsmith accompanies Marchand to the plague-stricken island, the cinematic atmospherics settle into what might be called "voodoo chiaroscuro," the foggy, noirish ambience of the African jungle, syncopated to the beating of drums and the chanting of natives. Amid the poverty and pestilence, the three heroes of health—Arrowsmith, Sondelius, and Marchand—set about treating the natives. As instructed, only half of the villagers receive the life-saving drug.

The plague dissipates, but not before consuming Sondelius, Marchand, and the devoted Leora. Mad with grief, Arrowsmith gives the serum to all the plague victims, curing the West Indians but failing Dr. Gottlief and betraying medical science. Back in New York, the medical community celebrates, but Arrowsmith thinks only of his violation of scientific method. Regaining a sense of mission in the film's last seconds, he rededicates himself to medical research and bounds into the future for an upbeat finale.

The racial politics of *Arrowsmith* are complex: in an era of simplistic stereotypes, this alone sets the film apart. Even amid the voodoo chiaroscuro, director Ford humanizes and individualizes the natives, pausing to capture the pain of a grieving plague victim whose baby has died in her arms. In a quiet and unobtrusive way, moreover, Dr. Marchand probably ranks as the most respectful portrait of an African-American male in Hollywood cinema of the 1930s. Played with quiet dignity by Clarence Brooks, Marchand is a well-spoken, educated, and self-sacrificing doctor on a plane of equality with

Heroes of medicine: black physician Dr. Oliver Marchand (Clarence Brooks), Dr. Martin Arrowsmith (Ronald Colman), and the Swedish Dr. Gustav Sondelius (Richard Bennett) in John Ford's
version of Sinclair Lewis's *Arrowsmith* (1931).

his colleagues ("Look in on my wife," requests Arrowsmith when Marchand
returns to the main island).

Delighted with the progressive portrait of the black doctor, Sinclair Lewis
wholeheartedly endorsed the film version of his novel. "*Arrowsmith* is the first
picture that hasn't made me a little sick watching 'him' get over 'her,'" said
the recent winner of the Nobel Prize for Literature. "The Negro doctor in
it, I think, is the first one of his kind on the screen who failed to come out
as a quaint and curious character. I've met dozens in Trinidad and the Bar-
bados. And the movies have presented him with the same honesty." Grateful
for small favors, the African-American press agreed. Two full years after the
film's release, the *New Age*'s Vere E. Johns remembered "Clarence Brooks as a
colored physician in *Arrowsmith*" as one of only two exceptions to the Hollywood rule of demeaning portraiture, the other being Clarence Muse as a
cabaret singer in *Safe in Hell* (1931).

Not for nothing, though, were black West Indians (read: African-Americans) consigned the role of human guinea pigs. The biological link to cattle,

with its echo of "chattel," implies that less-than-human status grants permission to medically experiment on the lower orders. In 1932, the year *Arrowsmith* circulated in release, the infamous Tuskegee experiments began in Alabama, where African-American patients afflicted with syphilis had treatment withheld from them by "heroes of science" employed by the federal government.

The other site for the drama of black-white interplay on screen, though not for real African-Americans, was the venerable theatrical tradition of blackface minstrelsy, wherein white performers donned burnt cork makeup and played Sambo. Just how deeply blackface was embedded in American popular entertainment is shown in the first talkie, itself a minstrel show within the assimilationist melodrama that was *The Jazz Singer*.

Freeman F. Gosden and Charles J. Correll translated the minstrel idiom into broadcasting as Amos 'n' Andy, the most famous radio characters of the day, a sensation Monday through Saturday from 7:00 to 7:15 P.M. EST. Counterintuitive though the concept of blackface on radio is (like the popularity of another unlikely broadcasting star, ventriloquist Edgar Bergen), Amos 'n' Andy achieved superstar status with an act built upon a caricature of black English vernacular whose punch line was mispronunciation and malapropism. On radio, however, Amos 'n' Andy were not whites in blackface but black characters. Listeners embraced the conceit and entered into the imaginative world of the Fresh Air Taxi Company and the zany get-rich-quick schemes of the blowhard con man, the Kingfish. For most Americans who knew Amos, Andy, and the Kingfish on a first-name basis, Gosden and Correll did not exist apart from the aural mask of their creations.

Sound on film transformed the radio stars into hot motion picture properties. In 1930 RKO won a frenzied bidding war for the services of Gosden and Correll as Amos 'n' Andy, promising them an initial payment of $250,000 and participation in the net profit from any film. The stated aim of the studio was to present Amos 'n' Andy "not merely as black face comedians but as authentic characters who will dwell immortally in the hearts of millions."

To ensure that Amos 'n' Andy not dwell too far afield, the contract that Gosden and Correll signed with RKO was called "one of the most rigid in the history of the industry and was drawn up to avoid offending Southern exhibitors and audiences." In an earlier blackface comedy from Moran and Mack, a second-tier version of Amos 'n' Andy who starred as "the Two Black Crows" in a series of popular short subjects, the pair had slapped white folk on the back and been guilty of other "untoward familiarities." Outraged southerners complained that such behavior gave indigenous

African-Americans "big ideas" about interracial comportment. Taking no chances, RKO carefully monitored the racial etiquette of the Amos 'n' Andy project and released no publicity stills featuring the blackface duo with whitefaces. Trailers concealed the faces of the pair, showing only their feet, a clever way to avoid regional taboos while piquing the curiosity of radio fans.

Due to "the southern angle," the plantation manners extended to the cinematic segregation of Duke Ellington's Cotton Club Orchestra, featured performers in the film and an act of enormous crossover appeal. Whenever Ellington struck up the band during rehearsals, however, the segregation on the RKO screen was breached on the RKO soundstage. "Every time the boys get hot everybody on the lot stops work to get an earful of the music," *Variety* reported. "When the boys play, it looks like a mass meeting of studio employees, with the execs and the stars in the front line."

Titled after a catchphrase the pair had contributed to the vernacular, *Check and Double Check* was released simultaneously in three hundred theaters nationwide on October 24, 1930, a marked departure from the standard distribution practice of exclusive premieres in New York and Los Angeles followed by platformed releases elsewhere. Timed to coincide with the most ambitious radio and newspaper publicity to date, a coast-to-coast, hour-long broadcast over NBC's "Red Network" kicked off the campaign. Gosden and Correll performed in character during the first fifteen minutes of the broadcast and then, on radio, did something they had never done before: dropped their (audio) blackface mask to speak as Gosden and Correll and tell anecdotes about their time in Hollywood.

The publicity punch paid off with huge audiences the first week, but in a pattern deemed "one of the most surprising records a picture has ever made in its first run," the spectacular first-week grosses were followed by precipitous drop-offs the second week. Insiders labeled *Check and Double Check* a "freak talker," a unique and unrepeatable phenomenon that managed to cash in, just once, on the radio-fueled curiosity about what Amos 'n' Andy looked like. A contemplated sequel never materialized. After months of contentious negotiations with Gosden and Correll, RKO decided the profit margin was too thin to venture a repeat.

Check and Double Check depicts a bizarre, racially fractured world, not so much segregated as ethereal, existing beyond the realm of Jim Crow or any identifiable American milieu. The film is a schizophrenic excursion through three separate and unequal diegetic universes: (1) the lily-white world of a family of rich upper-class Westchester millionaires, whose precocious daugh-

Radio blackface on the screen: Freeman F. Gosden and Charles J. Correll as Amos 'n' Andy in *Check and Double Check* (1930). (Courtesy of the Museum of Modern Art)

ter is being courted by two suitors, an avaricious scoundrel and a noble scion of the old Confederacy; (2) the world of Amos 'n' Andy and the Fresh Air Taxi Company, namely Gosden and Correll in blackface performing their radio shtick; and (3) the real world of Harlem screened in newsreel footage as establishing shots.

The mix and match of the realms is tense and troubled, as if the slightest misstep, any "untoward familiarity," will cause the delicate color-coded conceit to crumble. The newsreel Harlem, visibly inhabited by real African-Americans, dissolves into Amos 'n' Andy's realm of fake African-Americans *and* real African-Americans, who walk by as silent extras. Amos 'n' Andy, the whites in blackface, are the sole link between the white world and the black world: the real black world (of newsreel Harlem, of African-American actors and extras) and the white world (of Westchester and Caucasian actors) remain scrupulously isolated from each other.

The blackface and whiteface worlds collide when Amos 'n' Andy encounter the Confederate suitor, who turns out to be the son of their former employer back in Georgia, an old home "the boys" recall with a misty-eyed reverence worthy of an intertitle by D. W. Griffith. For reasons that need not be recounted, the pair must spend a night in a haunted mansion, an excuse for some labored spooks-in-the-spookhouse high jinks. Mainly, the pair recite dialogues from their radio show in static long takes.

With some poetic justice, an unexpected problem arose in the transition of the characters from radio to screen. The blackface makeup imported from the vaudeville stage looked grotesque and cartoonish on celluloid. Acceptable in short comedies and in limited doses in musical cavalcades, the blackface facade melted under the glare of klieg lights over the duration of a feature-length film. A disbelief willingly suspended on radio locked in again before the scrutiny of the high-definition motion picture medium. Make-up artists settled on a new kind of color scheme, more a shade of light charcoal than shoe polish black.

What was not suspended, however, was the belief in the separation of the races. Like real African-Americans, whites in blackface had to maintain a posture of craven deference toward their betters. When Gosden and Correll, as Amos 'n' Andy, confront a white youth, the pair tip their hats to him and grovel with due servility. Even under the false skin of ebony makeup, the blackface-whiteface codes of conduct were checked and double checked.

NERVE AND BRAINS: PAUL ROBESON AND *The Emperor Jones* (1933)

Though not the most famous, the singer Paul Robeson was surely the most uncompromising black performer of his generation. Virtually alone among entertainers of any color, he was willing to be disliked and unpopular. A communist in practice if not official membership, Robeson raised his booming bass voice not only in Negro spirituals but in radical labor songs and impassioned speeches for civil rights. In the long run, the Stalinist fellow traveling that mars his reputation even for admirers may be outweighed by his personal dynamism and unapologetic stance as a strong black man. In the early 1930s, a widespread and unfounded rumor whispered that the silent film actress Lillian Gish, the vessel of undefiled white womanhood in *The Birth of a Nation*, had played opposite Robeson as Desdemona in a production of *Othello*. The story said much about the true nature of the threat he represented and the fears he incited.

Othello aside, the only major theatrical role with a black man at center stage was Eugene O'Neill's *The Emperor Jones*, first produced by the Provincetown Players in New York in 1920. O'Neill's play had already been through several transformations when independent producers John Krimsky and Gifford Cochran approached O'Neill and proposed a screen version. In 1932 the pair had imported the German film *Maedchen in Uniform* (1931), a surprise commercial hit until anti-Nazi sentiment truncated its popularity in 1933. The playwright approved the Krimsky and Cochran project after hearing that DuBose Heyward, author of *Porgy and Bess* and *Mamba's Daughters*, would write the screen treatment.

Krimsky and Cochran immediately approached Robeson to play the lead for the motion picture. There was no second choice. As a press release for United Artists later claimed, the actor was "probably the only person adequately endowed racially, physically, histrionically, and temperamentally to play Brutus Jones in *The Emperor Jones*." Robeson had already played the part on stage in two revivals in New York as well as in London and Berlin. Fresh from his acclaimed performances on the New York stage in *Show Boat*, where he later pointedly changed the lyrics in "Ol Man River" from "you get a little drunk / and you land in jail" to "you show a little spunk / and you land in jail," he was the only African-American actor with sufficient backstory charisma to embody an emperor on screen.

Produced for United Artists at the Paramount studio in Astoria, New York, and directed by Dudley Murphy, *The Emperor Jones* came in for special scrutiny in the trade press. During production, Robeson reportedly proved difficult on one nonnegotiable point. Krimsky and Cochran wanted to shoot location exteriors down South, but Robeson "refused to budge below the Mason Dixon line. Anywhere, anytime, anything, he said, but not down South, where he would have to ride in Jim Crow cars and not be able to stop at the best hotels." All business as usual, *Variety* frowned at Robeson's flash of temperament: "The producers may have to build some costly sets and lose authenticity to placate the star."

Just as *Little Caesar* (1930) was a perverse Horatio Alger story for a time of stunted entrepreneurial options, *The Emperor Jones* was a black Horatio Alger story for a time of racist exclusion. Taglines traced the trajectory "from roaring Harlem buck to emperor—the Pullman porter who became a King." The color wheel was also part of the advertising spin for the tale of "throbbing jazz in gaudy Harlem flats ... of loving gals from darkest brown to highest yaller!"—though the wheel never rotated around to the next lightest shade on the spectrum. Like so many Depression protagonists, Brutus Jones is a doomed and deranged self-made man in a society closed to self-transformations.

From the title sequence onward, *The Emperor Jones* links African-Americans and primitive natives: a tribe of Caribbean natives thumping tom-toms and dancing in a frenzied voodoo ceremony dissolves into an equally ecstatic gospel service in a Baptist church. Bidding good-bye to his faithful girlfriend, Brutus Jones begins his journey already at the apex of achievement for African-Americans, wearing the spanking new uniform of a Pullman porter. On the train north, his friend Jeff introduces him to the ways of the big city, presumably Harlem. Jones immerses himself in the sporting life and soon forgets his country girl back in Georgia for the charms of the "high yaller" prostitutes up North. (Playing one of Brutus's girlfriends, black actress Fredi Washington was required to don a kind of blackface herself: she was so light-skinned that her scenes needed to be reshot in dark pancake makeup so audiences would not think Brutus/Robeson was consorting with a white woman.)

Jones rises fast. Promoted to the Pullman car of the railroad president, he profits from an insider stock market scam. Later, gambling in a more stereotypical manner in a high-stakes crap game, Jones kills Jeff in a knife fight. The grim aftermath starkly dramatizes the wall between white and black America. A fade-out on Jeff's lifeless body settles on a tableau showing the corpse still lying unattended on the floor, with the black clientele of the juke joint having resumed their entertainments. Music plays, a pool game progresses, and the crowd seems oblivious to the corpse at the party. In a high-angle long shot, a white policeman gingerly enters the black space and kneels beside the body. Unnerved as much by the dumb show around him as the dead man on the floor, he rushes out hurriedly to report the crime. No one pays the slightest attention to him.

The next sequence finds Jones in the prison stripes of a chain gang. A dynamic low-angle shot frames Robeson singing, shirtless, astride the landscape, his muscular bare torso and booming voice a picture of dominance and virility in image and sound. Ordered by a white straw boss to beat a fellow prisoner, Jones refuses. What happens next happens quickly, not only because it is an action sequence but because what happens cannot be rendered on screen. Suddenly, Jones bolts for a truck; the prison guard, barely visible backscreen, lies on the ground. Jones leaps into the back of a truck and orders a steam shovel full of rocks onto him. During the split seconds of the diegetic ellipsis, he has killed the guard, an incendiary act of black insurrection.

On the run, another fugitive from a chain gang, Jones stokes coal in the furnace room of a steamer until he spies a Caribbean island, jumps ship, and

Nerve and brains: the commanding presence of Paul Robeson in *The Emperor Jones* (1933). (Courtesy of the Museum of Modern Art)

swims to shore. Brought before the local chieftain, he is purchased by Smithers (Dudley Digges), a Cockney trader impressed with his smarts and unbowed backtalk. "Ain't afraid to stand up to your betters," Smithers notes, not unappreciatively. Jones begins a march up the economic ladder through crap games, bluff, and a full measure of "nerve and brains," as he puts it, the latter a combination never again given to a black man by the Hollywood studio system in the 1930s. His attitude to his Cockney sidekick is frankly one of a superior to a servant. "Talk polite, white man," he orders. "I'm boss here."

And he is: an active agent of his own destiny, the star performer, the black Gatsby. Like Tony Camonte in *Scarface* (1932), Jones dons regal threads and admires his self-image in the mirror but for a time at least the world really is his. Lord of all he surveys, he pumps the island dry with taxes and corruption, investing his ill-gotten gains offshore, not in America, but in a place "where there ain't no chain gangs and Jim Crow."

In the final sequence, an extended nightmare where Jones runs through the island jungle tormented by the sound of voodoo tom-toms, his past comes back to haunt him in ghostly double exposures: Jeff, whom he murdered in the crap game; the guard he killed on the chain gang; and the gospel choir of his Baptist church. Driven mad by the tom-toms, he collapses at last on the drum, dead, killed by a silver bullet.

Though allegedly a crossover production, the premiere of *The Emperor Jones* was orchestrated as a separate but equal affair. Given a rare "double premiere" on the night of September 19, 1933, it played midtown at the Rivoli Theater on Broadway and uptown at the Roosevelt Theater in Harlem. In the Harlem theater, black actors circulated among moviegoers and urged them to be tolerant of the racial stereotypes on screen because, after all, Krimsky and Cochran had given them something almost as desirable as professional respect: work. According to the *New Age*, at both theaters "the presentation was received with a few moments of dead silence followed by spontaneous applause after the spell had worn off."

No less than the screenings, the release prints of *The Emperor Jones* accommodated Jim Crow. Though thirty-four utterances of the word "nigger" remained in prints designated for white venues, the word was deleted from prints designated for the race circuit of "colored theaters" in deference to the wishes of African-Americans. However, special dispensation was granted for the uttering of another set of normally prohibited epithets. "The speeches using the words 'Lord" and 'God' are not objectionable for the reason that its use is characteristic of the Negro in moments of deep emotion and supplication, and not in a profane manner," a generous official of the Studio Relations Committee informed producer John Krimsky.

As a commercial product, *The Emperor Jones* was doubly cursed. Southern exhibitors wouldn't touch it because it depicted a strong black man ordering around a white man. From the other side of the tracks, the all-black theaters objected to the use of the word "nigger." Robeson notwithstanding, front-page stories in the Negro press assailed the film. Noting that a "storm of indignation and violent criticism has swept over Aframerica in the wake of *The Emperor Jones*," the *Pittsburgh Courier*, the premier African-American weekly, blasted the film. "It is bad enough to have 'nigger' and 'darky' shouted from the stage and screen by white actors, but coming from Negro actors it is abominable," seethed the editors. "Compared to this picture, the low comedy of Amos 'n' Andy is positively flattering and only *The Birth of a Nation* worse." Chappy Gardner, the black film critic for the *Chicago Defender* and the *Pittsburgh Courier*, explained that "colored folks feel that a man of their own race as prominent as Paul Robeson shouldn't be using [the slur]."

Nonetheless, the film did "turnaway business" in Harlem and was held over for a second week. Elsewhere, however, despite favorable critical notices, box office was tepid. White Southern audiences, in the words of one affronted exhibitor, did "not like this dressed up Negro."

What makes *The Emperor Jones* different from any other racial adventure film of the 1930s isn't its black protagonist and black milieu, but its integration of white and black life from the black perspective. Not unlike Rico Bandelli, himself named for a Roman emperor, Jones makes his own way in a hostile world and wears the mantle of authority as his birthright. It is this that made the film intolerable for Jim Crow: that in Paul Robeson, the Emperor Jones was not merely another scheming Kingfish but a man of nerve and brains.

BEAUTY AND THE BEAST: *King Kong* (1933)

Intimately known and instantly retrievable in image, plot, character, and dialogue, RKO's *King Kong* is the only pre-Code Hollywood picture that lives universally in the American imagination. No wonder: it is a perfect synthesis of the genres and tropes of the era, equal parts expeditionary film, nightmare picture, romantic melodrama, preachment yarn, special effects showcase, and sound-on-film innovator. Produced by former expeditionary filmmakers Ernest B. Schoedsack and Merian C. Cooper, *King Kong* self-reflexively glosses their own backstory. The high concept for the film grew out of a waking fantasy from Merian Cooper, the core of which was a single image: "a beast so large that he could hold the beauty in the palm of his hand, pulling bits of her clothing from her body until she was denuded." Symbolically, it partakes of the racial paranoia and forbidden lure of miscegenation with the most gargantuan realization of a coded figure swarming throughout American cinema of the 1930s, the gorilla.

Expeditionary filmmaker and impresario Carl Denham (Robert Armstrong) is the surrogate for Schoedsack and Cooper. Like them, he has a spotty record at the box office due to the lack of that essential ingredient, love interest. Determined to leaven his next documentary with sex appeal, Denham scans the streets of New York for a likely female to accompany the expedition. After first checking out a flophouse for women, he comes across Ann Darrow (Fay Wray) at a fruit stand. Faint from hunger, she reaches out to touch an apple, tempted to steal it, a preview of her role as the seductive Eve in the garden of a primeval Adam. Denham takes one look at her—

blonde, beautiful, and famished—and knows he has his girl. As in so many early Depression films, the male suitor courts the damsel not with flowers or refined manners but with the tangible proof of his breadwinner prowess, a square meal.

With Ann on board, Denham and company sail to an uncharted atoll west of Sumatra to encounter "something on that island that no white man has ever seen" and thus something not truly real until white eyes have verified it. Dark and murky, with few establishing shots for orientation, the voodoo chiaroscuro of Skull Island emerges, first spied through the fog, populated by excitable black tribesmen whose women wear coconut shell bras. A promethean cameraman who does his own hand-cranking (but who has not brought along sound equipment), Denham and crew come upon the natives preparing to sacrifice a black virgin. The tribal witchdoctor sets his sights on Ann, "the golden woman," and offers six black females in trade. "Blondes are scarce around here," deadpans Denham. Rebuffed, the natives sneak on board the vessel later that night and carry off the golden girl for sacrifice.

The middle act of *King Kong* is the psychic center of the film, a dark passage of sexual violation and subterranean fears. In the Jurassic jungle that is his realm, the bestial suitor spirits off the white maiden and solidifies his rights of possession by defending her, Tarzan-like, from tyrannosaur, alligator, and pterodactyl. The white men who follow to rescue her are impotent insects. In an iconic meshing of sexual and special effects, producer Cooper sees his kinky dream fulfilled in colossal proportions. Grasping Fay Wray's slender form in his hand, King Kong licentiously tears off pieces of her dress, intimating an unrequitable interspecies sexual liaison.

Western technology in the form of gas bombs subdues King Kong before he can act out his own fantasy. Taking a cue from expeditionary filmmaker Frank Buck, Denham decides to bring him back alive. Chained and sedated below the decks of the expeditionary ship, the enslaved beast will be ferried to America.

After the voodoo chiaroscuro of Skull Island, the lights and crowds of Broadway are jarring as the ballyhoo of a gala premiere unfolds. Milling customers complain about the hype and the cost of the tickets. "Are they responsible for those darling monkeys and tigers?" asks a ditzy society matron, probably thinking of Schoedsack's *Rango* (1931). Reporters crowd about backstage and photographers with flash cameras jostle for the best shot. The curtain parts to reveal the majestic figure of King Kong, standing with his arms outstretched above him, in chains, on a pedestal, evoking nothing so

Blonde sacrifice: the natives of Skull Island prepare Fay Wray for her consort in *King Kong* (1933). (Courtesy of the Museum of Modern Art)

much as an African slave on an auction block, just off-loaded from his Middle Passage across the Atlantic ocean.

Enraged by the flashbulbs, strangled by the confinement, Kong crashes out. A delirious act of personal liberation, the escape prompts a panicked call to the riot squad not the Army, a suggestion that the rampage is more a threat to domestic tranquility than national security. Kong runs amuck through New York City, peering into windows, hurling automobiles at the New York Stock Exchange, and disrupting mass transit on the Sixth Avenue El. Going for the high ground, he climbs up the side of the Empire State Building. A squadron of Army Air Corps biplanes buzzes about him like gnats and finally the machine gun bullets take their toll. Losing his grip on the building's antenna, Kong tumbles from the heights and crashes to the street below, like the stock market, the nation, flat on its back. "It was beauty killed the beast," intones Denham, bagging one of the best exit lines in Hollywood history.

With *King Kong*, Schoedsack and Cooper created a box office bonanza, an expeditionary film with love interest. Not least, though, the critical and commercial success of the film was also a timely reaffirmation of Hollywood's status as a dream factory in virtuoso command of the artistic and technological tools of motion picture making. Though stop motion animation, double exposures, and miniatures had been used since the dawn of cinema, Hollywood's last major outing in big-budget special effects was *The Lost World* (1925). Before *King Kong*, special effects had been used mainly for the pleasures of pure spectacle, not to aid the suspension of disbelief in a realistic narrative. The spectator delighted in the wonder of the image rather than becoming immersed in the fabula. Working in secret, FX pioneer Willis O'Brien oversaw the painstaking stop motion animation and special effects, which even in the age of computer graphic imaging still look remarkably good.

The expert deployment of sound also helped the fantastic attain a higher pitch of cinematic realism. At least one element (sound) if not the other (image) was not transparently fabricated. Orchestrated by soundman Murray Spivak, the sound effects (remixed and sweetened screeches of jungle beasts, especially Kong's lionlike roar) serve also as devices to "animate" the puppet of Fay Wray held in Kong's hand. Sound contributes to the illusion of life not only by giving the puppets voice but by suddenly depriving them of it. As Kong shakes a lineup of crewmen from a tree trunk and off a cliff, each in turn screams in terror for the duration of the fall, until abruptly silenced on impact.

No less than the sexual byplay between beauty and beast, the level of gore and sadism stretched the limits of pre-Code license. Blood gushes from the mouth of the Tyrannosaurus rex whose jaw Kong breaks, natives are squashed underfoot, and New Yorkers are chewed in his mouth. RKO benefited from the MPPDA double standard whereby the more prestigious the studio and the more expensive the production, the wider the latitude granted by the Code. Disreputable and low-budget B-level programmers were held to more rigorous standards.

Two years in production, as widely anticipated as any film in motion picture history, *King Kong* roared into Radio City to play both the Music Hall and the RKO Roxy, some ten thousand seats between them for ten showings a day. "Out of an enchanted corner of the world, a monster surviving seven million years of evolution crashes into the heart of civilization—onto the talking screen—to stagger the imagination," declared taglines that were, for once, basically true. Despite the bank holiday declared by President Roosevelt, the film played to nearly 200,000 paid admissions in the two venues that first week, a huge record that helped save the house from insolvency (insiders speculated that Kong's attack on the Sixth Avenue El came at Roxy's behest because the trains rumbled noisily past the two Radio City theaters).

King Kong went on to become a global phenomenon—with one notable exception. In Germany, Nazi propaganda minister Joseph Goebbels ultimately banned the film from import into the Fatherland. RKO distributors were bewildered by the decree, but perhaps the Nazis had rightly gleaned the subtextual threat to Aryan womanhood by the Untermensch turned Übermensch, King Kong.

11

Nightmare Pictures
The Quality of Gruesomeness

On November 2, 1931, two future pre-Code classics, W. S. Van Dyke's *Tarzan, the Ape Man* and Tod Browning's *Freaks*, began principal photography on the MGM lot at Culver City. The casts of the two films—becostumed African-Americans from Los Angeles supplemented with authentic Africans imported for racial verisimilitude, and circus freaks and performers collected from all over the world—made for a colorful pageant in the studio commissary. Nursing a wicked hangover, the journeyman screenwriter F. Scott Fitzgerald looked up from his meal and beheld the Siamese twin sisters from *Freaks* ordering lunch. "So, what do you think we should have today?" one sibling asked the other. Fitzgerald bolted to the bathroom and vomited.

The convergence in space and time between the racial adventure film and the horror film is too suggestive to brush aside. In both genres, man, beast, and beast-man trace an evolutionary regression from the normal, to the stunted, to the mutated. Like a Möbius strip where diverse motion pictures wind together, the outlines of the expeditionary film, the racial adventure film, and the horror film bleed into each other, jumping generic boundaries in a mesh of kindred tropes, images, and narratives. Let loose from the deepest recesses of the white imagination, the creatures rear their ugly heads and roar out equal measures of eros and thanatos. Naked African cannibals, virile yellow menaces, suave vampires, demons half man and half beast, all walk the earth over territory surveyed by Mary Shelley, Bram Stoker, Edgar Rice Burroughs, Sax Rohmer, H. G. Wells, and Robert Louis Stevenson, with Sigmund Freud along as navigator.

The aesthetic ambition of the horror film is single-minded: it aims to scare. In this it claims a kinship with other genres whose success is judged on physical reactions mechanically stimulated: comedy (laugh), melodrama (weep), horror (shudder). Horror is the stuff that nightmares are made of, the dreamscreen for subconscious desires and fears. Unlike science fiction, the technological genre of the age of the atomic bomb and the computer, set in well-lit laboratories and sparkling clean spacecraft, horror lurks in the psychic underbrush: in jungles and swamps, cobwebbed catacombs and pitch-black basements, dark castles in the mountains and remote estates in the forest, all stand-in locations for the subterranean landscapes of the mind.

Whereas science fiction is public and sociological in temper, horror is personal and psychological. But if the social dimension of the horror film is not as immediately apparent as the threat to the survival of the species posed by the man-made armaments and extraterrestrial armies of science fiction, the horror film too unmasks cultural fears, particularly when the monster himself is not a solo act but part of an organized collective, a countercultural force of groundlings rising up to challenge its betters.

Nurtured by the incipient sense of disorder and disintegration in American culture, the horror genre blossomed in the early 1930s. Whether in the form of torch-bearing peasants descending upon a mad doctor's lair or subhumans massing against their superiors to assert their inalienable rights, social chaos permeates the pre-Code horror film. With the rational pretenses of civilization askew, the superstitions of medieval Europe as transmitted through the post-Enlightenment prose of nineteenth-century novelists gained fresh currency. A tagline for *Dracula* (1931) compared the horror of the Great Depression favorably to the horror on the screen: "You'll be glad when the theater lights are turned on!" The specter haunting America was the fear that the natural order would be overthrown by nefarious creatures broken loose from their chains.

As a cultural index, the pre-Code horror film gave freer rein to psychic turmoil and social disorientation because it possessed a unique freedom from censorship. A singular thrill of the genre brought to light by *Franken-stein* (1931) was the "censorial oversight" regarding what was called "the quality of gruesomeness." "Picture producers have discovered what is the first loophole in all forms of censorship as well as in their own Hays Production Code," *Variety* announced in 1931. "There is no provision, it is officially conceded, in any censor law which rules on the quality or extent of gruesomeness. Sex, crime, ridicule, politics, church, and school—all are taken care of in the censor book. [Yet] the Hays Office admits that under the Code it is powerless to take a stand on the subject [of gruesomeness]."

State censor boards, however, were bound by no guidelines save the idiosyncratic tastes of a membership that sliced horror scenes, ex cathedra, as they saw fit. In Kansas, *Frankenstein* was banned on the grounds the film exhibited "cruelty and tended to debase morals." The state censor board objected specifically to thirty-two scenes that, if eliminated from the film, would have cut the running time in half. The *Kansas City Star* acidly described the mad methods of state censorship: "When it comes right down to cases, *Frankenstein*, the most popular picture of the year, is being kept from thousands of Kansans because it is not suitable for children and because three women do not like it."

Gruesomeness was to the horror film what sex was to the vice film, only sex was nominally under strict guidelines and rigorous surveillance. Gore and blood, forensic and medical sequences, and sundry putrescent effusions went unmentioned in the Code, probably because such Grand Guignol grisliness was beyond the ken of Father Lord, Martin Quigley, and Will Hays. In the queasy *Doctor X* (1932), for example, a mad scientist seeking a secret formula for "synthetic flesh" commits a series of cannibalistic murders to acquire the real item for experimentation. As long as monsters refrained from illicit sexual activity, respected the clergy, and maintained silence on controversial political matters, they might walk with impunity where bad girls, gangsters, and radicals feared to tread.

In 1931, two creatures with brand-name fame and aristocratic bloodlines, *Dracula* and *Frankenstein*, spawned the pre-Code horror cycle. Spurred into action by the success of the Universal twinpack, Paramount launched *Dr. Jekyll and Mr. Hyde* (1932), MGM gambled on Tod Browning's *Freaks* (1932), and Universal continued its run with *Murders in the Rue Morgue* (1932) and *The Mummy* (1932). "It looks like a weird winter for the moviegoers," cracked the *Hollywood Reporter*.

But the horror cycle was short-lived. Initially horror opened strongly at the box office, held its pace, and outgrossed expensive prestige productions such as *Abraham Lincoln* (1930) and *Cimarron* (1930). After a flurry of frenzied production activity in 1931–32, however, the horror cycle stagnated. Adjudging *The Mask of Fu Manchu* (1932) "not as good as some that were released a few months ago," an exhibitor articulated a theory of spectatorship that became the reigning wisdom for Hollywood in Depression America. "In these days of worry, people want light entertainment, comedy, drama; everyone has enough trouble. Why sit through a depressing picture? Let's have something that finishes up with adventure and optimism. People will leave our theater with their heads up, smiling, and we may expect them to return." Always counterintuitive, the horror cycle sagged badly by the end of the pre-Code era. Of the paltry box office returns for the voodoo-flavored horror film *Black Moon* (1934), a small town exhibitor remarked "the people out our way have had all the horror they can digest in their everyday life in the past few years and they just won't buy it."

Yet if the horror genre lies dormant, it never really dies. After 1934, Frankenstein would court a bride (and eventually Abbott and Costello), Dracula would rise from the grave with dreary regularity, and sundry wolf men, mummies, and zombies would howl at the moon, rise from the crypt, and walk the earth. However, when horror first dawned on the early sound screen in an era of lax censorship and social dislocation, the pioneer generation of weird creatures and mad scientists spread its own version of fear itself. They were a dark, perverse, and twisted lot, still new and unnerving to moviegoers, not yet familiar faces going through moves of kabuki-like ritualization.

Pre-Code horror fixated on gruesome imagery and sadistic scenarios built around creatures no longer fully human. The ur-theme was regression and de-evolution, a subtraction of human qualities for the monster alone or the beast in numbers. The archetypical incarnations were bred in *Island of Lost Souls* (1933), where the megalomaniacal geneticist Dr. Moreau created a tribe of loathsome animal-men. Reduced to a bestial state, the veneer of civilization torn away, denied the prerogatives of being an upright citizen, Americans whose evolutionary trajectory on the economic scale was all downward might well identify with the plight of a stunted, oppressed community. "Are we not men?" chant the lost souls on the island of Dr. Moreau, echoing the plea of the mournful lyric of the trademark song of the Great Depression: "Remember My Forgotten Man."

RUGGED INDIVIDUALISM: *Dracula* (1931), *Frankenstein* (1931), AND
THEIR PROGENY

Immigrants from Europe, two great American monsters defied the economic odds and prospered in 1931. Today, the creatures are as comfortably
familiar as members of the family, grist for comedic send-up and animated
yuks, their faces looking out benevolently from lunch boxes and postage
stamps. However, when first given screen life and beheld full figure, neither
was a funny man. *Dracula*, *Frankenstein*, and the cluster of horror films
spawned in their wake chilled their original audiences. Only later, in the
baroque sequels and B-level knock-offs, would even children feel brave
enough to laugh in the face of the monsters.

The tradition of German Expressionism molded the body cast for each.
Between them, F. W. Murnau's *Nosferatu* (1922) and Paul Wegener's *The
Golem* (1922) bequeathed the visual atmospherics to *Dracula* and *Frankenstein*
no less than Bram Stoker and Mary Shelley shaped the skeletal plot outline.
But where the silent German Expressionist creatures inhabited a dreamy
and moody landscape, sound technology and the Hollywood studio system
assembled a monster closer to modern specifications than the nineteenth-
century blueprint. Although the chiaroscuro and the mise-en-scène were
imported, the studio style tended to stabilize the line of sight, to maintain
the frame of vision on a level parallel with solid ground. The canted angles,
surrealist landscapes, and off-kilter perspectives of German Expressionism
kept the spectator off balance. Hollywood Expressionism wanted the spectator to sit still and then bolt upright. The lighting was foreign, the framing
was domestic.

As with so much vintage horror, *Dracula* is difficult to read retrospectively as anything besides unintentional comedy. The tropes of vampire
ethnography are so well known, the original body so mediated and domesticated by his many dim-witted descendants, that the original incarnation by
Bela Lugosi seems as harmless as Shirley Temple. When the lessons were new
and the creature just introduced, however, *Dracula* was a genuine horror
film. Even so, horror is the genre most easily satirized and joked about, as if
the moments of authentic terror must be soothed by the balm of laughter.
In the original *Dracula*, Bela Lugosi's thick Hungarian accent is ridiculed by
the British girls he threatens.

Crossing the images from Murnau's *Nosferatu* with the plot of Bram Stoker's novel, Tod Browning's *Dracula* is a moonlit adventure story set in Middle

Europe and the bedrooms of two female victims. The film imparts valuable lessons in vampire lore that will serve moviegoers in good stead throughout dozens of sequels, remakes, and offshoots. Ways to detect a vampire: no reflection in mirror, pallid skin, resides in native soil. Ways to repel a vampire: wolfsbane, garlic, and crucifixes. Strengths: shape shifting (bats, wolves), hypnotic eyes, and superhuman power. Weaknesses: sunlight and stakes. And though the blood-sucking aristocrat will be nailed with a stake in the heart, so profitable a star will not lie dead for long.

Each decade highlights that part of the Dracula legend most resonant with its own fears. Just as the Dracula cycle that arose in American film and literature in the mid-1980s coincided with the venereal horror of the AIDS epidemic, the original *Dracula* gave a prominent role to economic collapse in the character of Renfield, the bourgeois lawyer who becomes the sniveling factotum to the count. A self-possessed and prosperous professional, Renfield is summoned to the Transylvanian castle for a business proposition. He ignores the warnings of the local peasantry (always an ill-advised act of hubris in a horror film) and, after spending a night with the count and his three harpies, emerges a wide-eyed hysteric. Reduced from middle class to servant class, prosperity to penury, confidence to terror, Renfield is a deranged shell of his former self. Locked in an asylum cell, he cackles and eats flies, but only when he can't catch "nice, fat spiders."

Oddly, the usual rush to imitation on the sighting of a profitable formula did not occur immediately after *Dracula*. "Other studios are looking for horror tales—but very squeamishly," reported *Variety*. "Producers are not certain whether nightmare pictures have a box office pull, or whether *Dracula* is just a freak." Commercially at least, *Dracula* was no freak. Later that year, its surprise success was topped by *Frankenstein*, a more expensive and inventive portrait of a lone monster from the same studio. Universal became to the horror film what Warner Brothers was to preachment yarns.

Again, the well-known visage and stiff-backed shape of the creature breeds not terror but complacency, a ready affection for a monster once considered "the most startling bogey man ever conjured by make-up man." Noting the many walkouts during previews of *Frankenstein*, Universal highlighted the quality of gruesomeness so customers knew what to expect and the unwary would not be resentful. Not surprisingly, the pro- and anti-gruesome camps split along gender lines. The film drew "an excess of men" while "the femme trade specifically has been slightly retarded by the emphasis on the gruesome angle."

As a tongue-in-cheek precaution, *Frankenstein* begins with a prologue giving fair warning to the faint of heart. A gentleman in formal wear walks from behind a curtain. "Mr. Carl Laemmle feels it would be a little unkind to present the picture without just a word of friendly warning," he says in direct address. "We're about to unfold the story of Frankenstein, a man of science who sought to create a man after his own image without reckoning upon God. It is one of the strangest tales ever told. It deals with the two great mysteries of creation—life and death. I think it will thrill you. It may shock you. It might even horrify you. So if any of you feel that you do not care to subject your nerves to such a strain—now's your chance to, uh, well, we warned you."

Adapted freely "from the novel by Mrs. Percy B. Shelley" (thereby usurping the generative power of the female even in the credits), directed by James Whale (who screened *The Cabinet of Dr. Caligari* for homework), and featuring a question mark as the Monster ("?" reads the opening credit), *Frankenstein* is the most lucrative and best-remembered of the pre-Code horror films. A crown of black hair, bolts in the neck, scars on the face, animal grunts, stiff posture, and plodding forward perambulation: the motion picture image of the monster played by Boris Karloff (as the end credits confess) promoted the common verbal slip in which the doctor's surname is stolen by his creation, exposing the truth of the matter identity-wise. The monster is a projection of the desires of the man.

Frankenstein opens with an ashen interment scene set in a graveyard decorated with life-size statuary of the faces of death. Dr. Henry Frankenstein (a feverish Colin Clive) and his mentally challenged subaltern Fritz (Dwight Frye) await the ceremony to end so they can abscond with the decedent. As the camera pans across them, the pointed grates of the iron gate frame their heads in devil's horns. Frankenstein caresses the casket. "Just resting," he murmurs to the occupant. On the way back to the deserted windmill that serves as his laboratory, he and Fritz come upon a lynched body, reflected in silhouette. Fritz cuts down the body—thump!—but a broken neck makes the corpse unsuitable for recycling. "We must find another brain!"

The visual aids for an anatomy lecture at Goldstadt Medical College provide the missing ingredient. A pair of glass jars each contain a preserved brain, helpfully labeled "Normal Brain" and "Abnormal Brain." As instructed, Fritz grabs the former, but drops it. Using his own abnormal brain, he picks up the other jar and scurries away to Frankenstein's laboratory.

Meanwhile, Henry's dangerous experiments in "chemical galvanism and electro-biology" and "his insane ambition to create life" worry his bride-to-

Lurking outside the window: the monster kills the bride of Frankenstein in James Whale's *Frankenstein* (1931). (Courtesy of the Museum of Modern Art)

be Elizabeth (Mae Clarke), his friend Victor (John Boles), and his mentor Dr. Waldman (Edward Van Sloan, who also delivered the prologue warning). During a dark and very stormy night, they visit Henry's windmill laboratory. "Crazy am I?" screeches the mad scientist, and invites them inside to see his handiwork. As lightning cracks, thunder booms, and electrical thingamabobs crackle and sizzle, Henry unveils his vision and director Whale and set design artist Charles D. Hall showcase theirs: a nineteenth-century rendering of a twentieth-century science lab, with a shrouded figure on a slab. "I made it with my own hands," says the proud father, determined "to endow it with life." In a scene that makes good on the tagline promise of shocking thrills, the body ascends heavenward on its slab to attract the life-giving lightning. Lowered to floor level, the hand twitches ever so slightly. "It's alive!" shrieks Henry in hysterical glee. "It's alive! It's alive!"

Wisely, Whale prolongs the monster's entrance and parcels out the first glimpses sparingly. In the next scene, when the monster emerges from his cell walking stiffly upright, the camera jump-cuts to a tight close-up of his face for just a split second. Resentful of the child who has displaced him in the affections of the father, Fritz torments his makeshift sibling with fire. The monster roars in terror at the flames, but Fritz will not always have a torch to protect him. For Henry too the new addition to the family brings no paternal pride. Once confronted with the incarnation of his dark side, he realizes the enormity of his breach of divine law and resolves to kill the monster. After the creature is subdued with an injection, Dr. Waldman prepares to perform the euthanasia and dissection, but the monster revives and strangles his would-be coroner.

Returned to psychic health, Henry prepares to marry the beautiful Elizabeth. The entire community gaily celebrates the ceremony, the natural light of the Bavarian village a bright contrast to the murky Hollywood Expressionism of the first half of the film. However, the monster too has walked into sunlight and encounters a little girl by a river. Her fate was filmed but not screened in 1931: the monster grabs the child and drowns her. The elliptical murder is made clear enough when a traveling shot follows the girl's stricken father carrying her dead body through the village, quieting the festive mood as he walks by groups of jubilant peasants.

At that very moment, the monster is in Henry's house, lurking backframe in Elizabeth's bedroom, she as yet unaware of his presence. She screams, he roars, and by the time Henry breaks down the door the monster has taken his creator's bride. She lies dead on the bed. The tragic turn of events is faithful to the source novel, but faithful as well to the times: the impotency of a man unable to protect his wife from the beast at the door.

Henry and the villagers form a search party to hunt down the "horrible creation," but it is the monster who traps Henry and carries him to the windmill birthplace. A night-for-night scene of the torch-bearing peasantry shows the townspeople screaming, assaulting the citadel with fires and battering rams. The monster tosses the insensible Henry off the building and onto the blades of the windmill. Inside, flames close in on the roaring, terrified monster, as the building is consumed in a conflagration. Frankenstein, fils and père, have been reduced to ashes by the people.

In uniting Dr. Frankenstein's split personality within one body, Paramount's *Dr. Jekyll and Mr. Hyde* (1932) presumed that the Freudian-steeped 1920s had taught moviegoers to appreciate the psychological polarities warring within one ill-formed ego: charitable, responsible, and rational Dr. Jekyll (super-ego) versus vicious, impulsive, libidinal Mr. Hyde (id). It became the most honored of the pre-Code horror films, in part because of the Victorian pedigree from the novella by Robert Louis Stevenson (which el-

Id rising: Ivy (Miriam Hopkins) helps the good Victorian Dr. Jekyll (Fredric March) get in touch with his Hyde side in Rouben Mamoulian's *Dr. Jykell and Mr. Hyde* (1932). (Courtesy of the Museum of Modern Art)

evated the cultural brow from low to middle), in part because of Rouben Mamoulian's incessantly mobile, first-person camera (which locked spectators right behind the eyes of the monster from the id).

Like Dr. Freud, Dr. Jekyll (Fredric March) adheres to a philosophy of civilization and its discontents, where man is made up of dueling impulses for good and evil, but where the suppressed, subterranean self with its "dim animal relation with the earth" stains his soul. Only by releasing the evil inside will the ego be pure. "There are no bounds!" he shouts to his reserved medical colleagues.

On the subject of suppressed impulses, Dr. Jekyll knows whereof he speaks. His ardor for the beautiful Rose (Muriel Carew) is consistently frustrated by her father, who keeps his daughter out of Jekyll's reach. One night, wandering the gaslit, fog-shrouded streets of London (Paramount), Jekyll gallantly befriends the music hall girl Ivy (Miriam Hopkins), her name promising an embraceable alternative to the unattainable Rose. In her room, on her bed, she lifts her dress and bares her thigh. Jekyll watches as she bends over, exposes her bosom, and pulls off her garters and stockings. The next shot finds her under the covers with nothing on but a come-hither look. She kisses the good doctor but a comrade interrupts the as-yet social intercourse. "Come back," she whispers. Walking the street again, Jekyll cannot shake the memory of her leg, swaying temptingly on the bed and in double exposure in the corner of the film frame. He rushes to his fiancée. "Marry me *now*, my darling," he urges. "You don't know how much I *need* you." But she must obey her father's command and so will not satisfy Jekyll's need.

Jekyll returns to his laboratory, a Victorian curiosity shop cluttered with vials, beakers, and a cauldron, boiling over as an objective correlative for Jekyll's own juices. He resolves to conduct a fateful experiment on himself. The transformation into his alter ego is one of the most famous special effects sequences of the 1930s: a single shot where the contorted face of Jekyll metamorphoses into the brutish face of Hyde, a celluloid magic act performed with filters on the camera lens.

Another member of the populous tribe of pre-Code simians, Hyde is a dark-skinned neanderthal with furrowed brow, prominent forehead, and misshapen teeth. Agile and at ease with his body, he enters the nightlife of the London underground and makes Ivy the terrified object of his sado-masochistic lust. "I'll show you what horror means!" he threatens. "He ain't human—he's a beast!" cries Ivy.

Jekyll's preordained fate for playing with "dangerous knowledge" and releasing the beast within is to be suppressed by the forces of rational order. Chased through the streets of London by police and citizens alike, he is killed in his lair.

Fredric March's two-faced performance won an Oscar for Best Actor, a testimony to the stature of horror that year but also to the reassuring temper of the tale. Director Mamoulian claimed to be more interested in the conflict between Nature and Civilization than between Good and Evil, but either way the savage that escapes from the mind of man is easily run to ground and subdued once the alarm is sounded. With no explosion of insurrection in the city, no peasants bearing torches, no bestial collective rising up to overthrow authority, the threat is to the moral character of the individual doctor not the civic order of the Victorian community.

Based on "the immortal classic by Edgar Allan Poe," Universal's barely recognizable adaptation of *Murders in the Rue Morgue* (1932) continued the theme of sex-crazed horror with a perverse tale of interspecies miscegenation. In Paris in 1845 the deranged evolutionary biologist and sideshow impresario Dr. Mirakle (Bela Lugosi) displays Erik the Ape Man, also known as "the monster who walks upright" and "the beast with a human soul." (Erik's species-identity confusion may derive from the fact that in medium shots he is a man in a gorilla costume, in close-ups, a monkey.) Trembling spectators watch as Dr. Mirakle translates Erik's "Ape language." Erik relates how "hairless white apes" kidnapped him from his family and consigned him to a cage. "I'm in the prime of life and I'm lonely," says the lovelorn Erik via Dr. Mirakle. No mere sideshow charlatan, Dr. Mirakle is a radical Darwinian who seeks to prove man's "kinship with the ape" by the most direct of methods. "Erik's blood shall be mixed with the blood of a man!"

Or rather a woman: Dr. Mirakle wants nothing less than to mate his lonely gorilla with a human female. Seeking a suitable mate, he prowls the streets of Paris, kidnaps prostitutes, and acts out a ripe tableau of bondage and discipline: the silhouette of a woman, trussed up, tied to beams, her arms outstretched, is helpless before Dr. Mirakle, who looms over her with a hypodermic needle, injecting gorilla blood into her arm. But the woman of the streets is no genetic soulmate to Erik. "Your blood is rotten!" screams the doctor. "Black as your soul—your beauty was a lie!" A more likely match is the virginal Camille (Sidney Fox), whom Erik grunts with desire for. "You have made a conquest, my dear," Dr. Mirakle tells the unflattered Camille. "He can't forget you."

Dr. Mirakle dispatches Erik to retrieve the object of his affections from her boudoir. Feeling Erik's presence, the sleeping Camille awakens and screams, rousing her mother and the entire apartment building. What transpires during the cross-cut commotion—between the attack in the bedroom and the frenzied activity in the hallway as neighbors prepare to break down the door and rescue the women from the gorilla's clutches—can be interpreted in only one way: the gorilla is raping one of the women. Two brief shots repeat the same image: the gorilla's head and upper torso thrusting downward as grunts and shrieks fill the soundtrack.

Back in the lab, Dr. Mirakle is elated with Camille's bloodlines ("her blood is perfect!"), but Erik becomes agitated, kills the doctor, and darts off, precipitating a chase across the rooftops of Paris with Camille over his shoulder. Unlike *Frankenstein* and *Dr. Jekyll and Mr. Hyde*, however, the damsel is rescued and her attacker destroyed. Whatever his IQ, Erik possesses no supernatural powers and threatens only the virtue of women not the authority of man.

Compensating for the tactical misdirection in the Poe title (the crime haunting the Rue Morgue is not murder but rape), the publicity campaign

Interspecies violations: Erik the Ape Man prepares to take his mate (Sidney Fox) in *Murders in the Rue Morgue* (1932). (Courtesy of the Museum of Modern Art)

for the film insinuated the unholy link: "The story of Dr. Mirakle and the most terrible and mysterious crimes ever recorded in fiction or in fact! He roved Paris searching for the most perfect specimen of beautiful woman-hood to carry out the incredible diabolical experiment his mind conceived! Only people who can stand excitement and shock should dare see it." Be-musement not excitement characterized the reaction from most people who dared to see *Murders in the Rue Morgue*. "A cynical audience at the May-fair [in New York City] hooted the finale hokum, but away from Broadway the chase and its finish shouldn't meet such hard-boiled resistance," specu-lated the cosmopolitan reviewer for *Variety*.

As in the early nineteenth century, when the emergence of Gothic lit-erature expressed the loathing that a vital new middle class felt toward the tired blood of a dying aristocracy, the monster in the horror films of the early 1930s incarnated popular attitudes toward another class of remote elites: the engineer, the doctor, or the scientist, members of a profession with all the answers, who presumed to challenge even God, and who thereby rained down upon the whole community a supernatural vengeance. Like the bankers and politicians responsible for the universal horror of the Great Depression, megalomaniacal experts unleashed forces that preyed on mankind—though in the horror film mankind had the satisfaction of tracking down and killing both mentor and monster. Himself a victim of botched social planning, not one to abide his outcast fate without a roar of rebellion, the creature attracted a measure of sympathy and identification. But the arrogant creator, the true demon at large, was the agent of his own destruction. Chased down by his spawn and the citizenry alike, he deserved the death sentence meted out by popular demand in the last reel.

THE LOWER ORDERS RISE UP: *Island of Lost Souls* (1933) AND *Freaks* (1932)

The singular threats to the social order embodied in Dracula, Frankenstein's monster, Dr. Jekyll's worse half, and Dr. Mirakle's ape man were more readily subjugated, repressed, and enjoyed than the collective danger posed by mobs of monsters. The political symbolism has a connect-the-dots simplicity. Like the downtrodden masses, tribes of the misshapen and mutated exist on the fringes of mainstream culture and threaten to overturn it. Tellingly, the two most haunting depictions of aberrant societies in the early 1930s were commercial failures, as if certain kinds of revolutionary monstrosities were too horrible to contemplate. In *Island of Lost Souls*, directed by Erle C. Kenton from the novel by H. G. Wells, a bestial lumpenproletariat revolts against their tyrannical creator-ruler. In *Freaks* (1932), directed by Tod Browning from memories of backstage circus life, a subculture of stunted humanity overthrows a hierarchy not merely of power but of beauty.

The title credits of *Island of Lost Souls* wash over the screen in a seasick rhythm to light upon a castaway adrift in a lifeboat. Edward Parker (Richard Arlen) is not really rescued when he wakes up on a ship that resembles an ark. He is destined for "an island without a name, an island not on a chart." Barking and roaring fills the air as unfamiliar beasts prowl about their cages and the fog-enshrouded ship motors into unknown waters. Though the rumors of Dr. Moreau's island are discounted as "superstitious South Seas gossip," the deracinated deckhands lumbering about the ship—hairy men with malformed noses and ears, given to hoarse grunts and shambling gaits—are not reassuring. "Strange-looking natives here," observes Parker.

Dumped onto the island, Parker encounters the whispered-of Dr. Moreau, immaculate in a white plantation suit. As played by pudgy British stage actor Charles Laughton, he is a languid, degenerate homosexual who nonetheless skillfully brandishes his whip to beat back the uppity locals. Parker is introduced to Lota (Kathleen Burke), obviously the doctor's most successful experiment in cross-species fertilization. Lota is a beautiful well-endowed female who favors glossy lipstick, dark mascara, and fetching, bare-midriff outfits. She is also, says Dr. Moreau, "pure Polynesian, the only woman on the island" and thus of the only non-Caucasian blood type that a white man may mingle with. Laughton's slow, lascivious tones insinuate the true nature of his experiment: to see whether Lota has "a woman's emotional impulses."

She has. Dr. Moreau's own emotional impulses being purely voyeuristic, he watches as Lota bats her eyes at Mr. Parker ("I wish you would not go away"). Moreau's hungry eyes follow the romance furtively, glowing with excitement.

The idyll between Parker and Lota is interrupted by offscreen screeches emanating from the House of Pain, the laboratory where Dr. Moreau turns animals into men. An appalled Parker witnesses Moreau and his assistant bent over a bestial figure on an operating table, his torso hidden by hospital sheets but his black houndlike face contorted in agony. Moreau is "vivisecting a human being!"

Parker flees with Lota and runs smack into the village of the vivisected in the middle of the jungle. The inhabitants bound about a bonfire like hoboes in a Hooverville of mutant man-beasts. A gong strikes and the creatures converge from all directions, cringing and kneeling around the bonfire in a prehistoric ceremony. Looming from above in low angle, stark white against the dark jungle, Moreau surveys his minions, cracks his whip, and lays down the law. With an upright Sayer of the Law (Bela Lugosi) as mediating deacon, the lord and his vassals perform a ritual chant.

The whip cracks. "What is the law?" demands Dr. Moreau.

The Sayer of the Law replies: "Not to run on all fours. That is the law. Are we not men?"

The beast-men growl: "Are we not men?"

Crack! "What is the law?"

"Not to eat meat. That is the law. Are we not men?"

Growls and shuffling from the beast-men: "Are we not men?"

Crack! In more severe tones: "What is the law?"

"Not to spill blood. That is the law. Are we not men?"

Almost unintelligibly, they murmur: "Are we not men?"

The Sayer of the Law gestures to Moreau in supplication. This is his big moment. "*His* is the hand that makes! *His* is the hand that heals."

The camera cuts to a low-angle shot of Moreau, gripping his phallic whip, basking in the submission.

The lawgiver continues praising the awful majesty of Dr. Moreau. "*His* is the House of Paaa—iiin."

Taking the cue, the beast men also stress the final word: "His is the House of Paa-iiin."

With regal disdain, Moreau gestures and the assembly disperses.

The weird, spooky call-and-response invests Moreau as the supreme chieftain of a tribe of cowering, dependent subjects. "Do you know what it means to feel like God?" Moreau asks Mr. Parker. Like Dr. Frankenstein, he has usurped the prerogative of the Creator, but unlike Frankenstein, his purpose is social, to create not a single man but a body politic. A Hobbesian sovereign reigning over nasty and brutish creatures no longer in the state of nature, he is king by divine right ("*His* is the hand that makes/*His* is the hand that heals") and coercive force ("*His* is the house of pain").

Lota meanwhile is reverting to type ("the stubborn beast flesh creeping back!"), but Moreau remains determined to continue his experiment in procreation by keeping Parker on the island, figuring "time and monotony will do the rest." But when Parker's former girlfriend arrives on the island with a captain from the mainland, Moreau resorts to violence and dispatches one of his minions to kill the captain. The beasts realize that the ruler has broken his own social contract ("Law no more!"), and they are no longer bound by it. Having killed one man, they realize "He can die!" and the Nietzschean epiphany sparks a social and biological revolution.

Bearing torches, howling as one being, the beast-men surge forward to kill their lord and master. Individual faces of various animalistic configurations push into the camera lens as the rebels come for Dr. Moreau. Positioned atop them, he wields the whip but they are unbowed. The mass of "not men, not beasts, part men, part beast" rush forward, pushing Moreau back into his citadel. Suddenly they are upon him, lifting him high and carrying him into the House of Pain. Pinning the doctor upon his own operating table, the creatures crash through a glass case to seize his scalpels and medical implements. Now the doctor's tortured shrieks echo from the House of Pain.

An affront to the religious no less than the political order, *Island of Lost Souls* was doubly censorable. Where *Frankenstein* escaped the onus of blasphemy because the monster's genesis was dramatized as supernatural in origin, not as the result of human engineering, Dr. Moreau was condemned as

From servility to insurrection: the man-beasts rise up and kill their sovereign (Charles Laughton) in *Island of Lost Souls* (1933). (Courtesy of the British Film Institute)

a heretic who had usurped God's role by creating a human kind of life. Opposing the film for reasons of its own, the state joined in with the church. The insurrection of Moreau's minions, the murder of the sovereign, and the overthrow of the natural order were actions more politically dangerous than anything in *Frankenstein*, a singular threat incinerated by a citizen posse. A suggestive missing link between the horror film and the racial adventure film, between fears of personal violation and political insurrection, surfaced in Australia, where *Island of Lost Souls* was released with the special designation "N.E.N."—not to be exhibited to natives, else the aborigines too begin to ask, "Are we not men?"

As a case study in the censorship of the horror film, the fate of *Island of Lost Souls* well illustrates the contrast between the laxness of pre-Code regulation and the rigor of Breen Office monitoring. In 1932, Jason Joy of the Studio Relations Committee alerted Paramount chief B. P. Schulberg to the danger of "injecting the idea of crossing animals with humans" and warned that the project "should be abandoned, for I am sure you would never be allowed to suggest that sort of thing on screen." Schulberg knew the threat was toothless and the studio went ahead as planned with the experiment in horror. In 1935, under the Production Code Administration, Paramount applied for a Code seal in order to reissue the film. Joseph Breen flatly rejected the appeal. In 1941 an extensively reedited *Island of Lost Souls* finally passed muster after complying with Breen's demands to "eliminate from the picture the suggestion that Moreau considers himself on a par with God as creator, and reduce him to the status of a scientist conducting bio-anthropological experiments; remove any suggestion that Moreau attempts to mate the beast girl with a human being; [and] remove any suggestion that he encourages the mating of a beast man with a human being."

The dread of the inhuman creature embodied in the misshapen, deformed, and stunted inhabitants of the *Island of Lost Souls* emerged in another political allegory of enduring fascination, a unique film whose status is not so much pre-Code as beyond-Code Hollywood cinema. In Tod Browning's *Freaks*, the revolting creatures were bred not by modern science but Mother Nature. A cracked-mirror world where the strong and the beautiful are ignoble and cruel, the deformed and repulsive honorable and kind, *Freaks* is at once warmly humanist and starkly terrifying. The banality of the moral lesson (beauty is only skin deep) becomes profound through the audacity of the exploitation hook (real freaks).

Like Cecil B. DeMille, the pagan auteur of the biblical spectacle, director Tod Browning was one of a handful of Hollywood filmmakers whose name advertised a distinctive texture and tone. In 1931 Richard Watts, the film critic for the *New York Herald Tribune*, described Browning's touch as "grim and grotesque to an almost pathological degree: a cinematic rendition of the Edgar Allan Poe school" and called him a director who specialized in "ghostly, evil, slightly unhealthy and decidedly Poe-like narratives." The Poe comparison is apt for Browning's ouevre but not his outlook. Like Poe, Browning was drawn to the macabre, but unlike Poe, he was a humanist who sympathetically portrayed psychic torment and physical deformity. In the 1920s, with his alter ego Lon Chaney, he explored the outer limits of physical disability, psychic dementia, and self-inflicted amputations that expressed a castration complex of epic proportions. (In Browning's *The Unknown* [1927] Chaney plays the Armless Wonder in a circus sideshow, a serial killer whose real arms are trussed tight behind him. To win the love of a beautiful woman repulsed by the touch of a man's hands, he has his arms surgically removed. By then the lady has overcome her erotic phobia and leapt into the arms of the circus strong man.)

Unlike the fantastic horror of *Frankenstein, Dr. Jekyll and Mr. Hyde, Island of Lost Souls*, et al., where monsters are conjured with makeup and costuming, the freaks of *Freaks* are the real thing. At circuses and carnivals, they were familiar enough figures in the early 1930s. At the movies, they were strangers. The motion picture medium luxuriates in the close-up scrutiny of the human face and form, caressing smooth skin and chiseled profiles, an aesthetic hierarchy that spotlights the beautiful and banishes the blemished from sight. *Freaks* shoves the spectator's face in what is hidden from polite society and almost never permitted into sight on screen—the grotesque, not the ordinary or unconventional looking, who may serve as character actors and bit players, but faces and forms that are beyond ugly, that are viscerally repulsive, true freaks of cinematic nature. The freak lineup follows a scale of escalating disability and dread: midgets, dwarfs, hermaphrodites, Siamese Twins, the armless, the legless, and, most awful, the armless and legless man billed as the "living torso." The pinheads are lucky: mentally retarded, they do not know what the rest of the world thinks of them.

Freaks opens with an unusually long introduction; this "HIGHLY UN-USUAL ATTRACTION" requires some serious forewarning. Crackpot sociology aside, the explanatory (not exculpatory) preface subtly links political power and aesthetic status, leaping back and forth from the freak-as-scourge to the freak-as-victim:

> In ancient times, anything that deviated from the normal was considered an omen of ill luck or representative of evil. Gods of misfortune and adversity were invariably cast in the form of monstrosities, and deeds of injustice and hardship have been attributed to the many crippled and deformed tyrants of Europe and Asia.
>
> HISTORY, RELIGION, FOLKLORE, and LITERATURE abound in tales of misshapen misfits who have altered the world's course. GOLIATH, CALIBAN, FRANKENSTEIN, GLOUCHES-TER, TOM THUMB, and KAISER WILHELM are just a few, whose fame is world wide.

On balance, though, the misshapen misfits are more sinned against than sinning:

> The accident of abnormal birth was considered a disgrace and mal-formed children were placed out in the elements to die. If, perchance, one of these freaks of nature survived, he was always regarded with sus-

picion. Society shunned him because of his deformity, and a family so hampered was always ashamed of the curse put upon it.

Occasionally one of these unfortunates was taken to court to be jeered at or ridiculed for the amusement of the nobles. Others were left to eke out a living by begging, stealing or starving.

For the love of beauty is a deep seated urge, which dates back to the beginning of civilization. The revulsion with which we view the abnormal, the malformed, and the mutilated is the result of long conditioning by our forefathers. The majority of freaks themselves, are endowed with normal thoughts and emotions. Their lot is a truly heartbreaking one.

A brief lesson in the ethnography of freakdom then sets the stage for the thick description to come:

> They are forced into the most unnatural of lives. Therefore, they have built up among themselves a code of ethics to protect them from the barbs of normal people. Their rules are rigidly adhered to and the hurt of one is the hurt of all; the joy of one is the joy of all. The story about to be revealed is a story based on the effect of this code upon their lives. Never again will such a story be filmed, as modern science and technology is rapidly eliminating such blunders of nature from the world.
>
> With humility for the many injustices done to such people (they have no power to control their lot) we present the most startling horror story of the ABNORMAL and THE UNWANTED.

Whereupon a title card that doubles as a circus poster is ripped away by a carnival barker corralling customers into a tent. Like the respectable citizens who accompany the carny into the sideshow, the motion picture spectator follows along, knowing that the money shot awaits in the remotest corner of the midway. Stopping at a fenced-in pit, the crowd peeks over the fence. A woman screams. A flashback unveils the story of the freak in the pit, concealed as yet from the field of vision.

The lives of three couples intersect in a one-ring circus. Hans (Harry Earles) and Frieda (Daisy Earles) are two perfectly formed little people, refined in dress and manners, as delicate as porcelain miniatures. Towering above them physically though not morally are the thuggish Hercules (Henry Victor), the circus strongman, and the cruel Cleopatra (Olga Baclanova), the beautiful high-wire artist. Positioned midway in stature and serving as audience surrogates are kind-hearted Phroso the clown (Wallace Ford) and the sweet seal tamer Venus (Leila Hyams). As if sprung from a Middle European fairy tale, the normal couple plays the protective parents, the strongman and the goddess are the evil ogres, and the little people the vulnerable children. Projected in close-up on the big screen, however, Hans and Frieda can be the same size as anyone else, on a measurable scale of equality with the giants who loom above them.

Yet cinema can not do for shape what it does for size. A parade of physically deficient people fills out the cast. Immersed in circus life, the aberrant humans enjoy a normal existence. No carnival huckster, Browning pulls back the curtain on a complete sideshow pageant for no extra admission, stopping the story for moments of pure voyeuristic inspection: of the pinhead children (Zip and Pip), of the legless boy Johnny Eck scurrying across the ground by the palms of his hands, of the Siamese twins Daisy and Violet Hilton, British vaudeville stars, walking in tandem, and of the human torso Randian lighting a match and smoking a cigarette. Interludes of community warmth and authentic humor enliven life backstage. A running gag concerns the romance between a Siamese twin sister and her beau, whom her sister disapproves of. When the man bends to kiss his girlfriend, the other sister jerks upright, aroused.

First out of malice, then out of greed, the heartless Cleopatra toys with the lovelorn Hans, whose deficiencies as a suitor are of incurable proportions. (In his tragic love for a faithless blonde goddess, Hans recalls another proper German brought low by a gorgeous performer, the professor in Josef von Sternberg's *The Blue Angel* [1930], besotted with Marlene Dietrich's cold, cold Lola-Lola.) Learning that Hans is heir to a fortune, Cleopatra agrees to marry him. Hans alone cannot see the ugliness in the beauty he worships.

After the marriage, around a long table for the wedding dinner, the assembled freaks chant, "Gooble-gobble, gooble, gobble, one of us, one of us, now she is like one of us." Cleopatra looks down the table at her dining companions and surrogate in-laws, the society she has now joined. Suddenly repulsed, she shrieks and shouts insults at the members of the wedding. Drunk on wine, Hans passes out and Cleopatra carries her insensate husband across the threshold, like a small child, to the honeymoon bed. She plans to poison him for his money.

But Hans has wised up. The freaks exact revenge in an aesthetic insurrection where the ugly proletariat take up arms against the aristocracy of beauty. The dwarfs unsheathe tokens of phallic power. A switchblade clicks open; legless Johnny Eck caresses his gun with a handkerchief. Outside, in a

Freakish sexuality: an ad matte for *Freaks* (1932) sells what cannot be depicted.

nighttime thunderstorm, the freaks gather for attack. A long tracking shot hugs the ground, following the brisk, lateral movements of Johnny Eck whose arms serve as locomotion, his pawlike hands sweeping across the ground. At knee level, crawling forward into the camera frame, the lower orders move in and stab Hercules to death. Terrified, Cleopatra flees through the black forest, with the freaks hot on her trail.

The attack sequence dissolves to the present, back to the circus sideshow of the first reel and the curious onlookers, awaiting a glimpse of the creature in the pit, the framing device all but forgotten during the past seventy minutes of full immersion in freakdom. The shot does not disappoint: in the pit is the once haughty Cleopatra, metamorphosed into a squawking, feathered, ducklike monstrosity. Now she is like one of them.

Meeting expectations, the marketing campaign for *Freaks* was a model of tasteless ballyhoo. Advance publicity had Browning issuing a casting call "for all kinds of freaks. He wants one-legged men and three-legged women, men with faces and without heads, women with eyes crossed and otherwise. He wants giants and midgets, fat men and string beans." During filming, MGM leaked word that the film was being made "undercover" but that "on the set there is plenty of trouble with the freaks going haywire with temperament," that "there's more temperament in the mob of freaks than in a dozen picture stars."

The mysterious mechanics of freak sex became the main selling point. "Do the Siamese Twins make love? Can a full grown woman truly love a midget?" pondered the taglines. "Do the Pinheads think? What sex is the half-man half-woman?" The press kit pointed out redundantly that Marsha the Armless Woman "has no arms, just tiny feet on stubs of legs," but "with her toes, though, she can embroider and do anything another woman can do with her hands." In a standard horror come-on, advertising screamed: "WARNING! Children positively NOT admitted. Adults not in normal health advised not to see this picture." The "adults only" scam was a carnival ploy. "The kids turned out for the show and were let in," chuckled one exhibitor, "and we haven't heard of any one dying from heart failure."

To say that *Freaks* made for a tough sell in 1932 doesn't quite capture the level of revulsion the film incited. The critical reception was not just mixed or negative but downright unnerved. Women seemed particularly repulsed. "Ladies will not forgive this picture's cruel and crude bad taste in exploiting human deformity for sensationalism," asserted *Variety's* female expert on "the woman's angle." In the state of Georgia, *Freaks* was forced to withdraw from playdates and hastily replaced by a more conventional kind of big tent entertainment, *Polly of the Circus* (1932). One report noted that although "this odd and somewhat maligned picture" had played in many localities, it "has been held off in others." Paramount Publix balked at distributing a film that its own New York office deemed "disgusting." A directive went out to Paramount theater managers instructing them to follow scrupulously the "special and specific advertising campaign that is being prepared, otherwise great danger will be caused future patronage"—as if *Freaks* were so traumatic as to make an unprepared public swear off movies permanently. Commercially, *Freaks* bombed. According to one box office analysis, "Quiet word of mouth was against it on the aberrance angle."

Since the 1960s, when a generation of self-styled freaks rediscovered Browning's twisted fairy tale, *Freaks* has been a perennial cult classic. Aesthetics not politics is the key to its enduring appeal. Whatever the freakshow aspects of *Freaks*, of watching and inquiring into freak ethnography, Browning forces a recognition of sentience and humanity in the deformed while never for a minute flinching from the horror felt in the presence of the inhuman-looking human. Before the widespread use of medical names and euphemisms that blunt the dread of difference, before the legal protections for the "specially abled," *Freaks* was honest about the visceral horror that greets the spectacle of an armless and legless man, who can be looked at up close and at length. In an uninterrupted take, the camera watches the human torso Randian light a match with his teeth and smoke a cigarette. Take a good long look, *Freaks* seems to say, they cannot look back. In the age of the moving image, even in the Great Depression, the visibly repulsive make up the most reviled stratum of society and the lowest rung of humanity.

12

Classical Hollywood Cinema
The World According to Joseph I. Breen

After four years of gun-toting gangsters and smart-mouthed convicts, adulterous wives and promiscuous chorines, irreverence from the lower orders and incompetence from above, the immoral and insurrectionist impulses on the Hollywood screen were beaten back by forces dedicated to public restraint and social control. Though other media were more sexually explicit and politically incendiary, the domain of American cinema was panoramic and resonant, accessible to all, resisted by few. It was to Hollywood that politicians, clerics, and reformers looked when they detected a shredding of the moral fiber of the nation and a sickness in the body politic.

Toward the end of 1933, a cluster of political and cultural pressures brewing throughout the pre-Code era gathered momentum and, by mid-1934, had converged to transform the moral landscape of American cinema. The events leading to the curtailment of pre-Code license and the enshrinement of the Production Code were at once fixed and certain (a classic case of special interest groups hitting sensitive nerves for maximum impact) and hazy and atmospheric (a shift in zeitgeist intangible in outline but decisive in impact). The currents that flowed together in 1933–34 have identifiable names— the National Legion of Decency, the Motion Picture Research Council, and the New Deal—but what they represented was part of a stronger centrifugal force. Where pre-Code Hollywood vented the disorientations and despair of America in the nadir of the Great Depression, Hollywood after 1934 reflected the restoration of cultural equilibrium under FDR.

In December 1933, a front-page article in the *Hollywood Reporter* summarized the religious-political confluence. "The picture industry is going to be made to clean up or else—and that 'else' will be Federal censorship with no less a power than President Roosevelt ready to sponsor its passage through Congress." Reviewing the past few years, the trade paper asserted that "an important factor is also the attitude of the Catholic Church, which saved the industry from Federal censorship three years ago by listening to the promises of censorship [from] within the industry. The Hays Code of practice was largely the work of Father Daniel Lord, S.J.—and if producers had lived up to it, they would still have a strong ally." More than anything else, the alignment of church and state—the righteous opposition of a Roman Catholic hierarchy sternly admonishing parishioners to shun Hollywood combined with the threat of federal censorship under a new administration vigorously consolidating power in Washington, D.C.—forced the motion picture industry in 1934 to adopt in fact what in 1930 was adopted in name.

"The Storm of '34"

The Roman Catholic Church entered the fray first and most fiercely. After suffering years of noncompliance with Father Lord's Code, prelates felt duped by the Hollywood hustlers. "We believed we were dealing with moral gentleman," lamented George Cardinal Mundelein of Chicago in a letter to his flock. "We were mistaken. To them it was just another scrap of paper." Indignant, the Catholic leadership embarked upon a nationwide crusade to lead parishioners away from Hollywood's temptations.

In 1933 the Church hierarchy announced formation of the National Legion of Decency to spearhead a renewed and more aggressive crusade to clean up "the pest hole that infects the entire country with its obscene and lascivious moving pictures." During Sunday masses in cathedrals across America, Catholics took an oath to avoid objectionable movies as "occasions for sin." With the solemnity of an Act of Contrition, upwards of eleven million communicants recited the Legion pledge:

> I wish to join the Legion of Decency, which condemns vile and unwholesome moving pictures. I unite with all who protest against them as a grave menace to youth, to home life, to country, and to religion.
>
> I condemn absolutely those salacious motion pictures which, with other degrading agencies, are corrupting public morals and promoting a sex mania in our land.
>
> I shall do all that I can to arouse public opinion against the portrayal of vice as a normal condition of affairs, and against depicting criminals of any class as heroes and heroines, presenting their filthy philosophy of life as something acceptable to decent men and women.
>
> I unite with all who condemn the display of suggestive advertisements on billboards at theater entrances and the favorable notices given to immoral motion pictures.
>
> Considering these evils, I hereby promise to remain away from all motion pictures except those which do not offend decency and Christian morality. I promise further to secure as many members as possible for the Legion of Decency.
>
> I make this protest in a spirit of self-respect and with the conviction that the American public does not demand filthy pictures, but clean entertainment and educational features.

To assure that the covenant was kept, parish priests stationed themselves outside box office windows to eyeball wayward communicants contemplating a date with Mae West.

On June 8, 1934, Denis Cardinal Dougherty of Philadelphia raised the stakes by ordering good Catholics to avoid *all* motion pictures. "A vicious and insidious attack is being made on the very foundation of our Christian civilization," Dougherty wrote in a letter to parishes. "Perhaps the greatest menace to faith and morals in America today is the motion picture theater. Nothing is left for us except the boycott." The admonition to stay away, His Eminence concluded sternly, was "not merely a counsel, but a positive command binding all in conscience under pain of sin."

Although American Catholics were the best organized and most vocal of the religious groups condemning the movies, the crusade was very much an ecumenical movement. In fact, a shared hatred of Hollywood seemed to imbue Christians of all denominations with the spirit of brotherly love. "We feel that this move by our Catholic friends is one of the finest we have heard recently and we pledge them our unqualified support," said a Protestant spokesman for the Washington Federation of Churches. "We mean business in this thing. We have made up our minds to put an end to disgraceful and indecent motion pictures and I believe that with such a splendid start made by the Catholics, and with the Protestants joining hands, we shall be able to get results."

As Protestant clergy urged their congregations "to unite with Catholics in their campaign to raise the moral standards of pictures," the Central Conference of American Rabbis called for cooperation "with other religious and civic bodies in bringing home to the picture producers their responsibility for taking immediate steps to elevate the standards of pictures." American Jews had special reason to work shoulder to shoulder with Christian America. An antisemitism that was never too thinly veiled lay behind at least some of the attacks on Hollywood as the Sodom on the Pacific. Largely ruled and disproportionately populated by American Jews, the motion picture industry was a conspicuous national stage for a people whose every historical instinct counseled against conspicuous displays. Perhaps noting the significant omission of the "Judeo" from the possessive "our Christian civilization" in Cardinal Dougherty's pastoral letter, Rabbi Sidney E. Goldstein of the Central Conference of American Rabbis averred that Jews should be more concerned than other religious groups in making sure movies were wholesome, "for if the screen is not kept clean, the disgrace will fall on the shoulders of the Jews."

As clerics of all stripes fulminated against Hollywood impiety, sociology unexpectedly allied itself with religion. In 1933 the Motion Picture Research Council, under the auspices of the Payne Fund, issued the first results of a five-year investigation into the corrosive effects of motion pictures on the young. The study was summarized in an alarmist tome by Henry James Forman entitled *Our Movie-Made Children*. An immediate bestseller, it accused Hollywood of being "subversive to the best interests of society . . . nothing less than an *agent provocateur*, a treacherous and costly enemy let loose at the public expense." Couched in the jargon of white-coated researchers who had monitored sleeping children with a device called the "hypnograph" (a "sleep recorder" placed under the mattress to measure nocturnal jitters after exposure to horror movies) and ladled throughout with statistical precision (while 26 percent of delinquent boys reported "that pictures had taught them to act 'tough,' or to act like a 'big guy,' " no less than 72 percent of delinquent girls admitted to "having improved their attractiveness by imitating the movies"), the Payne Fund studies seemed to quantify what the matrons and clerics knew in their hearts. To editorial writers and city councilors for whom Catholic theology was but hearsay evidence, the authority of social science clinched the case.

Meanwhile, another quite different code was asserting itself over Hollywood. Like other businesses, the motion picture industry found itself subject to the elaborate guidelines and intrusive bureaucracy of the National Recovery Act, the New Deal legislation overseeing what had mainly been unfettered business practices in a laissez-faire economy. The arrival of the New Deal in Washington prompted no little panic about what kind of hand Hollywood would be left holding. On December 20, 1933, after months of wrangling between the motion picture industry and the federal government, the NRA promulgated a Code Authority for the Motion Picture Industry. It loomed to regulate not only business operations, everything from hourly wages for projectionists to ticket prices, but film content as well. The appointment to the NRA Code Authority of Dr. A. Lawrence Lowell, president emeritus of Harvard University and active president of the Motion Picture Research Council, was perceived as Washington's way of telling Hollywood to clean up its act.

Unlike the Production Code, the NRA Code was vague on matters of morality and, moreover, the legal status of its regulatory authority over film content was uncertain. But studios were leery of defying FDR's New Deal initiatives and running the risk of drawing fines or having their films banned. To motion picture executives who wondered what defined "off-color pix" or "dirt" in the eyes of federal regulators, an industry observer warned, "If they don't know [what dirt is], President Roosevelt will soon let them know." Or maybe President Roosevelt's mother would first let him know: Mrs. Sarah Delano Roosevelt served as honorary vice president of the Motion Picture Research Council.

In one sense, the prospect of New Deal censors was but the latest permutation on an old story. After all, the specter of federal censorship had shadowed the motion picture industry from its inception, or at least since 1915, when the Supreme Court disabused a consortium of producers of the notion that film possessed the same First Amendment rights as the press. Ruling in *Mutual Film Corporation v. Industrial Commission of Ohio*, the Court decreed that the upstart medium was "a business pure and simple, originated and conducted for profit, like other spectacles, not to be regarded . . . as part of the press of the country or as organs of public opinion." For blowhard congressmen, the introduction of bills to set up federal censorship boards had long been a reliable path to publicity and reelection. In 1932 a weary headline in *Variety* evoked the clockwork predictability of the harassment from Capitol Hill: "Congress Has 11 Legislative Film Bills Including Usual Nut Stuff."

The atmospherics of 1934 turned the empty threat into a dread possibility. The bills were not just grandstanding gestures, but ominous likelihoods. That summer a "drastic and far-reaching bill" introduced by Congressman Raymond Cannon (D-Wis.) was being weighed by the Committee on Interstate and Foreign Commerce, a measure that provided that "whosoever shall transport or cause to be transported in interstate or foreign commerce any moving picture film in which (a) any of the persons taking part in the film have ever been arrested and convicted of an offense involving moral turpitude; or (b) the actions of the persons taking part in the film are suggestive, unwholesome and or morally objectionable, shall be punished by a fine of not more than $5,000 or by imprisonment for not more than five years, or both." With the New Deal drawing governmental power once vested to the states into the hands of Washington bureaucrats, the stark threat of federal fines and imprisonment concentrated studio minds powerfully. Moreover, unlike most pending legislation in the Democratic Congress, the censorship bills claimed strong bipartisan support. "Steadily the stream of pollution which has flowed forth from Hollywood has become wilder and more turbulent," declared Francis D. Culkin (R-N.Y.), who estimated that 70 percent of Hollywood output was "salacious, criminal, or indecent" and protested "hectic stories of sex appeal, white slavery, and criminalistic vice."

As church, academe, and government pressed in upon the industry from the outside, internal differences prevented a united defense against the three-front war. The vertical integration of production, distribution, and exhibition worked in harmony as economics, but as social practice the exhibition end of the business took the hardest hit when Hollywood came under attack. The neighborhood theater manager functioned as the nearest available representative of all that was vile in American cinema and served as the face-to-face "squawk absorber" for brickbats from a disapproving public. Small town exhibitors faced community pressures big city exhibitors were insulated from: angry calls from customers they knew on a first-name basis, sharp lectures from lodge brothers and Chamber of Commerce associates, or a parish priest planting himself outside the theater front.

A small town exhibitor in Michigan complained about the personal grief he faced over *The Life of Vergie Winters* (1934), a women's weepie about the lifelong travails of a politician's mistress. "We took a terrible licking on the picture as it is one of the blacklisted and, believe me, these small town [clerics] are telling their congregations what pictures to not hop and see. If they don't clean them up, it will be curtains for us guys out in the sticks." Another Midwest theater manager agreed. "It may be okay for the large cities [but] out here in this small town and in all others it's bad medicine for our business and is going to bring down a lot of blue-nosed ladies before the local city council wanting something done about the matter." Of the risqué wisecracks in *Hot Pepper* (1933), a third manager complained: "Too 'hot' for small town patronage catering to respectable people and family trade. Every town has some people who like them 'hot,' but they won't keep you in business." The sophisticated diet of the urban crowd was deemed anathema to the guileless moviegoer from the heartland who preferred his film fare hearty and simple. "Producers are building their own funeral pyre by making films for the theater man and New York," said Cecil B. DeMille, the reigning expert on pagan rituals. From the hinterlands, the word came back that the sticks nixed sexed-up flicks.

By mid-1934, the sense of siege and impending crisis around Hollywood was palpable. "The cumulative effect of this movement is dangerous," warned one of a series of frightened front-page stories in the *Hollywood Reporter*. "The matter is beyond the annoyance stage; it is inflicting wounds at the box office." The trade press dubbed the uproar "the storm of '34," the sense that blasts from all sides were buffeting the motion picture industry in a whirlwind of destructive force. "The whole world has gotten the idea that Hollywood is Hell's home office and Hays is the District Manager," a flustered theater manager blurted out.

Desperate to stop box office boycotts by the Catholics, to forestall the controversy incited by the Motion Picture Research Council, and to preempt the imposition of federal censorship, the MPPDA reorganized the enforcement mechanism of the 1930 Code to give it coercive power over member producers. In an amendment proposed on June 13, 1934, and formally adopted by the MPPDA's Board of Directors on July 12, 1934, two key alterations in the 1930 Code changed the way Hollywood did business. First, the Producers Appeal Board, the Hollywood-based group of studio chiefs empowered to reverse decisions by the Studio Relations Committee, was abolished. Second, the Studio Relations Committee was itself supplanted by the Production Code Administration, an office whose decisions could be reversed only by a remote court of appeals back in New York, the full board of directors of the MPPDA. By redrawing the lines of authority away from the Hollywood moguls and toward their New York financiers, the MPPDA

"The Storm of '34": Hollywood slime merchants scoff at demands for a cleaner screen, May 17, 1934. (Courtesy of the *Chicago Tribune*)

granted the PCA autonomy and power. Bank of America president A. P. Giannini, one of Hollywood's most powerful financial backers, cemented the new arrangements by stating flatly that no film would receive financing without prior clearance from the PCA.

The watchword was "self-regulation," the promise that Hollywood itself would do what churchmen and politicians demanded, provided the former let up and the latter butt out. "Self regulation in the industry is the answer to clean pictures. It was evident in March 1934 that the place to do any cleaning up was at the source of the trouble—where the pictures were made and at the time they were made," declared Sol A. Rosenblatt, NRA division administrator in charge of amusement and transportation codes, putting the federal stamp of approval on the Code. "I myself do not believe in [government censorship]. Self regulation and education, under powerful and virile leadership, are the only effective mediums."

The powerful and virile leader appointed to head the Production Code Administration was Joseph I. Breen. In December 1931, Hays had brought Breen to Hollywood to work on public relations, and by January 1934 he had succeeded Dr. James Wingate as head of the Studio Relations Committee. Breen had immediately demonstrated a passionate and personal commitment to upholding the letter of the Code. Yet prior to July 1934, he had been stymied by having to answer to the very men he was trying to regulate. With the elimination of the Producers Appeal Board and the creation of the PCA, Breen's authority henceforth flowed not from a council of Hollywood-based executives but from the MPPDA board back in New York, the same men the studio moguls served. He could confront Jack L. Warner, Louis B. Mayer, or Sam Goldwyn on a plane of equality or maybe even a higher perch: as long as New York was happy, his position in Hollywood was secure.

Besides, as a prominent Roman Catholic himself, Breen was a human bulwark against the Legion of Decency. Jesuit-educated and studio wise, he acted as both mediator and missionary, a kind of Vatican envoy to the Hollywood heathen (to the Catholics) and a participant-observer conversant in the ways of gentile America (to the moguls). He could be a double agent, injecting Catholicism into the movies at the same time he instructed studio executives in the distinctions between venal and mortal, sins of omission and sins of commission. "I am the Code," Breen later said, not because the Code was whatever he said it was—it wasn't, everyone could read it—but because he enforced and embodied it.

If Breen's severe brand of Irish-Catholicism motivated his desire to fumigate Hollywood, his intricate knowledge of film grammar and the production process allowed him to enforce his dictates. Unlike most censors, Breen knew the art he bowdlerized. From story treatments and shooting scripts he spotted early warning signs of trouble and resolved difficulties before more expensive stages of production had proceeded. He made useful suggestions to producers on how to circumvent problem areas, permitting them to abide by the letter of the Code while keeping the spirit of their script. Breen may have been at the table by edict, but he was true player who relished his role as a creative collaborator in the filmmaking process. Moreover, he was a tireless and efficient bureaucrat who brought managerial order to the office and predictability to the review process.

In 1930, when the MPPDA first voted to abide by the Code, the decision was made as a placating gesture, an act taken seriously neither by the studio signatories nor the trade press. The Code, *Variety* quipped at the time, "prohibits or minimizes the use of all ingredients that have actually proven sure fire. If actually followed in a single feature release, said picture, it is officially observed, would bore in Rome, irritate in Palestine, and cause a riot in Moscow." Cynics on all sides viewed the revamped 1934 Code as another stalling maneuver, a tactical concession to violate as soon as the heat cooled. Four years later, however, the pressures to keep in line had become heavier and the penalties for noncompliance higher.

Having put in place the process and the person to make the 1934 Code in reality what the 1930 Code was in theory, the industry launched an advertising campaign to persuade the public of its sincere commitment to moral conduct. Breen went on radio and appeared before the newsreels to explain the Code and to assure Americans that Hollywood was putting its house in order. Shown by Pathé cameras visiting the set of RKO's *Dangerous Corner* (1934), Breen met with director Phil Rosen and actor Conrad Nagel and told the cast and crew, "I want you people really to understand what we are doing in the way of making clean pictures." On his feet and looking square into the camera in a clip released to all the newsreels, Breen clarified why "all of the motion picture companies of the United States have joined hands in adopting what has come to be known as a Production Code of ethics." An accomplished public speaker, he delivers his lines forcefully in an uninterrupted long take:

> Its broad general purpose is to insure screen entertainment which will be reasonably acceptable to our patrons everywhere—entertainment which is definitely free from offense. Now, of course, this does not mean that we are to impose upon you any unreasonable restrictions in the development of the art which is the motion picture. This does not mean that motion pictures are not to deal with live and vital subjects, stories based upon drama which is vigorous and stimulating as well as entertaining. Neither does it mean that we are to make pictures only for children.

As Breen winds up, he warms to his point:

> But it *does* mean *quite definitely* that the vulgar, the cheap, and the tawdry is out! There is no room on the screen at any time for pictures which offend against common decency—and these the industry will not allow.

A sure sign of the new order came in the form of a title card inserted before the credits of the first Code-approved releases of 1934. Superimposed over the oval seal of the MPPDA, the announcement read:

This Picture Approved by the Production Code Administration of the Motion Picture Producers & Distributors of America.

Certificate Number ###.

The message was underscored by Breen's force of personality, a polite way of saying he could be as obnoxious and intransigent as the producers he dealt with. Early on, the designated censor drew lines in the sand to assert his authority and to signal that he was no compliant Colonel Joy or befuddled Dr. Wingate, that a new regime with an alert sentinel had come to power. As Jack Vizzard recalled in *See No Evil: Life Inside a Hollywood Censor*, a witty memoir of his days as a Production Code official, "The mainspring of [Breen's] vitality was the fact that he nurtured not the slightest seed of self-doubt regarding his mission or his rectitude. He was right, the moviemakers were wrong, and that was that." Gradually, it dawned on studio executives that however insincerely they had pledged renewed fidelity to the Code, this time they really had meant it.

The first showdown between Breen and a studio came about over a small matter. MGM's *Forsaking All Others* (1934) was a zesty comedy of manners with Clark Gable, Joan Crawford, and Robert Montgomery entwined in a fairly standard romantic triangle. In Breen's view, however, the film treated the sacrament of marriage too lightly, an offense that dozens of pre-Code films had committed with impunity. The most troublesome scene involved a night in a mountain lodge spent together by single girl Crawford and married man Montgomery. Discovered the next morning by Gable, Crawford walks back into the lodge and says, "I forgot something," and Gable answers, "Well, it's in there, dressing," referring to Montgomery.

Though any adulterous conduct from the night before occurred only in the mind and not on the screen, Breen demanded dialogue that underscored the upright behavior of the heroine. Detailing his objections in a seven-page letter to Louis B. Mayer, Breen asserted that "in its present form the picture is definitely and specifically a violation of our Code because of its general low moral tone and specifically because of its very definite wrong reflection upon the institution of marriage." Trapped between the immovable enforcement mechanisms of the PCA and the invincible opposition of Joseph Breen, MGM caved. "[Studio manager Eddie] Mannix agreed today to make all cuts insisted upon by us in *Forsaking All Others*," Breen gloated in a telegram to Hays. "Peace Reigns Supreme." Director W. S. Van Dyke swallowed hard and shot the required retakes. "I shouldn't have seen you no matter how much I wanted to," Crawford says in a blatant editorial insert during her love scene with Montgomery. Later, referring to Gable's lectures on the sanctity of marriage, she confesses, "I was wrong yesterday. I thought I could knock the rules over, but I guess I'm not the type." Afterwards, Van Dyke penned a kiss-and-make-up letter to Breen but he couldn't resist a defiant postscript: "I still think I'm right!"

Besides saving MGM $100,000 on the cost of retakes with his uncredited dialogue contributions, Breen's successful intrusion into the process of motion picture editing marked a turning point in the balance of power. "Of course that censorship of *Forsaking All Others* will go down in the history of the picture business as something or other," predicted trade reporter W. R. Wilkerson, giving the devil his due. "We have heard Breen called everything in the world since he became the purifier of the screen, but not one person has accused him of doing other than what he honestly believes to be right." Moreover, Breen "will not weaken under fire" and when he issues an order, he "*makes it stick*." Around Hollywood, Breen's very name soon entered the vernacular as an ironic verb meaning "to purify" or "to whitewash." "Meticulous Breening" from "Purity Headquarters" was said to be hamstringing producers and creating films that must be "pure and simple at all costs." When MGM repainted their studios a bright new shade of alabaster, a sly headline in the *Hollywood Reporter* read: "MGM 'Breens' Plant."

Concerned that his profile as the "supreme pontiff of picture morals" had become too prominent too quickly, Breen filmed another newsreel spot in 1934 to assure moviegoers that "our Production Code Administration" was *not* an exercise in "one-man censorship." Rather "it represents the considered judgement of many persons of wide experience and a sincere interest in motion pictures." Shown sitting at the head of a table with three subordinates on either side, Breen invites moviegoers to "sit in with us at a meeting of the Production Code Administration in Hollywood, where we are working for finer and better motion pictures." He makes tactical use of the first-person plural as he explains something of the process: "From the very beginning of the picture we work with producers, authors, scenario writers, directors, and all who are connected with the production to the end that the finished product may be free from reasonable objection and that our pictures may be the vital and wholesome entertainment we all want them to be."

The "supreme pontiff of picture morals": Joseph I. Breen, head of the Production Code Administration and guardian of Hollywood's moral universe. (Courtesy of the Museum of Modern Art)

Now truly under the Code, the landscape of American cinema underwent a tectonic shift. In a matter of months, the genres, tones, and textures of pre-Code Hollywood were erased from the screen. The Breen Office refused passage to films bearing the stamp of the old epoch and called back from release those already in circulation. "Eliminate views of dancer wiggling her posterior at audience" and "re-edit the scene between George Raft and Carole Lombard so as definitely to remove present inference that they spent the night together," Breen demanded when Paramount applied to reissue *Bolero* (1934). Only after clearance from the Breen Office was a pre-Code Hollywood film let loose again: but of course then it was no longer pre-Code.

The toned-down quality of motion picture advertising reflected the modesty of the new regime. Advertising had always been a flash point because salacious taglines and lush illustrations were incandescent signs of vice. No matter that the films themselves were far tamer than the poster art and

A New Deal in motion pictures: Shirley Temple, mascot of the new morality, cradles the patriarch of the New Deal.

exclamatory blurbs; Hollywood sold the promise of immorality and insurrection. An unintended consequence, however, was that influential people who never went to the movies got their main impressions of the screen from the false advertising, the prime example being Cardinal Dougherty, provoked by a billboard to launch his boycott in Philadelphia.

Committed to "raising the standards of exploitation, promotion, and advertising copy," the Advertising Advisory Council of the MPPDA stanched the leering taglines, fleshy illustrations, and come-on trailers. The title of the next Jean Harlow vehicle underwent symbolic changes of heart, from the pre-Code *Born to Be Kissed* to the Code-approved *It Pays to Be Good*, before becoming the bland *The Girl from Missouri* (1934). Likewise, what was *Broadway Virgin* in preproduction crystallized into *Manhattan Butterfly* (1934) upon release. Before publication, studio advertising henceforth needed to be submitted and stamped with approval from the Hays Office. In the Warner Brothers publicity department, a sign was put up: "Did the Hays Office See It?" Caught in the gap between pre-Code production and post-Code advertising regulations, the publicity for *Tarzan and His Mate* (1934) is actually *less* titillating than the film. In billboards and one-sheets, Maureen O'-Sullivan wears an outfit containing a yard more cloth than the skimpy outfit she models in the film.

More than taglines and ad mattes, however, the new product line showed that the studios had made good on their promise to "say it with pictures." Historical and biographical films of a kind that warmed the hearts of librarians were exhibit A for the reformed Hollywood. The 1934–35 season, promised Hays, would see "a very large increase in the number of films being made from the great classics of literature and the stage and from books that have already won a place in the hearts of millions of readers." Fox took out nationwide ads trumpeting the commitment to family fare and literary excellence. "Thanks to [Will Rogers'] *David Harum* (1934) and *Little Women* (1933) for setting a new fashion in motion pictures—the extraordinary success of these two fine, wholesome movies was a mandate to the producers from the American public starting a new trend in motion picture entertainment and launching the screen on what promises to be its most worthwhile season." Moreover, the cycle of novels-into-films could be exploited with commercial tie-ins to elementary and junior high schools, helping at once to pump up box office and win over skeptical educators.

Six-year-old Shirley Temple rocketed to superstardom that year in *Stand Up and Cheer* (1934), *Little Miss Marker* (1934), and *Bright Eyes* (1934), the former Baby Burlesk toddler coming to personify the purity and wholesomeness of the new family-friendly fare. She was billed as "the perfect entertainment for every family in the land" and, not incidentally, "an attraction that will serve as an answer to many of the attacks that are being hurled at pictures." Temple's extraordinary success—she was by far the most lucrative human asset held by Hollywood throughout the 1930s—went a long way in proving that Code-approved films meant not just less trouble but more profit. No wonder Fox chief Winfield Sheehan trumpeted his product line for 1935 as "good music, clean comedy, and dramas of modern life built on strong simple stories."

Other studio heads spouted the same rhetoric. RKO-Radio president B. B. Kahane warned producers that "there is no need and no excuse whatsoever for productions which scoff at chastity and the sanctity of marriage, present criminals and wrong doers as heroes and heroines, or in which smut and salaciousness are deliberately injected for the appeal they may have to coarse and unrefined minds. The Production Code is comprehensive and clear. If we honestly carry out the spirit of the provisions, our productions will be unobjectionable." "Pictures for the entire family" was the keynote theme of Jack Warner's 1934–35 production schedule, "the absence of sophisticated and sex problem type features" being conspicuous in a program built around "adventure pictures jammed with action, musicals, dramas, romances, comedy dramas, and straight comedies." Adolph Zukor also pledged his wholehearted cooperation. "Paramount does not and will not make dirty pictures. Producers who make indecent pictures, who inject dirt into pictures, without excuse, should be driven out of the business." Chastened after straying into unsanctified realms, the motion picture industry adopted the guise of a prodigal medium, repentant and now ready to be welcomed back into the fold of hallowed American entertainment.

Not everyone praised the cleaner sheen of American cinema. Independent producers, seeing the Code as but another device to cut them out of the action, were defiant at first. "If the majors have not got the guts, if they are afraid of a few churchmen and a handful of professional reformers, we are not," said a spokesman for the Independent Motion Picture Producers Association. "We do not recognize and will give no thought to Mr. Joe Breen or anything he represents." After a month of inveighing against the "psalm singing politicians and professional reformers," however, the bluster turned to accommodation when the indies pledged to adhere to the Code and arranged cooperative oversight from the Breen Office.

Select cadres of critics and exhibitors also complained. "Breen can give the Church a picture that will be acceptable to the Legion of Decency, but not one that will be bought by the legions of movie fans," objected Fred Pasley in the *New York Daily News*. After tallying up the diminished returns for Mae West's misfiring in *The Belle of the Nineties* (1934), a rueful exhibitor sneered that "the Legion of Decency gummed things up—if I may be allowed that expression." A like-minded studio executive grumbled that under the Code "the leading woman must start out good, stay good, and be whitewashed for the finish." On Broadway and in Los Angeles, some audiences hissed when the Production Code seal appeared on the screen, a response that only laid bare the corrupt desires of the denizens of the big city against the homespun decency of small town folk.

But the recalcitrants were outnumbered by the accommodationists. By the end of 1934, three hard facts had created a consensus around the virtues of self-censorship.

First, the Code saved Hollywood huge sums on the editing and distribution of prints. Postproduction alterations demanded by the myriad of state and local censorship boards—groups with varying, shifting, and conflicting standards—cost plenty in money, hassle, and good will. Censorship boards in seven states and fifty-five cities bedeviled the industry, and no two seemed to have the same or even a consistent set of standards. In some regions, the town sheriff or the mayor's wife wielded mogul-like power to slice objectionable scenes before a film was permitted a local playdate. Moreover, an enormous amount of revenue was lost on films cut jagged beyond repair by the pruning sheers of local amateurs. In 1931 lost income on films "so drastically cut that the entertainment was washed out, with the resultant loss of patronage" was estimated at between $8,000,000 and $10,000,000. Worse, the rate of local censorship and its costs to the industry had actually *increased* since 1930, when the Code was adopted to forestall just such interference and expense. In achieving one of its central goals—placating the state and local censorship boards—the pre-Code experiment had been a woeful failure. Only with the Code as fortress and Breen as sentinel did the influence of the censorship boards wane. By the end of 1934, the studios calculated that over a million dollars on film alterations *alone* had already been saved via the expedient of the Code, a figure that did not estimate the box office revenues recouped on films that earlier would have been rendered unplayable by local interference.

Second, the wholesome family pictures took off at the box office. Shirley Temple was the preeminent example of virtue rewarded, but other stars and film cycles confirmed the profit in rectitude. Beginning with RKO's *Little Women* in November 1933, a pre-Code film in date only, a high school reading list's worth of literary classics was sanitized for a series of high-prestige and generally high-profit motion pictures: *Treasure Island* (1934), *Alice Adams* (1935), *Becky Sharp* (1935), *David Copperfield* (1935), *A Midsummer Night's Dream* (1935), and *A Tale of Two Cities* (1935). Guaranteed to be honored on Academy Awards night, the novels-into-films put Hollywood's best face forward and showcased its ideal sense of self to America. "Pictures based on great works of literature and drama are being presented without violating the screen's primary function of entertainment," declared a contented Will Hays, looking forward to 1935. "The screen is transforming class entertainment into mass entertainment." Hays didn't mention that in transferring the Anglo-American literary canon to the screen, the dark undertones of the classic texts were brightened and the supple ambiguities flattened out. A few proved incorrigible to the core. A contemplated version of Mark Twain's *Pudd'nhead Wilson* was suspended because the "miscegenation angle" was judged too integral to the plot line, "meticulous Breening" or not.

Third, and most persuasive, was the astonishing financial rebound of the motion picture industry by the close of 1934, the beginning of a rising arc of prosperity that Hollywood enjoyed until television ended the sweet ride in the late 1940s. The streamlining and belt-tightening forced upon the industry after 1929 had finally paid off. Fox endured a net loss of $226,346 in 1933; it earned profits of $2.4 million in 1934. Warner Brothers ended 1933 with losses of some $6.3 million; it closed out 1934 with earnings of nearly $3.8 million. Always the strongest of the big studios, even MGM-Loews weathered a slump in 1933; it rebounded strongly in 1934 with a net profit of $7.5 million. Most remarkably, Paramount, recently in bankruptcy, earned in excess of $5 million in 1934. Other studios were similarly flush. Hollywood, if not the rest of the nation, had turned the prosperity corner.

Whether because of the Code or not, the economic revival occurred immediately after the establishment of the Production Code Administration. Proponents noted the precipitous upswing and insisted upon a direct causal relationship between the new morality and the new prosperity. Audiences offended by the licentiousness of 1930–1934 had forgiven the industry and embraced it anew. "The Production Code Administration in its short period of functioning has eliminated at least two thirds of the costs of outside censorship and in the same movement reduced a loss at the ticket window," claimed a smug *Motion Picture Herald*. No one denied the motion picture industry was back in the black with the Code, and *post hoc ergo propter hoc*, the Code must have caused it.

Why quibble? The Code kept the Catholics happy, restored Hollywood to public respectability, greased the production machinery, and pumped up profits in the midst of a crippling Depression. Before the motion picture medium was granted First Amendment protection, before the temperamental "auteur" supplanted the job-of-work contract director, censorship was a basic assumption of moviemaking, a necessary item on the balance sheet, factored into the cost of doing business. As such, it had best be done in a businesslike manner, and the Production Code Administration under Joseph I. Breen was nothing if not businesslike.

HOLLYWOOD UNDER THE CODE

With the inauguration of President Franklin Delano Roosevelt on March 4, 1933, a fever burning in American culture since October 29, 1929, seemed suddenly to break. "I will never forget the electrifying effect of the phrase 'we have nothing to fear but fear itself,' " recalled CBS radio's H. V. Kaltenborn. "Here was a speech that seemed to lift a nation's spirit and change its mood." To scan the newspapers, to read the memoirs of artists and politicians, or to consult the memories of anyone alive during the Great Depression is to sense how indispensable FDR was as a unifying force and political lifeline. "The Houdini of Hyde Park," Will Rogers dubbed him. "That bird has done more for us in seven weeks than we've done for ourselves in seven years." Prosperity remained elusive, still tantalizingly out of sight behind that corner, but with the good father reigning in Washington and the New Deal reining in discontent, the crisis of American democracy had passed.

Admiring historians of the early days of FDR's first term of office speak of how the new president "saved capitalism in eight days," a lurch into hyperbole but not by much. "Roosevelt saved the system," recalled Sidney J. Weinberg, an industrial adviser during FDR's first two terms. "We were on the verge of something. You could have had a rebellion. You could have had a civil war." If not quite the avenging Gabriel over the White House barking out orders to solve every problem, the "fighting president" in the White House was working wonders with morale. By 1935, under orders from Moscow, even American communists had embraced the New Deal order in the coalition of liberals and progressives known as the Popular Front. No longer did cartoons in the *New Masses* picture the unholy trinity of Mussolini, Hitler, and FDR or label the president "a puppet of the monopolists" who would "bridge the gap to fascism" in America.

The motion picture industry colluded in the return to restraint and decorum, tradition and control. However unruly the streets of Great Depression America, however dire conditions remained for one-third of the nation, precious little of it worked its way onto the American screen after 1934. Hollywood undertook a wholesale depoliticizing of its subject matter and a desexualization of its atmosphere, language, and bodies. Political currents still welled up, but more calmly, with less radical force. Erotic sparks still flew but less visibly, with lower voltage.

The new political equilibrium in American cinema was official MPP-DA policy. "It is suggested in important places that the riots between police and the public in *Manhattan Melodrama* [1934] do harm," Will Hays confided in a communication to Joseph Breen, assuming a meaningful passive voice. "It is not suggested they be taken out of this picture since it is in and gone, but that we give some thought and time to the advisability of showing any riots at this time. You know the care which is exercised in the newsreels in this regard by the editors of the newsreels. I think the whole matter of care in this regard should be definitely in our minds from the angle of law and order." Breen agreed with his chief. "We shall endeavor in the future to persuade our people to delete all such scenes from their pictures," he assured Hays.

On the erotic front, the concealment of skin was the most visible sign of the new order. Maureen O'Sullivan's jungle outfit in *Tarzan and His Mate* (1934)—mere pieces of strategically placed leather—was cut to Mr. Breen's fashion in *Tarzan Escapes* (1936)—a modest, knee-length skirt. The chorus girls orchestrated for parade drill in Busby Berkeley's *Gold Diggers of 1935* (1935) are less carnal and more clothed than their sisters in *Gold Diggers of 1933* (1933). Jean Harlow covered her breasts, Clark Gable kept his shirt on, and even the cartoon gamin Betty Boop wore a longer hemline, sans garter.

Just as the conversion to talkies had doomed silent stars, the conversion to morality struck down actors incapable of a Code-approved personality transplant. Mae West took the hardest hit, the Code nearly doing to her what the microphone had done to John Gilbert. Her first Code-approved film was to be titled *It Ain't No Sin*, but Breen objected—not to the word "sin" but to the possible antecedents for the word "it." Only half facetiously, West suggested Paramount release the project with no title, just her name emblazoned on the credits. *The Belle of the Nineties* (1934), as it was eventually called, was a tepid imitation of earlier Mae West films. "It ain't no sin to see Mae West in *Belle of the Nineties*," assured ads, which was part of the problem. "Mae West is through, I'm afraid," reported a disappointed exhibitor. "The 'kick' audiences expected wasn't there" nor were the "expected 'cracks.' The Decency Campaign took the edge off Mae." West required rigid corsetting because most anything she said oozed sexual desire, any line reading packed with double meaning. Neutered without a free range of libidinous wisecracks, her film career sputtered and finally ended with the sadly titled *The Heat's On* (1943).

Gangsters were eliminated with deliberate speed on screen and off. In *G-Men* (1935) James Cagney himself switched allegiances from public enemy to government agent. For the balance of the 1930s, gangsters were magnetic intruders, as in *The Petrified Forest* (1936) and *Dead End* (1937), not centers of attraction whose rise and fall dictated the trajectory of the narrative. By the time of *The Roaring Twenties* (1939), when Cagney returned to type to revive a second wave of gangster films, the retrospective title signaled that the political dimension of the criminal threat had been safely relegated to the distant past.

The bloody deaths of real-life outlaws punctuated the terminus of the genre they had inspired. Almost on cue, the bullet-riddled bodies of colorful desperadoes began turning up in the newsreels. Within days of the creation of the Production Code Administration, John Dillinger was shot outside Chicago's Biograph Theater after watching the pre-Code gangster film *Manhattan Melodrama* ("Dillinger Died to See This Picture!" blared ads the next day). That November, Dillinger's successor as Public Enemy Number One, Baby Face Nelson, died in a hail of bullets outside Niles Center, Illinois, after a fierce gun battle in which two federal agents lost their lives. The newsreels need not protest that crime didn't pay when the death tableaux featured the contorted remains of Bonnie and Clyde in a stolen car honeycombed with bullet holes, the waxen corpse of Dillinger on a slab, or the perforated body of Baby Face Nelson in a wayside ditch. "1934 proved to be a bad year for the nation's public enemies, with John Dillinger heading the list the government swore to get," declared Hearst Metrotone News, concluding its year-end wrap-up on the FBI's war on crime with a montage of morgue shots of Dillinger and Baby Face Nelson ("the inevitable end of the killer—a grim warning indeed") and images of Al Capone and Machine Gun Kelly being transported to Alcatraz ("America's Devil's Island").

In the prison genre, the stoic stance of hardened convicts facing their final moment crumpled in *Angels with Dirty Faces* (1937) when Rocky Sullivan (James Cagney) is strapped to the electric chair screaming and slobbering in terror. His final act of sacrifice for his boyhood friend Father Connolly (Pat O' Brien) is to give up his reputation for stone courage, so the boys in the parish will not admire his criminal élan and follow his career path. The priest smiles when he sees the mocking obituary in the newspaper. Like Joseph Breen, he knows the facts of the matter, but he also knows he gets final edit when the medium prints the legend in a tabloid headline: "Rocky Dies Yellow!"

Turning away from racial and ethnic diversity, the Breen Office smoothed out the multicolored rawness of pre-Code Hollywood into a monochromatic monotony. In practice, the Code's injunction to respect non-Anglo-Americans generally meant to ignore them. The guiltless play of stereotypes in the central casting melting pots of *The Mayor of Hell* (1933), *This Day and Age* (1933), and *Wild Boys of the Road* (1933) was leavened out, the swarthy made white, the rough smoothed over. Trading on their kinship with the chief censor, the Irish alone were granted pride of place, free to drink, fight, and spout blarney.

Self-reflexive censorship: Father Connolly (Pat O'Brien) beams from backscreen as the Dead End Kids read the official version in *Angels with Dirty Faces* (1937). (Courtesy of the British Film Institute)

Not until the assimilationist requirements of the Second World War did a full complement of warm-blooded Americans gain admission into screen ensembles molded into military platoons. Still later, the postwar social problem film, the spiritual descendent of the preachment yarns of the Great Depression, began to depict antisemitism and racism with a modicum of verisimilitude. In *Gentleman's Agreement* (1947), when gentile reporter Gregory Peck decides to go undercover ethnically, he blurts out a word barely whispered in a Hollywood film since 1934. "I'll be a Jew!"

African-Americans continued to endure wide-eyed stereotypes throughout a racially unbalanced program of newsreels, shorts, cartoons, and A features. "Negroes can expect little from this crusade because the moralists themselves define 'cleanliness' in traditional terms," *The Crisis*, the official voice of the NAACP, observed bitterly and correctly in the wake of the storm of '34. "Hardly an organization in the present purity drive is opposed to Jim Crow and all that it means." The newsreels deemed African-American affairs worthy of note only when the camera caught a stereotype: ecstatic baptismal rituals, rhythmic bootblacks, and stuttering interviewees. If venomous racism imbued the portraits of servants and sidekicks, the main rule remained condescension and indifference. Among the black press and the civil rights community, *Gone with the Wind* (1939) was the most despised example of the status of African-Americans in classical Hollywood cinema, but one-tenth of the nation was more often just plain missing in action. Again, only after a world war against two racist empires did Hollywood initiate a slow, incremental change in an unquestioned racial hierarchy.

In political terms, the distance between pre-Code Hollywood and Hollywood under the Code is well registered in the gulf between *Gabriel Over the White House* (1933) and a like-themed film, Frank Capra's *Mr. Smith Goes to Washington* (1939). Both play out in the nation's capital, both indict congressional inaction and corruption, and both tackle the milestone crisis of the moment, one economic (the Great Depression) and one political (the totalitarian threat to democracy). The differences, however, mark the transition from an America that requires radical surgery to one that needs therapeutic rehabilitation.

Gabriel Over the White House has no faith in the tenets of American constitutional democracy. The film calls for a total redefinition of the government, institutionally and ideologically. The president must become a benevolent dictator because the solution to the present crisis cannot, in pre-FDR 1933, be envisioned from within the present system. The film is authentically radical in its utter contempt for the nation's economic and political underpinnings. Capitalism, the Congress, and the courts are tossed aside. Only the president remains as a vestige of the old constitutional machine, and he is no longer a president the Founding Fathers would recognize.

A reaffirmation not a rebuke, *Mr. Smith Goes to Washington* is a civics lesson in American values. "The more uncertain are people of the world, the more their hard-won freedoms are scattered and lost in the winds of chance, the more they need a ringing statement of America's democratic ideals," proclaimed director Frank Capra. Jefferson Smith is a common man who comes to reinvigorate the system not overthrow it: the foundation is solid and good; the men charged with preserving the structure are weak and corrupt. Like President Jud Hammond in *Gabriel Over the White House*, Jefferson Smith derives spiritual sustenance from Lincoln, but Smith's inspiration is the Lincoln of the better angels of our nature, the martyr for the Republic, not a demonic archangel of vengeance. Rogue elements temporarily betray their custodial duties as the people's representatives—governors pinned under the thumb of party bosses, senators selling their votes to special interests, newspapermen boozed up and up for sale—but in *Mr. Smith* it is men who fail the system; in *Gabriel* it is the system that fails the men. In *Mr. Smith*, the polis is set right by a reinfusion of common decency and traditional American values; in *Gabriel* nothing less than divine intervention can resurrect the terminal case that is America in the nadir of the Great Depression.

Mr. Smith Goes to Washington lives in American memory in a way *Gabriel Over the White House* never will because *Gabriel* has nothing to do with American culture after 1933 and everything to do with its terrifying historical moment, a moment so traumatic that Americans, or at least MGM and William Randolph Hearst, were willing to entertain seriously the prospect of a radical overthrow of constitutional democracy. Its unhinged like would not be seen again in Hollywood cinema until the turbulent 1960s, after the Code, when *Wild in the Streets* (1968) fantasized a futureworld where a rock star president puts everyone over thirty into concentration camps and spikes the drinking water with LSD. *Wild in the Streets* is a drug-addled satire; *Gabriel Over the White House* is dead serious.

POST-CODE HOLLYWOOD CINEMA

In 1934, with financial health restored, sound technology seamlessly woven into the grammar of cinema, and quality control of the product assured by Joseph Breen, the American motion picture began a high renaissance of artistic achievement and commercial good fortune. Until the cracking and eventual breakup of the Code's moral universe in the late 1950s, an explicit obeisance to Code authority influenced the nature of Hollywood cinema as much as its economic structure and aesthetic conventions.

From 1934 until 1954, save for a short interregnum at RKO in 1940–41, Breen oversaw the bureaucracy known to the public as the Hays Office and around Hollywood by his name. The causes célèbres and challenges to the Code that erupted on his watch—notably the case of *The Outlaw* (1943), where billboards pinpointing Jane Russell's breasts gave Breen two good reasons to deny the film a Production Code seal of approval—are anomalies, exceptions to the rule of studio compliance and smoothly operating censorship. During Breen's tenure, to go to the movies meant to see the world through Breen's eyes. In 1946, when Will Hays left his job as head of the newly renamed Motion Picture Association of America and turned over the reins to Eric Johnston, the effect on the content of Hollywood cinema was imperceptible.

The retirement of Breen in 1954 had more of an impact—not just because the founder and guardian of the moral universe was no longer at the helm, but because by then American culture too had changed. The social and cultural forces that transformed the nation in the postwar era, above all the cornucopia of earthly delights that survivors of the Great Depression never quite embraced as their birthright, broke up the old centers of moral authority. The greater personal freedom and private satisfactions that went hand in hand with economic prosperity offered Americans a wider selection of moral options no less than consumer items.

Throughout the 1950s, the Code was questioned, challenged, and ignored. Imports from overseas and a vibrant art house market applied pressure from the edges, but it was television, the new mass medium of the moving image, that pushed Hollywood to transgress its own laws. Having broken up the monopoly on moving image entertainment, television also precipitated the collapse of Hollywood's moral hegemony. At the same time, a series of idiotic decisions by the Legion of Decency and the Production Code turned motion picture censorship from a fair barometer of widely shared opinion into a laughing stock. In postwar America, the very notion of official morality, officially regulated, came to seem antiquated and intrusive. National security and economic prosperity, the obsessions of the 1930s and 1940s, now shared cultural space with freedom of expression and civil rights, the obsessions of the 1950s and 1960s.

The nicks and bruises the Production Code weathered in the 1950s, the creeping incursions of vulgar language, sexually explicit content, and violent imagery, were preludes to a mortal blow, a final brutal bloodletting. If classical Hollywood cinema was born in 1934, it was killed off in 1960 by a man nurtured in its bosom. The film was *Psycho* (1960), and the apostate in the ranks was director Alfred Hitchcock.

The notorious montage of murder in the bathroom of the Bates Motel is the scene of the crime, the place where Joseph Breen's moral universe went swirling down the drain. A naked woman steps into a shower and, as violins screech on the soundtrack, she is stabbed in a jump-cut danse macabre. At the end of the deed, the camera pulls back, absent a center of identification, Janet Leigh, the name-above-the-title star, being indisputably and shockingly dead. A surrogate for the suddenly unmoored spectator, the camera's gaze tracks sideways in search of a human to identify with until, finally, the tension is relieved with the screechy pitch of an offscreen voice: "Mother! Oh God! Mother, mother! Blood, blood!" The pyscho bursts into the hotel room and the film world will now be seen from his point of view.

Down the drain: Alfred Hitchcock and Janet Leigh plot the end of the moral universe of classical Hollywood cinema in a publicity still from *Psycho* (1960). (Courtesy of the Museum of Modern Art)

The impact of *Psycho* on Hollywood cinema is difficult to overstate. Hardened film critics, men who had championed Italian Neo-Realism, Swedish existentialism, and the French New Wave, who had inveighed for years against the puritanical hypocrisy of Production Code censorship, began having second thoughts about sex and violence and the linkage of the two unleashed on the American screen. "A nasty little film," Dwight Macdonald wrote, "a reflection of a most unpleasant mind, a mean, sly, sadistic little mind." Macdonald was not alone in seeing *Psycho* as the prototype and harbinger of a full-blown "sado-masochistic genre" nor was he the only liberal film critic who came to think, "I am against censorship on principle but this killing in the shower makes me wonder." The shock of the new Hollywood universe in *Psycho* remains a primal movie memory for generations of Code-bred Americans, a tribute to how well Joseph Breen had done his work and how completely Alfred Hitchcock had demolished it.

After *Psycho*, the Code was walking dead. Incrementally, cumulatively, the likes of *Lolita* (1962), *Kiss Me, Stupid* (1964), *Dr. Strangelove, or How I Learned to Stop Worrying and Love the Bomb* (1964), *The Pawnbroker* (1965), and

Who's Afraid of Virginia Woolf? (1966) vied to deliver the coup de grâce. Finally, facing the obvious in 1968, the Motion Picture Association of America adopted a new strategy, not a system of self-censorship but of ratings. Henceforth, American cinema would come with warning labels, for mature audiences, for children under seventeen, for parents and guardians. "Viewer beware," Hollywood now said, no longer, "Viewer be assured."

Today, scanning an entertainment bazaar with minimal limits on violence, sex, and end-reel nihilism, the world according to Joseph I. Breen may seem less a golden age of Hollywood cinema than a paleolithic interlude in American popular culture. In the family emporiums of the multiplex mall, on network television and cable channels, and across the World Wide Web of a wired planet, the images screened and the meanings affirmed abide no commandments and know no Codes. Some of the material that can be rented at the local video store or downloaded on the Internet is so appallingly graphic, so soul-deadeningly vicious, that, like Dwight Macdonald in post-traumatic shock from a screening of *Psycho*, it makes one, though against censorship on principle, wonder. Confronted with the right, or wrong, set of images, few spectators will not flinch and find a bit of Breen in themselves, itching to grasp final cut away from the hands of less moral sensibilities.

The story of pre-Code Hollywood traces the movement of that impulse from inchoate desire to operative reality. Defying expectations about the permissive forward trajectory of freedom of expression, films made *after* 1934 were censored with more rigor than films made before 1934. For those who deem censorship a word more profane than any of the utterances forbidden by the Production Code, the clampdown warns that repressive forces are always willing to restrain the free flow of information and images. Contrary to cliché, the genie can be put back in the bottle.

In comparing the relative value of the product lines, it would be tempting to sing a lament for the brief four-year flowering of a vital and liberating motion picture art in pre-Code Hollywood, to disdain Hollywood under the Code as a torrent of mindless dreck afraid to speak truth to power, and to celebrate the extinction of the Code as the aborning of a modern motion picture renaissance. The inconvenient truth is that Hollywood's output on the other side of the Code reveals no ready correlation between freedom of expression and aesthetic worth. To take an even longer view, and to look back over the first full century of the moving image, is to suspect that the most vivid and compelling motion pictures—glorious as art, momentous as texts—were created under the most severe and narrow-minded censorship ever inflicted upon American cinema.

Whatever the aesthetic rankings, motion pictures enjoy a rough equality as sites for historical investigation. Undeniably, though, the search for history in film tends to be more exciting when the territory has yet to be mined for cultural meaning. The world of pre-Code Hollywood is no virgin landscape, but it remains relatively uncharted and open to exploration, best so when the inhabitants are understood on their own terms. Throughout the early 1930s, long after it really needed to, Hollywood ballyhooed the breathless promise that the movies were now "all talking!" We know better: they speak their meanings selectively, sometimes inarticulately. Sometimes we have to strain to hear, and sometimes we hear what we want to hear, but sometimes too American cinema speaks loud and clear, expressing the worst fears and best hopes of its moments in time.

The Motion Picture Production Code of 1930

Author's Note: Though various texts of the Production Code have been reprinted over the years in trade journals, memoirs, and scholarly work, the Production Code Administration archives at the Margaret Herrick Library in Los Angeles contain no "definitive" copy of the Code as adopted in 1930 and enforced thereafter (the files for *Freaks* [1932] and *King Kong* [1933] have also disappeared). The extant versions of the Code vary somewhat in typographical details, layout, word choice, and arrangement of the text. Some omit the philosophical passages or lack a later amendment to the "working principles." Cross-checked against other versions for accuracy, the text below derives from the version printed in Olga J. Martin's *Hollywood's Movie Commandments*, published in 1937. As Joseph Breen's former secretary, Martin had access to the most complete, contemporaneous document consulted by Hollywood's in-house censors.

First Section

GENERAL PRINCIPLES

I. Theatrical motion pictures, that is, pictures intended for the theatre as distinct from pictures intended for churches, schools, lecture halls, educational movements, social reform movements, etc., are primarily to be regarded as *Entertainment.*
    Mankind has always recognized the importance of entertainment and its value in rebuilding the bodies and souls of human beings.

But it has always recognized that entertainment can be of a character either *helpful* or *harmful* to the human race, and, in consequence, has clearly distinguished between:

> *Entertainment which tends to improve* the race, or, at least, to recreate and rebuild human beings exhausted with the realities of life; and
>
> *Entertainment which tends to degrade human beings,* or to lower their standards of life and living.

Hence the *moral importance* of entertainment is something which has been universally recognized. It enters intimately into the lives of men and women and affects them closely; it occupies their minds and affections during leisure hours, and ultimately touches the whole of their lives. A man may be judged by his standard of entertainment as easily as by the standard of his work.

> So *correct entertainment raises* the whole standard of a nation.
>
> *Wrong entertainment lowers* the whole living condition and moral ideals of a race.
>
> NOTE, for example, the healthy reactions to healthful moral sports like baseball, golf; the unhealthy reactions to sports like cockfighting, bullfighting, bear-baiting, etc. Note, too, that effect on a nation of gladiatorial combats, the obscene plays of Roman times, etc.

II. Motion pictures are very important as *Art.*

Though a new art, possibly a combination art, it has the same object as the other arts, the presentation of human thoughts, emotions, and experiences, in terms of an appeal to the soul thru the senses.

> Here, as in entertainment:

Art *enters intimately* into the lives of human beings.

> Art can be *morally good,* lifting men to higher levels.

This has been done thru good music, great painting, authentic fiction, poetry, drama.

Art can be *morally evil* in its effects. This is the case clearly enough with unclean art, indecent books, suggestive drama. The effect on the lives of men and women is obvious.

> NOTE: It has often been argued that art in itself is unmoral, neither good nor bad. This is perhaps true of the *thing* which is music, painting, poetry, etc. But the thing is the *product* of some person's mind, and that mind was either good or bad morally when it produced the thing. And the thing has its *effect* upon

those who come into contact with it. In both these ways, as a product and the cause of definite effects, it has a deep moral significance and an unmistakable moral quality.

HENCE: The motion pictures which are the most popular of modern arts for the masses, have their moral quality from the minds which produce them and from their effects on the moral lives and reactions of their audiences. This gives them a most important morality.

(1) They *reproduce* the morality of the men who use the pictures as a medium for the expression of their ideas and ideals.

(2) They *affect* the moral standards of those who thru the screen take in these ideas and ideals.

In the case of the motion pictures, this effect may be particularly emphasized because no art has so quick and so widespread an appeal to the masses. It has become in an incredibly short period, *the art of the multitudes.*

III. The motion picture has special *Moral obligations*:

(A) Most arts appeal to the mature. This art appeals at once *to every class*—mature, immature, developed, undeveloped, law-abiding, criminal. Music has its grades for different classes; so has literature and drama. This art of the motion picture, combining as it does the two fundamental appeals of looking at a picture and listening to a story, at once reaches every class of society.

(B) Because of the mobility of a film and the ease of picture distribution, and because of the possibility of duplicating positives in large quantities, this art *reaches places* unpenetrated by other forms of art.

(C) Because of these two facts, it is difficult to produce films intended for only *certain classes of people.* The exhibitor's theatres are built for the masses, for the cultivated and the rude, mature and immature, self-restrained and inflammatory, young and old, law-respecting and criminal. Films, unlike books and music, can with difficulty be confined to certain selected groups.

(D) The latitude given to film material cannot, in consequence, be as wide as the latitude given to *book material.* In addition:

(a) A book describes; a film vividly presents.

(b) A book reaches the mind thru words merely; a film

reaches the eyes and ears thru the reproduction of actual events.

(c) The reaction of a reader to a book depends largely on the keenness of the reader; the reaction to a film depends of the vividness of presentation.

(E) This is also true when comparing the film with the newspapers. Newspapers present by description, films by actual presentation. Newspapers are after the fact and present things that have taken place; the film gives the events in the process of enactment and with apparent reality of life.

(F) Everything possible in a play is not possible in a film.

(a) Because of the larger audience of the film, and its consequently mixed character. Psychologically, the larger the audience, the lower the moral mass resistance to suggestion.

(b) Because thru light, enlargement of character presentation, scenic emphasis, etc., the screen story is brought closer to the audience than the play.

(c) The enthusiasm for and interest in the film *actors and actresses*, developed beyond anything of the sort in history, makes the audience largely sympathetic toward the characters they portray and the stories in which they figure. Hence they are more ready to confuse the actor and character, and they are most receptive of the emotions and ideals portrayed and presented by their favorite stars.

(G) Small communities, remote from sophistication and from the hardening process which often takes place in the ethical and moral standards of larger cities, are easily and readily reached by any sort of film.

(H) The grandeur of mass meetings, large action, spectacular features, etc., affects and arouses more intensely the emotional side of the audience.

IN GENERAL: The mobility, popularity, accessibility, emotional appeal, vividness, straight-forward presentation of fact in the films makes for intimate contact on a larger audience and greater emotional appeal.

Hence, the larger moral responsibilities of the motion pictures.

SECOND SECTION

WORKING PRINCIPLES

I. No picture should lower the moral standards of those who see it. This is done:

    (a)   When evil is made to appear *attractive*, and good is made to appear *unattractive*.

    (b)   When the *sympathy* of the audience is thrown on the side of crime, wrong-doing, evil, sin. The same thing is true of a film that would throw sympathy against goodness, honor, innocence, purity, honesty.

NOTE: *Sympathy with a person who sins,* is not the same as sympathy with the sin or crime of which he is guilty. We may feel sorry for the plight of the murderer or even understand the circumstances which led him to his crime; we may not feel sympathy with the wrong which he has done.

The presentation of evil is often essential for art, or fiction, or drama. This in itself is not wrong, provided:

    (a)   That evil is *not presented alluringly*. Even if later on the evil is condemned or punished, it must not be allowed to appear so attractive that the emotions are drawn to desire or approve so strongly that later they forget the condemnation and remember only the apparent joy of the sin.

    (b)   That thruout the presentation, *evil and good are never confused* and that evil is always recognized clearly as evil.

    (c)   That in the end the audience feels that *evil is wrong* and *good is right*.

II. Law, natural or divine, must not be belittled, ridiculed, nor must a sentiment be created against it.

    (A)   The *presentation of crimes* against the law, human or divine, is often necessary for the carrying out of the plot. But the presentation must not throw sympathy with the criminal as against the law, nor with the crime as against those who must punish it.

    (B)   The *courts* of the land should not be presented as *unjust*.

III. As far as possible, life should not be misrepresented, at least not in such a way as to place in the minds of youth false values on life.

> NOTE: This subject is touched just in passing. The attention of the producers is called, however, to the magnificent possibilities of the screen for character development, the building of right ideals, the inculcation in story-form of right principles. If motion pictures consistently held up high types of character, presented stories that would affect lives for the better, they could become the greatest natural force for the improvement of mankind.

PRINCIPLES OF PLOT

In accordance with the general principles laid down:

(1) No plot theme should definitely side *with evil and against good.*

(2) Comedies and farces should not make fun of good, innocence, morality or justice.

(3) No plot should be so constructed as to leave the question of *right or wrong in doubt or fogged.*

(4) No plot should by its treatment *throw the sympathy* of the audience with sin, crime, wrong-doing or evil.

(5) No plot should present evil alluringly.

Serious Film Drama

I. As stated in the general principles, sin and evil enter into the story of human beings, and hence in themselves are dramatic material.

II. In the use of this material, it must be distinguished between *sin* which by its very nature *repels*, and *sin* which by its nature *attracts*.

> (a) In the first class comes murder, most theft, most legal crimes, lying, hypocrisy, cruelty, etc.

> (b) In the second class come sex sins, sins and crimes of apparent heroism, such as banditry, daring thefts, leadership in evil, organized crime, revenge, etc.

> (A) The first class needs little care in handling, as sins and crimes of this class naturally are unattractive. The audience instinctively condemns and is repelled. Hence the one objective must be to avoid the hardening of the audiences, especially of those who are young and impressionable, to the thought and the fact

of crime. People can become accustomed even to murder, cruelty, brutality, and repellent crimes.

(B)   The second class needs real care in handling, as the response of human natures to their appeal is obvious. This is treated more fully below.

III. A careful distinction can be made between films intended for *general distribution*, and films intended for use in theatres restricted to a *limited audience*. Themes and plots quite appropriate for the latter would be altogether out of place and dangerous in the former.

NOTE: In general, the practice of using a general theatre and limiting the patronage during the showing of a certain film to "adults only" is not completely satisfactory and is only partially effective. However, maturer minds may easily understand and accept without harm subject matter in plots which does younger people positive harm.

HENCE: If there should be created a special type of theatre, catering exclusively to an adult audience, for plays of this character (plays with problem themes, difficult discussions and maturer treatment) it would seem to afford an outlet, which does not now exist, for pictures unsuitable for general distribution for exhibitions to a restricted audience.

PLOT MATERIAL

(1)   *The triangle*, that is, the love of a third party by one already married, needs careful handling, if marriage, the sanctity of the home, and sex morality are not to be imperiled.

(2)   *Adultery* as a subject should be avoided:

(a)   It is *never* a fit subject for *comedy*. Thru comedy of this sort, ridicule is thrown on the essential relationships of home and family and marriage, and illicit relationships are made to seem permissible, and either delightful or daring.

(b)   Sometimes adultery must be counted on as material occurring in serious drama.
    In this case:
    (1) It should not appear to be justified;
    (2) It should not be used to weaken respect for marriage;
    (3) It should not be presented as attractive or alluring.

(3) *Seduction and rape* are difficult subjects and bad material from the viewpoint of the general audience in the theatre.

   (a) They should never be introduced as subject matter *unless* absolutely essential to the plot.

   (b) They should *never* be treated as comedy.

   (c) Where essential to the plot, they must not be more than *suggested*.

   (d) Even the struggles preceding rape should not be shown.

   (e) The *methods* by which seduction, essential to the plot, is attained should not be explicit or represented in detail where there is likelihood of arousing wrongful emotions on the part of the audience.

(4) *Scenes of passion* are sometime necessary for the plot. However:

   (a) They should appear only where necessary and *not* as an added stimulus to the emotions of the audience.

   (b) *When not essential to the plot*, they should not occur.

   (c) They must *not* be *explicit* in action nor vivid in method, e.g. by handling of the body, by lustful and prolonged kissing, by evidently lustful embraces, by positions which strongly arouse passions.

   (d) In general, where essential to the plot, scenes of passion should *not* be presented in such a way as to *arouse or excite the passions of the ordinary spectator.*

(5) Sexual immorality is sometimes necessary for the plot. It is subject to the following:

GENERAL PRINCIPLES—regarding plots dealing with sex, passion, and incidents relating to them:

All legislators have recognized clearly that there are in normal human beings emotions which react naturally and spontaneously to the presentation of certain definite manifestations of sex and passion.

   (a) The presentation of scenes, episodes, plots, etc., which are deliberately meant to excite these manifestations on the part of the audience is always wrong, is subversive to the interest of society, and a peril to the human race.

   (b) Sex and passion exist and consequently must *sometimes enter* into the stories which deal with human beings.

      (1) *Pure love*, the love of a man for a woman permitted by the law of God and man, is the rightful subject

of plots. The passion arising from this love is not the subject for plots.

(2) *Impure love*, the love of man and woman forbidden by human and divine law, must be presented in such a way that:

    (a) It is clearly known by the audience to be wrong;

    (b) Its presentation does not excite sexual reactions, mental or physical, in an ordinary audience;

    (c) It is not treated as matter for comedy.

HENCE: *Even within the limits of pure love*, certain facts have been universally regarded by lawmakers as outside the limits of safe presentation. These are the manifestations of passion and the sacred intimacies of private life:

(1) Either before marriage in the courtship of decent people;

(2) Or after marriage, as is perfectly clear.

In the case of pure love, the difficulty is not so much about what details are permitted for presentation. This is perfectly clear in most cases. The difficulty concerns itself with the tact, delicacy, and general regard for propriety manifested in their presentation.

But in the case of impure love, the love which society has always regarded as wrong and which has been banned by divine law, the following are important:

(1) It must not be the subject of comedy or farce or treated as the material for laughter;

(2) It must not be presented as attractive and beautiful;

(3) It must not be presented in such a way as to arouse passion or morbid curiosity on the part of the audience;

(4) It must not be made to seem right and permissible;

(5) In general, it must not be detailed in method or manner.

(6) *The presentation of murder* is often necessary for the carrying out of the plot. However:

    (a) Frequent presentation of *murder* tends to lessen regard for the sacredness of life.

    (b) *Brutal killings* should not be presented in detail.

    (c) *Killings for revenge* should not be justified, i.e., the hero should not take justice into his own hands in such a way as to make his killings seem justified. This does not refer to killings in self-defense.

(d) *Dueling* should not be presented as right or just.

(7) *Crimes against the law* naturally occur in the course of film stories. However:

(a) *Criminals* should not be made heroes, even if they are historical criminals.

(b) *Law and justice* must not by the treatment they receive from criminals be made to seem wrong or ridiculous.

(c) *Methods of committing crime*, e.g., burglary, should not be so explicit as to teach the audience how crime can be committed; that is, the film should not serve as a possible school in crime methods for those who seeing the methods might use them.

(d) Crime need *not always be punished*, as long as the audience is made to know that it is wrong.

DETAILS OF PLOT, EPISODE, AND TREATMENT

Vulgarity

Vulgarity may be carefully distinguished from obscenity.

Vulgarity is the treatment of low, disgusting, unpleasant subjects which decent society considers outlawed from normal conversation.

Vulgarity in the motion pictures is limited in precisely the same way as in decent groups of men and women by the dictates of good taste and civilized usage, and by the effect of shock, scandal, and harm on those coming in contact with this vulgarity.

(1) *Oaths* should never be used as a comedy element. Where required by the plot, the less offensive oaths may be permitted.

(2) *Vulgar expressions* come under the same treatment as vulgarity in general. Where women and children are to see the film, vulgar expressions (and oaths) should be cut to the absolute essentials required by the situation.

(3) The name of *Jesus Christ* should never be used except in reverence.

Obscenity

Obscenity is concerned with immorality, but has the additional connotation of being common, vulgar and coarse.

(1)   *Obscenity in fact*, that is, in spoken word, gesture, episode, plot, is against divine and human law, and hence altogether outside the range of subject matter or treatment.

(2)   Obscenity should *not be suggested* by gesture, manner, etc.

(3)   An obscene reference, even if it is expected to be understandable to only the more sophisticated part of the audience, should not be introduced.

(4)   *Obscene language* is treated as all obscenity.

Costume

GENERAL PRINCIPLES

(1)   The effect of nudity or semi-nudity upon the normal man or woman, and much more upon the young person, has been honestly recognized by all lawmakers and moralists.

(2)   Hence the fact that the nude or semi-nude body may be *beautiful* does not make its use in the films moral. For in addition to its beauty, the effects of the nude or semi-nude on the normal individual must be taken into consideration.

(3)   Nudity or semi-nudity used simply to put a "punch" into a picture comes under the head of immoral actions as treated above. It is immoral in its effect upon the average audience.

(4)   Nudity or semi-nudity is sometimes apparently necessary for the plot. *Nudity is never permitted.* Semi-nudity may be permitted under conditions.

PARTICULAR PRINCIPLES

(1)   *The more intimate parts of the human body* are the male and female organs and the breasts of a woman.

    (a)   They should *never be uncovered*.

    (b)   They should not be covered with *transparent* or *translucent* material.

    (c)   They should not be clearly and unmistakably *outlined* by the garment.

(2)   *The less intimate parts of the body*, the legs, arms, shoulders and back, are less certain of causing reactions of the part of the audience. Hence:

    (a)   Exposure *necessary for the plot* or action is permitted.

    (b)   Exposure *for the sake of exposure* or the "punch" is wrong.

    (c)   *Scenes of undressing* should be avoided. When necessary for the plot, they should be kept within the limits of decency. When not necessary for the plot, they are to be avoided, as their effect on the ordinary spectator is harmful.

(d)　*The manner or treatment of exposure* should not be suggestive or indecent.

(e)　The following is important in connection with *dancing costumes*:

　　1.　Dancing costumes cut to permit *grace* or freedom of movement, provided they remain within the limits of decency indicated are permissible.

　　2.　Dancing costumes cut to permit indecent actions or movements or to make possible during the dance indecent exposure, are wrong, especially when permitting:

　　　(a)　Movements of the breasts

　　　(b)　Movements of sexual suggestions of the intimate parts of the body;

　　　(c)　Suggestion of nudity.

Dancing

(1)　Dancing in general is recognized as an *art* and a *beautiful* form of expressing human emotion.

(2)　Obscene dances are those:

　(a)　Which suggest or represent sexual actions, whether performed solo or with two or more;

　(b)　Which are designed to excite an audience, to arouse passions, or to cause physical excitement.

HENCE:　Dances of the type known as "Kooch" or "Can-Can," since they violate decency in these two ways, are wrong.

Dances with movements of the breasts, excessive body movement while the feet remain stationary, the so-called "belly dances"—these dances are immoral, obscene, and hence altogether wrong.

Locations

Certain places are so closely and thoroughly associated with sexual life or with sexual sin that their use must be carefully limited.

(1)　*Brothels and houses of ill-fame*, no matter of what country, are *not* proper locations for drama. They suggest to the average person at once sex sin, or they excite an unwholesome and morbid curiosity in the minds of youth.

IN GENERAL: They are dangerous and bad dramatic locations.

(2)   *Bedrooms.* In themselves they are perfectly innocent. Their suggestion may be kept innocent. However, under certain conditions they are bad dramatic locations.

    (a)   Their use in a comedy or farce (on the principle of the so-called bedroom farce) is wrong, because they suggest sex laxity and obscenity.

    (b)   In serious drama, their use should, where sex is suggested, be confined to absolute essentials, in accordance with the principles laid down above.

Religion

(1)   No film or episode in a film should be allowed to *throw ridicule* on any religious faith honestly maintained.

(2)   *Ministers of religion* in their characters or ministers should not be used in comedy, as villains, or as unpleasant persons.

NOTE: The reason for this is not that there are not such ministers of religion, but because the attitude toward them tends to be an attitude toward religion in general.

Religion is lowered in the minds of the audience because it lowers their respect for the ministers.

(3)   *Ceremonies* of any definite religion should be supervised by someone thoroughly conversant with that religion.

Particular Applications of the Code and the Reasons Therefore [Addenda to 1930 Code]

GENERAL PRINCIPLES

[BRIEF RE-STATEMENT]

1. No picture shall be produced which will lower the moral standards of those who see it. Hence the sympathy of the audience shall never be thrown to the side of crime, wrongdoing, evil or sin.

2. Correct standards of life, subject only to the requirements of drama and entertainment, shall be presented.

3. Law, natural or human, shall not be ridiculed, nor shall sympathy be created for its violation.

PARTICULAR APPLICATIONS

I.   *Crimes against the law*:

These shall never be presented in such a way as to throw sympathy with the crime as against law and justice or to inspire others with a desire for imitation.

The treatment of crimes against the law must not:

    a. Teach methods of crime.

    b. Inspire potential criminals with a desire for imitation.

    c. Make criminals seem heroic and justified.

    1. MURDER

    a. The technique of murder must be presented in a way that will not inspire imitation.

    b. Brutal killings are not to be presented in detail.

    c. Revenge in modern times shall not be justified. In lands and ages of less developed civilization and moral principles, revenge may sometimes be presented. This would be the case especially in places where no law exists to cover the crime because of which revenge is committed.

2. METHODS OF CRIME shall not be explicitly presented.

    a. Theft, robbery, safe-cracking, and dynamiting of trains, mines, buildings, etc., should not be detailed in method.

    b. Arson must be subject to the same safeguards.

    c. The use of firearms should be restricted to essentials.

    d. Methods of smuggling should not be presented.

3. ILLEGAL DRUG TRAFFIC must never be presented.

    Because of its evil consequences, the drug traffic should never be presented in any form. The existence of the trade should not be brought to the attention of audiences.

4. THE USE OF LIQUOR in American life, when not required by the plot or for proper characterization, should not be shown.

    The use of liquor should never be excessively presented even in picturing countries where its use is legal. In scenes from American life, the necessities of plot and proper characterization alone justify its use. And in this case, it should be shown with moderation.

II.   *Sex*

The sanctity of the institution of marriage and the home shall be upheld. Pictures shall not infer that low forms of sex relationship are the accepted or common thing.

1. ADULTERY, sometimes necessary plot material, must not be explicitly treated, or justified, or presented attractively. Out of regard for the sanctity of marriage and the home, the *triangle*, that is, the love of a third party for one already married, needs careful handling. The treatment should not throw sympathy against marriage as an institution.

2. SCENES OF PASSION must be treated with an honest acknowledgment of human nature and its normal reactions. Many scenes cannot be presented without arousing dangerous emotions on the part of the immature, the young or the criminal classes.

    a. They should not be introduced when not essential to the plot.

    b. Excessive and lustful kissing, lustful embraces, suggestive postures and gestures, are not to be shown.

    c. In general, passion should be so treated that these scenes do not stimulate the lower and baser element.

3. SEDUCTION OR RAPE

    a. They should never be more than suggested, and only when essential for the plot, and even then never shown by explicit method.

    b. They are never the proper subject for comedy.

4. SEX PERVERSION or any inference to it is forbidden.

5. WHITE SLAVERY shall not be treated.

6. MISCEGENATION (sex relationship between the white and black races) is forbidden.

7. SEX HYGIENE AND VENEREAL DISEASES are not subjects for motion pictures.

8. SCENES OF ACTUAL CHILDBIRTH, in fact or in silhouette, are never to be presented.

9. CHILDREN'S SEX ORGANS are never to be exposed.

III.   *Vulgarity*

The treatment of low, disgusting, unpleasant, though not necessarily evil, subjects should be subject always to the dictate of good taste and a regard for the sensibilities of the audience.

IV.   *Obscenity*

Obscenity in word, gesture, reference, song, joke, or by suggestion (even when likely to be understood only by part of the audience) is forbidden.

V.   *Profanity*

Pointed profanity (this includes the words, God, Lord, Jesus, Christ—unless used reverently—Hell, S.O.B., damn, Gawd), or every other profane or vulgar expression however used is forbidden.

VI.   *Costume*

1. COMPLETE NUDITY is never permitted. This includes nudity in fact or in silhouette, or any lecherous or licentious notice thereof by other characters in the picture.

2. UNDRESSING SCENES should be avoided, and never used save where essential to the plot.

3. INDECENT OR UNDUE EXPOSURE is forbidden.

4. DANCING COSTUMES intended to permit undue exposure or indecent movements in the dance are forbidden.

VII. *Dances*
1. DANCES SUGGESTING OR REPRESENTING SEXUAL ACTIONS or indecent passion are forbidden.
2. DANCES WHICH EMPHASIZE INDECENT MOVEMENTS are to be regarded as obscene.

VIII. *Religion*
1. NO FILM OR EPISODE MAY THROW RIDICULE on any religious faith.
2. MINISTERS OF RELIGION IN THEIR CHARACTER AS MINISTERS of religion should not be used as comic characters or as villains.
3. CEREMONIES OF ANY DEFINITE RELIGION should be carefully and respectfully handled.

IX. *Locations*
Certain places are so closely and thoroughly associated with sexual life or with sexual sin that their use must be carefully limited. Brothels and houses of ill-fame are *not* proper locations for drama.

X. *National feelings*
The just rights, history, and feelings of any nation are entitled to consideration and respectful treatment.
1. The use of the Flag shall be consistently respectful.
2. The history, institutions, prominent people and citizenry of other nations shall be represented fairly.

XI. *Titles*
Salacious, indecent, or obscene titles shall not be used.

Amendments

    I. BRUTALITY, HORROR AND GRUESOMENESS

    II. DRINKING

    III. GANGSTER STORIES

    IV. REGULATIONS RE CRIME IN MOTION PICTURES

> NOTE [*by Olga Martin*]: Rulings made by the Production Code Adminis-
> tration in the course of its work automatically become amendments
> to the Code. The regulation on drinking was necessary to indicate
> its manner of treatment after the repeal of Prohibition, since the
> original Code ruling had reference to Prohibition drinking.

I.   *Brutality, horror and gruesomeness*

Scenes of excessive brutality and gruesomeness must be cut to an absolute minimum. Where such scenes, in the judgment of the Production
Code Administration, are likely to prove seriously offensive, they will not be
approved.

II.   *Drinking in pictures*

"Drinking must be reduced to the absolute minimum essential for proper plot motivation."

The complaint is not so much against drinking when necessary for the
plot, as, for instance, when a character is portrayed definitely as an unfortunate drunkard, or is driven to drink by circumstances inherent in the story.

What is objected to is the incessant "smart" drinking apart from any story demands, or the exaggerated use of drinking for comedy purposes.

III. *Gangster stories*

Crime stories are not acceptable when they portray the activities of American gangsters, armed and in violent conflict with the law or law-enforcing officers.

IV. *Regulations re crime in motion pictures*
1. "Details of crime" must never be shown and care should be exercised at all times in discussing such details.
2. Action suggestive of wholesale slaughter of human beings, either by criminals, in conflict with police, or as between warring factions of criminals, or in public disorder of any kind, will not be allowed.
3. There must be no suggestion, at any time, of excessive brutality.
4. Because of the alarming increase in the number of films in which murder is frequently committed, action showing the taking of human life, *even in the mystery stories*, is to be cut to the minimum. These frequent presentations of murder tend to lessen regard for the sacredness of life.
5. Suicide, as a solution of problems occurring in the development of screen drama, is to be discouraged as "morally questionable" and as "Bad theatre"—unless absolutely necessary for the development of the plot.
6. There must be no display at any time, of *machine guns, sub-machine guns* or other weapons generally classified as illegal weapons, in the hands of gangsters, or other criminals, and there are to be no off-stage sounds of the repercussion of these guns. This means that even where the machine guns, or other prohibited weapons, are *not* shown, the effect of shots coming from these guns must be *cut to a minimum*.
7. There must be no new, unique or "trick" methods for concealing of guns shown at any time.
8. The flaunting of weapons by gangsters, or other criminals, will not be allowed.
9. All discussions and dialogue on the part of gangsters regarding guns should be cut to the minimum.
10. There must be no scenes, at any time, showing law-enforcing officers dying at the hands of criminals. This includes private detectives, and guards for banks, motor trucks, etc.

11. With special reference to the crime of kidnaping—or illegal abduction—it has been our policy to mark such stories as acceptable under the Code only when the kidnaping or abduction is (a) not the main theme of the story; (b) the person kidnaped is not a child; (c) there are no "details of the crime" of kidnaping; (d) no profit accrues to the abductors or kidnapers; and (e) where the kidnapers are punished.

 **Appendix 4**

The Critical and Commercial Hits of 1930–1934

The Ten Best Pictures, 1930–1934

Each year from 1930 until 1969, *The Film Daily* surveyed the nation's film critics and compiled an annual "Ten Best" list, ranking the films in order of votes. The list below encompasses those films during the period covered in this volume. (Note that because of extended release patterns, films might overlap a year.)

1930

All Quiet on the Western Front (Universal)
Abraham Lincoln (United Artists)
Holiday (RKO)
Journey's End (Tiffany)
Anna Christie (MGM)
The Big House (MGM)
With Byrd at the South Pole (Paramount)
The Divorcee (MGM)
Hell's Angels (United Artists)
Old English (Warner Brothers)

1931

Cimarron (RKO)
Street Scene (United Artists)
Skippy (Paramount)
Bad Girl (Fox)
Min and Bill (MGM)

The Front Page (United Artists)
Five Star Final (Warner Brothers)
City Lights (United Artists)
A Free Soul (MGM)
The Sin of Madelon Claudet (MGM)

1932

Grand Hotel (MGM)
The Champ (MGM)
Arrowsmith (United Artists)
The Guardsman (MGM)
Smilin' Through (MGM)
Dr. Jekyll and Mr. Hyde (Paramount)
Emma (MGM)
A Bill of Divorcement (RKO)
Back Street (Universal)
Scarface (United Artists)

1933

Cavalcade (Fox)
42nd Street (Warner Brothers)
The Private Life of Henry VIII (United Artists)
Lady for a Day (Columbia)
State Fair (Fox)
A Farewell to Arms (Paramount)
She Done Him Wrong (Paramount)
I Am a Fugitive from a Chain Gang (Warner Brothers)
Maedchen in Uniform (Film-choice)
Rasputin and the Empress (MGM)

1934

The Barretts of Wimpole Street (MGM)
The House of Rothchild (United Artists)
It Happened One Night (Columbia)
One Night of Love (Columbia)
Little Women (RKO)
The Thin Man (MGM)
Viva, Villa! (MGM)
Dinner at Eight (MGM)
The Count of Monte Cristo (United Artists)
Berkeley Square (Fox)

Box Office Champions, 1930–1934

The list below derives from the year-end calculations of the exhibitor-oriented trade journal *Motion Picture Herald*.

1930–1931

Cimarron (RKO)
Hell's Angels (United Artists)
Trader Horn (MGM)
Check and Double Check (RKO)
City Lights (United Artists)
Min and Bill (MGM)
Little Caesar (Warner Brothers)
Strangers May Kiss (MGM)
Reducing (MGM)
Daddy Long Legs (Fox)
The Man Who Came Back (Fox)
Politics (MGM)
Morocco (Paramount)
A Connecticut Yankee (Fox)
Animal Crackers (Paramount)

1932

Grand Hotel (MGM)
Emma (MGM)
Dr. Jekyll and Mr. Hyde (Paramount)
Mata Hari (MGM)
Delicious (Fox)
The Man Who Played God (Warner)
Hell Divers (MGM)
One Hour with You (Paramount)
Shanghai Express (Paramount)
Arrowsmith (United Artists)
Shopworn (Columbia)
Business and Pleasure (Fox)
Tarzan, the Ape Man (MGM)
Bring 'Em Back Alive (RKO)
Frankenstein (Universal)

1933

I'm No Angel (Paramount)
Cavalcade (Fox)
Gold Diggers of 1933 (Warner Brothers)
Be Mine Tonight (Gaumont-British Picture Corp.)
Tugboat Annie (MGM)
State Fair (Fox)
42nd Street (Warner Brothers)
Maedchen in Uniform (Film-choice)
Rasputin and the Empress (MGM)
Animal Kingdom (RKO)
The Kid from Spain (United Artists)
The Private Life of Henry VIII (United Artists)

1934

The House of Rothchild (United Artists)
It Happened One Night (Columbia)
Wonder Bar (Warner Brothers)
Roman Scandals (United Artists)
One Night of Love (Columbia)
The Gay Divorcee (RKO)
Dinner at Eight (MGM)
The Belle of the Nineties (Paramount)
Riptide (MGM)
Little Women (RKO)
Dames (Warner Brothers)
Chained (MGM)
Judge Priest (Fox)
Sons of the Desert (MGM)
The Barretts of Wimpole Street (MGM)
Queen Christina (MGM)
Girl of the Limberlost (Monogram)
Design for Living (Paramount)
She Loves Me Not (Paramount)
Flying Down to Rio (RKO)
The Lost Patrol (RKO)
The Son of Kong (RKO)
Kentucky Kernels (RKO)

Notes

This section lists research sources and a few observations, cued by page number and identifying phrase. Although not strictly necessary bibliographically, the trade press headlines were too evocative of the pre-Code era to omit.

1. ON THE CUSP OF CLASSICAL HOLLYWOOD CINEMA

Page 1. **On or about July 1934:** "Industry's Self-Regulation Starts This Week; Hays, Breen, Tellin' 'Em," *Variety*, July 10, 1934, 5; see also "Church, Films, Semi-Truce," *Variety*, July 3, 1934, 5, 45. The echo of Virginia Woolf's hyperbolic remark ("On or about December 1910 human character changed") is only partly ironic. Like the onset of modernism in the twentieth century, the exact starting date for the new morality in American cinema spans perhaps a month in the summer of 1934. The 1930 Code was amended to create the Production Code Administration on June 13, 1934, and formally approved by the executive board of the Motion Picture Producers and Distributors of America on July 12, 1934. Officially, the new regime was empowered on July 15, 1934, a Sunday. Since the fix was in from the start, however, the actual review process began earlier, on July 2, 1934. The first film to receive a Production Code seal was John Ford's aptly titled *The World Moves On* (1934), issued Production Code certificate No. 1 on July 11, 1934.

Page 2. **For four years:** "Picture 'Don'ts' for '30," *Variety*, February 19, 1930, 9.

Page 3. **Aptly dubbed:** Terry Ramsaye, "What the Production Code Really Says," *Motion Picture Herald*, August 11, 1934, 10.

Page 3. **the vital components of:** David Bordwell, Janet Staiger, and Kristen Thompson, *The Classical Hollywood Cinema: Film Style and Mode of Production to 1960.* (New York: Columbia University Press, 1985).

Page 4. **However, since the gambit:** For example, in arguing that early American cinema was not "simply a precursor of classical cinema but . . . a practice with its own logic and integrity," Charles Musser also demonstrates Edwin S. Porter's "far reaching exploration of cinema's manifold possibilities" within a series of narrative and institutional practices that, by 1908, sure look "classical." Musser, *Before the Nickelodeon: Edwin S. Porter and the Edison Manufacturing Company.* (Berkeley: University of California Press, 1991), 3, 11, 406–407.

Page 6. **In the context:** In an editorial in *Variety,* motion picture exhibitor Jack O'Connell directly asserted the connection between censorship and Prohibition. "A handful of political plum-seekers, ignorant of art and probably a lot of other things, is no more qualified to proscribe what the citizens of this free nation shall see on the screen than is the Anti-Saloon League to tell them what they should drink." O'Connell, "The Meddling Censor Menace," *Variety,* February 18, 1931, 32.

Page 7. **Pronouncing the document:** John Drinkwater, *The Life and Adventures of Carl Laemmle* (New York: Putnam's, 1931), 253.

Page 8. **"What constitutes decency:** "When a Picture Becomes Indecent— Shown for B.O.," *Variety,* November 3, 1931, 4.

Page 8. **Yet the men charged:** Formed in 1926, the Studio Relations Committee was designed to mediate relations between the MPPDA and member studios. In March 1930, Col. Jason S. Joy was assigned the task of monitoring compliance with the Production Code. In September 1932 he was succeeded by Dr. James Wingate, formerly director of the Motion Picture Division of the New York State Department of Education. By all accounts, both men were readily hoodwinked and sidestepped by the producers they allegedly regulated. Jack Vizzard, who served in the Production Code Administration from 1944 to its demise in 1968, quips that "Jason" was "quickly fleeced" and that Wingate "wrote letter after letter admonishing this studio and that regarding properties they were preparing, but his mood of bewilderment and of inability pervades the correspondence to this day." Jack Vizzard, *See No Evil: Life Inside a Hollywood Censor* (New York: Simon and Schuster, 1970), 39, 40.

Page 8. **"Does any producer pay attention:** "Producers War Brews," *Hollywood Reporter,* June 25, 1931, 1, 2.

Page 8. **"Producers have reduced:** "Deadline for Film Dirt," *Variety,* June 13, 1933, 1, 36.

Page 8. **The same year:** "Writers War on Filth," *Hollywood Reporter,* February 27, 1933, 2.

Page 9. **Upon his death:** Thomas M. Pryor, "Joe Breen, Sire of Code Ratings, Dies," *Variety,* December 8, 1965, 2.

Page 10. **Thus, just as the term:** Housed at the Margaret Herrick Library of the Academy of Motion Picture Arts and Sciences in Beverly Hills, California, the PCA's files first became readily available to researchers in 1983. Since then, a proliferating body of scholarly work on Hollywood censorship has profited from the careful recordkeeping of the Breen bureaucracy, notably Lea Jacobs, *The Wages of Sin: Censorship and the Fallen Woman Film, 1928–1942* (Madison: University of Wisconsin Press, 1991); Leonard J. Leff and Jerold L. Simmons, *The Dame in the Kimono: Hollywood, Censorship, and the Production Code from the 1920s to the 1960s* (New York: Grove Weidenfeld, 1990); Gregory D. Black, *Hollywood Censored: Morality Codes, Catholics, and the Movies* (New York: Cambridge University Press, 1995); Colin Schindler, *Hollywood in Crisis: Cinema and American Society* (New York: Routledge, 1996); and Frank Walsh, *Sin and Censorship: The Catholic Church and the Motion Picture Industry* (New Haven: Yale University Press, 1996).

Page 11. **Not for nothing:** Olga J. Martin, *Hollywood's Movie Commandments: A Handbook for Motion Picture Writers and Reviewers* (New York: H. W. Wilson, 1937), 35.

Page 11. **"Compensating moral value":** Martin, *Hollywood's Movie Commandments,* 99.

Page 13. **During the preproduction review:** Joseph Breen to John Hammel, November 30, 1936 (*Make Way for Tomorrow,* PCA file).

Page 19. **Nor, observed *Variety*:** "Inside Stuff—Pictures," *Variety,* October 25, 1932, 40.

Page 19. **the better portion:** Any survey purporting to register something as vaporous as the American movie memory is bound to be dubious, but the American Film Institute's list of the Top 100 Movies of the past century offers a fair reckoning. Announced in June 1998, the AFI list included just six films from the pre-Code era: *It Happened One Night* (1934) at no. 35, *King Kong* (1933) at no. 43, *All Quiet on the Western Front* (1930) at no. 54, *City Lights* (1931) at no. 76, *Duck Soup* (1933) at no. 85, and *Frankenstein* (1931) at no. 87.

With only two silent era films selected, *The Birth of a Nation* (1915) at no. 44 and *The Gold Rush* (1925) at no. 74, and with *Dances with Wolves* (1990) at no. 75 beating out *The Searchers* (1956) at no. 96, presentism and bad taste clearly skewed the results. Nonetheless, American cinema from the strict Production Code era of 1934–1960 heavily dominated the list, accounting for thirteen of the top twenty selections and forty-three of the total. Many of the balance—*Star Wars* (1977) at no. 15, *The Sound of Music* (1965) at no. 55, and *Close Encounters of the Third Kind* (1977) at no. 64—are Production Code films in spirit if not in date.

2. Breadlines and Box Office Lines

Page 22. **Fitzgerald could still:** F. Scott Fitzgerald, "Echoes of the Jazz Age," *Scribner's Magazine* (November 1931): 459, 465, 464.

Page 22. **The end of Coolidge-Hoover prosperity:** Frederick Lewis Allen, *Only Yesterday: An Informal History of the Nineteen-Twenties* (New York: Harper, 1931), xiii, 357, 339.

Page 22. **Even before the full pain:** See, for example, "Smash-Up," the final chapter in William E. Leuchtenburg, *The Perils of Prosperity, 1914–1932* (Chicago: University of Chicago Press, 1958): 241–64; and 265: "Never was a decade snuffed out so quickly as the 1920s."

Page 24. **To read the pronouncements:** The phrase had christened the decade by the publication of Lloyd M. Graves, *The Great Depression and Beyond* (New York: Brookmire Economic Service, 1932).

Page 24. **Nationally, 25 percent:** Michael A. Bernstein, *The Great Depression: Delayed Recovery and Economic Change in America, 1929–1939* (New York: Cambridge University Press, 1987), 48, 155–60.

Page 24. **"The great contraction":** Milton Friedman and Anna Jacobson Schwartz, *The Great Contraction, 1929–1933* (Princeton: Princeton University Press, 1965), 3, 5.

Page 24. **Anecdotal evidence:** Studs Terkel, *Hard Times: An Oral History of the Great Depression* (New York: Pantheon, 1970), 198, 442.

Page 25. **"You was handed a balloon:** Donald Day, *Will Rogers: A Biography* (New York: McKay, 1962), 286.

Page 25. **his surname christened:** Gene Smith, *The Shattered Dream: Herbert Hoover and the Great Depression* (New York: Morrow, 1970).

Page 25. **The only editorial response:** Edward Angly, *Oh Yeah?* (New York: Viking, 1931), 57.

Page 25. **The discrepancy between:** Gilbert Seldes, *The Years of the Locust (America, 1929–1932)* (Boston: Little, Brown, 1933), 11.

Page 25. **A Kansas farmer:** Roy V. Peel and Thomas C. Donnelly, *The 1932 Campaign: An Analysis* (1935; rpt., New York: Da Capo, 1973), 56.

Page 25. **In "The Hobo's Psalm"**: From the January 1932 issue of the *Hobo Magazine*, reprinted in *Film Daily*, May 3, 1932, 7.

Page 27. **Recalling the period**: Edmund Wilson, *The American Earthquake* (1958; rpt., New York: Da Capo, 1996), 12.

Page 27. **Writing in 1932**: Ernest Gruening, "Out of the Shuffle," *Saturday Review of Literature*, September 3, 1932, 75.

Page 27. **In 1930 Samuel Katz**: "Normalcy on Way But Waste Must Never Return, Says Katz," *Exhibitors Herald-World*, October 11, 1930, 23.

Page 27. **"Business is better.**: "Better Business Ahead, Says Franklin," *Exhibitors Herald-World*, August 30, 1930, 24.

Page 28. **By 1931 box office returns**: "Black Grosses in '31 if Coast Delivers on Quality and Theaters Handle It Properly," *Motion Picture Herald*, January 24, 1931, 26.

Page 28. **By the middle of 1932**: "6,500 Dark Film Houses Is All Time High," *Variety*, July 5, 1932, 1.

Page 28. **attendance plummeted**: Jack Alicoate, ed., *The Film Daily Year Book of 1934*, 35. Motion picture attendance figures should always be read skeptically and never more so than during the early days of the Great Depression when the motion picture industry had a good motive to float optimistic estimates to pump up its stock on Wall Street. *The Film Daily Year Book*'s annual lists of industry facts and figures retrospectively alter some figures from year to year before standardizing weekly attendance estimates for the pre-Code years as:

1930: 110 million
1931: 75 million
1932: 60 million
1933: 60 million
1934: 70 million

The figure for 1930 is ludicrously high given the daily hysteria throughout the industry that year over the "lost millions." The report from the *Film Daily Year Book of 1934* cited in the text seems the most reliable approximation, with the phrase "boom high" referring to the post-talkie, pre-Crash 1920s.

Page 28. **On Wall Street**: "Picture Stocks Hit Record Lows," *Motion Picture Herald*, May 23, 1931, 14.

Page 28. **In 1932 industry pioneer**: "Adolph Zukor Tells Stockholders Story of Paramount Today," *Motion Picture Herald*, April 30, 1932, 19.

Page 29. **Will Hays declared:** "New Films Increasing Potential for Audience, Hays Tells Directors," *Motion Picture Herald,* April 16, 1932, 21.

Page 29. **"There is no depression:** W. R. Wilkerson, "Tradeviews," *Hollywood Reporter,* June 1, 1931, 1.

Page 29. **avowed Universal's Carl Laemmle:** "Laemmle, 66, Says Action's the Thing," *Motion Picture Herald,* January 21, 1933, 20.

Page 29. **"Nothing would give me:** "That Turn in the Road," *Motion Picture Herald,* May 23, 1931, 9.

Page 29. **To the boosterism:** W. R. Wilkerson, "Tradeviews," *Hollywood Reporter,* April 8, 1931, 1.

Page 30. **By the close of 1931:** "Exhibitors Urge Quality Films to Bolster Box Office in 1932," *Motion Picture Herald,* January 2, 1932, 9.

Page 30. **The judgment from *Variety*:** Sid Silverman, "What the Grosses Say," *Variety,* December 29, 1931, 1, 169.

Page 30. **"The studios are in trouble:** W. R. Wilkerson, "Tradeviews," *Hollywood Reporter,* March 7, 1933, 1, 4.

Page 30. **"These Wall Street guys:** "Those Relatives," *Variety,* September 24, 1930, 5.

Page 30. **Taking note of:** "Production More Exacting and More Exact," *Motion Picture Herald,* January 3, 1931, 60–61.

Page 30. **Universal's Carl Laemmle:** "Laemmle, 66, Says Action's the Thing," *Motion Picture Herald,* January 21, 1933, 20.

Page 30. **Purchase a movie ticket:** "Rage for Giveaways Diminishing; False Stimulant in Present Form," *Motion Picture Herald,* October 1, 1932, 10.

Page 31. **"It's all bunk:** "Worried Authors Write Poor Stuff, Sez Sid Kent," *Variety,* December 1933, 3.

Page 31. **MGM president Nicholas Schenck:** W. R. Wilkerson, "Tradeviews," *Hollywood Reporter,* January 13, 1932, 1.

Page 31. **That a few big hits:** "Showman Only Can Run Show Business," *Variety,* December 22, 1931, 42.

Page 31. **Groucho Marx diagnosed:** Groucho Marx, "What's Wrong with the Movies," *Hollywood Reporter,* July 29, 1931, 1, 2.

Page 32. **Purely as an industrial revolution:** Scott Eyman chronicles the transition in *The Speed of Sound: Hollywood and the Talkie Revolution* (New York: Simon and Schuster, 1997).

Page 32. **By 1930 fully 70 percent:** "10,234 or 70 per cent of U.S. Theaters Are Wired for Sound," *Exhibitors Herald-World,* July 26, 1930, 15–16.

Page 32. **Most took pride:** "A Dirge to the Silents," *Film Daily,* October 15, 1930, 1; "The Mirror," *Film Daily,* May 21, 1930, 1.

Page 32. **To help close the margin:** "Scene Sketch Chart Evolved by Milestone," *Motion Picture Herald,* May 30, 1931, 40.

Page 32. **"In silent pictures:** "Two to Five," *Motion Picture Herald,* April 4, 1931, 64.

Page 33. **confessed B. P. Schulberg:** B. P. Schulberg, "Decentralized Production," *Film Daily,* December 20, 1932, 7.

Page 33. **The new model for production:** "Bulk of MGM Production Will Be Made by Unit Producers," *Hollywood Reporter,* February 10, 1933, 4.

Page 33. **But the sheer complexity:** Thomas Schatz discusses the art of the studio system in *The Genius of the System: Hollywood Filmmaking in the Studio Era* (New York: Random House, 1989).

Page 34. **As early as 1930:** "More Pantomime, Less Dialogue to Form Screen Technique, Says Laemmle," *Exhibitors Herald-World,* July 26, 1930, 20.

Page 34. **Ernst Lubitsch exclaimed:** "Lubitsch's Analysis of Pictures Minimizes Director's Importance," *Variety,* March 1, 1932, 2, 17.

Page 34. **A transcontinental causeway:** In April 1930, 40.3 percent of American homes owned radios; by January 1933 the figure had risen to 56.2 percent, a jump of 40 percent. Moreover, of the nine million new radio sets sold, nearly five million were purchased for homes that had previously not owned sets. The significant increase occurred not in markets where radio was already established by 1930 but remote rural areas and southern states. Radio penetration in Florida and Louisiana, for example, had increased by 140 percent. "17 Million Radio Receiver Sets Competing with Film Theaters," *Motion Picture Herald,* March 4, 1933, 9.

Page 34. **The relation of radio:** Michele Hilmes tracks the radio-studio relationship in *Hollywood and Broadcasting: From Radio to Cable* (Urbana: University of Illinois Press, 1990).

Page 35. **a series of alarmist articles:** "Radio Presents New Challenge to Theaters," *Motion Picture Herald,* February 11, 1933, 9–10; "17 Million Radio Receiver Sets Competing with Film Theaters," *Motion Picture Herald,* March 4, 1933, 9.

Page 35. **"The average family of five:** L. B. Wilson, "Film Theaters vs. Radio," *Variety,* January 2, 1934, 27.

Page 35. **Anticipating the media theories:** "Radio Presents a New Challenge to Theaters," *Motion Picture Herald,* February 11, 1933, 10.

Page 35. **Entertainers cross-pollinated:** "Broadcasting Grows as Film Publicity Aid," *Hollywood Reporter,* January 13, 1931, 4; "Warner Radio Hook Up," *Hollywood Reporter,* January 28, 1931, 1, 3.

Page 36. **In an earnest review:** Leo Meehan, *"Arrowsmith," Motion Picture Herald*, November 21, 1931, 48.

Page 37. **In the pre-Code era:** "Radio Presents New Challenge to Theaters," *Motion Picture Herald*, February 11, 1933, 9–10.

Page 37. **Many were said:** " 'Mike Fright' Terrorizes Many Celebrities into Silence with Radio Shows," *Variety*, January 12, 1932, 1, 50.

3. PREACHMENT YARNS

Page 40. **raved the** *New York World Telegram*: Quoted in an advertisement in *Variety*, August 8, 1932, 24.

Page 40. **"Individual fears," warned Lippmann:** Walter Lippmann, *Interpretations, 1931–1932* (New York: MacMillan, 1932), 12.

Page 41. **The story of the Bonus Army:** John Henry Bartlett, *The Bonus March and the New Deal* (New York: M. A. Donohue, 1937), 5, 70.

Page 41. **Will Rogers, the oracle:** Quoted in Edward Bliss, Jr., *Now the News: The Story of Broadcast Journalism* (New York: Columbia University Press, 1991), 55.

Page 42. **"That mob down there:** Gene Smith, *The Shattered Dream: Herbert Hoover and the Great Depression* (New York: Morrow, 1970), 32.

Page 42. **The next day:** Roy V. Peel and Thomas C. Donnelly, *The 1932 Campaign: An Analysis* (1935; rpt., New York: Da Capo, 1973), 175.

Page 43. **newsreel audiences hissed:** "Newsreel," *Variety*, August 2, 1932, 34.

Page 43. **"And the roaring flames:** Universal Newspaper Newsreel, July 28, 1932 (National Archives).

Page 43. **the films do not fit:** See Andrew Bergman, *We're in the Money: Depression America and Its Films* (New York: New York University Press, 1971), 92–109.

Page 44. **Taking stock:** Robert Sklar, *Movie Made America: A Cultural History of the Movies* (New York: Random House, 1975), 175.

Page 44. **"Playing soft music:** "Films Purer Than Plays," *Variety*, April 8, 1931, 9.

Page 44. **declared MPPDA secretary Carl Milliken:** "Milliken Tells Producers What Customers Want, Even If They Don't Believe Him," *Variety*, July 14, 1931, 2.

Page 45. **"The function of motion pictures:** "Code Is Improving Advertising Throughout Trade, Says Hays," *Motion Picture Herald*, April 23, 1932, 28.

Page 45. **C. C. Pettijohn argued:** "Tax Hearing Favorable Despite Exhib Discord," *Film Daily*, January 22, 1932, 1, 6.

Page 46. **"In the dark days:** "Film a Refuge Declares Hays," *Motion Picture Herald*, March 24, 1934, 44.

Page 46. **"We can't take sides:** "Novelty and the Pictures," *Motion Picture Herald*, May 28, 1932, 7.

Page 46. **In 1934, when the Theater Guild:** "Propaganda Too Hot for Use on Screen," *Hollywood Reporter*, March 1, 1934, 4.

Page 47. **"A movie with dialogue":** "Talker to Stay But No Better As Art, Says Writer in Nation," *Exhibitors Herald-World*, January 18, 1930, 39.

Page 47. **Lippmann ventured to pun:** Quoted in *Motion Picture Herald*, April 8, 1933, 7.

Page 47. **Gilbert Seldes asserted:** Gilbert Seldes, *The Movies Come from America* (New York: Scribner's, 1937), 52.

Page 47. **In 1937, shuddering to recall:** Olga J. Martin, *Hollywood's Movie Commandments: A Handbook for Motion Picture Writers and Reviewers* (New York: H. W. Wilson, 1937), 31.

Page 47. **In 1970, Jack Vizzard:** Jack Vizzard, *See No Evil: Life Inside a Hollywood Censor* (New York: Simon and Schuster, 1970), 38–39.

Page 48. **Audiences watched screens:** Wolf W. Moss, "The Movies and the Social Revolution," in William J. Perlman, ed., *The Movies on Trial: The Views and Opinions of Outstanding Personalities Anent Screen Entertainment Past and Present* (New York: MacMillan, 1936), 170.

Page 48. **Blind to the austere beauty:** Brian O'Neill, "Flaherty's *Man of Aran*," *The New Masses*, October 30, 1934, 29–30.

Page 48. **"Is it possible:** Harry Alan Potamkin, "Movies and Revolution," *The New Masses* (December 1932): 22; Harry Alan Potamkin, "*Shanghai Express*," *The New Masses* (May 1932): 28.

Page 48. **Formed in 1931:** "Workers Films and Photos," *The New Masses* (December 1931): 27; "Film and Photos," *The New Masses* (July 1931): 21.

Page 49. **"The political trend":** "Pictures Venture into New Fields for Cycles; Satires on Politics and Radio Hot," *Variety*, March 22, 1932, 3.

Page 49. **Testifying before Congress:** "The Motion Picture Producers and Distributors of America: 1932 Activities," in Jack Alicoate, ed., *The 1933 Film Daily Year Book of Motion Pictures*, 495.

Page 49. **Any film addressing any argument:** "Films Trying Propaganda," *Variety*, September 15, 1931, 7.

Page 50. **the KINO commissars:** "First American Talkie to Be Shown in Soviet Union," *Film Daily*, July 31, 1934, 1.

Page 54. **Audiences laughed out loud:** "Hollywood Error," *Variety*, November 29, 1932, 4.

Page 55. **In an eighteen-month period:** "Fastest of the Fast Set," *Variety*, August 1, 1933, 2.

Page 56. **Claudette Colbert flings:** The food theme in *It Happened One Night* is discussed by Stanley Cavell in *Pursuits of Happiness: The Hollywood Comedy of Remarriage* (Cambridge: Harvard University Press, 1981), 91–102.

Page 61. **The sure-fire material:** "Even Author Likes *Arrowsmith*," *Motion Picture Herald*, December 5, 1931, 12.

Page 62. **The *Hollywood Reporter* welcomed:** "*The Miracle Woman*," *Hollywood Reporter*, June 4, 1931, 3.

Page 63. **Timely enough to feature:** "Inside Stuff—Pictures," *Variety*, October 25, 1932, 40.

Page 64. **Columbia admitted:** "Inside Stuff—Pictures," *Variety*, October 4, 1932, 41.

Page 64. **Harry Cohn insisted:** "Political Worries," *Variety*, September 6, 1932, 4; "Gruesome Tag Stays in Merry-Go-Round," *Variety*, September 13, 1932, 7.

Page 64. **In the end, Columbia:** "Screen Won't Kid Politics," *Variety*, February 23, 1932, 5.

Page 65. **"I am not a radical:** Courtney Allison, "Cecil B. De Mille Talking," *Variety*, June 23, 1931, 3.

Page 65. **DeMille toured the USSR:** "DeMille Will Make Pictures in Russia," *Motion Picture Herald*, November 28, 1931, 31.

Page 67. **Wingate himself had cautioned:** James Wingate to A. M. Botsford, July 24, 1933; James Wingate to A. M. Botsford, May 11, 1933 (*This Day and Age*, PCA file).

Page 67. **Partly impressed, partly troubled:** "*This Day and Age*," *Hollywood Reporter*, July 18, 1933, 3.

4. DICTATORS AND DEMOCRATS

Page 69. **Standing-room-only crowds:** "Top Spot in Shorts Is 'Silly Symphony,'" *Variety*, August 8, 1933, 4.

Page 70. **Sometimes the tune:** "Newsreels," *Variety*, September 26, 1933, 12; "3 Little Pigs," *Variety*, October 10, 1933, 5.

Page 70. **"From what source come:** Lippmann, *Interpretations, 1931–1932* (New York: MacMillan, 1932), 30, 26, 29.

Pages 74–75. **Notwithstanding the powerhouse backing:** "Gabriel Retakes," *Hollywood Reporter*, March 20, 1933, 2.

Page 75. **antipathy to hectoring screen rhetoric:** "My Dear Mr. Hays," *Hollywood Reporter*, April 13, 1933, 8.

Page 76. **the week of FDR's inauguration:** "Mussolini Bookings Pour In," *Motion Picture Herald*, April 1, 1933, 29; *Motion Picture Herald*, April 8, 1933, 33.

Page 77. **Making a foray:** *Mussolini Speaks* press kit, New York Library for the Performing Arts, Lincoln Center, New York City.

Page 77. **Miriam Howell remarked:** Helen Gwynn, "Yesterday in New York," *Hollywood Reporter*, May 12, 1933, 3.

Page 78. **"Hoover can't speak:** Charles Peder, *Newsreel Man* (New York: Doubleday, Doran, 1932), 12. Note also the remark in "Newsreels," *Variety*, January 21, 1931, 46: "The president [Hoover] is photographed on the profile and never looks at the audience. Poor staging again."

Page 78. **Looking back from 1935:** Roy V. Peel and Thomas C. Donnelly, *The 1932 Campaign: An Analysis* (1935; rpt., New York: Da Capo, 1973), 51, 189.

Page 78. **Governor Roosevelt was deemed:** Peder, *Newsreel Man*, 12.

Page 79. **Shortly after his inauguration,** "Newsreels," *Variety*, April 11, 1933, 16.

Page 79. **"No chief executive:** Tom Waller, "Washington's Best Actors," *Variety*, May 30, 1933, 3, 14.

Page 79. **While tossing out:** "Newsreels," *Variety*, May 1, 1934, 19.

Page 79. **Jack Warner headed up:** "Inside Stuff—Pictures," *Variety*, September 20, 1932, 40.

Page 79. **As governor of New York:** Terry Ramsaye, "Industry Tries Again to Write Code," *Motion Picture Herald*, September 23, 1933, 9.

Page 79. **the candidate intervened:** "Newsreels an Issue in First Convention Tilt," *Motion Picture Herald*, July 9, 1932, 37.

Page 79. **two former newsreel editors:** "From Newsreels to the White House," *Motion Picture Herald*, March 11, 1933, 12.

Page 80. **"As an exhibitor:** "Inside Stuff—Pictures," *Variety*, September 5, 1933, 75.

Page 81. **Truman Talley of Fox Movietone:** James Cunningham, "Asides and Interludes," *Motion Picture Herald*, October 21, 1933, 23.

Page 81. **Pathé News made up:** Pathé News Special, the James A. Farley Collection, Motion Picture Division, Library of Congress (hereafter, MPD-LOC).

Page 81. **Within four months:** "Inside Stuff—Pictures," *Variety*, September 5, 1933, 75.

Page 81. **In many theaters:** "Inaugural Newsreels Cost Reaches $100,000," *Variety*, March 7, 1933, 4.

Page 82. **Al Smith responded:** Quoted in Hugh Gregory Gallagher, *FDR's Splendid Deception* (New York: Dodd, Mead, 1985), 95.

Page 82. **the acerbic H. L. Mencken:** H. L. Mencken, *Making a President: A Footnote to the Saga of Democracy* (New York: Knopf, 1932), 165, 170.

Page 82. **As late as 1944:** "White House Pictures," *Motion Picture Herald*, November 11, 1944, 8.

Page 83. **STAND BY YOUR PRESIDENT:** "Allied Suggests Trailers Urging Faith in Roosevelt," *Film Daily*, March 11, 1933, 1, 2.

Page 83. **a 15-second addition:** "NRA Trailers Ready for 6000 Houses August 20," *Hollywood Reporter*, August 9, 1933, 6.

Page 84. **Even MGM, repenting:** "Screen Propaganda Committee Forming," *Motion Picture Herald*, August 5, 1933, 18.

Page 84. **Powell sings a verse:** "Film Shorts for NRA Shown," *Variety*, September 5, 1933, 4.

Page 93. **the "fascinating fascism":** The phrase, of course, is from Susan Sontag, "Fascinating Fascism," reprinted in Bill Nichols, ed., *Movies and Methods* (Berkeley: University of California Press, 1976), 1:31–44.

Page 93. **By purging Jews:** According to *Variety*, the first notice of the Nazis in its pages occurred on June 15, 1932, when the paper reported on a band of Nazi thugs in Berlin breaking up a stage production of *Waterloo Bridge* by American playwright Robert E. Sherwood. "International Show Biz," *Variety*, September 5, 1933, 5.

Page 93. **Kathe deNagy was dismissed:** "Hitlerism Forces Standstill of U.S. Film Trade in Germany," *Motion Picture Herald*, April 15, 1933, 10; "Nazi Rule Driving Big German Players to US," *Hollywood Reporter*, December 29, 1934, 1, 3.

Page 93. **Wolf Kaufman tallied up:** Wolf Kaufman, "Hitlerized Show Biz," *Variety*, June 19, 1934, 1, 45. The *Motion Picture Herald* reported that the last of the remaining Jewish producers at Ufa—Arnold Pressburger and Gregor Rabinovitch—did not flee overseas until the end of 1934.

Page 94. **the Reichsfilmkammer demanded:** "Nazis Oust U.S. Film Men," *Variety*, April 18, 1933, 1, 17.

Page 94. **"American attitude on the matter:** "U.S. Film Units Yield to Nazis on Race Issue," *Variety*, May 9, 1933, 3.

Page 94. **a Faustian bargain:** "U.S. Filmers Protest Restrictions in Germany, but Carry on Trade," *Variety*, April 25, 1933, 13.

Page 94. **banned as a provocation:** Helen Gwynn, "Not That It Matters," *Hollywood Reporter*, May 11, 1934, 3.

Page 94. **source novelist Vicki Baum:** "Nazis Halt 'Hotel' Due to Race of Vicki Baum," *Variety*, May 16, 1933, 13.

Page 94. **Content notwithstanding:** "Nazi Minister Addresses German Film Industry, but Assurances Only Create More Uncertainties," *Variety*, April 11, 1933, 13.

Page 94. **the harmless Fox short subject:** "Banned," *Variety*, December 12, 1933, 12.

Page 95. **the number had dropped:** "1 German Film on Broadway; New Low," *Variety*, May 2, 1933, 17; "100 German Cinemas in U.S. Drop to 6; Bans Up All Over Continent," *Variety*, May 23, 1933, 13.

Page 95. **The deterioration of German cinema:** "Nazi Rule Puts German Film Industry on Rocks," *Hollywood Reporter*, December 1, 1934, 1, 7.

Page 95. **an embarrassed Goebbels:** "German Films So Bad Nazi Govt. Bans Them," *Hollywood Reporter*, December 17, 1934, 1, 5.

Page 95. **Goebbels personally banned:** "Hitler Gets Cold Feet on Picture Glorifying Horst Wessel, Nazi Hero," *Variety*, October 31, 1933, 11.

Page 95. **Variety helpfully explained:** "*S.A.-Mann Brand*," *Variety*, July 11, 1933, 15.

Page 96. **Released, though not widely:** "*S.A.-Mann Brand*," *Variety*, May 29, 1934, 12.

Page 96. **a British exhibitor expressed:** "Nazis Plan Propaganda Spread Through Films," *Hollywood Reporter*, October 2, 1933, 5.

Page 96. **the Nazis tactfully reedited:** The original version of *S.A.-Mann Brand* premiered in Berlin in 1933 and, according to accounts in the trade press, spouted fulsome antisemitic screeds and featured two coequal villains, the communists and the Jews. In the American version, the antisemitic dialogue has been eliminated and the prominence of the Jewish villain Neuberg, a factory owner who fires Fritz from his job, has been toned down. Neuberg appears as a Soviet agent who displays decadent modernist artwork on his desk, but he is not otherwise typed as Jewish.

Page 96. **distributors removed der Führer:** "*Hitlerjunge Quex*," *Variety*, July 17, 1934, 25.

Page 96. **In smuggled pamphlets:** "Smuggled Pamphlet Bars Hate," *Hollywood Reporter*, September 25, 1933, 4.

Page 97. **the official organ:** "Sacred Moustache Not to Be Insulted," *Hollywood Reporter*, September 9, 1933, 7.

Page 97. anti-Nazi plays: "Review of *The Shattered Lamp*," *Motion Picture Herald*, April 14, 1934, 15.

Page 97. the anti-Nazi plays flopped: "Hitler, Pro or Anti, a Blah Show Subject," *Variety*, November 1, 1933, 1.

Page 97. The Reichsfilmkammer held: "Nazi Picture Edict Most Stringent," *Variety*, February 20, 1934, 13.

Page 98. two Old Testament references: "Self-styled 'Hollywood Technical Directors Institute' also Wants Eisenstein Ousted from Country," *Exhibitors Herald-World*, June 28, 1930, 11.

Page 98. **Breen vented sentiments:** Black, *Hollywood Censored* (New York: Cambridge University Press, 1995), 70, 172. Breen's antisemitism seems to have informed his private correspondence but not his public actions or his oversight of Hollywood cinema. Moreover, most of the letters cited by Black and Frank Walsh (*Sin and Censorship* [New Haven: Yale University Press, 1996]) are from the early 1930s, none after 1935. Vizzard mentions that Breen put up his Malibu home as bond to help the Jewish producer Sam Spiegel. Vizzard, *See No Evil* (New York: Simon and Schuster, 1970), 76.

Page 99. an accusation directed: "*Are We Civilized?*" *Motion Picture Herald*, June 23, 1934, 119: "Obviously propaganda directed in opposition to the present regime and the current activity of Hitler and his henchmen in Germany."

Page 100. a ghastly image: No print of *Hitler's Reign of Terror* seems extant. This description is drawn from contemporary reviews and a short trailer for the film on deposit at MPD-LOC.

Page 100. LaGuardia ignored an appeal: "Denied License by Censor, Call Hitler News Film," *Film Daily*, April 30, 1934, 1, 3.

Page 100. after the title was truncated: "Modify Hitler Title," *Film Daily*, April 26, 1934, 2.

Page 100. the most prescient American film: "*Hitler's Reign of Terror*," *Film Daily*, April 27, 1934, 7.

Page 101. Jaffe took out full-page ads: Sam Jaffe, "To the Entire Motion Picture Industry," *Hollywood Reporter*, July 12, 1933, 4.

Page 101. Hays accused the pair: "Jaffe and Mankiewicz Flout Hays' 'Mad Dog' Ban," *Hollywood Reporter*, July 18, 1933, 1, 3.

Page 101. Rosen acquired several thousand feet: "Rosen All Set to Start Hitler Pic," *Variety*, January 2, 1934, 3.

Page 101. Hays later dispatched: "Rosen Intent on Filming Hitler Despite Hays Nix," *Variety*, October 17, 1933, 5.

Page 102. **Breen concluded his brief:** Joseph Breen to Sol Lesser, November 25, 1936 (*The Mad Dog of Europe*, PCA file).

5. VICE REWARDED

Page 104. **In 1932 Warner Brothers:** "Cycles Stale—WB Wants 'Em Hot," *Variety*, December 6, 1932, 4.

Page 104. *Variety* **estimated that:** "Deadline for Film Dirt," *Variety*, June 13, 1933, 1, 36.

Page 104. **Though Bow won:** Kenneth Anger, *Hollywood Babylon* (New York: Dell, 1975), 137–42.

Page 106 **"Why should some studios:** W. R. Wilkerson, "Tradeviews," *Hollywood Reporter*, March 23, 1931, 1.

Page 106. **three-word headline summed up:** "*The Man Who Played God*: Clean, Wholesome, and Dull," *Hollywood Reporter*, January 14, 1932, 3.

Page 106. **Vice-drenched films:** Robert H. Brown, "Sticks vs City on Pix," *Variety*, December 6, 1932, 21.

Page 106. **"As figures at the box office:** Sid Silverman, "U.S. Film Field for 1930," *Variety*, December 31, 1930, 7.

Page 106. **"There are more oversexed pictures:** "Over-Sexed Public Given Blame," *Variety*, June 13, 1933, 2.

Page 106. **"The more thoughtful among us:** "Femmes' Clean Films Drive," *Variety*, April 24, 1934, 3, 29. No film with the title *Lessons in Making Love* seems to exist.

Page 106. **"Illicit relations:** "Gangster Films Bring Most Cuts," *Motion Picture Herald*, April 11, 1934, 43.

Page 107. **blustered Martin Quigley:** Martin Quigley, "The Advertising Code," *Exhibitors Herald-World*, June 21, 1930, 42.

Page 108. **"For every person:** "Titles," *Motion Picture Herald*, January 19, 1931, 7.

Page 108. **Yet so widespread:** "Fumigating Titles," *Hollywood Reporter*, August 3, 1931, 1, 2.

Page 108. **Fox floated the title:** " 'Hooker' Title Banned," *Variety*, April 4, 1933, 2.

Page 108. **"We could not have shown:** "Phoney Come On," *Variety*, August 8, 1933, 23.

Page 108. **"If your Aunt Minnie:** "Inside Stuff—Pictures," *Variety*, May 9, 1933, 20.

Page 109. *Baby Face* **profited:** " 'Pinking' Baby Face Draws Heavy Black; No B.O. Blues in St. Louis," *Variety*, July 18, 1933, 3.

Page 110. **"I played this:** "What This Picture Did for Me," *Motion Picture Herald*, November 18, 1933, 57.

Page 110. **"Ballyhoo boys:** "Inside Stuff—Pictures," *Variety*, May 14, 1930, 31.

Page 110. **Such "pornographic stills":** "Pornographic Stills Flaunt Industry's Advertising Code," *Motion Picture Herald*, July 4, 1931, 9.

Page 111. **"Alluring, pursued:** Reverend Clifford Gray Twombly, *The Shamelessness of the Movies* (1932), quoted in Olga J. Martin, *Hollywood's Movie Commandments: A Handbook for Motion Picture Writers and Reviewers* (New York: H. W. Wilson, 1937), 26.

Page 111. **a set of twelve commandments:** "Hays' 12 Commandments to P.A.'s Just About Takes in Everything," *Variety*, December 26, 1933, 4.

Page 112. **"we'll supply the girls.":** "Inside Stuff—Pictures," *Variety*, January 1, 1934, 52.

Page 113. **the cardinal went:** Jack Vizzard, *See No Evil: Life Inside a Hollywood Censor* (New York: Simon and Schuster, 1970), 49.

Page 113. **The trade press summed up:** "Sex Stuff and Sad Finish Tiring," *Variety*, March 4, 1931, 5.

Page 114. **"What is the function:** "New York Critics Pan *Temple Drake*," *Hollywood Reporter*, May 8, 1933, 1.

Page 114. **Raft was under contract:** "Raft Will Quit Rather Than Play in Temple Drake," *Hollywood Reporter*, February 13, 1933, 1.

Page 119. **stylishly sophisticated directors:** "Wise Meggers Sidestepping Hays' Code," *Variety*, September 10, 1933, 3.

Page 120. **"The Code provides the laws:** "Milliken Tells Producers What Customers Want, Even If They Don't Believe Him," *Variety*, July 14, 1931, 2.

Page 121. **"The thirties were surprisingly:** Andrew Sarris, *The American Cinema: Directions and Directors, 1929–1968* (New York: Dutton, 1968), 249.

Page 121. **"Now the male magnolia:** "Banned from Bathroom by Hays Office, Pictures Hop into Pansy Stuff," *Variety*, February 2, 1932, 6.

Page 121. **What were called:** "Tsk, Tsk, Such Goings On," *Variety*, February 28, 1933, 2.

Page 122. **the lithe frauleins:** "*Maedchen in Uniform*," *Variety*, September 27, 1932, 17.

Page 122. **Arch Reeve salivated:** Quoted in James Cunningham, "Asides and Interludes," *Motion Picture Herald*, December 3, 1932, 19.

Page 125. **Paramount finally decided:** "Marlene's Wardrobe," *Variety*, December 13, 1932, 3; "Pants All Oke for Dietrich," *Variety*, January 24, 1933, 3; "Dietrich, Het Up Over Pants Publicity, Says She Wears Male Undies," *Variety*, January 31, 1933, 3.

Page 125. **Will Hays ordered:** "Hays Orders All 'Nance' Stuff Out," *Hollywood Reporter*, June 21, 1933, 4. The phrase comes from Vito Russo's pioneering study, *The Celluloid Closet: Homosexuality and Motion Pictures* (New York: Harper and Row, 1981).

Page 125. **Paramount filed for:** "Inside Stuff—Pictures," *Variety*, March 7, 1933, 41.

Page 125. **when Congressman Grant Hudson:** "New U.S. Censor Bill Would Bar 90 Per Cent of All Films Shown," *Exhibitors Herald-World*, February 22, 1930, 19.

Page 125. **"No program should be lowered:** "Women's Federation Starts Move on Balanced Bills and Cleaner Shorts," *Variety*, February 9, 1932, 23.

Page 126. **"the mind of the average man:** "Dirt Craze Due to Women," *Variety*, June 16, 1931, 1, 24.

Page 126. **Women "decide the fate:** Charles S. Aaronson, "B.O. Explodes Idea That Women Dislike War and Crook Pictures," *Exhibitors Herald-World*, September 6, 1930, 24.

Page 126. **"audiences are 75% female:** "Faking the Dame Angle," *Variety*, September 15, 1931, 3.

Page 126. **"When properly maneuvered:** *"Five Star Final,"* *Variety*, September 15, 1931, 14.

Page 126. ***Variety*'s resident expert:** Ruth Morris, "Sinful Girls Lead in 1931," *Variety*, December 29, 1931, 5, 37.

Page 127. **"It may do all right:** "Best Example of Bad Taste Yet Seen: *The Story of Temple Drake*," *Hollywood Reporter*, May 11, 1933, 4.

Page 127. **"they would run miles:** Ruth Morris, "Here's How Stahl Mixes Femme Cinematurgy with Psychology," *Variety*, October 11, 1932, 2, 43.

Page 127. **Thus, whereas the maudlin:** "The Woman's Angle," *Variety*, November 3, 1931, 17; "The Woman's Angle," *Variety*, December 29, 1931, 166.

Page 130. **"Charlie didn't attempt:** Cecelia Ager, "Special Studio Care Put 'Claudet' Over for Her, Explains Helen Hayes," *Variety*, February 2, 1932, 2.

Page 130. **"Every infant torn:** Ruth Morris, "Sinful Girls Lead in 1931," *Variety*, December 29, 1931, 37; Fred Stanley, "Figuring Only the B.O.," *Variety*, December 29, 1931, 10.

Page 131. **"We apologize to the men:** "Exhibs Censorship Def," *Variety*, August 22, 1933, 3.

Page 132. **cunning women worked:** "Bad Girl Film Cycle Earns Frown from Hays," *Variety*, April 18, 1933, 3.

Page 134. **Conceived as a reply:** "Baby Face Sapolioed," *Variety*, June 13, 1933, 4.

Page 136. **the package was too sordid:** Richard Maltby traces the censorship of the film in *"Baby Face* or How Joe Breen Made Barbara Stanwyck Atone for Causing the Wall Street Crash," *Screen* 27 (March–April 1986): 22–45.

6. CRIMINAL CODES

Page 137. **Hays fired off a cablegram:** Will H. Hays to Joseph I. Breen, March 20, 1934 (*Dillinger,* PCA file).

Page 138. **Inspiring "more laughs:** "Newsreels," *Variety,* March 13, 1934, 17.

Page 139. **the first authentic gangster:** *Time,* March 24, 1930. David E. Ruth examines the public face of Al Capone in *Inventing the Public Enemy: The Gangster in American Culture, 1918–1934* (Chicago: University of Chicago Press, 1996).

Page 139. **Warshow could rightly presume:** Robert Warshow, "The Gangster as Tragic Hero," *The Immediate Experience: Movies, Comics, Theater, and Other Aspects of Popular Culture* (New York: Atheneum, 1975), 130. See also Thomas Schatz, *Hollywood Genres: Formulas, Filmmaking, and the Studio System* (New York: Random House, 1981), 81–95.

Page 140. **As a communist critic:** Robert Forsythe, "Dillinger's Dilemma," *The New Masses,* May 15, 1934, 14.

Page 140. **Fitts decried reports:** "Capone Says No on Film Report," *Motion Picture Herald,* April 4, 1931, 32.

Page 140. **"I wouldn't go:** Lou Greenspan, "Capone Kids Gang Films," *Variety,* June 30, 1931, 19.

Page 140. **Capone was reportedly:** "Capone in Film at 200 G.s for Unemployed?" *Variety,* December 17, 1930, 1; W. R. Wilkerson, "Tradeviews," *Hollywood Reporter,* March 31, 1931, 1. Wilkerson asserts unequivocally he knew the screen offers to Capone "to be a fact."

Page 141. **"I've never willingly posed:** Lou Greenspan, "Capone Kids Gang Films," *Variety,* June 30, 1931, 19.

Page 141. **stormed out of the office.:** "Professional Pride," *The New Yorker,* December 12, 1931, 14.

Page 141. **a full page ad:** "Notice," *Hollywood Reporter,* March 7, 1934, 8. Paramount later disclaimed the ad, claiming it had been the work of an "individual scenarist" and that "the statements made by the advertiser were entirely false." However, as Martin Quigley pointed out, the studio's disclaimer was issued on March 29, 1934, only after Hays's anti-Dillinger decree had been issued to widespread editorial praise. " 'Rights' on Dillinger," *Motion Picture Herald*, April 7, 1934, 7.

Page 142. **The upbeat coverage:** "Newsreels," *Variety*, May 1, 1934, 19; "Newsreels," *Variety*, May 8, 1934, 23.

Page 142. **Outflanked in the court:** "Uncle Sam on Warpath in Crusade for Compulsory Cleanup of H'wood," *Variety*, June 6, 1934, 1.

Page 143. **Dillinger crashed out:** G. Russell Giradrin with William J. Helmer, *Dillinger: The Untold Story* (Bloomington: Indiana University Press, 1994), 103–108.

Page 144. **another sensational shoot-out:** John Toland, *The Dillinger Days* (New York: Random House, 1963), 286.

Page 144. **ready-made for tabloid headlines:** Curt Gentry, *J. Edgar Hoover: The Man and His Secrets* (New York: Norton, 1991), 172.

Page 147. **an incisive remark:** Warshow, *The Immediate Experience*, 133.

Page 149. **a "distinct feeling of nausea":** Jack Alicoate, "Scarface—A Mistake," *Film Daily*, April 14, 1932, 1.

Page 150. **To outmaneuver the outraged:** "Censors Ready to Make Concessions, Says Hughes," *Film Daily*, May 2, 1932, 1, 7.

Page 150. **Hughes's own ulterior motive:** "Dr. Wingate Denies Suit Caused Scarface Passing," *Motion Picture Herald*, May 28, 1932, 17.

Page 150. **a written directive:** "Worcester, Mass. Censors Forbid Any Gang Film in Local Houses," *Variety*, May 20, 1931, 4.

Page 151. **Darrow brought down the house:** Mae West, *Goodness Had Nothing to Do with It* (Englewood Cliffs, N.J.: Prentice-Hall, 1959), 96; "Darrow Eclipses John Sumner in Debate on Films," *Motion Picture Herald*, January 31, 1931, 65.

Page 151. *Variety* **pointed out:** "Dailies Load Gunman Stories; Tabs as Racketeers Trade Papers," *Variety*, May 13, 1931, 1, 55; "Local Censor as Censoring Solutions," *Variety*, May 20, 1931, 21.

Page 151. **"an Horatio Alger tale:** Quoted in *Hollywood Reporter*, January 16, 1931, 2.

Page 153. **glad to risk his life:** "For $25," *Variety*, November 29, 1930, 3.

Page 153. **the timely triple homicide:** "Inside Stuff—Pictures," *Variety*, August 2, 1932, 6.

Page 153. **the front office warned:** " 'Personal Artillery' Ruled Out in Gang Film Ballyhoo," *Motion Picture Herald*, May 23, 1931, 10.

Page 154. **According to this line:** "Capone Denied Preview, Says Hughes Office," *Motion Picture Herald*, October 17, 1931, 25.

Page 155. **"It is the function:** "The Gangster Genre Is Definitely Established Says Roy Del Ruth," *Hollywood Reporter,* June 29, 1931, 20.

Page 155. **"I have no excuse:** "Hays Declares Gang Films Are Right of Free Screen," *Motion Picture Herald,* July 4, 1931, 9.

Page 155. **In 1930 gangster themes:** "Crowley Case Publicity-Interest Turns Trade's Opinion on Gang Pictures—Another Cycle Now Due," *Variety,* May 13, 1931, 2.

Page 155. **a nineteen-hour grind:** "$50,000 Gross on 'Little Caesar,' " *Motion Picture Herald,* January 17, 1931, 34.

Page 155. **Under the circumstances:** "Gangster Opp. Bunk, Exhibs Want More," *Hollywood Reporter,* June 29, 1931, 1. See also "Gangsters on Spot Until Hays Ban Revived 'Em; Now Full Speed Ahead," *Variety,* August 18, 1931, 2.

Page 156. **Widespread outrage:** "Licking Gangsters All Way, New Style if Cycle Back as Suggested," *Variety,* February 14, 1933, 3.

Page 156. **the bent version:** "Producers Sadly Quit Gang Cycle; Clean Up in U.S., Tho Flop Abroad," *Variety,* August 11, 1931, 6.

Page 157. **The Federal reaction:** "Uncle Sam on Warpath in Crusade for Compulsory Cleanup of H'wood," *Variety,* June 6, 1934, 1, 57 (emphasis added).

Page 157. **Capone weighed in:** "Scarface Al Speaks," *Motion Picture Herald,* August 1, 1931, 15.

Page 163. **RKO permitted:** *"Hell's Highway,"* *Variety,* September 27, 1932, 21.

Page 163. **the true-life memoir:** Film historian John O'Connor relates the details of Burns's real story and the film's production history in O'Connor, ed., *I Am a Fugitive from a Chain Gang* (Madison: University of Wisconsin Press, 1981). Upon Burns's second recapture in 1932, the state of New Jersey refused to extradite him. Finally, in 1945, the state of Georgia commuted his sentence.

Page 164. **a naturalistic equality:** John Raeburn discusses the naturalist theme in "History and Fate in *I Am a Fugitive from a Chain Gang,*" *South Atlantic Quarterly* (Autumn 1986): 329–38.

Page 166. **In truth, LeRoy:** Working from production files and the shooting script, John O'Connor shows that the "I steal" line was in the final script written by Howard J. Green and Brown Holmes.

Page 166. **a brutal logic:** "If You Can Make 'Em Sit Forward, You've Got a Picture, Says LeRoy," *Variety,* December 26, 1933, 2.

Pages 166–67. **unfortunately no print:** The American Film Institute could not locate a copy of *Laughter in Hell* for its comprehensive *American Film In-*

stitute Catalogue, Feature Films, 1931–1940 (Berkeley: University of California Press, 1993).

Page 167. **"little has been glossed over:** *"Laughter in Hell,"* Motion Picture Herald, January 7, 1933, 26.

Page 167. **Johns also noted:** Vere E. Johns, "In the Name of Art," *The New Age*, March 25, 1933, 6.

Page 169. **A Dallas theater owner:** "Sensational Front Made by Paul Short on Chain Gang Film," *Motion Picture Herald*, December 10, 1932, 66.

Page 170. **Burns was prowling:** "Asides and Interludes," *Motion Picture Herald*, September 3, 1932, 29.

Page 170. **sentries of law and order censored:** Harry Turgend, "Tide of Prison Pictures Faces Backwash from Censorial Flood," *Exhibitors Herald-World*, June 21, 1930, 53.

Page 170. **The prison film "does not interest:** "What This Picture Did for Me," *Motion Picture Herald*, January 14, 1933, 44.

Page 170. **cautioned producers:** *"Laughter in Hell,"* Motion Picture Herald, January 7, 1933, 26.

Page 170. **"My personal opinion:** "What This Picture Did for Me," *Motion Picture Herald*, March 3, 1933, 36.

7. Comic Timing

Page 171. **the wisecrack thrived:** H. L. Mencken, the reigning expert on American vernacular and a mean wisecracker himself, first indexes the word "wise-crack" in the fourth edition of *The American Language: An Inquiry into the Development of English in the United States* (New York: Knopf, 1936). Mencken notes that the word and the practice had become lingua franca in the United States by 1926 and had even "entered the English slang vocabulary" by 1936.

Page 172. **"It's hard to make clear:** Pauline Kael, "Raising Kane," in *The Citizen Kane Book* (New York: Bantam Books, 1971), 18, 19.

Page 173. **"Humor has been:** Constance Rourke, *American Humor: A Study of the National Character* (New York: Harcourt, Brace, 1931), 297–98.

Page 174. **McNamee can't resist:** Universal Newspaper Newsreel, May 5, 1932.

Page 174. **"McNamee's lines are inclined:** Martin Quigley, "Pictures," *Exhibitors Herald-World*, August 2, 1930, 13.

Page 175. **"Let us hope:** "Dark and Silent," *Motion Picture Herald*, August 27, 1932, 7.

Page 175. **"The talk of these newsreels:** Vere E. Johns, "In the Name of Art," *The New Age*, April 29, 1933, 6.

Page 175. **Adventurer John Medbury:** "Newsreel," *Variety*, January 13, 1932, 17.

Page 178. **when Harold Lloyd sought:** "Inside Stuff—Pictures," *Variety*, May 30, 1933, 49.

Page 178. **"rapid fire farce":** "The Woman's Angle," *Variety*, December 26, 1933, 10.

Page 178. **Children shared the dimness:** "Inside Stuff—Pictures," *Variety*, June 4, 1930, 66.

Page 179. **Some lines went over:** "Inside Stuff—Pictures," *Variety*, August 16, 1932, 35.

Page 179. **Wallace pointed out:** "Old Line Directors Breathe Easily as Stage Recruits Fade Out of Picture," *Motion Picture Herald*, January 17, 1931, 31.

Page 179. **Sherwin A. Kane asserted:** Sherwin A. Kane, "Adapted Action Dramas Do Best Overseas; 'Wisecrack' Films Out," *Motion Picture Herald*, January 30, 1932, 12–13.

Page 179. **declared Carl Laemmle:** "25 Per Cent Dialogue Reduction Ordered for Universal Pictures," *Motion Picture Herald*, October 29, 1932, 12.

Page 179. **"We need more:** "The Curse of the Word," *Motion Picture Herald*, April 23, 1932, 7.

Page 180. **warned Dr. James Wingate:** "Adhere to Code, Chief Censor of New York Urges Producers," *Motion Picture Herald*, December 19, 1931, 13.

Pages 180–81. **"The theater patron:** " 'Smut' in Pictures," *Exhibitors Herald-World*, January 11, 1930, 58.

Page 181. **Terry Ramsaye declared:** "Naughty Words," *Motion Picture Herald*, August 4, 1934, 8.

Page 181. **"ultra-modern slanguists":** "Inside Stuff—Pictures," *Variety*, October 6, 1931, 54.

Page 181. **editor James Quirk:** "Here's a Censoress' Cinematic Dislikes," *Variety*, November 29, 1932, 3.

Page 181. **Hays requested a translation:** "The Lowdown," *Hollywood Reporter*, February 20, 1933, 2.

Page 182. **Sentenced to ten days:** Mae West, *Goodness Had Nothing to Do with It* (Englewood Cliffs, N.J.: Prentice-Hall, 1959), 97.

Page 182. **"Upholstered in the costumes:** Cecelia Ager, "The Elemental Lil," *Variety*, February 14, 1933, 17.

Page 183. "Hollywood has a sweetening: "Hollywood and CN," *Motion Picture Herald,* July 30, 1932, 23.

Page 183. "I've developed a different way: Cecelia Ager, "No Good Women in History, Mae West Says, During Hot Sex Selling Talk," *Variety,* January 31, 1933, 1, 42.

Page 183. "Nothing much changed: "*She Done Him Wrong,*" *Variety,* February 14, 1933, 12, 21; "Inside Stuff—Pictures," *Variety,* February 21, 1933, 49.

Page 184. Screen trailers teased: "Mae West Trailers," *Variety,* September 26, 1933, 34.

Page 184. a sure-fire lure for males: "Mae West's Saga of Barbary Coast Draws in Frisco," *Variety,* February 7, 1933, 8.

Page 184. West was the major exception: "*She Done Him Wrong*: The New York Press," *Hollywood Reporter,* February 14, 1933, 2.

Page 186. "This is dandy entertainment: "What This Picture Did for Me," *Motion Picture Herald,* February 24, 1934, 52; "What This Picture Did for Me," *Motion Picture Herald,* March 10, 1934, 76.

Page 186. "I cleaned up: Robert Welsh, "Tradeviews," *Hollywood Reporter,* November 4, 1933, 1.

Page 186. "Why in pictures: "Mae West Talks of Park Ave. Censorship," *Variety,* April 3, 1934, 3.

Page 187. "Yes," she admitted: James Cunningham, "Asides and Interludes," *Motion Picture Herald,* October 7, 1933, 49.

Page 187. When asked what she thought: James Cunningham, "Asides and Interludes," *Motion Picture Herald,* August 18, 1934, 27.

Page 187. "Schmucks with Underwoods": Cecelia Ager, "Hecht Sees Hollywood As Place Where the Kibitzers Play the Cards, But Always with Their Fingers Crossed," *Variety,* May 16, 1933, 2, 25.

Page 188. "And I heard language": Ben Hecht, *A Child of the Century* (New York: Donald Fine, 1954), 145–46.

Page 192. "The man in the street: Ruth Morris, "Capra Foresees Satirical Cycle; Many Subjects Ripe for Ridicule," *Variety,* February 2, 1932, 2.

Page 192. Harpo Marx confided: "Comrade Harpo," *Variety,* December 26, 1933, 3.

Page 193. Jenkins cautions: Henry Jenkins, *What Made Pistachio Nuts? Early Sound Comedy and the Vaudeville Aesthetic* (New York: Columbia University Press, 1992), 10.

Page 195. "Talk about your: "What This Picture Did for Me," *Motion Picture*

Herald, December 23, 1933, 62; "What This Picture Did for Me," *Motion Picture Herald,* February 10, 1934, 61.

8. NEWS ON SCREEN

Page 197. **five commercial newsreels:** The precise names of the five commercial newsreels changed periodically during their existence. The onset of sound inspired most of the newsreels to rechristen themselves accordingly. Paramount News changed its name to Paramount Sound News, Hearst News to Hearst Metrotone News, and Fox News to Fox Movietone News. The names given here were current throughout 1930–1934.

Page 198. **the newsreel provided:** Much of the information in this chapter is culled from *Variety's* reviews of the programs at New York's Embassy Newsreel Theater. Beginning in 1929, almost on a weekly basis, the trade paper's "Film House" review section commented on the 45-minute newsreel program. It is the single best record of what Americans actually saw in the newsreels and how they responded to them in theaters. One caution, however: trade press consensus reckoned the newsreel audiences in New York to be more "radical" in their sympathies than the average rung of motion picture audiences.

Page 198. **By September 1930:** "All Newsreels Will Dub Talk," *Hollywood Reporter,* September 9, 1930, 1.

Page 198. **McNamee narrated:** "Graham McNamee," *Exhibitors Herald-World,* January 18, 1930, 41; "Orchestra Fills Gaps Between Talks in Universal's Newsreel," *Exhibitor's Herald-World,* March 8, 1930, 50.

Page 200. **The 578-seat house:** "Newsreels," *Variety,* July 9, 1930, 41.

Page 200. **For a while the Embassy:** "Embassy Newsreel House, in Nine Months Grosses $380,000," *Exhibitors Herald-World,* August 9, 1930, 21; "Embassy Newsreel Celebrates First Anniversary," *Exhibitors Herald-World,* November 8, 1930, 57; "Los Angeles Newsreel Closes; Business Drops after Three Day Rush," *Exhibitors Herald-World,* September 20, 1930, 43.

Page 200. **a cost-efficient operation:** "Trans Lux Opens Twin Houses in New York on Friday," *Motion Picture Herald,* May 16, 1931, 26.

Page 201. **In 1928 in London:** "Movietone Portrays King George Speaking," *New York Times,* November 28, 1928, 2.

Page 201. **"Italy's Duce":** "Newsreels," *Variety,* May 14, 1930, 51.

Page 201. **Another signature politician:** "Newsreels," *Variety,* December 12, 1932, 13.

Page 201. **"It is hard for audiences:** "Newsreels," *Variety,* October 20, 1931, 37.

Page 201. **"As an actor:** "Newsreels," *Variety,* November 24, 1931, 31.

Page 201. **"God Bless:** "John D. Is Gagman Too; He Blesses All and Oil," *Exhibitors Herald-World,* January 8, 1930, 30.

Page 202. **"He is temperamental:** "Along the Rialto," *Film Daily,* May 31, 1931, 3.

Page 202. **a pair of congenial:** "Newsreels," *Variety,* March 11, 1931, 48.

Page 202. **The "ear entertainment:** "Fox Discards Silent Newsreels for U.S. and Canada Exhibitors," *Exhibitors Herald-World,* May 10, 1930, 16.

Page 202. **"There is deep silence:** "Newsreels," *Variety,* October 6, 1931, 42.

Page 203. **news of Edison's death.:** "Pathe on Edison," *Variety,* October 20, 1931, 5.

Page 203. **cumbersome, delicate, and expensive:** "Two More Newsreels," *Hollywood Reporter,* January 8, 1931, 4.

Page 203. **"I suspect we've sacrificed:** H. E. Jameyson, "A Showman Discusses the Shortcomings of the Short Feature!" *Motion Picture Herald,* April 23, 1932, 49.

Page 203. **not quite "pseudo events":** Daniel J. Boorstin, *The Image: A Guide to Pseudo-Events in America* (1961; rpt., New York: Atheneum, 1975), 11–12.

Page 204. **a worrisome instance:** Gilbert Seldes, *The Movies Come from America* (New York: Scribner's, 1937), 85.

Page 205. **a homicidal hyperbole:** Fred Ayer, "News Cameraman Comes into Own in Thriller Shot," *Motion Picture Herald,* July 1, 1933, 22.

Page 206. **"The Stallings comments:** Andre Sennwald, "*The First World War,*" *New York Times,* November 8, 1934, 27.

Page 208. **an exciting historical pageant.":** "New York Reviews: *This Is America,*" *Hollywood Reporter,* August 1, 1933, 2.

Page 208. **"I say there is more:** Harry Lawrenceson, "Behind the Newsreel," *Film Daily,* March 27, 1932, 8.

Page 209. **Unable to obtain footage:** "English Burn Over Newsreel Blanket," *Hollywood Reporter,* October 6, 1933, 5.

Page 209. **Sensational sports footage:** James Cunningham, "Asides and Interludes," *Motion Picture Herald,* January 2, 1932, 21.

Page 209. **a monthly listing:** "Fox-Hearst No. 1 with May's Scoops," *Variety,* May 31, 1932, 20.

Page 209. **"Under current methods:** "Asleep at the Desk," *Motion Picture Herald,* April 14, 1934, 7.

Page 210. **"Efforts to establish:** "Drop Censor Formula Ideas of Newsreels," *Variety,* August 30, 1932, 5.

Page 210. In 1931, New York: "Exempt Newsreels from Censorship," *Hollywood Reporter*, February 2, 1931, 5; "Newsreel Censorship Is Terminated in Ohio," *Film Daily*, April 11, 1933, 1, 6.

Page 210. By 1934, Chicago: "Newsreel Will Ignore Censorial Meddling; Constitutional Rights," *Variety*, March 20, 1934, 6.

Page 210. "Scenes of actual death: "Inside Stuff—Pictures," *Variety*, May 31, 1932, 10; "Inside Stuff—Pictures," *Variety*, May 24, 1932, 66.

Page 210. "the all-time shocker: "Newsreels," *Variety*, April 10, 1934, 12.

Page 211. "in the eyes of the law: "Newsreel Status" and "Prison Guards Censor Newsreel; Cameraman Held," *Motion Picture Herald*, December 19, 1931, 7, 12.

Page 212. Ramsaye criticized: Terry Ramsaye, "News and Corpses," *Motion Picture Herald*, September 1, 1934, 7–8.

Page 212. The total costs: Tom Waller, "Lowdown on the Newsreels," *Variety*, January 3, 1933, 4. The article declares that the profitable mathematics for the newsreels were "uncovered here publicly for the first time."

Page 212. "the one product: "Selling the Newsreel," *Motion Picture Herald*, July 11, 1931, 7.

Page 212. "drawing the best: "Newsreels," *Variety*, July 9, 1930, 41.

Page 212. the Prohibition-weary veterans: "Newsreels," *Variety*, September 29, 1931, 141.

Page 213. develop a backbone": "Newsreel Status" and "Prison Guards Censor Newsreel; Cameraman Held," *Motion Picture Herald*, December 19, 1931, 7, 12.

Page 214. managers were instructed: "Inside Stuff—Pictures," *Variety*, September 22, 1931, 48.

Page 214. The unscreenable material: "Fox Screen Deletions," *Variety*, March 4, 1931, 11, 27. The report also notes that "anything that [exhibitors] cut [from the newsreels] is to be preserved and returned to the film exchange with the rest of the reel." Again, then, the newsreel images of the Great Depression that survive in motion picture archives were not necessarily seen during the Great Depression itself.

Page 214. "Fear instilled: Tom Waller, "Checking the Newsreels," *Variety*, January 2, 1934, 5.

Page 214. a prime motivation: "The Film Forum," *The New Masses* (February 1933): 29.

Page 214. cheerful economic forecasts: Universal Newspaper Newsreel, September 5, 1932, and September 19, 1932.

Page 215. **job tips:** "The Newsreel as a Civic Force," *Film Daily*, December 10, 1932, 6.

Page 215. **"By preaching:** "The Screen as a Medium for Gospel of Optimism," *The Billboard*, November 15, 1930, quoted in ads for Fox Movietone News in *Variety*, November 19, 1930, 17.

Page 215. **"We'll take a cab.":** Ibid.

Page 215. **"a riot of catcalls:** "Newsreels," *Variety*, December 20, 1932, 12.

Page 215. **audiences hooted:** "Newsreels," *Variety*, September 26, 1933, 12.

Page 216. **The changing political winds:** Responses to Prohibition speakers culled from the "Newsreels" review section in *Variety*, July 2, 1930, 55; October 15, 1930, 45; December 17, 1930, 37; January 14, 1931, 14; January 29, 1932, 36.

Page 216. **Rogers sparked rueful laughter:** "Newsreels," *Variety*, February 16, 1932, 53.

Page 216. **clips that dared:** "Cutting Depression from Reels," *Film Daily*, January 8, 1932, 2.

Page 216. **violence nearly erupted:** "Inside Stuff—Motion Pictures," *Variety*, January 21, 1931, 54.

Page 217. **deleted clips of Hitler:** "Boycott of German Pictures Is Deplored," *Motion Picture Herald*, April 1, 1933, 16.

Page 217. **Unlike Mussolini:** "Newsreels," *Variety*, July 24, 1934, 18 ("Mussolini is provoking raucous laughter by posing as a hay shaker before a Hearst camera").

Page 217. **"Death of Dillinger:** "Newsreels," *Variety*, July 31, 1934, 17.

Page 218. **a terrifying effect:** "Those Newsreel Shots," *Motion Picture Herald*, December 22, 1934, 58.

Page 218. **"The world's most famous baby:** Lowell Thomas, *History As You Heard It* (Garden City, N.Y.: Doubleday, 1957), 19.

Page 218. **"the greatest concentration:** "Newsreels Set a Service Record in Kidnapping of Lindbergh Baby," *Motion Picture Herald*, March 12, 1932, 23–24.

Page 218. **seven crews on duty:** "Paramount Sound News Claims Series of Beats," *Film Daily*, March 27, 1932, 4.

Page 218. **private pictures were "conscripted:** "Newsreels," *Variety*, March 8, 1932, 36.

Page 219. **McNamee voiced:** Contemporaneous commentary adjudged Universal's coverage of the kidnapping the most affecting. "I believe I can state authoritatively that McNamee created a feeling of sympathetic understanding not equaled in any other expressed method of screen or press," observed exhibitor Fred S. Meyer, who saw all five newsreel accounts. Meyer, " 'Double' or 'Trouble Features'—Does This Answer the Riddle?" *Motion Picture Herald*, April 23, 1932, 56.

9. REMOTE KINSHIPS

Page 223. **ruminated Winston Churchill:** Quoted in Paul Johnson, *Modern Times: The World from the Twenties to the Eighties* (New York: Harper and Row, 1983), 14.

Page 224. **director John Ford:** "The Lowdown," *Hollywood Reporter*, July 2, 1931, 2.

Page 225. **a critic rebuked:** Leo Meehan, *"Around the World in Eighty Minutes,"* *Motion Picture Herald*, November 7, 1931, 50.

Page 225. **by forbidding "any scene:** The double standard was too much even for the Victorian Martin Quigley. "Presumably an educated Tahitian mother would be barred while her wilder and more nubile sister Morea would be eligible," he speculated. "Save the Wild Flowers," *Motion Picture Herald*, September 19, 1931, 7.

Page 227. **enchanted with the sound:** *"Trader Horn* a Great Bet: It Has Everything," *Hollywood Reporter*, January 6, 1931, 3.

Page 232. **"No shots of anyone:** *"Rango,"* *Hollywood Reporter*, December 11, 1930, 4.

Page 232. **riding a crest:** "Goona's an Indie Producer's Dream," *Variety*, December 20, 1932, 33.

Page 235. **"the house was nearly full:** *"Virgins of Bali,"* *Variety*, December 13, 1932, 15.

Page 235. **"This simple little nature story:** "What This Picture Did for Me," *Motion Picture Herald*, December 23, 1933, 64.

Page 235. **a quasi-documentary record:** *"Ubangi* Investigated by Better Business Bureau," *Film Daily*, February 15, 1932, 2.

Page 237. **a "stag population":** "Gorilla Dough Getter and Three Film Premieres Only Talk in LA," *Variety*, April 16, 1930, 9; "Gag 'Ingagi'? It's Up to Theaters Themselves, Says Milliken," *Exhibitors Herald-World*, June 21, 1930, 58.

Page 237. **roving bands of gorillas:** "Ballyhoo Made New Film Break Record," *Variety*, April 16, 1930, 5.

Page 238. **Unable to avoid smirking:** "Gorilla Film Can't Show on Big Circuits," *Variety*, May 21, 1930, 2, 58.

Page 238. **"After long efforts:** Unsigned memorandum to Will H. Hays, October 27, 1929 (*Ingagi*, PCA file).

Page 238. **"Behind the walls:** "In Fight to Stay, Says Spitzer in Suing MPPDA Over 'Ingagi,' " *Exhibitors Herald-World*, June 28, 1930, 21.

Page 239. **"At last:** "Ingagi a Find for the Indies," *Variety*, May 28, 1930, 15.

Page 239. **Audiences were unanimous:** "Patrons Vote on Banned 'Ingagi,' " *Variety*, August 13, 1930, 19.

Page 239. **"The MPPDA gently reminds:** "Will Hays Making Moral Code 100% Effective; Curbing 'Dirt' by Sexy Indie-Legit Producers," *Variety*, August 27, 1930, 25, 58.

Page 239. **Audiences were invited:** "Lions and Social Lions Figure in Preview of *Africa Speaks* at Chicago House," *Exhibitors Herald-World*, September 27, 1930, 54.

Page 240. **the company contended:** "Charges of Fraud Made Against *Africa Speaks*," *Hollywood Reporter*, October 13, 1930, 1, 2.

Page 240. **"Columbia is not advertising:** "Columbia, Hays, Along with 'Africa Speaks,' a Coincidence—Minus," *Variety*, October 1, 1930, 4.

Page 240. **"one of the best films:** "Faked Animal Film 'Nice Deception!' Says 'Tribune'—Leave Them Alone," *Variety*, June 13, 1933, 6.

Page 240. **an out-of-court settlement:** "Charge Congo Pictures Used 'Heart of Africa' in Producing Ingagi," *Exhibitors Herald-World*, August 2, 1930, 13; "Ingagi Writ Dropped; 150,000 Payment Is Involved in Settlement," *Exhibitors Herald-World*, October 25, 1930, 27.

Page 240. **filed a complaint:** "FTC Files Complaint on Ingagi," *Film Daily*, May 27, 1931, 1.

Page 241. **Even the etymology was bogus:** Francis L. Burt, "Officially 'Fake' Now," *Motion Picture Herald*, May 5, 1933, 14.

Page 241. **Filmed in the Bronx:** " 'Jungle Hazards' Alleged to Be 'Jango' with Cannibal from Harlem," *Variety*, July 21, 1931, 7.

Page 243. **Cool and unruffled:** "*Bring 'Em Back Alive*," *Motion Picture Herald*, June 4, 1932, 35.

Page 244. **the battles had been supervised:** "Inside Stuff—Pictures," *Variety*, January 24, 1933, 47.

Page 244. **Ramsaye dryly dissected:** Terry Ramsaye, "*Eskimo*," *Motion Picture Herald*, November 18, 1933, 36.

Page 244. **(The female lead:** "Inside Stuff—Pictures," *Variety*, September 26, 1933, 6.

Page 245. **"It would seem reasonable:** "Rawer Than Nature," *Motion Picture Herald*, February 17, 1934, 7.

Page 245. **devouring his opponent:** "Grim Nature Film Well Produced," *Hollywood Reporter,* May 15, 1933, 3.

Page 246. **she married him:** Osa Johnson, *I Married Adventure: The Lives and Adventures of Martin and Osa Johnson* (1940; rpt., New York: Morrow, 1989).

10. PRIMITIVE MATING RITUALS

Page 255. **connected the dots:** "*The Blonde Captive,*" *Variety,* March 1, 1932, 21.

Page 255. **"It's a pity:** "Inside Stuff—Pictures," *Variety,* October 22, 1930, 63.

Page 255. **"sold on the strength:** George Brown, " 'Blonde Captive' Campaign Was Columbia Standout," *The 1933 Film Daily Year Book of Motion Pictures,* 674.

Page 261. **"the verdict of this office:** Joseph Breen to Will Hays, April 10, 1934 (*Tarzan and His Mate,* PCA file).

Page 262. **an appreciative critic:** "Tarzan and His Mate," *Hollywood Reporter,* April 7, 1934, 3.

Page 267. **the critical response to *Massacre:*** "*Massacre* Reviews," *Hollywood Reporter,* January 27, 1934, 2.

Page 267. ***Variety* demurred:** "*Massacre,*" *Variety,* January 23, 1934, 13.

Page 268. **filled with Occidentals.":** "All White Cast,' *Variety,* October 4, 1932, 7.

Page 273. **"The whole purpose:** John V. Wilson to Will Hays, January 21, 1933 (*The Bitter Tea of General Yen,* PCA file).

Page 274. **business fell off:** "Colored Houses 65% Off as Maids, Chauffeurs Out of Work," *Variety,* December 17, 1930, 12.

Page 274. **white pictures with white casts":** "Inside Stuff—Pictures," *Variety,* August 11, 1931, 52.

Page 274. **With mercenary egalitarianism:** "Colored Screen Players in Person for Builder Uppers for Balcony Biz," *Variety,* June 28, 1932, 1, 30.

Page 275. **a "few get a chance:** Vere E. Johns, "In the Name of Art," *The New Age,* January 14, 1933, 6; Vere E. Johns, "In the Name of Art," *The New Age,* March 18, 1933, 6.

Page 275. **"One scene depicts:** Loren Miller, "Uncle Tom in Hollywood," *The Crisis* (November 1934): 329.

Page 275. **a portion of the patronage.":** "*Black Moon,*" *Motion Picture Herald,* July 7, 1934, 48.

Page 275. **insiders readily linked:** "*The Emperor Jones,*" *Variety,* September 26, 1933, 15.

Page 280. **said the recent winner:** "Even Author Likes Arrowsmith," *Motion Picture Herald*, December 5, 1931, 12.

Page 280. **only two exceptions:** Vere E. Johns, "In the Name of Art," *The New Age*, January 14, 1933, 6.

Page 281. **venerable theatrical tradition:** See Michael Paul Rogin, *Blackface, White Noise: Jewish Immigrants in the Hollywood Melting Pot* (Berkeley: University of California Press, 1996).

Page 282. **Taking no chances:** "Color Issue Finessed in Amos 'n' Andy Contract," *Exhibitors Herald-World*, September 20, 1930, 41.

Page 282. **"Every time the boys get hot:** " 'Amos 'n' Andy' Film Jams Studio Routine," *Variety*, August 20, 1930, 4.

Page 282. **Gosden and Correll performed:** "Record Tieups on Amos 'n' Andy; Opens Oct. 24 in 300 Theaters," *Exhibitors Herald-World*, October 11, 1930, 26; "Amos 'n' Andy Tell of Hollywood Over the Air as RKO Film Is Released," *Exhibitors Herald-World*, October 25, 1930, 34.

Page 282. **The publicity punch:** "Amos 'n' Andy Is Record for Week But Then Falls Off" and "Box Office Reports on Amos 'n' Andy Picture from Cities Across U.S.," *Exhibitors Herald-World*, November 22, 1930, 19, 61.

Page 282. **a "freak talker":** "Inside Stuff—Pictures," *Variety*, December 10, 1930, 55; see also "Opinions on Publicity," *Variety*, November 12, 1930, 11, 28.

Page 282. **RKO decided:** "Amos 'n' Andy as Radio Stars Cold," *Hollywood Reporter*, June 11, 1932, 1.

Page 284. **rumor whispered:** "O'Neill's *Emperor Jones* on U.A. List," *Hollywood Reporter*, July 17, 1933, 8.

Page 285. **a press release:** Karl Krug, "Paul Robeson Endowed with Culture, Talents," *Pittsburgh Courier*, September 30, 1933, sec. 2: 6.

Page 285. **All business as usual:** "Inside Stuff—Motion Pictures," *Variety*, June 6, 1933, 21.

Page 285. **The color wheel:** *The Emperor Jones* press kit, New York Public Library for the Performing Arts, Lincoln Center, New York City.

Page 286. **actress Fredi Washington:** "*The Emperor Jones*," *American Film Institute Catalogue, Feature Films, 1931–1940* (Berkeley: University of California Press, 1993), 574.

Page 286. **No one pays:** The sequence showing the policeman enter the juke joint and fleeing has been cut from many surviving prints of *The Emperor Jones*.

Page 288. **at both theaters:** Vere E. Johns, "Harlem and Broadway Acclaim Robeson in Emperor Jones," *The New Age*, September 23, 1933, 6.

Page 288. the word was deleted: James Cunningham, "Asides and Interludes," *Motion Picture Herald*, October 28, 1933, 17.

Page 288. a generous official: Vincent G. Hart to John Krimsky, June 15, 1933 (*The Emperor Jones*, PCA file).

Page 288. a "storm of indignation: "Maligning the Negro," *Pittsburgh Courier*, October 7, 1933, sec. 1: 10. See also J. A. Rogers, "O'Neill's Masterpiece *The Emperor Jones* Flayed by J. A. Rogers as Portraying False Negro Type; Appeals to Nordic Prejudice," *Pittsburgh Courier*, September 30, 1933, sec. 2: 1.

Page 288. Chappy Gardner: "Harlem Raps 'Jones' But Pays to See Pix; Criticize Robeson," *Variety*, October 3, 1933, 11.

Page 289. "turnaway business": Ibid.

Page 289. one affronted exhibitor: "What This Picture Did for Me," *Motion Picture Herald*, April 24, 1934, 63.

Page 289. a single image: " 'King Kong' a Winner," *Hollywood Reporter*, February 15, 1933, 1, 6.

Page 293. a huge record: "More Than 8,000,000 Attended Radio City Houses in First Year," *Motion Picture Herald*, January 13, 1934, 27; James Cunningham, "Asides and Interludes," *Motion Picture Herald*, February 4, 1933, 33.

Page 293. distributors were bewildered: "Berlin Bans Kong," *Hollywood Reporter*, September 20, 1933, 5.

11. NIGHTMARE PICTURES

Page 295. Fitzgerald bolted: David J. Skal and Elias Savada, *Dark Carnival: The Secret World of Tod Browning* (New York: Anchor, 1995), 168.

Page 297. "Picture producers have discovered: "Inside Stuff—Pictures," *Variety*, November 17, 1931, 49.

Page 297. acidly described: "Kansas in Arms as *Frankenstein* Is Barred," *Motion Picture Herald*, December 19, 1931, 13.

Page 297. a weird winter: W. R. Wilkerson, "Tradeviews," *Hollywood Reporter*, December 19, 1931, 1.

Page 298. an exhibitor articulated: "What This Picture Did for Me," *Motion Picture Herald*, December 17, 1932, 49.

Page 298. "the people out our way: "What This Picture Did for Me," *Motion Picture Herald*, October 17, 1934, 49.

Page 300. "**Other studios are looking:** "U Has Horror Cycle All to Self," *Variety*, April 8, 1931, 2.

Page 300. "**the most startling:** "Inside Stuff—Pictures," *Variety*, September 15, 1931, 49.

Page 300. "**an excess of men**": "Frankenstein Loop Wow," "Frankenstein's $50,000 Will Establish New Mayfair Record," and "Inside Stuff—Motion Pictures," *Variety*, December 8, 1931, 9, 10, 48.

Page 305. **Director Mamoulian:** Tom Milne, *Mamoulian* (Bloomington: Indiana University Press, 1969), 39–50.

Page 307. "**A cynical audience:** "*Murders in the Rue Morgue*," *Variety*, February 16, 1932, 24.

Page 311. **the special designation:** "Inside Stuff—Pictures," *Variety*, April 11, 1933, 41.

Page 312. **remove any suggestion:** Jason Joy to B. P. Schulberg, June 3, 1932; Luigi Luraschi to Joseph Breen, March 15, 1941 (*Island of Lost Souls*, PCA file).

Page 312. "**grim and grotesque:** Richard Watts, Jr., "The Directorial Stylist— Has He Passed from the Picture?" *Motion Picture Herald*, March 28, 1931, 20.

Page 317. **a casting call:** "A Freak Call," *Hollywood Reporter*, September 21, 1931, 3.

Page 317. **MGM leaked word:** "Metro's Freaks 'Tougher Than Prima Donnas,'" *Variety*, November 24, 1931, 1, 19.

Page 317. "**The kids turned out:** "Real Circus Bally Put Freak Picture Over for W. Burns," *Motion Picture Herald*, August 13, 1932, 57.

Page 317. "**Ladies will not forgive:** "The Woman's Angle," *Variety*, July 12, 1932, 15.

Page 317. **In the state of Georgia:** 19. "*Freaks* Has Censor Trouble in Georgia," *Variety*, February 23, 1932, 5.

Page 318. **an unprepared public:** " 'Freaks' Giving Publix Headaches," *Hollywood Reporter*, February 23, 1932, 1, 4.

Page 318. "**Quiet word of mouth:** "*Freaks* a Disappointment in L.A.," *Variety*, February 23, 1932, 9.

12. CLASSICAL HOLLYWOOD CINEMA

Page 320. **a front-page article:** "Pres. Backs Censorship," *Hollywood Reporter*, December 6, 1933, 1, 6.

Page 320. **another scrap of paper.":** "Production Code Scrap of Paper Says Mundelein," *Motion Picture Herald,* June 9, 1934, 40.

Page 320. **In 1933 the Church:** Gerald B. Donelly, S.J., "The Bishops Rise Against Hollywood," *America,* May 26, 1934, 152, cited in Gregory D. Black, *Hollywood Censored: Morality Codes, Catholics, and the Movies* (New York: Cambridge University Press, 1995), 164. Announced in late 1933, the National Legion of Decency was formally established on April 11, 1934. See Black, *Hollywood Censored,* 149–97, and Frank Walsh, *Sin and Censorship: The Catholic Church and the Motion Picture Industry* (New Haven: Yale University Press, 1996), 95–142.

Page 321. **I make this protest:** A shorter version of the Legion pledge was adopted in November 1934:

> I condemn indecent and immoral pictures, and those which glorify crime or criminals.
>
> I promise to do all that I can to strengthen public opinion against the production of indecent and immoral films, and to unite with all who protest them.
>
> I acknowledge my obligation to form a right conscience about pictures that are dangerous to my moral life. As a member of the Legion of Decency, I pledge myself to remain away from them. I promise, further, to stay away altogether from places of amusement which show them as a matter of policy.

Both versions of the pledge are quoted in Paul W. Facey, *The Legion of Decency: A Sociological Analysis of the Emergence and Development of a Social Pressure Group* (1945; rpt., New York: Arno, 1974), 144–45.

Page 321. **a positive command:** "Cardinal Bans All Pix," *Hollywood Reporter,* June 9, 1934, 1; "Cardinal Dougherty's Broadside," *Variety,* June 12, 1934, 27.

Page 322. **a splendid start:** "Protestants Join Catholics in Wash. on Film Boycott," *Variety,* June 12, 1934, 4.

Page 322. **called for cooperation:** "Protestant Clergy Back Catholic War" and "Jewish Conference Joins War on Dirt," *Hollywood Reporter,* June 19, 1934, 1.

Page 322. **the disgrace will fall:** " 'Decency' Move Spreads," *Hollywood Reporter,* July 19, 1934, 1, 7.

Page 323. **the Payne Fund studies:** Henry James Forman, *Our Movie-Made Children* (New York: MacMillan, 1933), 195, 72–74, 189, 232. For a full account of the Payne Fund contretemps, see Garth S. Jowett, Ian C. Jarvie, and Kathryn H. Fuller, *Children and the Movies: Media Influence and the Payne Fund Studies* (Cambridge: Cambridge University Press, 1996).

Page 323. **"If they don't know:** "Make Pix Clean as Radio," *Variety*, December 5, 1933, 1, 63. Lowell ultimately refused to serve on the NRA Code Authority for the Motion Picture Industry because of his moral opposition to block booking. Moreover, Sol A. Rosenblatt, NRA division administrator for amusements, stated publicly that the New Deal sought no control over motion picture content. "The federal government in its NRA program is not interested in censorship," he told a gathering of industry officials in 1934. Yet with Congress debating various censorship bills and with the woman closest to FDR supporting the Motion Picture Research Council, neither Lowell's resignation nor Rosenblatt's rhetoric offered assurance that Washington regulators had not set their sights on Hollywood content. See, for example, "Pres. Backs Censorship," *Hollywood Reporter*, December 6, 1933, 1, 6, which noted: "Political observers here [in Washington] are amazed at the fact that film men will not take this threat seriously. It is no secret here: Administration intimates are outspoken. They will tell you that the first sign of obstreperousness on the part of the industry towards Dr. Lowell's attitude will see the Federal bill in Congress."

Page 323. **"a business pure and simple:** Quoted in Kevin Brownlow, *Behind the Mask of Innocence: Sex, Violence, Prejudice, Crime, Films of Social Conscience in the Silent Era* (Berkeley: University of California Press, 1990), 10.

Page 324. **a weary headline:** "Congress Has 11 Legislative Film Bills Including Usual Nut Stuff," *Variety*, February 16, 1932, 6.

Page 324. **a "drastic and far-reaching bill":** "Drastic House Bill Is Aimed at Immoral Pictures," *Film Daily*, June 14, 1934, 1, 7.

Page 324. **protested "hectic stories:** "Congressmen Denounce Films," *Variety*, June 19, 1934, 7.

Page 324. **"squawk absorber":** The phrase is from "Studios on the Remake," *Variety*, January 21, 1931, 26.

Page 325. **it will be curtains:** "What This Movie Did for Me," *Motion Picture Herald*, August 11, 1934, 45.

Page 325. **it's bad medicine:** " 'Smut' in Pictures," *Exhibitors Herald-World*, January 11, 1930, 58.

Page 325. **"Too 'hot':** "What This Picture Did for Me," *Motion Picture Herald*, April 22, 1933, 53.

Page 325. **the reigning expert:** "De Mille DeClares," *Motion Picture Herald*, August 4, 1934, 8.

Page 325. **"The cumulative effect:** Frank Pope, "Tradeviews," *Hollywood Reporter,* June 7, 1934, 1, 4; see also W. R. Wilkerson, "Tradeviews," *Hollywood Reporter,* May 26, 1934, 1, 4.

Page 325. **a flustered theater manager:** "Favors Radio Exploitation," *Motion Picture Herald,* September 22, 1934, 64.

Page 326. **A. P. Giannini:** "Clean Scripts or No Cash Says Gianinni," *Hollywood Reporter,* July 27, 1934, 3.

Page 326. **"Self regulation:** "Rosenblatt Against Federal Censorship," *Motion Picture Herald,* October 20, 1934, 12.

Page 328. **a riot in Moscow.":** "Hays Plagued by Religionists But Issues 'Don'ts' on Schedule," *Variety,* April 2, 1930, 2.

Page 328. **"I want you people:** "Joe Breen Makes Newsreel Debut," *Hollywood Reporter,* August 16, 1934, 8.

Page 328. **he warms to his point:** "Motion Picture Official Explains Code," Universal Newsreel, September 5, 1934.

Page 329. **a witty memoir:** Vizzard, *See No Evil: Life Inside a Hollywood Censor* (New York: Simon and Schuster, 1970), 75.

Page 330. **a defiant postscript:** Joseph Breen to Louis B. Mayer, November 27, 1934; Joseph Breen to Will H. Hays, December 1, 1934; Willard S. Van Dyke to Joseph Breen, December 6, 1934 (*Forsaking All Others*, PCA file).

Page 330. **Breen's successful intrusion:** Helen Gwynn, "Not That It Matters," *Hollywood Reporter,* December 6, 1934, 3.

Page 330. **Breen "will not weaken:** W. R. Wilkerson, "Tradeviews," *Hollywood Reporter,* December 6, 1934, 1.

Page 330. **"Meticulous Breening":** "Business Good All Over," *Hollywood Reporter,* September 10, 1934, 1, 2.

Page 330. **a sly headline:** "MGM 'Breens' Plant," *Hollywood Reporter,* October 4, 1934, 4.

Page 330. **another newsreel spot:** Universal Newsreel, September 19, 1934.

Page 331. **"re-edit the scene:** Joseph Breen to John Hammel, August 30, 1935 (*Bolero*, PCA file).

Page 332. **symbolic changes:** "Same Thing," *Variety,* July 17, 1934, 5.

Page 332. **Likewise, what was:** "Sanforth 'Breens' 'Virgin' to 'Butterfly,' " *Hollywood Reporter,* October 8, 1934, 4.

Page 332. **a sign was put up:** "Breen on Radio, Says Films Are Much Improved," *Motion Picture Herald,* September 8, 1934, 7.

Page 333. **the great classics:** "Historical Films Increasing: Hays," *Motion Picture Herald,* October 20, 1934, 39.

Page 333. **"Thanks to [Will Rogers']:** *Motion Picture Herald*, September 8, 1934, 14.

Page 333. **"the perfect entertainment:** "Shirley Temple a Sensation; 'Little Miss Marker' Cashes," *Hollywood Reporter*, May 29, 1934, 7.

Page 333. **strong simple stories.":** "1935 Product," *Motion Picture Herald*, December 15, 1934, 34.

Page 333. **B. B. Kahane warned:** "Kahane on Bat on Film Cleanup; Issues Ultimatum to His Producers," *Variety*, July 3, 1934, 5, 43; see also "Kahane Orders Radio Pictures Be Kept Clean," *Hollywood Reporter*, June 29, 1934, 4.

Page 334. **the keynote theme:** "Warner Bros. Promises Pictures for Family," *Hollywood Reporter*, June 18, 1934, 2.

Page 334. **"Paramount does not:** Frank Pope, "Tradeviews," *Hollywood Reporter*, May 17, 1934, 1.

Page 334. **said a spokesman:** "Indies Snub Mr. Breen," *Hollywood Reporter*, July 25, 1934, 1, 3.

Page 334. **the indies pledged:** "Indies Accept Hays Offer to Give Them Purity Seals," *Hollywood Reporter*, August 23, 1934, 3.

Page 334. **objected Fred Pasley:** "N.Y. Daily News Fights," *Hollywood Reporter*, August 10, 1934, 1, 3.

Page 334. **a rueful exhibitor:** "What This Movie Did For Me," *Motion Picture Herald*, December 8, 1934, 75.

Page 334. **A like-minded studio executive:** "Pure," *Variety*, July 24, 1934, 1.

Page 334. **some audiences hissed:** "Hisses," *Motion Picture Herald*, September 8, 1934, 7; "Audience Hisses New Purity Seal," *Hollywood Reporter*, August 7, 1934, 1.

Page 335. **lost income on films:** "Big Censorship Loss," *Hollywood Reporter*, April 3, 1931, 1, 3.

Page 335. **Worse, the rate:** "Hot and Cold Censoring," *Variety*, December 29, 1932, 7.

Page 335. **the studios calculated:** "Censorship at the Source," *Variety*, January 1, 1935, 37.

Page 335. **"Pictures based on great works:** Will Hays, "The Year Ahead," *The 1935 Film Daily Year Book of Motion Pictures*, 35.

Page 335. **A contemplated version:** "Breen Bans Twain's Pudd'nhead Wilson," *Hollywood Reporter*, August 20, 1934, 1.

Page 336. **Other studios were:** "Earnings Largest in Several Years Indicated by End of the Year," *Motion Picture Herald*, December 8, 1934, 15, 18.

Page 336. reduced a loss: Victor M. Shapiro, "The Hollywood Scene," *Motion Picture Herald*, December 22, 1934, 49.

Page 336. "I will never forget: H.V. Kaltenborn, *Fifty Fabulous Years, 1900–1950* (New York: Putnam, 1950), 171.

Page 337. "The Houdini of Hyde Park": Quoted in Edward Bliss, Jr., *Now the News: The Story of Broadcast Journalism* (New York: Columbia University Press, 1991), 55.

Page 337. "saved capitalism: New Dealer Raymond Moley, quoted in William E. Leuchtenburg, *Franklin D. Roosevelt and the New Deal, 1932–1940* (New York: Harper and Row, 1963), 45.

Page 337. "Roosevelt saved: Studs Terkel, *Hard Times: An Oral History of the Great Depression* (New York: Pantheon, 1970), 73.

Page 337. the unholy trinity: Mauritz A. Hallgren, *Seeds of Revolt: A Study of American Life and the Temper of the American People During the Depression* (New York: Knopf, 1933), 312.

Page 338. "We shall endeavor: Will Hays to Joseph Breen, May 15, 1934; Breen to Hays, May 18, 1934 (*Manhattan Melodrama*, PCA file).

Page 338. the possible antecedents: "Sin Is Kicker in West Title," *Variety*, June 19, 1934, 2.

Page 338. her name emblazoned: "Inside Stuff—Pictures," *Variety*, July 7, 1934, 43, 59.

Page 338. "Mae West is through: "What This Picture Did for Me," *Motion Picture Herald*, November 24, 1934, 48.

Page 339. Dillinger was shot: "Along the Rialto," *Film Daily*, July 28, 1934, 3.

Page 340. the official voice: Loren Miller, "Uncle Tom in Hollywood," *The Crisis* (November 1934): 329.

Page 341. a ringing statement: Frank Capra, *The Name Above the Title* (New York: MacMillan, 1971), 291.

Page 344. "A nasty little film": Dwight Macdonald, *On Movies* (New York: Da Capo, 1981), 51.

Abbott and Costello, 298
Academy ratio, 33
adultery, 13–14, 114
"adults only," 109–10, 184
Advertising Advisory Council
    (MPPDA), 332
Advertising Code, 107, 109 (photo), 110
advertising, 107–13, 153–54, 169–70,
    184, 185, 186, 317, 331–33
Africans and African-Americans, 161,
    167, 168, 241, 246; in comedies,
    177–78; in expeditionary films,
    236–41, 245–51; in newsreels, 175,
    340–41; in racial adventure films,
    253–56, 260, 262, 263, 264, 267,
    269, 274–89
Ager, Cecelia, 182
Ager, Milton, 26
Akron, 210
Algonquin Round Table, 172, 173
Alicoate, Jack, 149–50
Allen, Frederick Lewis, 21, 22
Allen, Robert Sharon, 64
American Cinema, The (Sarris), 121
American Film Institute's Top 100
    Movies, 376*n*
American Humor (Rourke), 173
American Indians, 223, 224, 225,
    231–32, 256, 262–67
American Legion, 70
American Movie Classics, 20

Amos 'n' Andy, 35, 37, 281–84, 288
Anderson, Eddie "Rochester," 178
Anderson, Maxwell, 64
androgyny, 123–25
Angly, Edward, 25
Anson, A. E., 278
antisemitism, 93–95, 96–97, 98, 322,
    340
archival documentaries, 204–208
Arlen, Richard, 308
Armstrong, Robert, 289
Arthur, Nils, 271, 273 (photo)
Asians and Asian-Americans, 223, 224,
    256, 267–74, 276
"As Time Goes By," 10
Astor, Mary, 14
attendance, motion picture, 18, 378*n*
Ayres, Lew, 146

Baclanova, Olga, 314
bad girl films, 104, 131–36
Baer, Max, 94
Bakewell, William, 23
Bali, 232–35
Barker gang, 140
Barrat, Robert, 87
Barrow, Clyde, 339
Barrymore, John, 36, 54, 55 (photo), 60
Barrymore, Lionel, 55 (photo)
Barthelmess, Richard, 51, 52 (photo),
    86, 119, 263, 265 (photo), 267, 268

Baum, Vicki, 94
Beery, Wallace, 160
Beetson, Frederick W., 260
Benchley, Robert, 173
Benedict, Ruth, 223
Bennett, Constance, 119, 128, 129, 131, 176, 177 (photo), 182
Bennett, Richard, 278, 280 (photo)
Benny, Jack, 37, 178
Bergen, Edgar, 281
Bergman, Ingrid, 3
Berkeley, Busby, 40, 131, 338
Berlin book burnings, 93, 99
Better Business Bureau, 235, 241
Better Films Committee, 106
Bickford, Charles, 66
Billboard, The, 215
Biograph Theater (Chicago), 139, 144, 339
Black, Gregory, 98, 387n
blackface, 281–84, 286
block booking, 238–39
Blondell, Joan, 11, 56, 118, 152, 176
Blue Eagle, 83, 92, 184, 194, 196, 266
Bogart, Humphrey, 145
Boles, John, 302
Bondi, Beulah, 12 (and photo)
Bonus Army, 41–43, 42 (photo), 63, 74
Boop, Betty, 64, 338
Boorstin, Daniel, 203
Booth, Edwina, 254 (photo)
Bordwell, David, 3, 4, 5
Borzage, Frank, 114
Bow, Clara, 104, 108, 263
Boyer, Charles, 134
Brabin, Charles, 269
breadlines, 28 (and photo)
Breen Office, 10, 331, 334, 339
Breen, Joseph I., 9–11, 13, 19, 20, 47, 98, 101–102, 125, 195, 210, 260–61, 311, 312, 327–31, 334, 335, 336, 337–38, 339, 342–43, 345, 387n
Brent, George, 135
Bridge, The (Crane), xii

Brisbane, Arthur, 77
Brooks, Clarence, 279, 280 (and photo)
Browning, Tod, 295, 297, 299, 308, 312, 317
Buck, Frank, 243–44, 290
Buck, Pearl S., 224
Buffalo Child Long Lance, Chief, 264
Burke, Kathleen, 309
Burns and Allen, 37
Burns, Robert E., 163, 166, 169, 170, 393n
Burroughs, Edgar Rice, 256, 269, 296,
businessmen, 58–60
Butterfield, Allyn, 209
Byrd, Rear Admiral Richard E., 227, 228, 229

Cabot, Bruce, 119
Cagney, James, 8, 54, 91, 146, 148, 150, 154 (photo), 169, 178, 180, 338, 339
Cahn, Edward L., 166
Cannon, Congressman Raymond, 324
Cantor, Eddie, 37
Capone, Al, 28, 74, 138 (photo), 139, 140–41, 145, 146, 148, 153, 157, 174, 339
Capra, Frank, 40, 61, 62, 188, 191–92, 270, 271, 341
Carew, Muriel, 304
Carewe, Edwin, 99
cartoons, 69
Carver, H. P., 225–31
Casey, Harry, 254
Catholics and Catholicism, 7, 8–9, 10, 100, 101, 320–22, 323, 325, 327, 336
Cavanagh, Paul, 259
censorship, 2, 5–15, 105–107, 139–40, 155–57, 210, 297, 320, 323–24, 325, 326 (photo), 327, 334–35, 343–44, 345; in newsreels, 213–20
Central Conference of American Rabbis, 322
Cermak, Anton, 158
chain gang films, 161–67

Child of the Century, A (Hecht), 188
Chaney, Lon, 312
Chaplin, Charles, 53–54, 97, 120, 128, 217
cheesecake, 110, 111 (photo)
Chicago Board of Censors, 106
Chicago Daily Journal, 188
Chicago Daily News, 151
Chicago Defender, 288
Chicago Tribune, 326
Chicago World's Fair, 263
Chinese, 66, 224, 225, 268–69, 270–74
Churchill, Berton, 51
Churchill, Winston, 223
CinemaScope, 33
Clarke, Mae, 130, 150, 302 (and photo)
Classical Hollywood Cinema, The (Bordwell, Staiger, and Thompson), 3–4
Clive, Colin, 301
Cochran, Gifford, 285, 288
Cody, Buffalo Bill, 263
Cohn, Harry, 64
Cohn, Jack, 76
Colbert, Claudette, 10, 56, 122, 191
Colman, Ronald, 120, 278, 280 (photo)
Columbia Pictures, 4, 64, 76, 240, 270
Coming of Age in Samoa (Mead), 223
commentative music, 198–99
communists and communism, 48–49, 70, 87, 88, 140, 151, 178, 214, 337
Congo pictures, 236, 237, 240
Conley, Onest, 278
Connolly, Walter, 272, 273 (photo)
Conrad, Joseph, 221
Conway, Jack, 118, 132
Coolidge, Calvin, 172
Coonan, Dorothy, 90, 91 (photo)
Cooper, Anita, 12 (photo)
Cooper, Jackie, 247
Cooper, James Fenimore, 245, 262
Cooper, Merian C., 223, 232, 289, 290, 292
Cormack, Bartlett, 141

Correll, Charles J., 281–84, 283 (photo)
Coughlin, Father Charles E., 84–85
Coward, Noel, 172
Crane, Hart, xii
Crawford, Joan, 23 (and photo), 54, 55 (photo), 60, 120, 182, 329, 330
Criminal Code (Falvin), 158
Crisis, The, 275, 340
Cromwell, John, 119
Cromwell, Richard, 66
Crosby, Bing, 6, 37
Crosland, Alan, 263
Culkin, Congressman Francis D., 324
Cummings, Constance, 41 (photo)
Cunningham, Cecil, 121
Curley, James Michael, 79
Curry, Nathan, 260
Curtiz, Michael, 50, 51, 55, 161

Dall, Anna Roosevelt, 83
Daniels, Bebe, 178
Darro, Frankie, 89, 91 (photo), 92
Darrow, Clarence, 8, 151
Davis, Bette, 51, 119
Davis, James J., 25
Day of the Locust, The (West), 26
de Cordoba, Pedro, 207, 208
Dead End Kids, 340 (photo)
Del Rio, Dolores, 119
Del Ruth, Roy, 55–56, 71, 155
DeMille, Cecil B., 26, 32, 65, 67, 114, 120, 122, 123, 141, 278, 312, 325
deNagy, Kathe, 93
Denny, Reginald, 114
Deutsches Theater (Berlin), 93
DeVoe, Daisy, 104
Diamond Lil (West), 183
Dickason, Deane H., 234–35
dictator craze, 70–77
diegesis, 10
diegetic ellipsis, 12–15
Dietrich, Marlene, 48, 56, 123–25, 124 (photo), 129, 182, 255, 315

Digges, Dudley, 168, 287
Dillinger, John, 137–39, 140, 141–46, 143 (photo), 145 (photo), 212, 217, 218, 339
Dionne Quintuplets, 220
Disney, Walt, 69, 232
Dix, Richard, 162 (photo), 163
doctors, 61
Dougherty, Cardinal Denis, 113, 321, 322, 332
Dreiser, Theodore, 201
Drinkwater, John, 7
Dumont, Margaret, 194
Dunne, Irene, 119, 129
Durante, Jimmy, 267
Dvorak, Ann, 149 (and photo), 264
Dymov, Ossip, 97

Earles, Daisy, 314
Earles, Harry, 314
Early, Stephen T., 79
Eastman Kodak, 33
"Echoes of the Jazz Age" (Fitzgerald), 22
Eck, Johnny, 315
Edison, Thomas, 4, 5, 203
Einstein, Albert, 202
Eisenhower, Maj. Dwight D., 42
Eisenstein, Sergei, 98, 207
Eldridge, Florence, 116 (and photo)
Eliot, T. S., 224
Ellington, Duke, 282
Elliot, Clyde, 244
Elmer Gantry (Lewis), 61
Embassy Newsreel Theater (New York), 200, 202, 212, 216
Emperor Jones, The (O'Neill), 284–85
Eskimos, 229–30, 244
Estill, Robert, 143 (and photo)
evangelists, 61–62
Evans, Madge, 168
Evans, Walker, 89
exculpatory preface, 50, 154–55, 162

exhibitors, 30–31, 35, 153, 170, 216, 218, 324–25
expeditionary films, 204, 222–51, 296

Fairbanks, Douglas, 241–43, 247 (photo)
Fairbanks, Douglas, Jr., 57, 146
fallen women films, 104, 113, 123, 128–30, 131
Fallon, William Joseph, 60
Falvin, Martin, 158
Fanck, Dr. Arnold, 230
Farewell to Arms, A (Hemingway), 114
Farley, James, 80 (photo), 81
Farm Security Administration, 89
Farnum, William, 99
Farrell, Charles, 202
fascism, 76–77, 337
Faulkner, William, 114
FBI (Federal Bureau of Investigation), 137, 142, 144, 145, 339
Federal Communications Act, 18
Federal Trade Commission, 240
Fein, Sammy, 84
Fenton, Leslie, 269
Fields, W. C., 37
5th Avenue Playhouse (New York), 216
figurative literalness, 118–20
Film Daily Year Book, The, 28
Film Daily, 32, 100, 149, 369
Film Forum, 214
Fish, Hamilton, 216–17
Fitts, Buron, 140
Fitzgerald, F. Scott, 21–22, 148, 172, 295
Flaherty, Robert, 48, 229, 232
Fleischer, Max, 64
Fleming, Victor, 14, 55 (photo), 242, 243
Ford, John, 3, 120, 224, 278, 279, 280
Ford, Wallace, 314
Forman, Henry James, 322
Fowler, Gene, 60, 172

Fox Movietone News, 78, 81, 141, 198, 199, 200, 201, 202, 209, 215
Fox Film Corp., 4, 71, 84, 104, 108, 141, 260, 336, 333
Fox, Sidney, 306, 307 (photo)
Franklin, Harold B., 27–28, 29
French, Daniel Chester, 74
Freud, Sigmund, 296
Friedman, Milton, 24
Frye, Dwight, 301
Futter, Walter, 239

Gable, Clark, 14, 15 (and photo), 48, 54, 61, 129, 158, 188, 191, 216, 276, 329, 330, 338
gangsters and gangster films, 137–57, 217–18, 338–39
Garbo, Greta, 48, 54, 123, 124, 128–29, 182
Gardner, Chappy, 288
Gargan, William, 115
Garner, John Nance, 199, 216
Garnett, Tay, 230
Gaynor, Janet, 202
Gemora, Charles, 238
General Federation of Women's Clubs, 106, 125
Gentlemen Prefer Blondes (Loos), 132
German Expressionism, 299
Germans, 98
Germany in Flames (Dymov), 97
Ghandi, Mahatma, 201–202, 208
Giannini, A. P., 326
Gilbert, John, 338
Gish, Lillian, 268, 284
Goebbels, Joseph, 93, 95, 293
Goldstein, Rabbi Sidney E., 322
Goldwyn, Sam, 2, 46, 49, 52, 327
Good Earth, The (Buck), 224
Gosden, Freeman F., 281–84, 283 (photo)
gore, 292–93
Grant, Cary, 3, 184

Great Depression, 15, 16–17, 18, 19, 20, 21–27, 40, 43, 44–45, 47, 52, 53, 56, 59, 70, 73, 74, 75, 81, 82, 84, 85, 91, 123, 131, 139, 140, 151, 158, 161, 166, 168, 173, 192, 193, 208, 212, 213–17, 220, 224, 225, 242, 243, 264, 274, 285, 290, 296, 298, 308, 318, 320, 336, 337, 341, 343, 399n; economic impact on Hollywood, 27–31, 37
Great Gatsby, The (Fitzgerald), 148
Great Mouthpiece, The (Fowler), 60
Green, Harry, 66
Griffith, D. W., 4, 108, 268, 284
Gruening, Ernest, 27
gruesomeness, 170, 297, 300
"Guy What Takes His Time, A" 184

Hamilton, Neil, 257
"Happy Days Are Here Again," 26–27
Harding, Warren G., 6, 73
Harlow, Jean, 14, 15 (and photo), 111 (illustration), 118, 132–34, 133 (photo), 176, 178, 181, 182, 183, 192, 276, 332, 338
Harris, Theresa, 135, 276, 277 (photo)
Hawks, Howard, 153, 188
Hayakawa, Sesue, 268
Hayes, Helen, 130, 268, 278
Hays Code. *See* Production Code
Hays Office, 1, 10, 45, 47, 75, 101, 108, 114, 115, 121, 140, 181, 183, 214, 238, 240, 297, 332, 342
Hays, Will H., 6, 9 (and photo), 29, 45, 46, 79, 101, 111–12, 125, 137, 150, 156, 181, 183, 237, 238, 239, 261, 297, 325, 327, 330, 333, 335, 337–38
Hearst Metrotone News, 142, 198, 199, 200, 210
Hearst, William Randolph, 73, 74, 75, 342
Heart of Darkness (Conrad), 221, 251

Hecht, Ben, 130, 146, 148, 172, 187, 188–89
Hemingway, Ernest, 114
Hepburn, Katharine, 128
Hersholt, Jean, 270
Heyward, DuBose, 285
Hill, Edwin C., 99
Hilton, Daisy and Violet, 315
Hirohito, 208
Hitchcock, Alfred, 3, 343, 344 (photo)
Hitler, Adolf, 93, 97, 99, 100, 208, 217, 337
Hoeffler, Paul L., 239
Holley, Lillian, 143
"Hollow Men, The" (Eliot), 224
Hollywood Reporter, 8, 29, 30, 62, 67, 106, 127, 155, 227, 262, 297, 320, 325, 330
Hollywood's Movie Commandments (Martin), 347
Holmes, Burt, 242
homosexuality, 7, 120–25, 146–47, 309
Hoover, Herbert, 19, 24–26, 27, 41, 42, 47, 52, 54, 70,71, 73, 78 (and photo), 79, 81, 82, 85, 199, 212, 215, 216
Hoover, J. Edgar, 137, 144, 145, 218
Hope, Bob, 37
Hopkins, Miriam, 115, 116 (photo), 304 (and photo)
Horner, Dr. Harlan T., 8
horror films, 295–318
House Committee on Un-American Activities, 65
Howard, William K., 71
Howell, Miriam, 77
Hubbard, Wyant D., 246
Hudson, Grant, 125
Hughes, Howard, 108, 150, 153
hunger, 56–58, 224, 225
Hurst, Fannie, 100
Huston, Walter, 41 (photo), 73, 75 (photo), 77
Hyams, Leila, 132, 315

Hyman, Bernard, 260

"I'm Against It," 194
Independent Motion Picture Producers Association, 334
independents, 239
Inuits, 223. See also Eskimos
Irish and Irish-Americans, 66, 117, 140, 146, 179, 339
Irish Catholicism, 6, 327
Italians and Italian-Americans, 66, 140, 146, 177
"I Wonder Where My Easy Rider's Gone," 184

Jacko, Firpo, 241
Jaffe, Sam, 101
Jameyson, H. E., 203
Japanese, 242
Jazz Age, 21–23, 48
Jazz Age prelude, 50, 89, 151
Jenkins, Henry, 193
Jews and Jewish Americans, 66, 93, 94, 95, 96–98, 101–102, 140, 146, 177, 178, 179, 190, 217, 276, 322, 340
Jim Crow, 276–77, 285, 287, 288, 289
"Jim Crow roosts," 274–75
Johns, Vere E., 167, 275, 280
Johnson, Martin, 175, 225, 240, 246–51, 248 (photo)
Johnson, Osa, 225, 240, 246–51, 247 (photo), 248 (photo)
Johnston, Eric, 342
Jolson, Al, 37
Jordan, Dorothy, 51
Joy, Col. Jason S., 8, 311, 329, 375n
Joyzelle, 122 (and photo)
juvenile, 168–70

Kael, Pauline, 172
Kahal, Irving, 84
Kahane, B. B., 260, 261, 333
Kaltenborn, H.V., 337
Kane, Sherwin A., 179

Kansas City Star, 297
Karloff, Boris, 211, 269, 271 (photo), 301 (and photo)
Katz, Samuel, 27, 29
Kaufman, Wolf, 93
Keeler, Ruby, 56
Keller, Harry, 97
Kelly, Machine Gun, 339
Kenton, Erle C., 308
Kibbee, Guy, 63, 118
Klingenberg, Heinz, 95 (photo), 96
Koster and Bial Theater (New York), 9
Krimsky, John, 285, 288
Kroll, Harry Harrison, 50
Kruega, Ivar, 58

La Cava, Gregory, 73
Laemmle, Carl, 29, 30, 34, 179, 230, 301
Laemmle, Carl, Jr., 260
LaGuardia, Fiorello, 100, 216
Landi, Elissa, 122 (and photo), 123
Lang, Fritz, 94, 139
Lange, Dorothea, 89
LaRue, Jack, 115, 116 (photo)
Lasky, Jesse L., 30, 98
Last Mile, The (Wexley), 158
"Last Roundup, The" 144
Laughton, Charles, 309, 311
Laurel and Hardy, 192
Lawes, Lewis E., 161
Lawrenceson, Harry, 208–209
Lawson, John Howard, 151
lawyers, 58, 60–61
Leatherstocking Tales (Cooper), 262
Legion of Decency, 320–21, 327, 334, 338, 343
Legion of Decency pledge, 321, 407*n*
Leigh, Janet, 343, 344 (photo)
Lenin, Vladimir, 207
LeRoy, Mervyn, 55, 146, 163, 164, 166, 189, 190
lesbians, 121–23
Lewis, Chuck, 242
Lewis, Meriwether, 249

Lewis, Sinclair, 61, 119, 278, 280
Lincoln, Abraham, 74, 84, 341
Lindbergh baby, 209, 218–20, 219 (photo)
Lindbergh, Anne Morrow, 218
Lindbergh, Charles, 202, 209, 218–20
Lippman, Walter, 40–41, 47, 70
Lipton, Sir Thomas, 202
Lloyd, Harold, 36, 178
Longworth, Alice Roosevelt, 172
Loos, Anita, 132
Lord, Father Daniel, S.J., 6, 7, 8, 297, 320
Lord, Robert, 86
Lowell, Dr. A. Lawrence, 323, 408*n*
Loy, Myrna, 120, 132, 270, 271 (photo)
Lubitsch, Ernst, 34, 94
Lugosi, Bela, 299, 306, 309
Luke, Keye, 268
Lyon, Ben, 61

MacArthur, Charles, 130, 172, 188
MacArthur, Maj. Gen. Douglas, 42
Macdonald, Dwight, 344, 345
Mackenzie, Byron P., 240
MacMahon, Aline, 60, 87, 190
Macy, Dora, 61
Madman (Keller), 97
Mamba's Daughters (Heyward), 285
Mamoulian, Rouben, 34, 94, 304, 305
Mankiewicz, Herman J., 100, 101, 172
Mannix, Eddie, 260, 329
March, Fredric, 122 (and photo), 304 (and photo), 305
marriage, 113–14, 329–30
Marsh, Marian, 26
Martin, Olga J., 47, 347, 365
Marx Brothers, 37, 44, 179, 192–96
Marx, Chico, 193, 195, 196
Marx, Groucho, 31, 171, 175, 179, 181, 193, 194, 195, 196
Marx, Harpo, 44, 192, 193, 195
Marx, Zeppo, 193, 195
Maugham, Somerset, 148

Mayer, Louis B., 54, 79, 260, 327, 329
Mayfair Theater (New York), 307
Mayo, Archie, 55, 168
McAdoo, Sen. William, 80 (photo)
McCarey, Leo, 11, 12, 13
McCarthy, Charlie, 37
McCrea, Joel, 119, 132
McIntyre, Col. Marvin Hunter, 79
McKim, Josephine, xi, 260
McLuhan, Marshall, 35
McNamee, Graham, 36, 43, 174, 198,
   219, 400–401n
McPherson, Aimee Semple, 61, 62, 215
Mead, Margaret, 223
Medbury, John, 175
Mencken, H. L., 82, 394n
Merkel, Una, 118
Merriam, Charlotte, 62 (photo)
Meyer, Fred S., 401n
MGM (Metro-Goldwyn-Mayer
   Corp.), 4, 31, 33, 49, 54, 55–56, 84,
   134, 193, 260–61, 295, 317, 329, 330,
   336, 342
Micheaux, Oscar, 274
Milestone, Lewis, 32, 34, 188
Milliken, Carl, 44, 120
Million and One Nights, A (Ramsaye),
   211
Mindlin, Michael, 99
miscegenation, 7, 254–55, 289
Mizner, Wilson, 86
Montgomery, Robert, 54, 160, 329, 330
Moore, Victor, 11
moral universe of classical Hollywood
   cinema, 5–6, 10–11, 342–45
Moran and Mack, 281
Morley, Karen, 270
Morris, Chester, 132, 133 (photo), 160
Morris, Ruth, 126–27
Motion Picture Association of
   America (MPAA), 342, 345
Motion Picture Herald, 35, 36, 82, 107,
   110, 126, 167, 170, 174, 209, 211,
   217, 275, 336, 371

Motion Picture Producers and
   Distributors of America. See
   MPPDA
Motion Picture Research Council, 8,
   320, 322–23, 325
MPPDA, 2, 6, 8, 9, 49, 106, 137, 156,
   237, 238, 239, 240, 261, 325, 327,
   329, 332, 337
Mundelein, George Cardinal, 320
Muni, Paul, 57, 146, 149 (photo), 164,
   165 (photo)
Munson, Ona, 190
Muray, Doleres, 110
Murnau, F. W., 232, 299
Murphey, Dudley, 285
Muse, Clarence, 263, 280
Musser, Charles, 375n
Mussolini, Benito, 76–77, 201, 202,
   208, 217, 337
Mutual Film Corp. v. Industrial
   Commission of Ohio, 323

Nagel, Conrad, 328
Nation, The, 47
National Association for the Advance-
   ment of Colored People, 340
National Geographic, 225
National Recovery Act (NRA), 83,
   323
Nazism, 76, 93–102, 205, 231, 285, 293
Nelson, Baby Face, 140, 217, 218, 339
New Age, 167, 175, 275, 280, 288
New Deal, 8, 53, 54, 83–84, 85, 162,
   174, 266, 267, 320, 323, 324, 337; in
   preachment yarns, 85–92
New Masses, 48, 140, 337
New York American, 77
New York Censor Board, 180
New York Daily News, 334
New York Herald Tribune, 25, 267, 312
New York Mirror, 184, 267
New York News, 114, 208
New York Post, 151
New York Times, 206

New York World Telegram, 40
New Yorker, The, 172
newspaper films, 187–92
newsreel theaters, 200
newsreels, 77–85, 93, 141, 197–220,
  328, 330, 338, 339, 340, 397*n*, 399*n*
Nori, Toshia, 272
nudity, 118–19, 225, 233–35, 260–62

O'Banion, Dion, 140, 148
O'Brien, Pat, 6, 167, 339, 340 (photo)
O'Brien, Willis, 292
O'Connell, Jack, 374*n*
O'Neill, Eugene, 128
Oh Yeah? (Angly), 25
Oland, Warner, 268
"Old Man River," 285
Olsen and Johnson, 192
Only Yesterday (Allen), 22
Oomoolu, Mutia, 254 (photo)
O'Sullivan, Maureen, xi, 59, 109
  (photo), 119, 257, 258 (photo), 261,
  262, 333, 338
Othello, 284
Our Movie-Made Children (Forman),
  322
Owsley, Monroe, 105

Palace Theater (New York), 77
Pangborn, Franklin, 121
"Paramount Hour," 35
Paramount Publix Corporation, 27,
  29, 318
Paramount Sound News, 79, 199, 200,
  213, 215, 218, 227
Paramount Theater (New York), 19
Paramount Pictures, 4, 29, 30, 33, 35,
  67, 84, 114, 124, 125, 141, 182, 183,
  193, 312, 338, 334, 336
Pare, Lorentz, 89
Parker, Bonnie, 140, 339
Pasley, Fred D., 151, 334
Pathé News, 79, 80, 81, 121, 138, 141,
  175, 198, 200, 214, 220, 328

Patterns of Culture (Benedict), 223
Payne Fund, 322, 323
"Peanut Vendor, The," 36
Pearson, Drew, 64
Pease, Maj. Frank, 98
Peder, Charles, 78
Pettijohn, C. C., 45–46
Phillips, Edwin, 89, 91 (photo)
Photoplay, 181
Pickford, Mary, 114, 202
Pittsburgh Courier, 288
Poe, Edgar Allan, 305, 306, 312
Poland, O. S., 216
politicians, 63–64, 73–77
Ponting, Herbert, 227–28, 228–29
Popular Front, 337
Porgy and Bess (Heyward), 285
Porter, Edwin S., 5, 375*n*
Potamkin, Harry Alan, 48
Powell, Dick, 84
Powell, William, 60
pre-Code Hollywood, defined, xii,
  2–3, 15–20
preachment yarns, 49–50, 52–53
Presley, Elvis, 185
prison films, 157–70, 339
Producers Appeal Board, 9, 325, 327
Production Code Administration, 1, 9,
  19, 47, 113, 156, 186, 260, 312, 325–
  26, 327, 329, 330, 331, 336, 339
Production Code, 5–11, 13–14, 19, 47,
  91, 106, 107, 110, 117, 173, 195, 210,
  239, 261, 273, 276, 293, 297, 320,
  323, 327–29, 331–42, 342–45; text
  of, 347–67
Production Code seal, 329, 334, 342
profanity, 7
Prohibition, 6, 48, 49, 212, 214, 216,
  375*n*
Promethean cameraman, 226, 227
  (photo)
Protestants, 100, 332
pseudo-events, 203–204
Pudd'nhead Wilson (Twain), 335

Quigley, Martin, 6, 7, 107, 108, 174, 297, 401*n*
Quirk, James, 181

"race houses," 274–75
racial adventure films, 253–93, 295, 296
Radio City Music Hall (New York), 69, 293
radio, 16, 17–18, 34–37, 74, 77, 85, 174, 199, 220, 281, 282, 284, 328, 380*n*
Raft, George, 114, 141, 149
Rain (Maugham), 148
Ramsaye, Terry, 82, 175, 181, 211–12, 213, 217, 244, 245
Randian, 315, 318
Read, Barbara, 12
Reade, Leslie, 97
Reed, Tom, 166
Reichsfilmkammer, 93, 94, 97
Riefenstahl, Leni, 257
Reinhardt, Max, 93
"Remember My Forgotten Man," 298
Renaldo, Duncan, 254 (photo)
Rin Tin Tin, 199
Rivoli Theater (New York), 288
RKO Radio Pictures, 9, 29, 35, 84, 141, 260, 281, 282, 292
RKO Roxy (New York), 293
"Road Is Open Again, The" (Fein and Kahal), 84
Robeson, Paul, 284–89, 287 (photo)
Robinson, Edward G., 146, 147 (photo), 189 (and photo), 268
Rockefeller, John D., 201, 202
Rogers, Will, 25, 41, 80 (photo), 144, 216, 263, 333, 337
Rohmer, Sax, 269, 296
Roosevelt Theater (New York), 288
Roosevelt, André, 233
Roosevelt, Eleanor, 81, 266
Roosevelt, Franklin Delano, 24, 27, 40, 47, 52, 53, 71, 72, 75, 76, 77–85, 80 (photo), 93, 158, 173, 191, 195, 196, 199, 204, 208, 216, 293, 320, 323, 332 (photo), 336–37, 341, 342
Roosevelt, James, 80
Roosevelt, Sarah Delano, 323
Rosen, Al, 101
Rosen, Phil, 328
Rosenblatt, Sol A., 326, 408*n*
Roth, Lillian, 122
Rotter, Alfred, 93
Rourke, Constance, 173
Ruben, J. Walter, 151
Rucker, Joseph, 227
Rule, A. J., 205, 206
Russell, Jane, 342
Russell, Mildred Lewis, 106

Sale, Chic, 152
Sanctuary (Faulkner), 114
Sanger, Margaret, 203
Sarnoff, David, 203
Sarris, Andrew, 121
Schaeffer, Gus, 94
Schenk, Nicholas, 31
Schmelling, Max, 94
Schoedsack, Ernest B., 232, 223, 289, 290, 292
Schulberg, B. P., 33, 311, 312
Schwartz, Anne Jacobson, 24
Scott, Ewing, 229
Scott, Capt. Robert, 228–29
Scottsboro Boys, 46–47, 167, 255
Seabury, Samuel, 100
See No Evil (Vizzard), 329
Seldes, Gilbert, 25, 26, 47, 204
self-censorship, 326–27, 334
self-regulation. *See* self-censorship
Sex (West), 182, 186
sex films, 103, 297. *See also* vice films
Sharp, Henry, 242
Shattered Lamp, The (Reade), 97
Shaw, George Bernard, 19, 201
Shearer, Norma, 54
Sheehan, Winfield, 202, 260, 333
Shelley, Mary, 296, 299, 301

Sherman, Lowell, 101
Sherwood, Robert E., 130
Showboat, 285
Shurlock, Geoffrey, 260
silent cinema, 5, 31–32, 172
Sinclair, Upton, 49
Smith, Al, 82
Smith, C. Aubrey, 229, 257
Smith, Courtland, 214
Smith, Kate, 37
social problem films, 52–53, 340
sound and sound cinema, 5, 16, 17,
    29–30, 31–34, 37, 47, 121, 172, 175,
    197, 198, 200–203, 222, 227, 246,
    247–48, 276, 268, 281, 292, 298
Soviet Union, 48, 50, 65, 70, 192, 205
spectatorship, 18–19
Spitzer, Nat H., 237, 238, 240
Spivak, Murray, 292
St. Valentine's Day Massacre, 148
Stahl, John, 127
Staiger, Janet, 3, 4, 5
Stalin, Joseph, 70
Stallings, Laurence, 206
Standing, Sir Guy, 115
Stanwyck, Barbara, 61, 62 (photo),
    111 (photo), 118, 122, 134–36, 135
    (photo), 183, 271, 273 (photo), 277
Starr, Francis, 190
Starrett, Charles, 270, 271 (photo)
Steinbeck, John, 3
Stephenson, Henry, 134
Stepin Fetchit, 178, 278
Stevenson, Robert Louis, 296, 303
stock market crash, 48
Stoker, Bram, 296, 299
Stone, George E., 147 (and photo), 190
Stone, Lewis, 55 (photo), 270, 271
    (photo)
Strand Theater (New York), 155
Stuart, Gloria, 167
Studio Relations Committee, 8, 9,
    66–67, 150, 210, 260, 261, 272–73,
    288, 311, 325, 327, 375*n*

Sturges, Preston, 71
Sumner, John S., 151
Sunday, Billy, 61

taglines, 108–109
Talbot, Lyle, 131
Talking Picture Epics, 240
"talking reporters," 174, 198
Talley, Truman, 206
Teasdale, Verree, 59
television, 18, 20
Temple, Shirley, 299, 332 (photo), 333,
    335
Terkel, Studs, 24
Thalberg, Irving, 33, 260, 261
Theater Guild, 46, 48
"Theater of the Air," 35
Thomas, Lowell, 76, 218
Thompson, Kristen, 3, 4, 5
Thou Shalt Not Die (Wexley), 46
Tibbet, Lawrence, 37
Time, 139
Title Registration Bureau, 107
titles, 107–108
Toomey, Regis, 131
Tracy, Lee, 63
Tracy, Spencer, 6, 27, 71, 161
Trans-Lux (New York), 200, 212
travelogues, 204, 222
Trotsky, Leon, 201
Turner Classic Movies, 20
Tuskegee experiments, 281
Twain, Mark, 335
Twelvetrees, Helen, 105
Twombly, Rev. Clifford Gray, 110
Tynan, Kenneth, 128

Ufa, 93, 94
unit production, 32–33
United Artists, 285
Universal Newspaper Newsreel, 43,
    142, 174, 197, 200, 203, 209, 210–
    11, 214, 217, 219
Universal Pictures, 30, 260, 300

Vallee, Rudy, 24

Van der Veer, Willard, 227

Van Dyke, W. S., 230, 295, 330

Van Sloan, Edward, 302

Vanderbilt, Cornelius, Jr., 99, 100

Variety, 8, 9, 19, 30, 44, 49, 79, 80, 93, 94, 95, 104, 106, 110, 111, 120, 121, 126, 142, 155, 156, 178, 183, 200, 201, 202, 209, 210, 212, 214, 215, 217, 235, 238, 239, 255, 274, 282, 285, 297, 300, 307, 317, 324, 328

vice films, 103–36

Victor, Henry, 314

violence, 217–18, 149–51, 245, 343–44

Vizzard, Jack, 47–48, 329, 375*n*, 387*n*

voice-over narration, 174–75, 227

von Sternberg, Josef, 48, 123, 146, 315

voodoo chiaroscuro, 279

Wallace, Richard, 179

Waller, Tom, 202, 210–11, 215, 217

Walsh, Frank, 387*n*

Walsh, Raoul, 145

Wanger, Walter, 73

Warner, Harry M., 83

Warner, Jack, 55, 54, 79, 161, 187, 327, 334

Warner Bros. Pictures, 4, 35, 49, 50, 52, 54–57, 79, 84, 85, 89, 104, 134, 141, 161, 168, 169, 170, 266, 300, 336

Warner Brothers social consciousness, 43

Warshaw, Robert, 139, 147

Washington Federation of Churches, 322

Washington Merry-Go-Round (Allen and Pearson), 64

Washington, "Blue," 275

Washington, Fredi, 286

Washington, George Lincoln, 256

Watts, Richard, 312

Wayne, John, 275

Wegener, Paul, 299

Weinberg, Sidney J., 337

Weismuller, Johnny, xi, 109 (photo), 119, 257, 258 (photo), 261, 262

Weiss, Hymie, 140

Wellman, William, 55, 61, 85, 86, 89, 147, 152, 154 (photo)

Wells, H. G., 201, 296, 308

"We're Going to War," 194

West, Mae, 8, 110, 123, 125, 171, 172, 179, 181, 182–87, 185 (photo), 193, 277, 321, 334, 338

West, Nathanael, 26

Westcott, Gordon, 86

Wexley, John, 46, 158

Whale, James, 130, 301, 302

Wheeler and Woolsey, 167, 192

"Who's Afraid of the Big Bad Wolf," 69–70

Wilde, Oscar, 172

Wilder, Billy, 171

Wilkerson, W. R., 330

William, Warren, 59, 60, 63, 71 (and photo)

Williams, Robert, 191

Wilson, Carey, 73

Wilson, Dr. Clarence True, 216

Wilson, Edmund, 27

Wilson, John V., 273

Wilson, Woodrow, 79

Winchell, Walter, 97

Wingate, Dr. James, 8, 67, 150, 180, 261, 327, 329

Winters, Mrs. Thomas G., 106

Winthrop, John, 16

Wise, Rabbi Stephen S., 100

Wise, Ray, 244

wisecracks, 85, 171–96, 394*n*

Withington, Paul, 255

women's melodramas, 128–30

women, 113, 125–28, 150, 176, 300

Wong, Anna Mae, 244, 268

Wong, Lulu, 244

Wood, Gen. Robert E., 24

Woodcock, Col. Amos Walter Wright,
216
Workers Film and Photo League, 48
World War I, 65, 85, 86, 129–30, 194,
195, 205–208, 223–24, 256
World War II, 16, 23, 24, 40, 81, 94, 97
Wray, Fay, 56, 289, 290, 291 (photo),
292
Wynn, Ed, 37

Yellin, Jack, 26

Yellow Cloud, Chief, 232
Yiddish, 180
Yorkville Theater (New York), 96
Young, Loretta, 54, 72, 87, 131, 192,
268
Young, Robert, 105

Zangara, Guiseppi, 158
Zanuck, Darryl, 134
Zip and Pip, 315
Zukor, Adolph, 28–29, 334

Abraham Lincoln (1930), 58, 108, 298

Adventures in Africa (1931), 246

Africa Speaks (1930), 239–40, 242, 255

Alexander Hamilton (1931), 58

Alice Adams (1935), 335

All Quiet on the Western Front (1930), 34, 188, 375*n*

American Madness (1932), 40, 41 (photo), 49

Angels with Dirty Faces (1937), 339, 340 (photo)

Animal Crackers (1930), 193

Ann Vickers (1933), 119, 129

Anna Christie (1930), 128

Applause (1929), 34

Are We Civilized? (1934), 99

Around the World (1931), 225

Around the World with Douglas Fairbanks (aka *Around the World in Eighty Minutes*) (1931), 224, 224–25, 241–43, 247 (photo)

Arrowsmith (1931), 36, 61, 120, 278–81, 280 (photo)

Baby Face (1933), 3, 101, 108–10, 132, 134–36, 135 (photo), 183, 277 (and photo)

Back Street (1932), 127

Bad One, The (1930), 170

Battle of Gallipoli, The (1931), 127

Beauty and the Boss (1932), 56

Beauty for Sale (1933), 132

Becky Sharp (1935), 335

Bed of Roses (1933), 132

Belle of the Nineties, The (1934), 334, 338

Ben-Hur (1926), 35

Best Years of Our Lives (1946), 53

Betty Boop for President (1932), 64

Big City Blues (1932), 56

Big Drive, The (1933), 205–206, 206 (photo)

Big House, The (1930), 158, 159 (photo), 160–61, 169, 170

Bird of Paradise (1932), 119, 261

Birth of a Nation, The (1915), 4, 276, 284, 288, 375*n*

Bitter Tea of General Yen, The (1933), 2, 270–74, 273 (photo)

Black Moon (1934), 275, 298

Blessed Event (1932), 56

Blonde Captive, The (1932), 254–55

Blonde Crazy (1931), 56

Blonde Venus (1932), 2, 56, 57 (photo), 123, 129, 255

Blondie Johnson (1933), 152–53

Blue Angel, The (1930), 123, 315

Bolero (1934), 331

Born to Love (1931), 129

Bright Eyes (1934), 333

Bring 'Em Back Alive (1932), 243–44, 244 (photo)

Broken Blossoms (1920), 268
Bureau of Missing Persons (1933), 56

Cabin in the Cotton (1932), 50–52, 52
    (photo), 119
Cabinet of Dr. Caligari, The (1919), 301
Call Her Savage (1932), 3, 104, 108, 181,
    263
Cannons or Tractors, 49
Captured! (1933), 56
Casablanca (1942), 10
Cavalcade (1933), 80, 121
Champ, The (1931), 277
Chang (1927), 232
Check and Double Check (1930), 282–
    84, 283 (photo)
Christopher Strong (1933), 128
Cimarron (1930), 298
Citizen Kane (1941), 71
City Lights (1931), 53–54, 375n
City Streets (1931), 155
Cleopatra (1934), 65
Close Encounters of the Third Kind
    (1977), 376n
Cock of the Air (1932), 108
Cocoanuts (1929), 193
Common Law, The (1931), 2, 110, 119,
    131–32, 261
Congorilla (1932), 175, 246–50, 247
    (photo), 248 (photo)
Convention City (1933), 108, 178
Convict's Code (1939), 159
Criminal Code, The (1931), 159

Dance, Fools, Dance (1931), 23 (and
    photo)
Dances with Wolves (1990), 375n
Dark Horse, The (1932), 63
David Copperfield (1935), 335
David Harum (1934), 333
Day at the Races, A (1937), 193
Dead End (1937), 338
Destiny Unknown (1933), 83

Devil Is Driving, The (1932), 103
Dillinger—Public Enemy No. 1 (1934),
    142–45
Dinner at Eight (1933), 128, 176
Dishonored (1931), 123
Doctor X (1932), 297
Doorway to Hell (1930), 146, 153–54
Dr. Jekyll and Mr. Hyde (1932), 94, 297,
    303–305, 304 (photo), 306, 313
Dr. Strangelove, or How I Learned to Stop
    Worrying and Love the Bomb (1964),
    344
Dracula (1931), 19, 296, 297, 299–300
Duck Soup (1933), 171, 175, 193–96,
    375n

Eat 'Em Alive (1933), 245
Eight Girls in a Boat (1934), 106
Emperor Jones, The (1933), 2, 284–89,
    287 (photo), 403n
Employee's Entrance (1933), 56, 71–73,
    72 (photo), 131, 176
Eskimo (1933), 229, 230, 231 (photo),
    235, 244–45
Explorers of the World (1931), 227

Faithless (1932), 54
Fighting President, The (1933), 82–83
Fighting Priest, The (1934), 84–85
Finishing School (1934), 176
First World War, The (1934), 205, 206–208
Five Star Final (1931), 187, 188, 189–91,
    189 (photo)
Footlight Parade (1933), 107, 176, 178
Forsaking All Others (1934), 329–30
42nd Street (1933), 56, 118, 131, 178
Frankenstein (1931), 19, 31, 297, 299–
    303, 302 (photo), 306, 310–11, 313,
    375n
Freaks (1932), 295, 297, 308, 313–18,
    316 (photo)
Free Love (1931), 103
Front Page, The (1931), 10, 187, 188, 191

Gabriel Over the White House (1933), 2, 40, 73–75, 75 (photo), 341–42
Gentleman's Agreement (1947), 53, 340
Gentlemen of the Press (1929), 187
Gentlemen Prefer Blondes, 132
Girl from Missouri (1934), 332
Girl of the Limberlost, A (1934), 218
G-Men (1935), 338
Gold Diggers of 1933 (1933), 56, 338
Gold Diggers of 1935 (1935), 338
Gold Rush, The (1925), 375n
Golem, The (1922), 299
Gone with the Wind (1939), 341
Goona-Goona (1932), 232–33
Grand Hotel (1932), 54, 55 (photo), 59, 94
Grapes of Wrath, The (1940), 3
Grass (1925), 223, 232
Great Dictator, The (1940), 97
Great Edition, The (1932), 187
Great Train Robbery, The (1903), 5
Great White Silence, The (1924), 229

Half-Naked Truth, The (1932), 108
Hansel and Gretel (1933), 94
Hatchet Man, The (1932), 268–69
Haunted Gold (1932), 275
Headline Shooter (1933), 213
Heart of Africa, The (1914), 240
Heat's On, The (1943), 338
Hell's Highway (1932), 162–63, 162 (photo), 169
Hell's Holiday (1933), 205
Heroes for Sale (1933), 27, 40, 61, 85–89, 164
High Sierra (1941), 145–46
His Girl Friday (1940), 188
Hitler's Reign of Terror (aka *Hitler's Reign*) (1934), 99–100
Hitlerjunge Quex (aka *Our Flags Lead Us Forward*) (1934), 96
Hold 'Em Jail (1932), 167
Hold Your Man (1933), 178, 276

Horse Feathers (1932), 44, 193
Horst Wessel (1933), 95
Hot Pepper (1933), 325
How to Sleep (1935), 173

I'm No Angel (1933), 183, 184–87
I Am a Fugitive from a Chain Gang (1932), 49, 56–57, 161–62, 163–66, 165 (photo), 169–70, 267, 392n
If I Had a Million (1932), 53
Igloo (1932), 229–30, 245
Inauguration of Franklin D. Roosevelt, The (1933), 81
Inflation (1933), 84
Ingagi (1929), 236–41, 242, 243
Iron Horse, The (1925), 262
Island of Lost Souls (1933), 298, 308–13, 311 (photo), 313
It (1928), 121
It Happened One Night (1934), 56, 188, 191–92, 375n

Jango: Exposing the Terrors of Africa in the Land of Trader Horn (1930), 241
Jazz Singer, The (1927), 17, 31, 180, 281
Jungle Hazards (1931), 241
Jungle Virgins (aka *Virgins of Bali*) (1932), 175, 232, 233–35, 234 (photo)

King Kong (1933), 19, 31, 56, 181, 232, 289–93, 291 (photo), 375n
King of Kings, The (1927), 35
Kiss Me, Stupid (1964), 344
Kiss, The (1896), 5

Ladies of the Big House (1931), 167
Ladies They Talk About (1933), 122
Lady for a Day (1933), 53
Larceny Lane (1931), 155
Last Flight, The (1931), 181
Last Parade, The (1931), 154
Laughing Sinners (1931), 103, 120

Laughter in Hell (1933), 103, 162–63, 166–67

Lawyer Man (1932), 60

Leftover Ladies (1931), 108

Life in the Raw (1933), 108

Life of Vergie Winters (1934), 324

Little Caesar (1930), 31, 146, 147 (photo), 151, 153–55, 285

Little Giant, The (1933), 56

Little Miss Marker (1934), 333

Little Women (1933), 195, 333, 335

Lolita (1962), 344

Lost Weekend, The (1945), 53

Lost World, The (1925), 292

Love Is a Racket (1932), 104–105

M (1930; released in U.S. in 1933), 94

Mad Dog of Europe, The (unproduced), 101–102

Madame Satan (1930), 2, 26, 114

Maedchen in Uniform (1931; released in U.S. in 1932), 94, 122, 285

Make Way for Tomorrow (1937), 11–14; 12 (photo)

Man of Aran (1934), 48

Man Who Played God, The (1932), 106

Manhattan Butterfly (1934), 332

Manhattan Melodrama (1934), 139, 158, 337, 339

Mary Stevens, M.D. (1933), 61, 129

Mask of Fu Manchu, The (1932), 269–70, 271 (photo), 298

Massacre (1934), 2, 61, 262–67, 265 (photo)

Match King, The (1932), 58

Mayor of Hell, The (1933), 40, 167, 168–69, 180, 339

Melody Cruise (1933), 101

Men in White (1934), 61, 176

Men, The (1950), 53

Merrily We Go to Hell (1932), 103, 108

Metropolis (1926), 159

Midsummer Night's Dream, A (1935), 335

Mind Reader, The (1933), 56

Miracle Woman, The (1931), 61–62, 181

Morning Glory (1933), 44

Morocco (1930), 123

Mouthpiece, The (1932), 60

Mr. Deeds Goes to Town (1936), 173

Mr. Smith Goes to Washington (1939), 63, 173, 341–42

Mummy, The (1932), 297

Murders in the Rue Morgue (1932), 297, 305–307, 307 (photo)

Mussolini Speaks (1933), 76–77

Mystery of Life, The (1931), 8

Mystery of the Wax Museum (1933), 44

Nanook of the North (1922), 229

Night After Night (1932), 183

Night at the Opera, A (1935), 193, 195–96

Night Nurse (1931), 61, 62 (photo), 118

90° South (1933), 227, 228–29, 243

Ninotchka (1939), 128

No More Women (1934), 175

No Way Out (1950), 53

Nosferatu (1922), 299

Notorious (1946), 3

Numbered Men (1930), 159, 170

Office Wife, The (1930), 11

Old Morals for New (1932), 2, 132

Other Men's Women (1931), 176

Our Betters (1932), 121

Our Flags Lead Us Forward (aka *Hitlerjunge Quex*) (1934), 96

Outlaw, The (1943), 342

Paid (1931), 60–61

Pawnbroker, The (1965), 344

Penthouse (1933), 132

Petrified Forest, The (1936), 338

Picture Snatcher, The (1933), 150, 180

Platinum Blonde (1931), 191–92

Polly of the Circus (1932), 318

Power and the Glory, The (1933), 71, 80

Prizefighter and the Lady, The (1933), 94
Prodigal, The (1930), 113
Psycho (1960), 343–45, 344 (photo)
Public Enemy, The (1931), 146–48, 150, 153, 154 (photo), 155

Rain or Shine (1930), 26
Rango (1931), 232, 290
Red Dust (1932), 14–15, 15 (photo)
Red Headed Woman (1932), 2, 118, 132–34, 133 (photo), 183
Registered Nurse (1933), 181
Road Is Open Again, The (1933), 84
Road to Ruin, The (1934), 103
Roaring Twenties, The (1939), 338
Roosevelt—the Man of the Hour (1933), 82

Safe in Hell (1931), 103, 280
Sailor's Luck (1932), 121
S.A.-Mann Brand (1933), 95–96, 95 (photo), 385*n*
Scandal Sheet (1931), 187
Scarface (1932), 145, 146, 148–50, 149 (photo), 153, 154, 155, 156, 287
Searchers, The (1956), 375*n*
Secrets (1933), 114
Shadow of the Law (1930), 159
Shame of Temple Drake, The (aka *The Story of Temple Drake*) (1933), 108, 114–18, 116 (photo), 127
Shanghai Express (1932), 48, 123
She Done Him Wrong (1933), 2, 110, 171, 183–84, 185 (photo)
She Had to Say Yes (1933), 131
Shopworn (1932), 132
Sign of the Cross, The (1932), 10, 65, 122–23, 122 (photo)
Silent Enemy, The (1930), 225, 231–32, 264
Simba (1928), 246
Sin of Madelon Claudet, The (1931), 127, 130

Skyscraper Souls (1932), 59, 176
Smart Money (1931), 155
Son-Daughter, The (1933), 268
S.O.S. Iceberg (1933), 229, 230–31
Sound of Music, The (1965), 376*n*
So This Is Africa (1933), 101
Speedy (1928), 36
Squawman, The (1931), 32
Stand Up and Cheer (1934), 333
Star Wars (1977), 376*n*
Star Witness, The (1931), 152
State's Attorney (1932), 36, 60
Storm Over Asia (1928; released in U.S. in 1930), 49
Story of Temple Drake, The (aka *The Shame of Temple Drake*) (1933), 108, 114–18, 116 (photo), 127
Strange Justice (1933), 253
Success at Any Price (1934), 151
Susan Lennox: Her Fall and Rise (1931), 128–29

Tabu (1930), 232
Tale of Two Cities, A (1935), 335
Tarzan and His Mate (1934), xi, 109 (photo), 119, 256, 257 (photo), 259–62, 333, 338
Tarzan Escapes (1936), 338
Tarzan, the Ape Man (1932), 256–59, 295
Taxi! (1931), 54–55, 56, 180
They Learned About Women (1930), 36, 177
Thief of Baghdad (1925), 243
This Day and Age (1933), 2, 65–67, 141, 277–78, 339
This Is America (1933), 206, 208
Three Little Pigs, The (1933), 69–70
Tol'able David (1921), 86
Trader Horn (1930), 227, 243, 254 (photo), 255, 275
Treasure Island (1934), 335
Triumph of the Will (1935), 231
Trouble in Paradise (1932), 94

20,000 Years in Sing Sing (1933), 27, 161

Ubangi (1931), 235
Unashamed (1932), 2, 104–105
Under 18 (1932), 26
Underworld (1928), 146
Unguarded Girls (1929), 110
Union Depot (1932), 57–58
Unknown, The (1927), 312

Virgins of Bali (aka *Jungle Virgins*) (1932),
    175, 232, 233–35, 234 (photo)
Volga to Gastonia, 49

Washington Merry-Go-Round (1932),
    63–64
Waterloo Bridge (1931), 130
We're Rich Again (1934), 53
West of Singapore (1933), 253
Wet Parade, The (1932), 49

What Men Want (1930), 108
What Price Hollywood? (1932), 128, 176,
    177 (photo)
White Hell of Pitz Palleu (1929), 230
White Shadows of the South Sea (1928),
    261
Who's Afraid of Virginia Woolf? (1966),
    345
Wild Boys of the Road (1933), 2, 40, 89–
    92, 91 (photo), 180, 339
Wild Cargo (1934), 244
Wild in the Streets (1968), 342
Winner Take All, 56
With Byrd at the South Pole (1930),
    227–28, 228 (photo), 235
World Moves On, The (1934), 373n
World in Revolt (1933), 206
World's Greatest Thrills, The (1933), 209

Young Sinners (1931), 113

600066410X

 University of
fordshi

Pre-Code Hollywood

FILM AND CULTURE / JOHN BELTON, GENERAL EDITOR

Film and Culture / A Columbia University Press series / Edited by John Belton

What Made Pistachio Nuts?
Henry Jenkins

Showstoppers: Busby Berkeley and
the Tradition of Spectacle
Martin Rubin

Projections of War:
Hollywood, American Culture, and
World War II
Thomas Doherty

Laughing Screaming:
Modern Hollywood Horror
and Comedy
William Paul

Laughing Hysterically: American
Screen Comedy of the 1950s
Ed Sikov

Primitive Passions: Visuality,
Sexuality, Ethnography, and
Contemporary Chinese Cinema
Rey Chow

The Cinema of Max Ophuls:
Magisterial Vision and the Figure
of Woman
Susan M. White

Black Women as Cultural Readers
Jacqueline Bobo

Picturing Japaneseness: Monumental
Style, National Identity, Japanese Film
Darrell William Davis

Attack of the Leading Ladies: Gender,
Sexuality, and Spectatorship in Classic
Horror Cinema
Rhona J. Berenstein

This Mad Masquerade: Stardom and
Masculinity in the Jazz Age
Gaylyn Studlar

Sexual Politics and Narrative Film:
Hollywood and Beyond
Robin Wood

The Sounds of Commerce: Marketing
Popular Film Music
Jeff Smith

Orson Welles, Shakespeare, and
Popular Culture
Michael Anderegg

Pre-Code Hollywood: Sex, Immorality, and
Insurrection in American Cinema, 1930–1934
Thomas Doherty

Sexual Technology and the American
Cinema: Perception, Representation,
Modernity
James Lastra